Central Bank Communication, Decision Making, and Governance

CESifo Seminar Series
Edited by Hans-Werner Sinn

See http://mitpress.mit.edu for a complete list of titles in this series.

Central Bank Communication, Decision Making, and Governance

Issues, Challenges, and Case Studies

edited by Pierre L. Siklos and Jan-Egbert Sturm

 Seminar Series

The MIT Press
Cambridge, Massachusetts
London, England

MIT Press books may be purchased at special quantity discounts for business or sales promotional use. For information, please email special_sales@mitpress.mit.edu or write to Special Sales Department, The MIT Press, 55 Hayward Street, Cambridge, MA 02142.

This book was set in Palatino by Toppan Best-set Premedia Limited, Hong Kong. Printed and bound in the United States of America.

Library of Congress Cataloging-in-Publication Data

Central bank communication, decision making, and governance : issues, challenges, and case studies / edited by Pierre L. Siklos and Jan-Egbert Sturm.
    p.   cm. — (CESifo seminar series)
Includes bibliographical references and index.
ISBN 978-0-262-01893-7 (hbk. : alk. paper)
1. Banks and banking, Central.   2. Business communication.   I. Siklos, Pierre L., 1955–
II. Sturm, Jan-Egbert, 1969–
HG1811.C44   2013
332.1'10684—dc23
                                                                                    2012037154

10   9   8   7   6   5   4   3   2   1

Contents

Series Foreword

This book is part of the CESifo Seminar Series. The series aims to cover topical policy issues in economics from a largely European perspective. The books in this series are the products of the papers and intensive debates that took place during the seminars hosted by CESifo, an international research network of renowned economists organized jointly by the Center for Economic Studies at Ludwig-Maximilians-Universität, Munich, and the Ifo Institute for Economic Research. All publications in this series have been carefully selected and refereed by members of the CESifo research network.

1 Introduction and Overview

Pierre L. Siklos and Jan-Egbert Sturm

1.1 Background, Motivation, and Contribution to the Literature

Central bankers have for some time now understood and emphasized the importance of communication. They have expanded communication not only through the age-old practice of giving more speeches but also by greatly increasing the volume of information provided to the public. The result, as documented by Dincer and Eichengreen (2008, 2009) and Siklos (2011),[1] among others, has been a sharp rise in central bank transparency. This is not surprising as the worldwide movement toward greater central bank independence, which gathered pace during the 1990s, was met by the monetary authorities' recognition that with greater responsibilities comes greater accountability.

Of course, more transparency need not translate into greater clarity. Paralleling the rise in transparency has been an increased emphasis on explaining to the public how monetary policy ought to work in practice and the processes central banks employ both in making and in communicating their policy decisions to financial markets and the public more generally. Indeed, several central banks (e.g., Bank of England, the Riksbank) have asked outside experts to critically evaluate the manner in which decisions are taken, especially the models and methods used to generate and communicate forecasts of macroeconomic activity, while the International Monetary Fund, to give another example, has extensively examined and reviewed the governance structures of many central banks (e.g., see Lybek and Morris 2004; Berger, Nitsch, and Lybek 2006).

Along with the relatively recent interest in central bank communication there has been recognition that this function is complex, consisting of several elements that can conceivably come into conflict with each other (e.g., see Jeanneau 2009). Moreover, even if almost every central bank has become more transparent over the past decade, there are both institutional and practical limitations on their capacity to provide more and clearer information about the outlook for the economy. Nevertheless, central banks strive to improve their ability to steer expectations, balancing this essential function with their natural caution not to commit in advance how future monetary policy will be set. Nowhere is this more apparent than in considering the question of how forthcoming they should be about the likely future path of the policy rate. Before the global financial crisis began around 2007, a large number of central banks relied on an interest rate as the central instrument of monetary policy. Only a few central banks (viz., Sweden's Riksbank, Norway's Norges Bank, New Zealand's Reserve Bank) were prepared to provide the public with explicit data about the future path the policy rate might take. Indeed, the issue has sometimes been cast as the "last frontier" in central bank communication. It is notable therefore that, beginning in 2012, the US Federal Reserve, very much preoccupied with the issue of transparency and how best to communicate the views of the Federal Open Market Committee (FOMC; e.g., see Bernanke 2007), decided to publish its members' views about future policy rate settings and to provide markets with an indication of when the Fed might escape the zero lower bound for the federal funds rate.[2] While this development suggests that there continues to be some scope for greater transparency, Fed officials themselves are quick to point out that each attempt to be more forthcoming carries risks in the form of a loss of clarity or reputation if the audience is neither receptive nor convinced that the central bank intends to use such devices to improve the delivery of monetary policy.

Recognition of the importance of communication in central banking is evident from the recent survey on the subject by Blinder et al. (2008). Indeed, interest in what central banks say and why they say it is not new (e.g., Siklos 2002; Fracasso, Genberg, and Wyplosz 2003). What has caught the attention of the profession is the recognition that not only deeds matter; that words—and the various channels available to convey and tailor messages about monetary policy in public—are equally important. However, despite the greater attention in economic research devoted to this field, it is instructive that Blinder et al. (2008) conclude by highlighting many areas where future research is needed. In particular, they note the following:

(i) There is no consensus on what works best in central bank communication.

(ii) "Distinctions among forms of communication merits further empirical evaluation" (940).

(iii) There are too few studies dealing with the directional intent of central bank communication. Indeed, the authors stress that "we have little empirical knowledge of its effects" (i.e., projected paths of the policy rate) (941).

(iv) The survey highlights the need for research on the links between central bank communication and other macro variables.

(v) Finally, the profession needs to pay attention not only to financial market reactions but to public perceptions of central bank communication.

Clearly, filling the gaps in the research is an ambitious goal. Nevertheless, this volume is an attempt to move the literature in this direction. The contributions that follow offer a wide variety of approaches, data, and insights on what works best in central bank communication, covering both the large economies as well as the experiences of small open economies. Examinations of the experiences of smaller economies has been notably absent from the literature. This collection also investigates distinctions among forms of communication, with several papers examining the implication that certain forms of communication matter more than others. Some papers examine speeches and decode words, while others study the role of providing more guidance to markets in various ways. In particular, two chapters in this volume explore the impact of the release of forward guidance on interest rates.

The first two chapters that open the volume address directly, in an analytical manner, how central bank communication interacts and impacts with the general macroeconomic environment, thereby addressing the fourth area of concern raised by Blinder et al. (2008). Further, a couple of the contributors to this volume use new data to examine how the public perceives the actions and decisions of some central banks. In so doing, the present volume goes at least part way to asking what implications arise from monetary policies that must be sensitive to the public's views about the decisions of the monetary authorities.

Clearly, a single volume will not do justice to all of the various facets relevant to a comprehensive study of central bank communication. In particular, one may reasonably ask whether the results presented in this volume resonate in light of the events that have transpired since the start of the US and euro-area financial crises. For example, the governor of the Bank of Canada, Mark Carney, suggested at the height of the so-called global financial crisis that a central bank's communication strategy in crisis times may need to differ from that relied upon in more "normal" times (Carney 2009). However, one might want to be careful about drawing such conclusions.

Other than the obvious fact that we have yet to emerge from a crisis environment, there are at least three other observations that can be made about communicating during a crisis versus in normal times. First, if the objective of the communication function is to provide clarity about the outlook for the monetary policy stance, it is far from clear why or how the central bank talks should be different in crisis times. Indeed, if anything, the premium on clarity should be higher in crisis times. Therefore, a solid understanding of the communication function in normal times ought to be a prerequisite for communicating in more turbulent times. Second, while the sheer scale of the US and euro-area crises dwarf others in recent memory, one has only to look at Reinhart and Rogoff's (2009) magisterial contribution to recognize that crises of various kinds are not rare events. Hence, there is something to be gained from a deeper understanding of the communication function when comparatively rare events of the kind the world economy has experienced since 2008 are under-emphasized. Nevertheless, one of the contributions in this volume explicitly inquires about the role of communication when financial markets are under stress. Third, the crisis did not leave central banks unscathed. Quite the contrary, as these institutions now struggle to grasp the significance of and responsibilities for macro-prudential policies. As Born, Ehrmann, and Fratzscher (2011) and Siklos (2010) point out, it needs to be stressed that communicating monetary policy need not change during a crisis. Rather, central banks have to invest resources into developing a separate communication strategy for macro-prudential concerns. Indeed, Svensson (2012) also stresses the need to separate monetary policy from financial stability objectives. It is clearly too early (and beyond the scope of this volume) to draw conclusions about this line of research. No doubt the topic of central bank communication during crisis times will elicit a separate body of work that should eventually complement the contributions in this volume.

1.2 How the Volume Is Organized

The chapters in this volume were selected from papers that were submitted to the 2010 edition of CESifo's Venice Summer Institute. The volume is divided into five parts. First, we included some theoretical papers that address the problems and challenges faced by monetary policy when it must simultaneously be transparent and communicate the uncertainties of monetary policy in an environment where the volume of available information to both agents and policymakers is large and growing over time. How transparent should a central bank be, and are there limits to the revelation of information that can potentially be counterproductive to the delivery of good monetary policy? Are there additional questions that need to be considered when, as the events since 2007 clearly demonstrate, the monetary authorities also need to worry about more than just price stability?

Since central banks also vary according to how decisions are made, including the composition and authority of the committee responsible for making monetary policy decisions, some chapters explore the record and consequences of particular governance structures to see what lessons can be learned in an era that is likely to lead to greater complexity in how monetary policy is conducted. A separate part of the volume considers a variety of novel empirical approaches that address, from a broad perspective, how central banks communicate and to what effect. This section is followed by two parts that offer a series of illustrations and empirical evidence centering on two quite different, but overwhelmingly important, central banks: the US Federal Reserve and the European Central Bank (ECB). The contrast between the two banks permits one to highlight the idiosyncratic elements of both institutions as they pertain to how monetary policy is communicated and delivered in public. The ECB is a relatively young institution that operates as a supranational authority inside a common currency area, while the much older US Fed has had a largely enviable record in recent decades, but must operate under a dual mandate that requires both price stability and full employment objectives to be met. In spite of the institutional differences, common to both central banks are their shared and significant responsibilities for providing good monetary policy with obvious global implications.

The final part of the volume considers the international experience. Whereas the extant literature has naturally focused on the experiences of the Fed and the ECB, there is a wealth of useful knowledge to be gained from the communication, decision-making, and governance practices of smaller and more open economies.

1.3   An Overview of the Contributions

De Grauwe begins the volume by pointing out that models in which communication plays a role still rely heavily on the rational expectations assumption. He reaches back to the work of Hayek to revive the distinction between top-down and bottom-up models, which allows for variety in the ability of individuals to process and model information. Of course, this is not the only available approach that deals with the problem of asymmetric information. For example, in addition to the learning approach, the Mankiw-Reis approach can also be used to explain anomalies in consumption spending, which is based on the notion that some individuals are inattentive to incoming information.

One way of thinking of individuals who are less attentive or knowledgeable about underlying macroeconomic conditions is to assume that some extrapolate inflation based on past performance. This is essentially the view that there is a substantial inertial component to inflation which, incidentally, is the approach used in a variety of intermediate and more advanced macroeconomics textbooks. The difference, in De Grauwe's view, is that agents can learn over time and, hopefully, make better decisions or improve their knowledge of the underlying economic environment.

De Grauwe's setup also includes an inflation target which, depending on the reliability and credibility of the central bank, is capable of pinning down inflation; however, it is unclear whether it matters if such an objective is explicit or not. One type of target might be more helpful than another in anchoring inflation expectations. Also, it is not necessarily the case that extrapolative expectations need to be "irrational" if one accepts Alan Greenspan's definition of price stability as "that state in which expected changes in the general price level do not effectively alter business or household conditions."[3]

Since De Grauwe's aim is to explain the emergence of waves of booms and busts, akin to the notion of animal spirits (e.g., as in Akerlof and Shiller 2009), any psychologically based approach must also confront the fact that it cannot accommodate the irrational exuberance stemming from developments in the financial sector, except indirectly through aggregate demand shocks that somehow spill over from the financial sector into the goods sector. Communication therefore creates challenges for the central bank not only because of parameter uncertainty—popularly assumed to generate something that can lead to some form of irrational exuberance—but because the same shock can produce cycles in economic performance as some agents are inattentive.

The prediction that a temporary change in the inflation target also creates communication challenges and can exacerbate cycles helps explain why central banks are careful with their words, but it is not the only lesson learned. The other lesson not explicitly considered by De Grauwe is that perhaps this is a road that ought to be less traveled. In particular, there is a lesson for emerging market economies that have a tendency to change inflation targets when they seemingly fail to be consistently attained.

In the next essay, Geraats argues that the publication of information—in particular, inflation forecasts—provides the central bank with added flexibility in dealing with economic shocks. Hence, contrary to the conclusion of Morris and Shin (2002), central bank transparency is welfare-improving. Why? It all has to do with what the central bank is thinking. If the public knows that the central bank is attempting to attain a specific stabilization objective, then knowing what the central bank is thinking is a superior strategy to obfuscation about its true motives. Moreover, in the Morris and Shin setup, agents focus on the public signal and become complacent through a coordination motive, unlike Geraats's model where there are no such distortion-inducing motives.

One might object to the view that a central bank is subject to Kydland and Prescott's (1977) time-inconsistency problem. After all, Alan Blinder (1998) has convincingly argued that central banks do not "think" in this fashion or base their decisions on this kind of calculus. Nevertheless, it is equally well known that central banks need to respond differently to aggregate demand shocks than to aggregate supply shocks, which, of course, the central bank is assumed to be able to readily identify. Yet since at least Orphanides (2001), identifying whether shocks are primarily driven by supply or by demand has been a difficult task, and failure to make this determination results in more than just a forecast error—it implies that the precise nature of disturbances is not known when monetary policy decisions are being made. Hence, if the central bank is able to communicate the distinction, and this does require a significant form of transparency, then it follows that the transparency of central banks is desirable. Ultimately, one is still left asking: What is the desirable or optimal amount of transparency? Finally, there is the role of the rational expectations hypothesis. Geraats touches on the points raised by De Grauwe and acknowledges that there may well be instances where transparency can be detrimental to welfare, but, ultimately, this depends on how clearly the central bank communicates with the public—a theme that several papers in the volume address.

Finally, the assumption that central banks have a comparative informational advantage, though an assumption not shared by everyone, seems plausible if only because Romer and Romer (2000), among others, have convincingly demonstrated that central bank forecasts are typically superior to most alternatives, although perhaps not to combinations of forecasts (e.g., see Siklos 2010 and references therein). It is also interesting to note that more transparency, especially of the perfect variety (i.e., the central bank recognizes aggregate demand shocks and can distinguish them from supply shocks), leads to more interest rate volatility, that is, less interest rate persistence. Since there is an ongoing debate about whether monetary authorities smooth interest rates, one should be able to ascertain whether more-transparent central banks are less apt to smooth interest rates. Casual empirical evidence suggests that the answer is a qualified yes.

Blix Grimaldi's contribution to this volume picks up a theme that has increasingly preoccupied central banks since the global financial crisis of 2007–2009, namely, how to formulate a communication strategy when the financial system experiences considerable amounts of stress. While the development of indicators of financial stress has attracted considerable attention in recent years for obvious reasons, proxies for financial stability remain largely in their infancy (e.g., Hatzius et al. 2010 is a recent survey). One question immediately comes to mind: Why rely on a single indicator? Is valuable information either omitted or subsumed by resorting to indicators, as opposed to central banks' claims that they "look at everything"? While bounded rationality and cognitive limitations are typically used to motivate such an approach—and this is the argument on which Blix Grimaldi's work rests—there is perhaps another compelling reason to adopt such a strategy that is not highlighted in the chapter. To put it simply, as long as the profession has not settled on a consensus definition of what is meant by "financial system stability," it is entirely unclear how various bits of data may or may not be related to financial stability. In the absence of such a consensus, an indicator approach seems to provide a way forward, at least for the time being.

Financial system stress is assumed to indicate the "fragility" of financial markets to shocks. Given the speed with which economic shocks can lead to full-blown financial crises, it is also helpful if such an indicator can be constructed using fairly high-frequency data. Invariably, however, it is useful if an indicator of this kind mixes qualitative and quantitative elements. To illustrate the qualitative component of such an indicator, one can perform a word search of a central bank publication, such as the ECB's *Monthly Bulletin,* to identify periods when there is heightened concern over weaknesses in the financial system. Clearly, one has to be careful with the selection of words to avoid confusing concerns about certain developments in the economy with true signals of a looming weakness in the financial system. The fact that central bank publications generally choose their words carefully—a point underscored by Blix Grimaldi—helps mitigate any subjective element in any word count. Moreover, the efficacy of such an approach can be cross-checked, as is also done here, against periods when there is no doubt that significant financial instability took place (e.g., the dotcom episode). Finally, as other indicators of "stress" exist in the euro area, though not exclusively of the financial stability variety (such as the CEPR EuroCOIN index), this can also help one to avoid arbitrary classifications of periods of high versus low weakness in the financial system. Data covering a period since 1999, combined with 18 financial variables chosen to match those used by others who have studied episodes of financial instability, are examined. Among the variables chosen are the usual suspects: varieties of interest rate spreads, share prices, and their volatility, to name just a few typical examples.

The various constituents of an indicator of financial stress are aggregated into subindices which, following estimation of a logit-based modeling approach, yield an estimate of Blix Grimaldi's financial stress indicator (FSI). Since the "proof of the pudding is in the eating," the resulting FSI is put through its paces with robustness checks against similar or competing indicators and is tested for its ability to predict known events associated with high levels of financial stress or fragile financial markets. In most cases the proposed FSI performs quite well.

Lamla and Sturm's chapter suggests that while markets generate expectations of the future path of monetary policy in the form of expected interest rates or based on the information content of the yield curve, there are other ways of generating expectations and influencing household and firm behavior. Indeed, for young central banks such as the ECB, one can well imagine that the way the media interprets and views central bank decisions might well constitute another form of useful information.

An organization called Media Tenor codes media statements from the widely read and circulated *Financial Times Europe* that portend the future path of monetary policy in the euro area; this coding serves as a proxy for expected future interest rates. In effect, this is a counterpart to the market-based expected interest rate indicators that exist elsewhere, as in the case considered by Karagedikli and Siklos's contribution (chapter 13). Certain checks are put into place to ensure that the coding is performed in as objective a manner as possible. Since multiple statements are made surrounding a press release in a window of a few days following a meeting of the ECB's Governing Council, one is able to measure the balance of opinion in the media concerning the likely future direction of interest rates.

Clearly, how the media feels about the likely course of future monetary policy will also be influenced both by the past performance of the ECB as well as by how well the ECB communicates policy. We have already seen in this volume that several indicators exist for the quality of ECB communication, and Lamla and Sturm examine how sensitive the determinants of the balance of opinion over interest rate developments are to a variety of alternative proxies for central bank communication. Finally, since the dependent variable is bounded between −1 and +1, there are some econometric issues stemming from the authors' specification that need to be addressed before the econometric results can be presented.

Lamla and Sturm conclude that, when it comes to monetary policy, both deeds and words matter, though the signaling value of deeds has a greater weight than that of words. Moreover, and in line with the ECB's mandate to maintain stable prices, signals that focus on future price developments are generally more influential than other forms of signaling considered by the authors. Just as interesting, the value of the signal is very much in the eye of the beholder. Journalists interpret interest rate signals clearly, while ECB officials consistently reinforce the policy rate decision of the Governing Council. The evidence presented in this chapter provides a first look at the impact of media reports on how the public interprets the conduct of monetary policy and is a useful counterpart to a rich literature that attempts to measure and draw conclusions from media-generated information (e.g., see Mullainathan and Shleifer 2005; Gentzkow and Shapiro 2006, 2010).

The chapter by Berger, Ehrmann, and Fratzscher, "Extreme Views Make News," centers on a simple but important aspect of central bank communication that resonates especially with some of the challenges faced by central banks such as the ECB. The media can be biased because, depending on their readership, income, and a host of other factors, there are built-in incentives to slant stories in one way or another to favor a certain point of view. If, as Lamla and Sturm argue (this volume), actions do speak louder than words, one is led to ask whether the media must in effect "shout" not only to be heard but to influence the public. Consequently, as the title of Berger et al.'s chapter suggests, "extreme" views can indeed make news. One can well imagine that a greater propensity toward extreme views would exist in a single-currency area that includes a divergent set of countries all governed by one monetary policy, as is the case in the euro area.

Relying on a survey of a large number of newspapers, the authors construct a data set that evaluates how favorably the media view the monetary policy of the ECB. Both qualitative and quantitative indices are constructed. The former is based on an interpretation of the content of ECB-related news item that is then scaled, while the latter represents an aggregation of characteristics of news items that include characteristics such as the length of the story and its placement in a publication.

Berger et al. conclude that negative views are more likely to receive attention and that the link between how favorably the ECB is viewed in the media and how widely this kind of news is covered is nonlinear. Hence, extreme views do make news, and if the news is negative, all the more reason to cover it. Moreover, it seems that for the ECB to be heard, at least by the media, it is far better for the ECB to change the policy rate than to leave it unchanged. Now, it may well be the case that the authors' findings are heavily influenced by the sample, in which policy rate changes took place fairly regularly, as well as by the fact that the data consist of media reports from the ECB's beginnings in 1999, when it was a new and untested institution. It will be interesting in the future to determine how extreme views change when policy rates either change infrequently or fall to within the proximity of the zero lower bound, and how one can control for the crisis-like atmosphere that has reigned in Europe and elsewhere since 2008. Answers to these questions await future research.

The following two chapters (part III of the volume) add to the literature on decision making and communication by the US Federal Reserve by providing new insights into the lengthy and eventful tenure of Alan Greenspan as chair of the FOMC. Bligh and Hess's chapter points out that the US experience is fascinating for several reasons. Unlike the ECB or many other central banks in the industrialized world, the US Federal Reserve did not have a stated inflation objective until January 2012, but rigorously adhered to the dictates of its dual mandate. Second, although the Fed, like many other central banks, has become more transparent, former Fed Chairman Alan Greenspan emphasized that he did not want to be too clear or too transparent about the likely future direction in monetary policy. With these considerations in mind, Bligh and Hess seek to evaluate how predictable Fed forward guidance was during the Greenspan era.

Focusing on data at the daily frequency, the authors examine how Greenspan's verbal communications influenced a variety of financial market asset prices—namely interest rates, including the critical federal funds rate that is at the center of Fed policy actions, and equity prices. Additional controls are required to capture the impact of a variety of news releases that frequently signal changes in the overall state of the US economy. Perhaps the best-known example is the role played by the release of data about developments in nonfarm payrolls.

Since Greenspan generally communicated via FOMC statements, speeches, and congressional testimony, the authors focus on the language content of his public pronouncements in order to quantify what Greenspan said and the importance of his comments. Bligh and Hess rely on Diction software, an algorithm that allows one to determine the relative importance of certain key words or terms. They focus on words that capture whether the chairman is certain (i.e., certainty) or pessimistic (i.e., pessimism) and the degree to which he is concerned with macroeconomic aspects of fed policy (i.e., the term "macro"). Bligh and Hess are aware of the risks entailed in relying on any such algorithm, since the meaning of any term can easily be changed by the simple addition of a negative, and they are careful to remove these instances lest they convey the exact opposite of what was intended.

While a rich set of results are presented, a couple are especially notable. Statements that convey certainty tend to be strongly associated with periods of rising federal funds rates, whereas pessimistic statements are more likely to significantly influence equity markets and the exchange rate. Also interesting is the finding that, of all forms of communication considered, the chairman's congressional testimony has the least impact on financial markets. In other words, the "news" content of this type of information is comparatively low. Finally, language directed at macroeconomic analysis was found to reduce the volatility of financial market asset prices.

Chirinko and Curran's contribution to the volume essentially relies on the same sources of information used in Bligh and Hess's chapter, but their focus is on the "ultra"-high-frequency response of financial markets to the verbal utterances of former Chairman Greenspan. Owing to some of the challenges that arise in dealing with this type of data, and their goal of identifying whether Greenspan's words just add "noise" versus the predictive content of his communication activities, Chirinko and Curran focus their research on the bond market's reaction from 1997 to 1999. This sample covers a total of 24 FOMC meetings and is therefore smaller than the dataset constructed by Bligh and Hess. The timing of any response is also important because, if the information communicated by the chairman is news, then it should impact financial markets very quickly after the communication takes place. If, on the other hand, bond markets react in anticipation of Greenspan's verbal communication, the impact reflects a form of coordination which renders verbal forms of communication much less effective, if not potentially counterproductive.

To evaluate the impact of the FOMC's utterances, the authors adopt an event study approach to estimate how speeches, FOMC statements, and testimonies affect prices and quantities in the bond market. Consistent with the results of Bligh and Hess, though using very different methodology, Chirinko and Curran find that Greenspan's speeches and other forms of communication have different effects on the bond market. Equally interesting is their finding that bond markets react not only after the event but also in anticipation of such events. In addition, a battery of statistical tests finds that much of what Greenspan says is news and that the FOMC serves as a coordination device. As a result, policy rate changes during the period considered were largely expected. It is important to underscore the fact that the effective number of FOMC meetings considered is rather small and that macroeconomic conditions were especially stable, which is likely to have reduced the element of surprise in the first place.

The finding that verbal communications during a portion of the Greenspan era can indeed be shown to potentially "crowd out" private information is directly relevant to the ongoing debate over whether there can be too much transparency. Even if one is skeptical about the period selected and the focus on Greenspan, who, as noted previously, aimed not to be too clear, it is notable that some empirical evidence is favorable to the Morris and Shin (2002) "anti"-transparency result, once again stressing not only the role of clarity, an aspect not directly addressed by Chirinko and Curran, but the role of the form of central bank communication.

Previous chapters have considered the overall consequences of transparency and the type and volume of information generated by central banks. However, equally important is the overall quality of that information and how consistently a central bank communicates with the public. Although difficult to define, in principle the term "transparency" refers to an expression that has a clear meaning in a variety of situations and is unlikely to confuse the consumer of information. Using the example of the ECB, a fledgling central bank with an especially difficult communication challenge as it attempts to steer a single monetary policy for a diverse group of sovereign countries, De Haan and Jansen's chapter explores the impact of subtle but potentially significant changes in wording emanating from the ECB by relying on an algorithm that "scores" the relative salience of certain terms used in its "Introductory Statement" that accompanies the release of the policy rate setting by the Governing Council. This form of communication is widely perceived as the single most important communication device the ECB relies on to convey its policy stance and intentions. The authors assume that individual consumers of central bank information are either easily distracted or have limited time and resources to digest the vast amounts of information produced by a central bank; for these reasons, De Haan and Jansen argue, consumers will seek out important pieces of information and attempt to extrapolate their understanding of policy based on limited data.

Interestingly, De Haan and Jansen find that while the overall correlation between words and deeds is not that strong, there is considerably higher correlation when there is tightening than when monetary policy is apt to become looser over time. While the results do not appear to be overly sensitive to alternative ways of measuring tightness or looseness of policy, they can be sensitive to the choice of words used in the analysis. For example, the term "vigilance" is more likely to be associated with expectations of tightening of monetary policy. It should also be noted that the reliability of the algorithm chosen by the authors is dependent on the word content of a document that serves as a reference or a benchmark. Nevertheless, it seems that ECB statements are generally consistent through time.

Bulíř, Čihák, and Šmídková's chapter takes on the difficult issue raised by several authors in this volume, namely how to measure the clarity of monetary policy and whether its impact can be separately identified from the usual sets of characteristics that make up most notions of central bank transparency. As in the preceding chapters, the proposed measure is applied to the ECB since it is a young central bank that must communicate to a very diverse audience, a situation that puts a premium on the clarity of communication. The challenge of communicating monetary policy effectively is further complicated by the fact that the ECB is not an inflation-targeting central bank, even though it has set for itself a numerical objective for inflation; nor does it explicitly consider a role for developments in the real side of the economy, although it has adopted a so-called "two-pillar" strategy that seeks to distinguish between short-run and long-run determinants of monetary policy.

The authors construct a series of indicators that attempt to quantify, in as simple a manner as possible, the risks that what the ECB does, or says it will do, will confuse the public. The public is assumed to follow something akin to a rule of thumb in evaluating whether the current setting of the stance of monetary policy is appropriate given the staff's estimates of, say, future inflation. Since there are a variety of reasons the central bank will not follow the simple rule to the letter—such as caution and the resulting smoothing of interest rates, not to mention overarching uncertainties about future shocks likely to hit the euro area—Bulíř, Čihák, and Šmídková next adjust their rule of thumb to permit a "substantial" amount of tolerance for failure to precisely follow the rule at all times. Since central banks use a vast amount of verbal communication which also needs to be consistent with the message of policy rate decisions and staff projections, the authors subsequently construct indicators based on the content of the introductory statement that follows the ECB's Governing Council's decision as well as the contents of the *Monthly Bulletin*s.

ECB communication is generally found to be clear and consistent around 80% of the time. Nevertheless, the authors find that the ECB achieves clarity not with a single signal but with a variety of meaningful signals, such as projections and the ECB's introductory statement as well as its *Monthly Bulletin*. The potential implications of this result are significant because it emphasizes that good monetary policy requires multiple complementary signals. Single sources of central bank news are insufficient. Two other interesting findings are worthy of mention. First, the ECB need not confuse the public by simply stating that it is, at times, ignorant about the risks to future economic prospects. Second, communicating in the context of a two-pillar approach actually reduces the clarity of communication.

Moving to the international experience, Mayes and Montagnoli's contribution begins with the observation that modern monetary policy-making recognizes that there exists a tradeoff between inflation and output volatility; they argue that central banks, recognizing that policy has to be conducted in an uncertain world, should devote their efforts to minimizing its unintended consequences. Nevertheless, parameters in models, the associated forecasts, macroeconomic data that are fed into various models, and various forms of communication undertaken by central banks are all influenced by the presence of uncertainty. Yet to date there has been no attempt to evaluate what central bankers believe is the level of ongoing uncertainty. Mayes and Montagnoli analyze the contents of meetings of central bank monetary policy committees, and seek to quantify whether the incipient uncertainty that is the stuff of committee deliberations is also somehow reflected in the policy rate decisions of central banks.

By necessity, the authors' indicator requires that a qualitative measure be employed, and they choose the frequency with which the term "uncertainty" is uttered in the minutes of central bank meetings. Since relatively few central bank minutes are published promptly, the empirical work is limited to examining the experiences of the Czech Republic, Sweden's Riksbank, and the Bank of England. All three central banks share the distinction of being inflation-targeting (IT) central banks as well as making decisions in a committee-type setting. It is a pity that additional comparisons with a non-inflation-targeting central bank (e.g., the US Fed) could not be presented, though later chapters in this volume fill the gap to a large extent. Moreover, because their respective IT regimes began at different times, the samples considered are not identical. Indeed, the three central banks differ in terms of how they view inflation targeting and in how transparent they are; in addition, the Czech National Bank is a candidate for entry into the euro area. These differences between the three banks provide considerable scope for differences in how uncertainty influences the conduct of monetary policy in the three countries considered.

Adding the resulting uncertainty indicator to an eponymous Taylor rule, the authors conclude that the interest rate response to inflation and output gap uncertainty is largely significant, though central banks appear more aggressive when there is more output gap uncertainty than when the concern is greater inflation uncertainty. It is important to note that the period since the global financial crisis is excluded in order to avoid contaminating the results with a shift in emphasis away from traditional central bank concerns and toward maintaining the stability of the financial system. Finally, it is possible that uncertainty is reflected in the voting dispersion of Monetary Policy Committee (MPC) decisions. It appears that this is generally not the case, so one must conclude that voting reflects concerns that are perhaps not directly related to uncertainty—though the authors do not draw firm conclusions about the implications of their results regarding the role of MPC voting.

In evaluations of the quality of central bank decisions, increased attention is being paid to voting records and the associated minutes of central bank monetary policy committees (also see, for example, Maier 2010). This is the concern of the contribution by Horváth, Šmídková, and Zápal. In principle, this type of information permits observers to determine, on an individual basis, policymakers' leanings in setting the policy rate. Moreover, one is able to measure how much disagreement or dispersion exists within the committee. This kind of information may also provide some insights about how much uncertainty there is in the outlook for the economy in question. Alternatively, knowledge about the internal functioning of MPC meetings may be helpful in isolating the determinants of any consensus or factors that can limit the potential for groupthink. Other issues that pertain to how the voting is structured (i.e., whether the chair votes first, which member formulates the policy rate motion, and so on) potentially have consequences for governance structures of central banks.

Decision making on monetary policy is likely to be especially challenging in emerging markets, such as in Central and Eastern Europe where the states admitted into the European Union in 2004 are expected to eventually join the euro area and meet the Maastricht Treaty convergence requirements. This is true for the Czech Republic, Hungary, and Poland, the three countries that are considered in the chapter by Horváth, Šmídková, and Zápal. To gain additional insights from other central banks, the authors add the United Kingdom and Sweden to the data set they examine. Neither country belongs to the European Monetary Union, but both target inflation. Since the US experience is also a useful benchmark—the Fed does not target inflation and its committee is relatively large compared to those of many central banks—the authors also consider evidence based on FOMC decisions.

Monetary policy, of course, is a two-sided coin; that is, while observers are interested in what MPCs think and how they vote, financial markets are also keenly interested in how much disagreement there is in the setting of the policy instrument. Hence, Horváth, Šmídková, and Zápal's empirical work considers how expectations of future interest rates are influenced by committee disagreements. The results point to a strong and significant link between the voting record of MPCs and interest rate expectations. In addition, the findings are robust to a number of modifications to the baseline specification and to the choice of sample periods.

Inflation targeting (IT) is popular among small open economies with flexible exchange rates. New Zealand was the first country to adopt IT in 1990 and has led the way in becoming one of the most transparent central banks in the world (e.g., see Siklos 2002; Dincer and Eichengreen 2008, 2009). Arguably, the last bastion of transparency concerns the release of a forward interest rate track. The reason, as Karagedikli and Siklos point out in their chapter, is that some observers of central bank policies believe that this is transparency gone too far. After all, doesn't a forecast of short-term interest rate, let alone a policy rate, risk committing a central bank to following a policy path a priori? Supporters of the release of interest rate forecasts contend that all such indicators are conditional and that the central bank is in no way committed to carrying out a specific interest rate path if, in the event, circumstances warrant a different policy. Indeed, a forward interest rate track can serve as a powerful communication device that can foreshadow a possible change in stance, especially if the stated inflation objective is threatened. It is also, in principle, a vital piece of information that is easier to communicate with a reduced chance of generating confusion in financial markets.

One way of testing the information content of forward interest rate tracks is to ask whether the release of such information creates surprise changes in exchange rates. This seems to be a natural test, particularly for a small open economy where exchange rate considerations have loomed large in recent years. Karagedikli and Siklos perform a series of event studies that ask: Conditional on the wide array of macroeconomic information that affects exchange rates, does the central bank's release of a future interest rate path produce more movements in the exchange rates than would otherwise take place?

The event study approach also has the advantage of relying on high-frequency data (i.e., data at intervals ranging from a few minutes to one day), which allows for easier control of variables that can influence the exchange rate.

The authors conclude that despite the significant amount of transparency associated with the work of the Reserve Bank of New Zealand (RBNZ), monetary policy surprises persist and have significant effect on the USD-NZD and AUD-NZD exchange rate in spite of the release of a forward interest rate track. Moreover, consistent with the work of Clarida and Waldman (2008), "bad" inflation news is "good" news for the exchange rate. Perhaps even more interesting is their finding that, at least in the case of New Zealand, in a period when observed inflation is rising, financial markets consistently overestimate the possibility that future policy rates will rise. Either financial markets do not perform well at forecasting the future course of interest rates or there is a residual lack of credibility in the policies of the RBNZ. Hence, more research is needed. Future studies should be directed, for example, at identifying the sources of discrepancies between future observed rates and their conditional forecasts, as this finding is likely one that holds for other central banks that publish forward interest rate tracks, such as the Norges Bank (Norway) and the Riksbank (Sweden).

Notes

The first author is grateful for financial support from a CIGI-INET grant.

1. Annual data on central bank transparency since 1998 for over 100 countries is available from the Central Bank Communication Network, http://www.central-bank-communication.net/links/.

2. The federal funds rate has been at the effective zero lower bound since December 2008.

3. The comment was made by Greenspan in a July 1996 FOMC meeting.

References

Akerlof, G., and R. Shiller. 2009. *Animal Spirits*. Princeton: Princeton University Press.

Berger, H., V. Nitsch, and T. Lybek. 2006. Central Bank Boards around the World: Why Does Membership Size Differ? IMF working paper 06/281, December.

Bernanke, B. 2007. Federal Reserve Communications. Speech at the Cato Institute 25th Annual Monetary Conference, Washington, D.C., November 14.

Blinder, A. S. 1998. *Central Banking in Theory and Practice*. Cambridge, MA: MIT Press.

Blinder, A. S., M. Ehrmann, M. Fratzscher, J. De Haan, and D.-J. Jansen. 2008. Central Bank Communication and Monetary Policy: A Survey of Theory and Evidence. *Journal of Economic Literature* 46 (12):910–945.

Born, B., M. Ehrmann, and M. Fratzscher. 2011. How Should Central Banks Deal with a Financial Stability Objective? The Evolving Role of Communication as a Policy Instrument. In *Handbook of Central Banking, Financial Regulation and Supervision: After the Financial Crisis*, ed. S. Eijffinger and D. Masciandaro, 244–267. Cheltenham, UK: Edward Elgar.

Carney, M. 2009. Some Considerations on Using Monetary Policy to Stabilize the Economy. Remarks presented at the Symposium Sponsored by the Federal Reserve Bank of Kansas City, Jackson Hole, August 22, available from www.bankofcanada.ca.

Clarida, R., and D. Waldman. 2008. Is Bad News for Inflation Good News for Exchange Rate? And, If So, Can That Tell Us Anything about the Conduct of Monetary Policy? In *Asset Prices + Monetary Policy*, ed. J. Y. Campbell, 371–392. Chicago: University of Chicago Press.

Dincer, N., and B. Eichengreen. 2008. Central Bank Transparency: Where, Why and with What Effects? In *Central Banks as Economic Institutions*, ed. J.-P. Touffut, 105–141. Cheltenham, UK: Edward Elgar.

Dincer, N., and B. Eichengreen. 2009. Central Bank Transparency: Causes, Consequences and Updates. NBER working paper w14791.

Fracasso, A., H. Genberg, and C. Wyplosz. 2003. How Do Central Banks Write? An Evaluation of Inflation Reports by Inflation Targeting Central Banks. Geneva Reports on the World Economy Special Report 2, May.

Gentzkow, M., and J. Shapiro. 2006. Media Bias and Reputation. *Journal of Political Economy* 114 (4):280–316.

Gentzkow, M., and J. Shapiro. 2010. What Drives Media Slant? Evidence from U.S. Daily Newspapers. *Econometrica* 78 (1):35–71.

Hatzius, J., P. Hooper, F. Mishkin, K. Schoenholtz, and M. Watson. 2010. Financial Conditions Indexes: A Fresh Look after the Financial Crisis. NBER working paper w16150.

Jeanneau, S. 2009. Communication of Monetary Policy Decisions by Central Banks: What Is Revealed and Why. BIS working paper no. 47, May.

Kydland, F. E., and E. C. Prescott. 1977. Rules Rather Than Discretion: The Inconsistency of Optimal Plans. *Journal of Political Economy* 85 (3):473–491.

Lybek, T., and J. Morris. 2004. Central Bank Governance: A Survey of Boards and Management. IMF working paper 04/226, December.

Maier, P. 2010. How Central Banks Take Decisions: An Analysis of Monetary Policy Meetings. In *Challenges in Central Banking*, ed. P. L. Siklos, M. T. Bohl, and M. E. Wohar, 320–356. Cambridge: Cambridge University Press.

Morris, S., and H. Shin. 2002. Social Value of Public Information. *American Economic Review* 92 (12):1521–1534.

Mullainathan, S., and A. Shleifer. 2005. The Market for News. *American Economic Review* 95 (9):1031–1053.

Orphanides, A. 2001. Monetary Policy Rules Based on Real-Time Data. *American Economic Review* 91 (9):964–985.

Reinhart, C., and K. Rogoff. 2009. *This Time Is Different*. Princeton: Princeton University Press.

Romer, C., and D. Romer. 2000. Federal Reserve Information and the Behavior of Interest Rates. *American Economic Review* 90 (6):429–457.

Siklos, P. L. 2002. *The Changing Face of Central Banking*. Cambridge: Cambridge University Press.

Siklos, P. L. 2010. Communication for Multi-Taskers: Perspectives on Dealing with Both Monetary Policy and Financial Stability. Unpublished working paper.

Siklos, P. L. 2011. Central Bank Transparency: Another Look. *Applied Economics Letters* 18 (10–12):929–933.

Svensson, L. 2012. Central-Banking Challenges for the Riksbank: Monetary Policy, Financial-Stability Policy and Asset Management. CEPR discussion paper DP8789, February.

I Central Bank Communication: Some Theoretical Considerations

2 Central Bank Communication When Agents Experience Cognitive Limitations

Paul De Grauwe

2.1 Introduction

Academic discussions of the value of communication by central banks have been greatly influenced by the theory of inflation targeting as developed by Svensson (1997), Bernanke and Mishkin (1997), and Woodford (2003), among others. Inflation targeting as conceived by these authors implies transparency, i.e., a willingness of the central bank to communicate as much information as possible, including its own forecasts of the rate of inflation. Under the influence of the "inflation-targeting revolution," central banks have opened up their boardrooms and have provided vastly more information than they used to do. It is not an exaggeration to say that the inflation-targeting revolution has transformed central banks from the secretive institutions that they used to be into transparent institutions.

Against this background of increasing openness, some recent academic thinking has stressed the limitations of transparency and open communication. The seminal contribution of Morris and Shin (2002) is important in this connection. Based on a model in which individual agents use private information about the fundamentals while at the same time second-guessing the intentions of other agents, Morris and Shin showed that public information, if sufficiently noisy, can lead private agents to coordinate on this public information, thereby reducing the weight placed on valuable private information. The authors concluded that central banks should be circumspect about providing information to the market. However, Svensson (2006) argued that this conclusion depends on the assumption that public information is less precise than private information, an assumption that reduces the practical importance of Morris and Shin's analysis.

Most of the analysis of the value of communication created by central banks has been performed using models with rational expectations. In my view this is a serious limitation. Clearly, communication by a central bank in a world where agents have the cognitive abilities to understand the complexity of the world in which they live (rational expectations) will be inherently different from communication that occurs when agents understand only small bits and pieces of the complex world.

In this paper I present a model in which agents have a limited understanding of the underlying model and therefore use simple rules to forecast. I analyze the implications of this model for the communication of the central bank. In section 2.2, I contrast the traditional rational expectations model, which I call a top-down model, with a bottom-up model in which agents have limited cognitive abilities. In section 2.3, I present the bottom-up (behavioral model), and in sections 2.4 and 2.5, I derive some implications of this model about the effects of communication by the central bank.

2.2 Top-Down versus Bottom-Up Models

In its most general definition, a top-down system is one in which one or more agents fully understand the system. These agents are capable of representing the whole system in a blueprint that they can store in their mind. Depending on their position in the system, they can use this blueprint to take command of the system or to optimize their own private welfare. These are systems in which there is a one-to-one mapping of the information embedded in the system with the information contained in the brain of one or more individuals. An example of such a top-down system is a building that can be represented by a blueprint and is fully understood by the architect.

Bottom-up systems are very different in nature. These are systems in which no individual understands the whole picture. Instead, each person understands only a very small part of the whole. These systems function as a result of the application of simple rules by the individuals populating the system. Most living systems follow this bottom-up logic. The market system is also a bottom-up system. The best description of this bottom-up system is still the one made by Hayek (1945). Hayek argued that no individual exists who is capable of understanding the full complexity of a market system; individuals understand only small bits of the entire system. The main function of markets consists in aggregating this diverse information. If there were individuals capable of understanding the whole picture, we would not need markets. This was in fact Hayek's criticism of the "socialist" economists who took the view that the central planner understood the whole picture, and would therefore be able to compute the whole set of optimal prices, making the market system superfluous. (For further insightful analysis, see Leijonhufvud 1993.)

My contention is that macroeconomic models that use the rational expectations assumption are the intellectual heirs of these central-planning models—not in the sense that individuals in these rational expectations models aim at planning the whole, but in the sense that, like the central planner, they understand the whole picture. Individuals in these rational expectations models are assumed to know and understand the complex structure of the economy and the statistical distribution of all the shocks that will hit the economy. These individuals then use this superior information to obtain the *optimum optimorum* for their own private welfare. In this sense they are top-down models.

A bottom-up macroeconomic model is very different. This is a model in which agents have cognitive limitations and do not understand the whole picture (the underlying model). Instead, they understand only small bits and pieces of the whole model and use simple rules to guide their behavior. I will introduce rationality in the model through a selection mechanism in which agents evaluate the performance of the rule they are following and decide whether to switch or to stick to the rule depending on how well the rule performs relative to other rules.

The modeling approach presented in this paper is not the only possible one to model agents' behavior under imperfect information. In fact, a large literature has emerged attempting to introduce imperfect information into macroeconomic models. These attempts have been based mainly on the statistical learning approach pioneered by Sargent (1993) and Evans and Honkapohja (2001). This literature leads to important new insights (see, e.g., Gaspar, Smets, and Vestin 2006; Orphanides and Williams 2004; Milani 2007; Branch and Evans 2011). However, I feel that this approach still loads individual agents with more cognitive skills than they probably possess in the real world.[1]

2.3 A Behavioral Macroeconomic Model

In this section the behavioral model is presented. (This section is based on De Grauwe 2012.) The novel feature of the model is that agents use simple rules, or heuristics, to forecast the future. These rules are subjected to an adaptive learning mechanism, i.e., agents endogenously select the forecasting rules that have delivered the highest performance ("fitness") in the past. This selection mechanism acts as a disciplining device on the kind of rules that are acceptable. Since agents use different heuristics, one obtains heterogeneity which, as will be shown, creates endogenous business cycles.

2.3.1   The Model

The model consists of an aggregate demand equation, an aggregate supply equation, and a Taylor rule.

The aggregate demand equation is specified in the standard way, i.e.,

$$y_t = a_1 \tilde{E}_t y_{t+1} + (1 - a_1) y_{t-1} + a_2 (r_t - \tilde{E}_t \pi_{t+1}) + \varepsilon_t, \tag{2.1}$$

where y_t is the output gap, r_t is the nominal interest rate, π_t is the rate of inflation, and ε_t is a white-noise disturbance term. $\tilde{E}_t$ is the expectations operator where the tilde above E refers to expectations that are not formed rationally. This process will be specified subsequently. I follow the procedure introduced in DSGE models of adding a lagged output in the demand equation.

The aggregate supply equation can be derived from profit maximization of individual producers. As in DSGE models, a Calvo pricing rule and some indexation rules used in adjusting prices are assumed. This leads to a lagged inflation variable in the equation.[2] The supply curve can also be interpreted as a New Keynesian Phillips curve:

$$\pi_t = b_1 \tilde{E}_t \pi_{t+1} + (1 - b_1) \pi_{t-1} + b_2 y_t + \eta_t. \tag{2.2}$$

Finally, the Taylor rule describes the behavior of the central bank:

$$r_t = c_1 (\pi_t - \pi^*) + c_2 y_t + c_3 r_{t-1} + u_t, \tag{2.3}$$

where π^* is the inflation target which for the sake of convenience will be set equal to 0. Note that, as is commonly done, the central bank is assumed to smooth the interest rate. This smoothing behavior is represented by the lagged interest rate in equation (2.3).

Introducing heuristics in forecasting output   Agents are assumed to use simple rules (heuristics) to forecast the future output and inflation. The way I proceed is as follows. I start with a very simple forecasting heuristic and apply it to the forecasting rules of future output.

I assume two types of forecasting rules. The first rule can be called a "fundamentalist" one. Agents estimate the steady state value of the output gap (which is normalized at 0) and use this to forecast the future output gap. The second forecasting rule is an "extrapolative" one. This is a rule that does not presuppose that agents know the steady state output gap. Instead, they are doubtful about it and extrapolate the previous observed output gap into the future.

The two rules are specified as follows. The fundamentalist rule is defined by

$$\tilde{E}_t^f y_{t+1} = 0. \tag{2.4}$$

The extrapolative rule is defined by

$$\tilde{E}_t^e y_{t+1} = y_{t-1}. \tag{2.5}$$

This kind of simple heuristic has often been used in the behavioral finance literature when agents are assumed to use fundamentalist and chartist rules (see Brock and Hommes 1997; Branch and Evans 2006; De Grauwe and Grimaldi 2006). It is probably the simplest possible assumption one can make about how agents, experiencing cognitive limitations, use rules that embody limited knowledge to guide their behavior. In this sense they are bottom-up rules because they only require agents to use information they understand, and do not require them to understand the whole picture. There is now increasing scientific evidence that in a complex world that is beyond the understanding of any one individual, agents are likely to use simple rules, or heuristics, to forecast the future (see, e.g., Damasio 2003; Kahneman 2002; Camerer, Loewenstein, and Prelec 2005). Such behavior should not be interpreted as being "irrational." In a very uncertain world, it is rational to use trial-and-error learning processes based on simple rules (heuristics).[3]

Thus, the specification of the heuristics in (2.4) and (2.5) should not be interpreted as a realistic representation of how agents forecast. Rather, it is a parsimonious representation of a world where agents do not know the "Truth" (i.e., the underlying model). The use of simple rules does not mean that the agents are dumb or do not want to learn from their errors. They use simple rules only because the real world is too complex to understand, but they are willing to learn from their mistakes, i.e., they regularly subject the rules they use to some criterion of success. There are essentially two ways this can be done. The first approach is called "statistical learning," as pioneered by Sargent (1993) and Evans and Honkapohja (2001), and consists of assuming that agents learn in the same way as econometricians do. The statistical learning literature leads to important new insights (see, e.g., Bullard and Mitra 2002; Gaspar, Smets, and Vestin 2006; Orphanides and Williams 2004; Milani 2007; Branch and Evans 2011). However, this approach loads individual agents with a lot of cognitive skills that they may or may not have. I will instead use another learning strategy that can be called "trial and error" learning. It is also often labeled "adaptive learning" and describes agents continuously trying to correct for their errors by switching from one rule to the other.

The market forecast is obtained as a weighted average of these two forecasts, i.e.,

$$\tilde{E}_t y_{t+1} = \alpha_{f,t} \tilde{E}_t^f y_{t+1} + \alpha_{c,t} \tilde{E}_t^e y_{t+1}, \tag{2.6}$$

$$\tilde{E}_t y_{t+1} = \alpha_{f,t} 0 + \alpha_{c,t} y_{t-1}, \text{ and} \tag{2.7}$$

$$\alpha_{f,t} + \alpha_{e,t} = 1, \tag{2.8}$$

where $\alpha_{f,t}$ and $\alpha_{e,t}$ are the probabilities that agents use a fundamentalist or extrapolative rule, respectively.

As indicated earlier, agents are rational in the sense that they continuously evaluate their forecast performance. I apply notions of discrete choice theory (see Anderson, de Palma, and Thisse 1992; Brock and Hommes 1997) in specifying the procedure agents follow in this evaluation process. Discrete choice theory analyzes how agents decide between different alternatives. The theory takes the view that agents are boundedly rational, i.e., utility has a deterministic component and a random component. Agents compute the forecast performance of the different heuristics as follows:

$$U_{f,t} = -\sum_{k=1}^{\infty} \omega_k \left[y_{t-k} - \tilde{E}_{f,t-k-1} y_{t-k} \right]^2, \tag{2.9}$$

$$U_{e,t} = -\sum_{k=1}^{\infty} \omega_k \left[y_{t-k} - \tilde{E}_{e,t-k-1} y_{t-k} \right]^2, \tag{2.10}$$

where $U_{f,t}$ and $U_{e,t}$ are the forecast performances (utilities) of the fundamentalists and extrapolators, respectively. These are defined as the mean squared forecasting errors (MSFEs) of the optimistic and pessimistic forecasting rules; ω_k are geometrically declining weights.

Applying discrete choice theory, the probability that an agent will use the fundamentalist forecasting rule is given by the expression (Anderson, de Palma, and Thisse 1992; Brock and Hommes 1997)

$$\alpha_{f,t} = \frac{\exp(\gamma U_{f,t})}{\exp(\gamma U_{f,t}) + \exp(\gamma U_{e,t})}. \qquad (2.11)$$

Similarly, the probability that an agent will use the extrapolative forecasting rule is given by

$$\alpha_{e,t} = \frac{\exp(\gamma U_{e,t})}{\exp(\gamma U_{f,t}) + \exp(\gamma U_{e,t})} = 1 - \alpha_{f,t}. \qquad (2.12)$$

Equation (2.11) says that as the past forecast performance of the fundamentalists improves relative to that of the extrapolators, agents are more likely to select the fundamentalist rule about the output gap for their future forecasts. As a result, the probability that agents use the fundamentalist rule increases. Equation (2.12) has a similar interpretation. The parameter γ measures the "intensity of choice." It parametrizes the extent to which the deterministic component of utility determines actual choice. When $\gamma = 0$, utility is purely stochastic. In that case agents decide to be fundamentalist or extrapolator by tossing a coin, and the probability of being fundamentalist (or extrapolator) is exactly 0.5. When $\gamma = \infty$, utility is fully deterministic and the probability of using a fundamentalist rule is either 1 or 0. The parameter γ can also be interpreted as expressing a willingness to learn from past performance. When $\gamma = 0$, this willingness is zero; it increases with the size of γ.

It should also be stressed that although individuals use simple rules in forecasting the future, this does not mean that they fail to learn. In fact the fitness criterion used should be interpreted as a learning mechanism based on "trial and error." When observing that the rule they use performs less well than the alternative rule, agents are willing to switch to the better-performing rule. Put differently, agents avoid making systematic mistakes by constantly being willing to learn from past mistakes and to change their behavior. This also ensures that the market forecasts are unbiased.

The mechanism driving the selection of the rules introduces a self-organizing dynamics in the model. It is a dynamics that is beyond the capacity of any one individual in the model to understand. In this sense it is a bottom-up system. It contrasts with the mainstream macroeconomic models in which it is assumed that some or all agents can take a bird's eye view and understand the whole picture. These agents not only understand the whole picture but also use this whole picture to decide about their optimal behavior. Thus, there is a one-to-one correspondence between the total information embedded in the world and the individual brains.

Introducing heuristics in forecasting inflation Agents also have to forecast inflation. A similar simple heuristic is used as in the case of output gap forecasting, with one rule that could be called a fundamentalist rule and the other an extrapolative rule. (See Brazier et al. 2006 for a similar setup.) The fundamentalist rule is based on the announced inflation target, i.e., agents using this rule have confidence in the credibility of this rule and use it to forecast inflation. The extrapolative rule is used by agents who do not trust the announced inflation target and instead extrapolate inflation from the past into the future.

The fundamentalist rule will be called an "inflation-targeting" rule. It uses the central bank's inflation target to forecast future inflation, i.e.,

$$\tilde{E}_t^{tar}\pi_{t+1} = \pi^*,\tag{2.13}$$

where the inflation target π^* is normalized to be equal to 0. The "extrapolators" are defined by

$$E_t^{ext}\pi_{t+1} = \pi_{t-1}.\tag{2.14}$$

The market forecast is a weighted average of these two forecasts, i.e.,

$$\tilde{E}_t\pi_{t+1} = \beta_{tar,t}\tilde{E}_t^{tar}\pi_{t+1} + \beta_{ext,t}\tilde{E}_t^{ext}\pi_{t+1}\tag{2.15}$$

or

$$\tilde{E}_t\pi_{t+1} = \beta_{tar,t}\pi^* + \beta_{ext,t}\pi_{t-1} \text{ and}\tag{2.16}$$

$$\beta_{tar,t} + \beta_{ext,t} = 1.\tag{2.17}$$

The same selection mechanism is used as in the case of output forecasting to determine the probabilities of agents trusting the inflation target and those who do not trust it and revert to extrapolation of past inflation, i.e.,

$$\beta_{tar,t} = \frac{\exp(\gamma U_{tar,t})}{\exp(\gamma U_{tar,t}) + \exp(\gamma U_{ext,t})},\tag{2.18}$$

$$\beta_{ext,t} = \frac{\exp(\gamma U_{ext,t})}{\exp(\gamma U_{tar,t}) + \exp(\gamma U_{ext,t})},\tag{2.19}$$

where $U_{tar,t}$ and $U_{ext,t}$ are the weighted averages of past squared forecast errors from using targeting and extrapolating rules, respectively. These are defined in the same way as in (2.9) and (2.10).

This inflation-forecasting heuristic can be interpreted as a procedure of agents to find out how credible the central bank's inflation targeting is. If it is very credible, using the announced inflation target will produce good forecasts and, as a result, the probability that agents will rely on the inflation target will be high. If, on the other hand, the inflation target does not produce good forecasts (compared to a simple extrapolation rule), the probability that agents will use it will be small.

The solution of the model is found by first substituting (2.3) into (2.1) and rewriting in matrix notation. This yields

$$\begin{bmatrix} 1 & -b_2 \\ -a_2c_1 & 1-a_2c_2 \end{bmatrix}\begin{bmatrix} \pi_t \\ y_t \end{bmatrix} = \begin{bmatrix} b_1 & 0 \\ -a_2 & a_1 \end{bmatrix}\begin{bmatrix} \tilde{E}_t\pi_{t+1} \\ \tilde{E}_t y_{t+1} \end{bmatrix} + \begin{bmatrix} 1-b_1 & 0 \\ 0 & 1-a_1 \end{bmatrix}\begin{bmatrix} \pi_{t-1} \\ y_{t-1} \end{bmatrix}$$
$$+ \begin{bmatrix} 0 \\ a_2c_3 \end{bmatrix}r_{t-1} + \begin{bmatrix} \eta_t \\ a_2u_t + \varepsilon_t \end{bmatrix}$$

or

$$A Z_t = B \tilde{E}_t Z_{t+1} + C Z_{t-1} + b\, r_{t-1} + v_t, \tag{2.20}$$

where bold characters refer to matrices and vectors. The solution for Z_t is given by

$$Z_t = A^{-1}\left[B \tilde{E}_t Z_{t+1} + C Z_{t-1} + b\, r_{t-1} + v_t \right]. \tag{2.21}$$

The solution exists if the matrix A is nonsingular, i.e., if $(1 - a_2c_2)a_2b_2c_1 \neq 0$. The system (2.21) describes the solution for y_t and π_t given the forecasts of y_t and π_t. The latter have been specified in equations (2.4) to (2.12) and can be substituted into (2.21). Finally, the solution for r_t is found by substituting y_t and π_t obtained from (2.21) into (2.3).

2.3.2 Calibrating the Model

The model was calibrated in such a way that the time units can be considered to be months. I will present a sensitivity analysis of the main results to changes in some of the parameters of the model. The three shocks (demand shocks, supply shocks, and interest rate shocks) are i.i.d. with standard deviations of 0.5%.

2.4   Animal Spirits, Learning, and Forgetfulness

In this section, simulations of the behavioral model in the time domain
are presented and interpreted. (This section is based on De Grauwe
2012.) The upper panel of figure 2.1 shows the time pattern of output
produced by the behavioral model. A strong cyclical movement in the
output gap can be observed. The lower panel of figure 2.1 shows a
variable called "animal spirits."[4] It represents the evolution of the fraction of agents who extrapolate a positive output gap. Thus, when the
curve reaches +1, all agents are extrapolating a positive output gap;
when the curve reaches 0, no agents are extrapolating a positive output

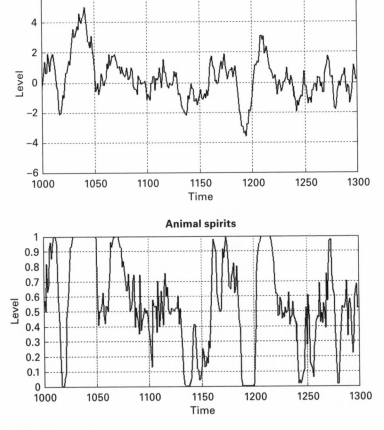

Figure 2.1
Output gap and animal spirits.

gap. In fact, in that case, they all extrapolate a negative output gap. The curve thus shows the degree of optimism and pessimism of agents who make forecasts about the output gap.

Combining the information from the two panels in figure 2.1, we can see that the model generates endogenous waves of optimism and pessimism. During some periods, optimists (i.e., agents who extrapolate positive output gaps) dominate, and this translates into above-average output growth. These optimistic periods are followed by pessimistic ones when pessimists (i.e., agents who extrapolate negative output gaps) dominate and the growth rate of output is below average. These waves of optimism and pessimism are essentially unpredictable. Other realizations of the shocks produce different cycles with the same general characteristics.

These endogenously generated cycles in output are made possible by a self-fulfilling mechanism that can be described as follows. A series of random shocks creates the possibility that one of the two forecasting rules, say the extrapolating one, delivers a higher payoff, i.e., a lower mean squared forecast error (MSFE). This possibility attracts agents that were using the fundamentalist rule. If the successful extrapolation happens to be a positive extrapolation, more agents will start extrapolating the positive output gap. The "contagion effect" leads to an increasing use of the optimistic extrapolation of the output gap, which in turn stimulates aggregate demand. Optimism is therefore self-fulfilling, and a boom is created. At some point, negative stochastic shocks and/or the reaction of the central bank through the Taylor rule make a dent in the MSFE of the optimistic forecasts. Fundamentalist forecasts may become attractive again, but it is equally possible that pessimistic extrapolation becomes attractive and therefore fashionable again. The economy turns around.

These waves of optimism and pessimism can be understood to be searching (learning) mechanisms of agents who do not fully understand the underlying model but are continuously searching for the truth. An essential characteristic of this searching mechanism is that it leads to systematic correlation in beliefs (e.g., optimistic extrapolations or pessimistic extrapolations). This systematic correlation is at the core of the booms and busts created in the model. Note, however, that when computed over a significantly large period of time, the average error in the forecasting goes to 0. In this sense, the forecast bias tends to disappear asymptotically.

The dynamics of booms and busts generated in this behavioral model is also illustrated in table 2.1, which shows the result of causality

Table 2.1
Pairwise Granger Causality Tests: Behavioral Model

Null hypothesis	Obs	F-statistic	Probability
Output does not Granger Cause optimism	1948	31.0990	5.1E-14
Optimism does not Granger Cause output		32.8553	9.3E-15

Note: Computed using the data generated in figure 2.1.

tests (in the sense of Granger). It shows that the causality between animal spirits and the output gap runs both ways, i.e., the output gap is caused by animal spirits but the reverse is equally true (i.e., the output gap causes animal spirits). This is the result of the self-fulfilling dynamics in which waves of optimism and pessimism drive the business cycle. The latter then in turn influences optimism and pessimism.

The results concerning the time path of inflation are shown in figure 2.2. First concentrate on the lower panel of figure 2.2. This shows the fraction of agents using the extrapolator heuristics, i.e., the agents who do not trust the inflation target of the central bank. One can identify two regimes. There is a regime in which the fraction of extrapolators fluctuates around 50%, which also implies that the fraction of forecasters using the inflation target as their guide (the "inflation targeters") is around 50%. This is sufficient to maintain the rate of inflation within a narrow band of approximately ±1% around the central bank's inflation target. However, there is a second regime which occurs when the extrapolators are dominant. During this regime, the rate of inflation fluctuates significantly more. Thus, the inflation targeting of the central bank is fragile, and can be undermined when forecasters decide that relying on past inflation movements produces better forecast performances than relying on the central bank's inflation target. This can occur quite unpredictably as a result of stochastic shocks in supply and/or demand. We will return to the question of how the central bank can reduce this loss of credibility.

The existence of these two regimes depends on the calibration of the model. In De Grauwe (2012) it is shown that it depends, among other things, on the intensity with which the central bank applies inflation targeting (the inflation coefficient in the Taylor rule). With increasing intensity of inflation targeting, the second regime occurs less frequently.

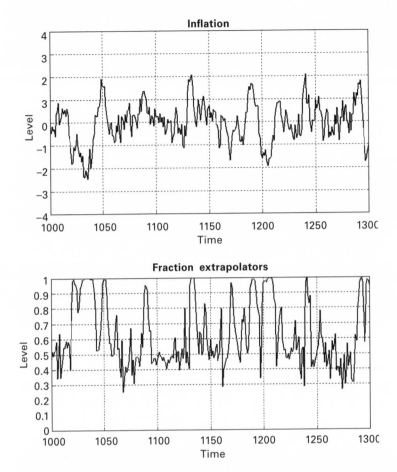

Figure 2.2
Inflation and fraction extrapolators.

2.5   Communication in a Behavioral Model

In the model presented in the previous section, waves of optimism and pessimism (animal spirits) alternate and influence the movements in output and inflation. In such an environment, the actions and words of the central bank are likely to be very much influenced by these animal spirits, or "market sentiments." We show the importance of this influence by first analyzing the dependence of the central bank's actions on market sentiments.

2.5.1 Actions and Market Sentiments

The action we consider here is an unanticipated increase in the interest rate. We compute the impulse responses to a positive interest rate shock. These describe the path of one of the endogenous variables (output gap, inflation) following the occurrence of the shock in the interest rate. To make this computation, we simulate two series of these endogenous variables. One is the series without the shock (the benchmark series); the other is the series with the shock. We then subtract the first from the second one. This yields a new series, the impulse response that shows how the endogenous variable that embodies the shock evolves relative to the benchmark. These impulse responses are expressed as "multipliers," i.e., the output and inflation responses to the shock are divided by the shock itself (which is one standard deviation of the error term in the Taylor rule equation).

The behavioral model is nonlinear. Therefore, during the post-shock period we continue to allow for random disturbances. The impulse response thus measures the response to the exogenous shock in an environment in which the random disturbances are the same for the series with and without the shock.

The exercise was repeated 500 times with 500 different realizations of the random disturbances. The mean impulse response together with the standard deviation was then computed. We define the interest rate shock to be a one-standard-deviation shock of the random disturbances of the Taylor rule equation. We show the results in figure 2.3. We find the traditional result concerning the effects of an increase in the interest rate; the output gap and the rate of inflation decline following the increase in the interest rate. The decline in output, however, is swifter and more intense than the decline in the rate of inflation, owing to the built-in wage and price rigidities in the model.

The most important aspect of the impulse responses in figure 2.3 is the wide variation in the short-term effects of the interest rate shock. This can be seen from the fact that dotted lines representing ±2 standard deviations from the mean are very far from the mean. As a result, it is very difficult to predict how the same interest rate shock affects the output gap and inflation in the short run. This uncertainty can also be illustrated by presenting the frequency distribution of the short-term output gap and inflation effects of the interest rate shock. We show these in figure 2.4. We have defined "the short term" to mean the effect after five periods, which corresponds to a little more than a year. The divergence in the effects of the same interest rate shock is striking. We

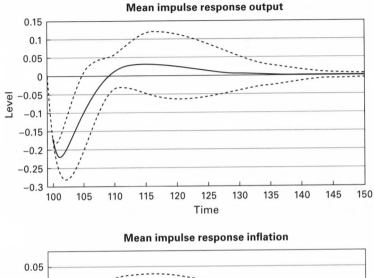

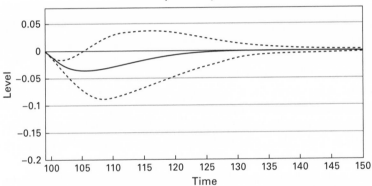

Figure 2.3
Impulse responses to positive interest rate shock.

also note that the statistical distribution of these short-term effects is far from the normal distribution and exhibits fat tails. Thus, the same interest rate shock can lead to strong outlying effects. The non-normal distribution of the short-term effects adds to the unpredictability of these effects, causing the transmission of the shock to be shrouded by the veil of uncertainty (in the sense of Frank Knight).

Where does this uncertainty come from? Not from parameter uncertainty. The same parameters are used in constructing all our impulse responses. The answer is that in this behavioral model each realization of the shocks creates different waves of optimism and pessimism—that is, animal spirits, or "market sentiments." Thus, a shock that occurs in

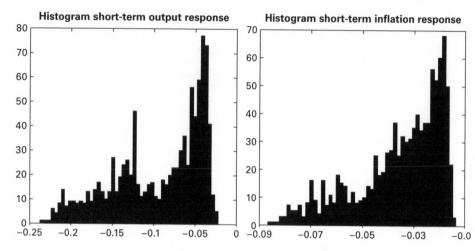

Figure 2.4
Frequency distribution of short-term effects of interest rate shock (kurtosis = 5.7).

one simulation happens in a different market sentiment than the same shock in another simulation. In addition, the shock itself affects market sentiments. As a result, the short-term effects of the same interest rate shock become very hard to predict.

Note that the uncertainty about the impulse responses tends to disappear in the long run, as the effect of short-term differences in market sentiments disappears.

Finally, we also analyzed the question of how the transmission of the interest rate shock is influenced by the market sentiments (animal spirits). We show the importance of these market sentiments in figure 2.5. On the horizontal axis we plot the mean value of the animal spirits index up to the fifth period after the productivity shock (remember that we defined the short-term effect to be the effect five periods after the shock). On the vertical axis, the short-term output and inflation effects (respectively) are shown. Thus, these figures show the relation between market sentiments prevailing during the adjustment period following the shock (including the period of the shock) and the size of the short-term effect of the interest rate shock. The most striking aspect of this relation is that animal spirits have a great influence on the intensity of the effects of a productivity shock.

The results of figure 2.5 lend themselves to the following interpretation. First, animal spirits have a strong impact on the short-term output effect of the same interest rate shock. In general, the stronger the animal

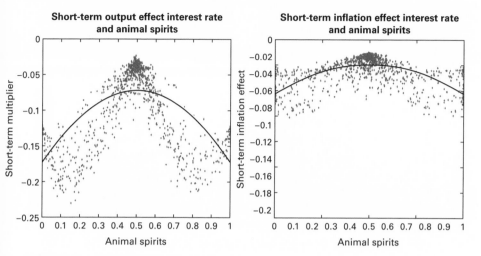

Figure 2.5
Effects of monetary policy depend on market sentiments.

spirits, i.e., the stronger optimism and pessimism are, the greater is the short-term impact of the interest rate shock on output. In contrast, when animal spirits are weak (the index is close to 0.5), the impact is weakest. When the market is dominated by either optimism or pessimism, the monetary authorities' interest rate instrument has the greatest impact on output (in the short run). Thus, animal spirits tend to amplify the short-term effects of monetary policies. These effects tend to disappear in the long run, however.

Second, the animal spirits have a much lower impact on the effectiveness of monetary policy in moving inflation. This is made clear by contrasting the two graphs in figure 2.5, which shows a low sensitivity of animal spirits to the impact of an interest rate shock on inflation.

The preceding analysis leads to the following insights. In a world where agents have cognitive limitations and in which their attempts at understanding the world lead to periods of optimism alternating with periods of pessimism, the same action by a central bank will have very different short-term effects on output and inflation. Put differently, the same news about monetary policy is interpreted very differently depending on market sentiments. This contrasts with the role of news in mainstream rational expectations models, where news means the same thing for everybody and forever. In our behavioral model, this is not the case: news is not something objective that is understood the same way by everybody. Instead, the meaning and the importance of the same news varies across individuals and across time. This feature makes the communication problem of central banks much more complicated than it appears from mainstream rational expectations models.

2.5.2   Words and Market Sentiments

We now analyze how an announcement by a central bank affects the economy. We do this by assuming that the central bank announces a temporary increase in the inflation target by 0.5%. "Temporary" means here that the inflation target is raised during one period. We perform the same analysis as in the previous section: we compute the impulse responses of output gap and inflation to this announcement (figure 2.6) and the frequency distribution of the short-term effects of the announcement on output gap and inflation (figure 2.7). We obtain results that are similar to those in the previous section, but with an even greater variation of the short-term effects of the announcement. Thus, the effects of the announcement are shrouded in even more uncertainty than the effects of a policy action.

Again, market sentiments appear to play an important role in determining how the same announcement will affect the economy. This can be seen from figure 2.8, which plots the short-term effects against the effects of animal spirits. Here we obtain a similar conclusion as in the previous section. The same announcement can be interpreted in many different ways by the market, creating very different short-term effects on output gap and inflation. There is no such thing as an objective announcement that will be interpreted in the same way across agents and across time. Movements of optimism and pessimism "color" the way an announcement is processed by agents. This phenomenon creates great uncertainty for the central bank about how its announcement will be interpreted and therefore how it will affect the economy (see Sturm and De Haan 2009 on this). Central banks in general are aware of this effect, and as a result they usually take great care in the way they make announcements.

2.6   Conclusion

The academic discussion of communication and central bank transparency has been dominated by the paradigm of rational expectations. This has led to models in which individuals who are confronted with private and public information signals have no problem interpreting

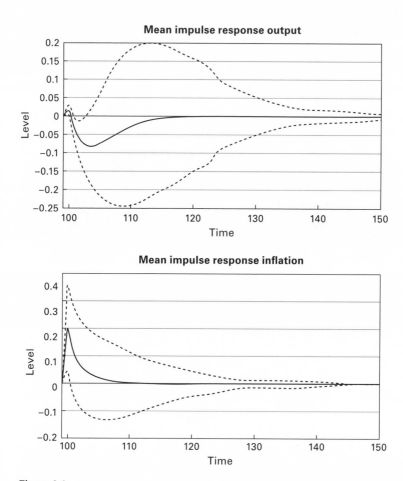

Figure 2.6
Impulse responses to temporary increase in inflation target.

the true meaning of these signals. The signals in these models are objective and have only one interpretation. Morris and Shin (2002) have shown that this approach can induce agents to disregard their own private signals, leading to the conclusion that central banks should not always provide public information signals.

The information problem in a world where agents struggle to understand its complexity is of a very different nature from the one analyzed in rational expectations (RE) models. Individuals with limited cognitive abilities face an overwhelming amount of unstructured information that they find difficult to understand. These individuals want to

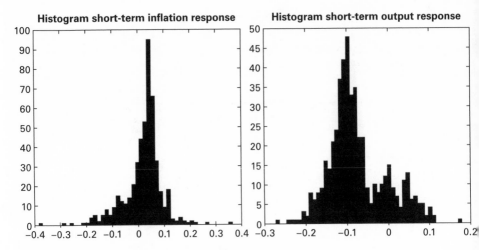

Figure 2.7
Frequency distribution of short-term effects of announcement.

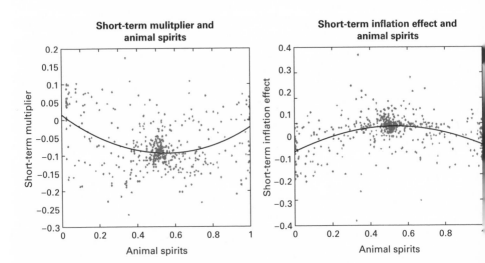

Figure 2.8
Effects of announcement depend on market sentiments.

make sense of this information. When confronted with news, they first have to select those pieces they think are relevant. This selection process is influenced by their moods and sentiments (animal spirits). In addition, the news has to be interpreted. There is no news that will be interpreted in the same way by all agents. Whereas RE models assume that news has the same significance for all agents, this cannot be true in a world of agents with cognitive limitations. Agents always have to interpret news; and they will do it in different ways, and in ways that change over time, because they are influenced by movements of optimism and pessimism.

We have analyzed this information problem in the context of a behavioral macroeconomic model. This model produces endogenous movements of optimism and pessimism (animal spirits). We found that these animal spirits color the way agents interpret and use news and announcements by the central bank. As a result, the effect of news and of central bank announcements is very hard to predict. There is no such thing as an objective announcement that will be interpreted in the same way across agents and across time. This fact creates great uncertainty for the central bank about how the announcement will be interpreted and thus how it will affect the economy. This explains the care central banks usually attach to the way they make announcements.

Our results also cast doubt on the skepticism introduced by Morris and Shin about whether the central bank should pursue a policy of full transparency. In macroeconomics there is no such thing as objective private and public information signals. All information is in the public domain. But agents struggle to understand these signals, leading to different private and subjective interpretations of the same signals. In such a world, the central bank can, by making its intentions clear, reduce the degree of confusion agents experience. It is difficult to see how this would be welfare-reducing. This being said, our results also show that even in a world of great transparency, there will still be a great deal of uncertainty about the meaning of announcements made by the central bank.

Notes

1. See the fascinating book by Gigerenzer and Todd (1999) on the use of simple heuristics as compared to statistical (regression) learning. Much of the behavioral economic literature has been very much influenced by the work of Kahneman and Tversky. See, e.g., Kahneman (2002) and Tversky and Kahneman (1981).

2. It is now standard in DSGE models to use a pricing equation in which marginal costs enter on the right-hand side. Such an equation is derived from profit maximization in a world of imperfect competition. It can be shown that under certain conditions the aggregate supply equation (2.3) is equivalent to such a pricing equation (see Galí 2008; Smets and Wouters 2003).

3. See Gigerenzer and Todd (1999), which argues that individual agents experience great difficulties in using statistical learning techniques.

4. See Farmer (2006) and the recent book of Akerlof and Shiller (2009) on the different interpretations of "Animal Spirits." The locus classicus is Keynes (1936).

References

Akerlof, G., and R. Shiller. 2009. *Animal Spirits: How Human Psychology Drives the Economy and Why It Matters for Global Capitalism*. Princeton: Princeton University Press.

Anderson, S., A. de Palma, and J.-F. Thisse. 1992. *Discrete Choice Theory of Product Differentiation*. Cambridge, Mass.: MIT Press.

Bernanke, B., and F. Mishkin. 1997. Inflation Targeting: A New Framework for Monetary Policy? *Journal of Economic Perspectives* 11 (2):97–116.

Branch, W., and G. Evans. 2006. Intrinsic Heterogeneity in Expectation Formation. *Journal of Economic Theory* 127:264–295.

Branch, W., and G. Evans. 2011. Monetary Policy with Heterogeneous Expectations. *Economic Theory* 47:365–393.

Brazier, A., R. Harrison, M. King, and T. Yates. 2006. The Danger of Inflating Expectations of Macroeconomic Stability: Heuristic Switching in an Overlapping Generations Monetary Model. Working paper no. 303, Bank of England, August.

Brock, W., and C. Hommes. 1997. A Rational Route to Randomness. *Econometrica* 65:1059–1095.

Bullard, J., and K. Mitra. 2002. Learning about Monetary Policy Rules. *Journal of Monetary Economics* 49 (6):1105–1129.

Camerer, C., G. Loewenstein, and D. Prelec. 2005. Neuroeconomics: How Neuroscience Can Inform Economics. *Journal of Economic Literature* 63 (1):9–64.

Damasio, A. 2003. *Looking for Spinoza: Joy, Sorrow and the Feeling Brain*. Orlando: Harcourt.

De Grauwe, P. 2012. *Lectures on Behavioral Macroeconomics*. Princeton: Princeton University Press.

De Grauwe, P., and M. Grimaldi. 2006. *The Exchange Rate in a Behavioral Finance Framework*. Princeton: Princeton University Press.

Evans, G., and S. Honkapohja. 2001. *Learning and Expectations in Macroeconomics*. Princeton: Princeton University Press.

Farmer, R. E. A. 2006. Animal Spirits. *Palgrave Dictionary of Economics*. London: Macmillan.

Galí, J. 2008. *Monetary Policy, Inflation and the Business Cycle.* Princeton: Princeton University Press.

Gaspar, V., F. Smets, and D. Vestin. 2006. Adaptive Learning, Persistence and Optimal Monetary Policy. Working Paper Series, no. 644, European Central Bank.

Gigerenzer, G., and P. M. Todd. 1999. *Simple Heuristics That Make Us Smart.* New York: Oxford University Press.

Hayek, F. 1945. The Use of Knowledge in Society. *American Economic Review* 35 (4):519–530.

Kahneman, D. 2002. Maps of Bounded Rationality: A Perspective on Intuitive Judgment and Choice. Nobel Prize Lecture, Stockholm, December 8.

Keynes, J. M. 1936. *The General Theory of Employment, Interest and Money.* London: Macmillan.

Leijonhufvud, A. 1993. Towards a Not-Too-Rational Macroeconomics. *Southern Economic Journal* 60 (1):1–13.

Milani, F. 2007. Learning and Time-Varying Macroeconomic Volatility. Mimeo, University of California, Irvine.

Morris, S., and H. Shin. 2002. Social Value of Public Information. *American Economic Review* 92 (5):1521–1534.

Orphanides, A., and J. Williams. 2004. Robust Monetary Policy with Imperfect Information. Discussion Paper, Board of Governors of the Federal Reserve System.

Sargent, T. 1993. *Bounded Rationality in Macroeconomics.* New York: Oxford University Press.

Smets, F., and R. Wouters. 2003. An Estimated Dynamic Stochastic General Equilibrium Model. *Journal of the European Economic Association* 1 (5):1123–1175.

Sturm, J. E., and J. De Haan. 2009. Does Central Bank Communication Really Lead to Better Forecasts of Policy Decisions? New Evidence Based on a Taylor Rule Model for the ECB. KOF Working Paper 2009, no. 236.

Svensson, L. 1997. Inflation Forecast Targeting: Implementing and Monitoring Inflation Targets. *European Economic Review* 41:111–146.

Svensson, L. 2006. Social Value of Public Information: Morris and Shin (2002) Is Actually Pro Transparency, Not Con. *American Economic Review* 96 (1):448–452.

Tversky, A., and D. Kahneman. 1981. The Framing of Decisions and the Psychology of Choice. *Science* 211:453–458.

Woodford, M. 2003. *Interest and Prices: Foundations of a Theory of Monetary Policy.* Princeton: Princeton University Press.

3 Transparency, Flexibility, and Macroeconomic Stabilization

Petra M. Geraats

3.1 Introduction

There has been a remarkable rise in the transparency of monetary policy during the last two decades. A majority of central banks throughout the world nowadays regularly publish their macroeconomic forecasts. This paper shows that such transparency gives the central bank greater flexibility to offset macroeconomic disturbances. In contrast, opacity forces the central bank to limit the stabilization of macroeconomic shocks to prevent upsetting the private sector's inflation expectations. Thus, an opaque central bank mutes its interest rate response and no longer fully offsets aggregate demand shocks it anticipates. As a result, greater transparency about macroeconomic forecasts leads to more effective stabilization and is welfare-improving.

Intuitively, the policy rate set by the central bank reflects both its inflationary intentions and the stabilization of aggregate demand and supply shocks. Transparency about the macroeconomic shocks to which the central bank responds allows the private sector to infer the central bank's inflationary intentions from its policy actions. But when there is opacity, the private sector confuses the central bank's stabilization efforts with changes in policy intentions, thereby causing greater volatility in private sector inflation expectations. This makes opaque central banks more reluctant to use the policy rate to stabilize macroeconomic shocks.

This paper analyzes a two-period model of discretionary monetary policy in the tradition of Kydland and Prescott (1977) and Barro and Gordon (1983). The structure of the economy is described by an expectations-augmented Phillips equation and an aggregate demand equation, where the central bank sets the policy rate. The public is uncertain about the central bank's inflationary intentions and faces asymmetric information about the aggregate demand and supply shocks observed by the central bank. Thus, the model is similar to Geraats (2005), except that it features a central bank objective function that is quadratic in both inflation and output, does not exhibit an inflation bias, and allows for intermediate degrees of transparency about macroeconomic shocks. Following Geraats (2002), the latter is referred to as "economic transparency" and describes the extent to which the private sector faces no asymmetric information about the macroeconomic information used by the central bank for monetary policymaking.

Although Geraats (2005) shows that economic transparency is beneficial because it reduces the inflation bias, much of the rest of the literature has found it to be detrimental. For instance, Cukierman (2001) and Gersbach (2003) show that the release of aggregate supply shocks negatively affects private sector inflation expectations in a simple static model. Using a two-period model with a New Keynesian Phillips curve and uncertainty about the central bank's output gap target, Jensen (2000, 2002) finds that greater transparency hampers the stabilization of supply shocks. Walsh (2007a, 2007b, 2008), who analyzes announcements to a fraction of agents in the New Keynesian model, also finds that imperfect economic transparency is generally desirable. In contrast to these studies, the present paper shows that transparency about aggregate supply shocks could actually be beneficial and enhance the stabilization of macroeconomic shocks. Thus, it helps to explain why economic transparency has been embraced by so many central banks (Geraats 2009).

Regarding the remainder of the paper, the model is presented in section 3.2 and the solution in section 3.3. Section 3.4 examines the effects of greater macroeconomic transparency on the volatility of the interest rate, inflation and output, and expected social welfare. The results are further discussed in section 3.5, and section 3.6 concludes.

3.2   Model

The central bank has the objective function

$$W_t = -\frac{1}{2}\alpha(\pi_t - \tau)^2 - \frac{1}{2}(y_t - \bar{y})^2, \tag{3.1}$$

where π_t is the rate of inflation; y_t is the level of real output; τ is the central bank's inflation target, which is stochastic but time-invariant

($\tau \sim N(\bar{\tau}, \sigma_\tau^2)$ with $\sigma_\tau^2 > 0$); $\bar{y}$ equals the natural rate of output; α is the relative weight on inflation stabilization ($\alpha > 0$); and the subscript t denotes the time period, $t \in \{1, 2\}$. The central banker is in office for two periods and maximizes the expected value of

$$U = W_1 + \delta W_2, \tag{3.2}$$

where δ is the intertemporal discount factor ($0 < \delta \leq 1$).

The structure of the economy is described by the aggregate demand relation

$$y_t = \bar{y} - (i_t - \pi_t^e - \bar{r}) + d_t, \tag{3.3}$$

where i_t is the nominal interest rate; π_t^e denotes inflation expectations formed by the private sector; d_t is an aggregate demand shock: $d_t \sim N(0, \sigma_d^2)$ with $\sigma_d^2 > 0$; and $\bar{r}$ is the long-run, ex ante real interest rate. Aggregate supply is described by the price adjustment relation

$$\pi_t = \pi_t^e + (y_t - \bar{y}) - s_t, \tag{3.4}$$

where s_t is a (beneficial) aggregate supply shock: $s_t \sim N(0, \sigma_s^2)$ with $\sigma_s^2 > 0$. It is assumed that τ, d_t, and s_t are independent. The structure of the economy is kept simple to keep the algebra tractable and obtain analytical results, in contrast to much of the related literature, which depends on numerical findings. For analytical convenience, the slopes of the aggregate demand and supply equations have been normalized to 1, but all the qualitative results in this paper continue to hold when this assumption is dropped.

The central bank is assumed to observe the aggregate demand and supply shocks (d_t, s_t). Although central bank forecasts in practice are far from perfect, allowing for noisy forecasts in the model would increase algebraic clutter without affecting the key conclusions.

A crucial assumption is that the private sector does not have the same information as the central bank. There are two sources of asymmetric information. First, the private sector only observes a signal of the (central bank forecasts of the) demand and supply shocks. More precisely, the economic shocks can be decomposed into an unbiased public signal (ξ_t^d, ξ_t^s) and an independent white noise shock (η_t^d, η_t^s) only observed by the central bank:

$$d_t = \xi_t^d + \eta_t^d, \tag{3.5}$$

$$s_t = \xi_t^s + \eta_t^s. \tag{3.6}$$

The public's forecast errors depend on the extent of the information asymmetry: $\eta_t^d \sim N(0, (1 - \kappa_d)\sigma_d^2)$ and $\eta_t^s \sim N(0, (1 - \kappa_s)\sigma_s^2)$, where $0 \leq \kappa_d \leq 1$, $0 \leq \kappa_s \leq 1$, and η_t^d and η_t^s are assumed to be independent of τ. The parameters κ_d and κ_s provide a measure of the degree of economic transparency. They reflect the extent to which the central bank communicates the macroeconomic shocks to the public. In the special case of $\kappa_d = \kappa_s = 0$, the public is completely ignorant about the economic disturbances ($\xi_t^d = \xi_t^s = 0$); for $\kappa_d = \kappa_s = 1$, perfect transparency about the macroeconomic shocks prevails ($\xi_t^d = d_t$, $\xi_t^s = s_t$).

For analytical simplicity, the central bank is assumed to have superior economic information, which is consistent with empirical evidence provided by Peek, Rosengren, and Tootell (1999) and Romer and Romer (2000). Instead, the private sector could have an information advantage, in which case indeterminacies may arise if the central bank attempts to infer information from private sector inflation expectations (Bernanke and Woodford 1997). If the central bank would refrain from such attempts, the conclusions of the present model would still apply. The key assumption is that the information that the central bank uses for its policy decisions (how imperfect it may be) is generally not fully observed by the private sector (for instance because it includes central bankers' private judgments). The transparency parameters κ_d and κ_s measure the extent to which the private sector observes the macroeconomic information used for monetary policy decisions.

The second source of asymmetric information is that the private sector faces some initial uncertainty about the inflation target τ that the central bank pursues. This could be the case even if there exists an explicit inflation target, as the latter is often formulated as a range and need not be perfectly credible. In addition, the central bank's preferences cannot be directly observed. So, the absence of complete certainty about preferences appears plausible and a tiny amount of ex ante uncertainty $\sigma_\tau^2 > 0$ already suffices to obtain the results in this paper. Although other forms of preference uncertainty may be more appealing, for instance about the relative weight on inflation stabilization, this would come at the loss of analytical tractability.

The timing of events is as follows. Before the first period, the central bank's inflation target τ is drawn by nature but is only observed by the central bank. In addition, private sector inflation expectations π_1^e are formed using its prior on τ. In the first period, the public signals ξ_1^d and ξ_1^s are revealed, and the central bank observes the economic disturbances d_1 and s_1, and sets the nominal interest rate i_1 accordingly. At the end of the first period, the private sector updates its prior on τ using the nominal interest rate i_1 and public signals (ξ_1^d, ξ_1^s). So, its first-period posterior of τ depends on the degree of economic transparency (κ_d, κ_s) and is incorporated into private sector inflation expectations π_2^e. At the beginning of the second period, the levels of inflation π_1 and output y_1 are observed. In addition, the public signals ξ_2^d and ξ_2^s are revealed, and the central bank observes the economic disturbances d_2 and s_2, and sets the nominal interest rate i_2. After this last period, inflation π_2 and output y_2 are known.

The assumption that information on inflation π_1 and output y_1 is not available when the private sector forms its inflation expectations π_2^e is due to lags in the effect of monetary policy decisions. Since the macroeconomic outcome of a previous decision is not yet known, the private sector uses the policy instrument and its information about economic disturbances to determine inflation expectations, which are relevant for the next policy decision. This captures the prevalent practice of the private sector paying close attention to the central bank's interest rate decisions to infer its intentions.

It is assumed that people have rational expectations. Formally, the information set available to the public when it forms its inflation expectations π_1^e and π_2^e equals $\Omega \equiv \{\bar{r}, \bar{y}, \alpha, \delta, \kappa_d, \kappa_s, \bar{\tau}, \sigma_\tau^2, \sigma_d^2, \sigma_s^2\}$ and $\{i_1, \Omega_1\}$, respectively, where $\Omega_1 \equiv \{\xi_1^d, \xi_1^s, \Omega\}$. The next section provides the solution to the model.

3.3 Solution

The model is solved by backward induction. In period two, the central bank maximizes W_2 with respect to i_2 subject to (3.4) and (3.3), and given π_2^e, d_2, and s_2. The first-order condition implies

$$i_2 = \bar{r} + \pi_2^e - \frac{\alpha}{1+\alpha}(\tau - \pi_2^e) + d_2 - \frac{\alpha}{1+\alpha}s_2. \tag{3.7}$$

Using (3.3) and (3.4), this yields

$$y_2 = \bar{y} + \frac{\alpha}{1+\alpha}(\tau - \pi_2^e) + \frac{\alpha}{1+\alpha}s_2, \tag{3.8}$$

$$\pi_2 = \pi_2^e + \frac{\alpha}{1+\alpha}(\tau - \pi_2^e) - \frac{1}{1+\alpha}s_2. \tag{3.9}$$

An inflation target above the expected rate of inflation has an expansionary effect and reduces the interest rate and increases output and inflation. Demand shocks d are fully offset by an increase in the interest rate, whereas the effect of a (deflationary) supply shock s is partially neutralized by a decrease in the interest rate that raises output. A more conservative central bank (higher α) has a stronger interest rate response to supply shocks, which therefore have a larger effect on output but a smaller impact on inflation.

Substituting (3.8) and (3.9) into (3.1) and taking expectations conditional on τ and π_2^e gives

$$E[W_2 \mid \tau, \pi_2^e] = -\frac{1}{2}\frac{\alpha}{1+\alpha}[(\pi_2^e - \tau)^2 + \sigma_s^2]. \tag{3.10}$$

The expected payoff to the central bank in period two is maximized when the private sector perfectly anticipates the central bank's type: $\pi_2^e = \tau$. Thus, it is in the central bank's interest to reveal its type through its policy action i_1.

Facing imperfect information, the private sector uses the nominal interest rate i_1 and the public signals ξ_1^d and ξ_1^s to update its prior on τ and form its inflation expectations π_2^e. Suppose that the private sector uses the following updating equation:

$$\pi_2^e = u_0 + u_i i_1 + u_d \xi_1^d + u_s \xi_1^s. \tag{3.11}$$

Below it is shown that this is consistent with a rational expectations equilibrium.[1] The simple linear structure follows from the normality assumptions on τ, η_1^d, and η_1^s.

In the first period, the central bank maximizes the expected value of (3.2) with respect to i_1 subject to (3.4) and (3.3), given π_1^e, d_1, and s_1, and using (3.1), (3.10), and (3.11). The first-order condition implies

$$\begin{aligned} i_1 = \frac{1}{(1+\alpha)^2 + \delta\alpha u_i^2}&[(1+\alpha)^2(\bar{r} + \pi_1^e) - \alpha(1+\alpha)(\tau - \pi_1^e) + \delta\alpha u_i(\tau - u_0) \\ &- \delta\alpha u_i(u_d \xi_1^d + u_s \xi_1^s) + (1+\alpha)^2 d_1 - \alpha(1+\alpha)s_1]. \end{aligned} \tag{3.12}$$

The updating coefficients u_0, u_i, u_d, and u_s can be found by using the condition for rational expectations: $\pi_2^e = E_1[\pi_2 \mid i_1]$, where a moment operator with subscript 1 is conditional on the information set Ω_1. Taking expectations and rearranging (3.9) gives $\pi_2^e = E_1[\tau \mid i_1]$. Before tackling the general case, it is instructive to first consider the special case of perfect economic transparency.

3.3.1 Perfect Economic Transparency

In the case of perfect economic transparency, which is indicated by superscript T, $\kappa_d = \kappa_s = 1$, so that $d_t = \xi_t^d$ and $s_t = \xi_t^s$. In that case, (3.12) can be used to infer the central bank's inflation target τ from the interest rate i_1: $E_1^T[\tau|i_1] = \tau$. Hence, $(\pi_2^e)^T = E_1^T[\tau|i_1] = \tau$. Solving (3.12) for τ, matching coefficients with (3.11), and rearranging yields:[2]

$$u_0^T = (\pi_1^e)^T + \frac{1+\alpha}{\alpha}[\bar{r} + (\pi_1^e)^T], \tag{3.13}$$

$$u_i^T = -\frac{1+\alpha}{\alpha}, \tag{3.14}$$

$$u_d^T = \frac{1+\alpha}{\alpha}, \tag{3.15}$$

$$u_s^T = -1. \tag{3.16}$$

Intuitively, a higher interest rate i_1 reduces inflation expectations ($u_i^T < 0$), as it is (correctly) attributed to a lower inflation target τ. In addition, a higher (perceived) demand shock ξ_1^d leads to higher inflation expectations π_2^e for a given interest rate i_1 ($u_d^T > 0$) as the inflation target τ implied by i_1 rises. Similarly, a higher (perceived) supply shock ξ_1^s lowers inflation expectations π_2^e given i_1 ($u_s^T < 0$) as the implied inflation target τ declines.

Substituting these updating equations into (3.12), using $\xi_t^d = d_t$ and $\xi_t^s = s_t$, and simplifying produces the nominal interest rate under perfect economic transparency:

$$i_1^T = \bar{r} + (\pi_1^e)^T - \frac{\alpha}{1+\alpha}[\tau - (\pi_1^e)^T] + d_1 - \frac{\alpha}{1+\alpha}s_1. \tag{3.17}$$

Substituting (3.17) into (3.3) and (3.4), and imposing rational expectations (so that $(\pi_1^e)^T = \bar{\tau}$) gives

$$y_1^T = \bar{y} + \frac{\alpha}{1+\alpha}(\tau - \bar{\tau}) + \frac{\alpha}{1+\alpha}s_1, \tag{3.18}$$

$$\pi_1^T = \bar{\tau} + \frac{\alpha}{1+\alpha}(\tau - \bar{\tau}) - \frac{1}{1+\alpha}s_1. \tag{3.19}$$

These expressions are similar to the ones for the second period. Demand shocks are again completely offset by monetary policy.

Finally, the expected payoff to the central bank under perfect economic transparency can be found using (3.2) after substituting (3.18) and (3.19) into (3.1) and $(\pi_2^e)^T = \tau$ into (3.10):

$$\mathrm{E}[U^T \mid \tau] = -\frac{1}{2}\frac{\alpha}{1+\alpha}(\tau - \overline{\tau})^2 - \frac{1}{2}\frac{\alpha}{1+\alpha}(1+\delta)\sigma_s^2. \tag{3.20}$$

This shows that the expected payoff to the central bank is decreasing in the difference between the inflation target τ and the public's prior of it $\overline{\tau}$, and in the variance of supply shocks σ_s^2. The variance of demand shocks σ_d^2 is immaterial, as they are fully offset under economic transparency.

3.3.2   General Case

Except for the special case of perfect economic transparency, the nominal interest rate i_1 and the public signals ξ_1^d and ξ_1^s generally do not suffice to infer the central bank's inflation target τ. To find the updating coefficients, use the fact that (3.12) implies that i_1 and τ have a jointly normal distribution, so that

$$\pi_2^e = \mathrm{E}_1[\tau \mid i_1] = \mathrm{E}_1[\tau] + \frac{\mathrm{Cov}_1\{i_1, \tau\}}{\mathrm{Var}_1[i_1]}(i_1 - \mathrm{E}_1[i_1]), \tag{3.21}$$

where moment operators with subscript 1 are conditional on Ω_1. Using (3.12), (3.5), and (3.6), and matching coefficients between (3.21) and (3.11), and rearranging gives the following expression for u_i:[3]

$$-\delta\alpha^2\sigma_\tau^2 u_i^2 + (1+\alpha)[\alpha(\alpha-\delta)\sigma_\tau^2 + (1+\alpha)^2(1-\kappa_d)\sigma_d^2$$
$$+ \alpha^2(1-\kappa_s)\sigma_s^2]u_i + \alpha(1+\alpha)^2\sigma_\tau^2 = 0.$$

This equation has two real roots, $u_i^- < 0$ and $u_i^+ > 0$. However, the positive root u_i^+ can be excluded based on an argument by McCallum (1983). The reason is that u_i^+ is not valid for all admissible parameter values, because $\lim_{\kappa_d,\kappa_s\to1} u_i^+ \neq u_i^T$. The remaining negative root can be written as

$$u_i = \frac{(1+\alpha)}{2\delta\alpha^2\sigma_\tau^2}\left\{ \alpha(\alpha-\delta)\sigma_\tau^2 + (1+\alpha)^2(1-\kappa_d)\sigma_d^2 + \alpha^2(1-\kappa_s)\sigma_s^2 \right.$$
$$\left. - \sqrt{\begin{array}{l}[\alpha(\alpha+\delta)\sigma_\tau^2 + (1+\alpha)^2(1-\kappa_d)\sigma_d^2 + \alpha^2(1-\kappa_s)\sigma_s^2]^2 \\ -4\delta\alpha[(1+\alpha)^2(1-\kappa_d)\sigma_d^2 + \alpha^2(1-\kappa_s)\sigma_s^2]\sigma_\tau^2 \end{array}} \right\}. \tag{3.22}$$

From this it follows that $u_i \geq -(1+\alpha)/\alpha$ with a strict inequality if $\kappa_d \neq 1$ and/or $\kappa_s \neq 1$. Hence, $|u_i| \leq |u_i^T|$; the magnitude of the effect of the interest rate on inflation expectations is smaller under opacity because it is a noisier signal of the inflation target. Concerning intermediate degrees of transparency, $du_i / d\kappa_m \leq 0$, with strict inequality if $\sigma_m^2 > 0$, where $m \in \{d, s\}$ denotes the macroeconomic shock. So, the magnitude of the sensitivity u_i of private sector inflation expectations π_2^e to the policy rate i_1 is increasing in the degree of economic transparency κ_m as the policy rate becomes a more accurate signal of the inflation target.

Regarding the other updating coefficients, matching coefficients and rearranging gives

$$u_0 = \bar{\tau} + u_i \frac{\alpha}{1+\alpha}(\bar{\tau} - \pi_1^e) - u_i(\bar{r} + \pi_1^e), \tag{3.23}$$

$$u_d = -u_i, \tag{3.24}$$

$$u_s = \frac{\alpha}{1+\alpha}u_i. \tag{3.25}$$

Intuitively, a higher interest rate i_1 reduces inflation expectations ($u_i < 0$) as it is partly attributed to a lower inflation target τ. In addition, a higher perceived demand [supply] shock ξ_i^d [ξ_i^s] leads to higher [lower] inflation expectations π_2^e for a given interest rate i_1 ($u_d > 0$, $u_s < 0$) as the inflation target τ implied by i_1 rises [falls]. Compared to perfect economic transparency, these effects are qualitatively the same, but they are more muted since the private sector faces greater uncertainty about these signals.

Substituting these updating coefficients into (3.12), using (3.5) and (3.6), and simplifying gives the nominal interest rate:

$$i_1 = \bar{r} + \pi_1^e - \frac{\alpha}{1+\alpha}(\tau - \pi_1^e) + (1-\mu)\left(\frac{\alpha}{1+\alpha} + \frac{1}{u_i}\right)(\tau - \bar{\tau})$$
$$+ (\xi_1^d + \mu\eta_1^d) - \frac{\alpha}{1+\alpha}(\xi_1^s + \mu\eta_1^s), \tag{3.26}$$

where $\mu \equiv \dfrac{(1+\alpha)^2}{(1+\alpha)^2 + \delta\alpha u_i^2}$ ($0 < \mu < 1$). Note that in the special case of perfect economic transparency, $u_i = -(1 + \alpha)/\alpha$, $d_1 = \xi_1^d$, $s_1 = \xi_1^s$, and $\eta_1^d = \eta_1^s = 0$, so that (3.26) reduces to (3.17). Demand and supply shocks that are publicly anticipated (ξ_1^d and ξ_1^s) have the same effect as under transparency. However, the responsiveness of the interest rate to economic disturbances that are not anticipated by the private sector (η_1^d and η_1^s) is smaller under opacity. The reason is that the central bank is concerned about affecting private sector inflation expectations. As a consequence, (publicly unanticipated) demand shocks are no longer completely offset.

Substitute (3.26) into (3.3) and (3.4), use (3.5) and (3.6), and impose rational expectations (which yields $\pi_1^e = \overline{\tau}$) to get output and inflation:

$$y_1 = \overline{y} + \left[\frac{\alpha}{1+\alpha} - (1-\mu)\left(\frac{\alpha}{1+\alpha} + \frac{1}{u_i}\right) \right](\tau - \overline{\tau}) + (1-\mu)\eta_1^d + \frac{\alpha}{1+\alpha}(\xi_1^s + \mu\eta_1^s),$$

(3.27)

$$\pi_1 = \overline{\tau} + \left[\frac{\alpha}{1+\alpha} - (1-\mu)\left(\frac{\alpha}{1+\alpha} + \frac{1}{u_i}\right) \right](\tau - \overline{\tau})$$
$$+ (1-\mu)\eta_1^d - \frac{1}{1+\alpha}(\xi_1^s + [1+(1-\mu)\alpha]\eta_1^s).$$

(3.28)

Although demand shocks anticipated by the public (ξ_1^d) are perfectly offset, the central bank reduces its response to publicly unanticipated demand shocks (η_1^d), which therefore affect both output and inflation. A publicly anticipated (deflationary) supply shock (ξ_1^s) leads to more expansionary monetary policy, which raises output and partly offsets the effect of the shock on inflation. The central bank responds less to publicly unanticipated supply shocks (η_1^s), so the effect on output is smaller and the impact on inflation is larger. Note that $u_i < 0$ and $0 < \mu < 1$ imply that the coefficient of $(\tau - \overline{\tau})$ is positive. Intuitively, if the inflation target τ is higher than the public's prior $\overline{\tau}$, the central bank implements more expansionary policy than anticipated, which increases both output and inflation. In the special case of perfect economic transparency, $u_i = -(1 + \alpha)/\alpha$, $d_1 = \xi_1^d$, $s_1 = \xi_1^s$, and $\eta_1^d = \eta_1^s = 0$, so that (3.27) and (3.28) reduce to (3.18) and (3.19), respectively.

Using (3.26), $\pi_1^e = \overline{\tau}$, and the fact that $\mathrm{Var}[\eta_t^m] = (1 - \kappa_m)\sigma_m^2$ and $\mathrm{Var}[\xi_t^m] = \kappa_m\sigma_m^2$, where $m \in \{d, s\}$ denotes the macroeconomic shock, the volatility of the interest rate i_1 (for a given inflation target τ) equals[4]

$$\mathrm{Var}[i_1 \mid \tau] = [1 - (1-\mu^2)(1-\kappa_d)]\sigma_d^2 + \frac{\alpha^2}{(1+\alpha)^2}[1 - (1-\mu^2)(1-\kappa_s)]\sigma_s^2. \quad (3.29)$$

In the case of perfect economic transparency ($\kappa_d = \kappa_s = 1$), this reduces to $\mathrm{Var}[i_1^T \mid \tau] = \sigma_d^2 + \frac{\alpha^2}{(1+\alpha)^2}\sigma_s^2$. Clearly, $\mathrm{Var}[i_1 \mid \tau] \le \mathrm{Var}[i_1^T \mid \tau]$, with a strict inequality in the case of some economic opacity ($\kappa_d \neq 1$ or $\kappa_s \neq 1$). Intuitively, the lack of economic transparency induces the central bank to limit its adjustment of the policy rate in response to macroeconomic shocks to avoid affecting private sector inflation expectations. As a result, economic opacity leads to a muted interest rate response.

Regarding the volatility of output and inflation (given the inflation target τ), (3.27) and (3.28) imply that

$$\text{Var}[y_1 \mid \tau] = (1-\mu)^2(1-\kappa_d)\sigma_d^2 + \frac{\alpha^2}{(1+\alpha)^2}[1-(1-\mu^2)(1-\kappa_s)]\sigma_s^2, \tag{3.30}$$

$$\text{Var}[\pi_1 \mid \tau] = (1-\mu)^2(1-\kappa_d)\sigma_d^2 + \frac{1}{(1+\alpha)^2}[\kappa_s + [1+(1-\mu)\alpha]^2(1-\kappa_s)]\sigma_s^2. \tag{3.31}$$

In the case of perfect economic transparency ($\kappa_d = \kappa_s = 1$), this reduces to $\text{Var}[y_1^T \mid \tau] = \dfrac{\alpha^2}{(1+\alpha)^2}\sigma_s^2$ and $\text{Var}[\pi_1^T \mid \tau] = \dfrac{1}{(1+\alpha)^2}\sigma_s^2$. This shows that economic transparency reduces output volatility due to demand shocks, but increases it for supply shocks, so the net effect is ambiguous. The variance of inflation is unambiguously lower under economic transparency for both demand and supply shocks, so that $\text{Var}[\pi_1 \mid \tau] \geq \text{Var}[\pi_1^T \mid \tau]$.[5] The intuition is that the enhanced flexibility under economic transparency allows the central bank to respond more vigorously to demand shocks, which decreases the variance of both output and inflation, and to supply shocks, which increases output volatility but reduces inflation variability.

The degree of opacity also affects macroeconomic volatility in the second period due to the noise it creates in private sector inflation expectations π_2^e. Substituting (3.23), (3.24), (3.25), and (3.26) into (3.11) produces

$$\pi_2^e = \tau - \mu\left(1 + \frac{\alpha}{(1+\alpha)}u_i\right)(\tau - \bar{\tau}) + u_i\mu\eta_1^d - \frac{\alpha}{(1+\alpha)}u_i\mu\eta_1^s. \tag{3.32}$$

Intuitively, economic shocks η^d and η^s that are unanticipated by the public affect their inflation expectations because the corresponding interest rate response is partially attributed to the central bank's inflation target. In the case of perfect economic transparency, $u_i = -(1+\alpha)/\alpha$ and $\eta_1^d = \eta_1^s = 0$, yielding $(\pi_2^e)^T = \tau$, as in section 3.3.1. The volatility of private sector inflation expectations (for a given inflation target τ) are equal to

$$\text{Var}[\pi_2^e \mid \tau] = u_i^2\mu^2(1-\kappa_d)\sigma_d^2 + \left(\frac{\alpha}{1+\alpha}\right)^2 u_i^2\mu^2(1-\kappa_s)\sigma_s^2. \tag{3.33}$$

Clearly, $\mathrm{Var}[\pi_2^e \mid \tau] \geq \mathrm{Var}[(\pi_2^e)^T \mid \tau] = 0$, with a strict inequality in the case of some economic opacity ($\kappa_d \neq 1$ or $\kappa_s \neq 1$).

Regarding the variability of the interest rate, output and inflation in the second period, (3.7), (3.8), and (3.9) yield

$$\mathrm{Var}[i_2 \mid \tau] = \left(1 + \frac{\alpha}{(1+\alpha)}\right)^2 \mathrm{Var}[\pi_2^e \mid \tau] + \sigma_d^2 + \left(\frac{\alpha}{1+\alpha}\right)^2 \sigma_s^2,$$

$$\mathrm{Var}[y_2 \mid \tau] = \left(\frac{\alpha}{1+\alpha}\right)^2 \left\{ \mathrm{Var}[\pi_2^e \mid \tau] + \sigma_s^2 \right\},$$

$$\mathrm{Var}[\pi_2 \mid \tau] = \left(\frac{1}{1+\alpha}\right)^2 \left\{ \mathrm{Var}[\pi_2^e \mid \tau] + \sigma_s^2 \right\}.$$

So, $\mathrm{Var}[i_2 \mid \tau] \geq \mathrm{Var}[i_2^T \mid \tau]$, $\mathrm{Var}[y_2 \mid \tau] \geq \mathrm{Var}[y_2^T \mid \tau]$, and $\mathrm{Var}[\pi_2 \mid \tau] \geq \mathrm{Var}[\pi_2^T \mid \tau]$, with a strict inequality in the case of some economic opacity ($\kappa_m \neq 1$). As a result, the greater stability of private sector inflation expectations under economic transparency contributes to lower overall macroeconomic volatility in the second period.

3.4   Effects of Greater Macroeconomic Transparency

The previous section has derived how perfect transparency about macroeconomic shocks affects the interest rate, inflation (expectations), and output. This section examines intermediate degrees of transparency and shows the effect of greater macroeconomic transparency on the volatility of the interest rate, inflation (expectations), and output (in section 3.4.1) and on expected social welfare (in section 3.4.2).

3.4.1   Macroeconomic Volatility

The analysis so far has shown that perfect economic transparency (i.e., $\kappa_d = \kappa_s = 1$) leads to greater interest rate variability ($\mathrm{Var}[i_1 \mid \tau]$), but reduces the volatility of inflation and inflation expectations ($\mathrm{Var}[\pi_1 \mid \tau]$ and $\mathrm{Var}[\pi_2^e \mid \tau]$), while the effect on output volatility ($\mathrm{Var}[y_1 \mid \tau]$) is ambiguous. For intermediate degrees of transparency, (3.29), (3.30), (3.31), and (3.33) show that the effect of a change in κ_m depends on $d\mu/d\kappa_m$. Since $d\mu/du_i > 0$ and $du_i/d\kappa_m < 0$, it follows that $d\mu/d\kappa_m < 0$.[6] So, the effect of κ_m on macroeconomic volatility is in principle ambiguous.

To facilitate the analysis, assume that $\kappa_d = \kappa_s = \kappa$, i.e., the degree of economic transparency is the same for demand and supply shocks. Then

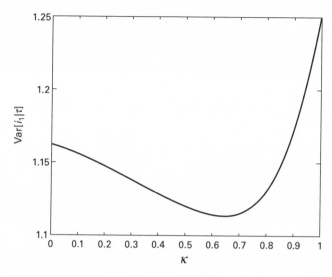

Figure 3.1
The effect of economic transparency κ on interest rate variability, for parameter values $\alpha = \delta = 1$ and $\sigma_\tau^2 = \sigma_d^2 = \sigma_s^2 = 1$.

it is straightforward to show that $\lim_{\kappa \to 1} d\mathrm{Var}[i_1 \mid \tau]/d\kappa > 0$, $\lim_{\kappa \to 1} d\mathrm{Var}[\pi_1 \mid \tau]/d\kappa < 0$, and $\lim_{\kappa \to 1} d\mathrm{Var}[\pi_2^e \mid \tau]/d\kappa < 0$. Thus, greater macroeconomic transparency increases interest rate variability but decreases the volatility of inflation and inflation expectations for sufficiently high κ. For lower κ the effects tend to be reversed. This is illustrated in figures 3.1, 3.2, and 3.4 for the parameter configuration $\alpha = \delta = 1$ and $\sigma_\tau^2 = \sigma_d^2 = \sigma_s^2 = 1$.

Figure 3.1 shows that starting from complete opacity ($\kappa = 0$), higher macroeconomic transparency κ initially reduces and subsequently increases interest rate variability. Intuitively, for low levels of economic transparency, the interest rate i_1 is dominated by the central bank's response to publicly unanticipated shocks η_1^m. As the degree of economic transparency rises, the public rationally increases its reliance on the interest rate i_1 to update its inflation expectations π_2^e, and so the central bank reduces its response to unanticipated shocks to prevent upsetting private sector expectations. Hence, the variability of the interest rate i_1 initially declines. But for a sufficiently high level of economic transparency, publicly anticipated shocks ξ_1^m start prevailing. Since the central bank need not mute its response to these shocks, the variance of the interest rate increases as anticipated shocks become more

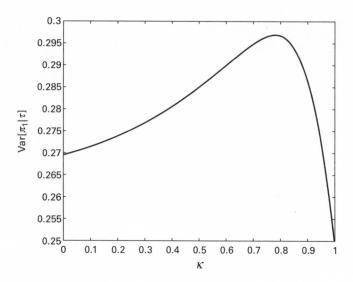

Figure 3.2
The effect of economic transparency κ on inflation volatility, for parameter values $\alpha = \delta$ = 1 and $\sigma_\tau^2 = \sigma_d^2 = \sigma_s^2 = 1$.

important at higher levels of economic transparency. As a result, there is a U-shaped effect on interest rate volatility.

Figure 3.2 shows that more macroeconomic transparency κ initially raises and subsequently reduces inflation volatility in period one. As explained above, a rise in economic transparency causes the central bank to reduce its interest rate response to publicly unanticipated shocks, which therefore cause greater inflation volatility. But for higher levels of economic transparency, publicly anticipated shocks start becoming more important. These are adequately offset by the central bank, resulting in a reduction of the variability of inflation.

The effect of higher macroeconomic transparency κ on output volatility in period one exhibits a more peculiar pattern. For the baseline case of $\alpha = \delta = 1$ and $\sigma_\tau^2 = \sigma_d^2 = \sigma_s^2 = 1$ shown in figure 3.3, the variance of y_1 is initially decreasing, then increasing, and finally decreasing again. However, this result is very sensitive to the parameter values. In particular, for higher values of α or σ_s^2, or lower values of σ_d^2, the response becomes U-shaped, whereas for higher values of σ_τ^2, the response becomes hump-shaped. Clearly, the effect of macroeconomic transparency on first-period output volatility critically depends on the precise parameter configuration.

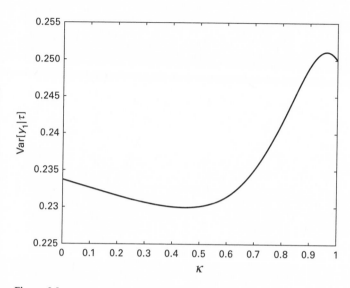

Figure 3.3
The effect of economic transparency κ on output volatility, for parameter values $\alpha = \delta = 1$ and $\sigma_\tau^2 = \sigma_d^2 = \sigma_s^2 = 1$.

In the second period, greater macroeconomic transparency κ initially raises and subsequently reduces the volatility of private sector inflation expectations, as shown in figure 3.4. The same holds for the volatility of the interest rate, output, and inflation in period two. Intuitively, only macroeconomic shocks η_1^m that are not anticipated by the public affect its expectations. When the degree of economic transparency goes up, the public rationally relies more on the interest rate i_1 to update its inflation expectations π_2^e, since it becomes a better signal of the central bank's intentions τ. This also raises the response of expectations to the noise caused by unanticipated shocks, which initially increases the volatility of inflation expectations. However, as the degree of economic transparency further rises, the unanticipated shocks start diminishing in importance and the variance of private sector inflation expectations declines.

The U-shaped effect of macroeconomic transparency κ on $\mathrm{Var}[i_1 \mid \tau]$ in figure 3.1 and the hump-shaped effect for $\mathrm{Var}[\pi_1 \mid \tau]$ and $\mathrm{Var}[\pi_2^e \mid \tau]$ in figures 3.2 and 3.4 are fairly typical for reasonable parameter values, but they are by no means universal. Intuitively, the U-shaped and hump-shaped patterns arise from the differential effects of publicly unanticipated macroeconomic disturbances η_1^m, which dominate when economic transparency is low, and publicly anticipated shocks ξ_1^m,

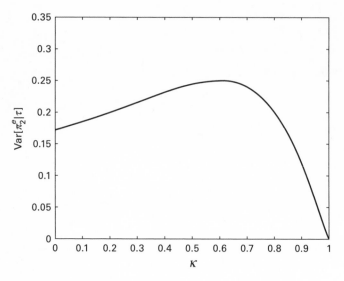

Figure 3.4
The effect of economic transparency κ on the volatility of inflation expectations, for parameter values $\alpha = \delta = 1$ and $\sigma_\tau^2 = \sigma_d^2 = \sigma_s^2 = 1$.

which prevail when economic transparency is high. But the latter may already dominate straightaway, depending on the parameter values.

To assess the robustness of the results, a grid search was conducted for $\alpha \in \{0.1, 0.25: 0.25: 10\}$, $\delta \in [0.5: 0.1: 1]$, $\sigma_\tau^2 \in \{0.1, 0.25: 0.25: 10\}$, $\sigma_d^2 \in \{0.1, 0.25: 0.25: 10\}$, and $\sigma_s^2 \in \{0.1, 0.25: 0.25: 10\}$, covering 16,954,566 parameter configurations.[7] For this parameter space, the result of a U-shaped effect on the variability of the interest rate i_1 and/or the hump-shaped effect on the volatility of inflation π_1 and inflation expectations π_2^e does not hold for 14.99% of parameter values. Although the exceptions occur throughout the parameter space, there is a systematic deviation from the usual pattern when σ_τ^2 is large relative to σ_d^2 and/or σ_s^2. In particular, when macroeconomic volatility σ_m^2 is sufficiently small compared to preference uncertainty σ_τ^2, $\text{Var}[i_1 \mid \tau]$ is monotonically increasing in κ, and $\text{Var}[\pi_1 \mid \tau]$ and $\text{Var}[\pi_2^e \mid \tau]$ are monotonically decreasing. More formally, for $\sigma_m^2 \to 0$, $du_i/d\kappa \to 0$, so $d\mu/d\kappa \to 0$.[8] Hence, (3.29), (3.31), and (3.33) yield $\lim_{\sigma_m^2 \to 0} d\text{Var}[i_1 \mid \tau]/d\kappa > 0$, $\lim_{\sigma_m^2 \to 0} d\text{Var}[\pi_1 \mid \tau]/d\kappa < 0$, and $\lim_{\sigma_m^2 \to 0} d\text{Var}[\pi_2^e \mid \tau]/d\kappa < 0$. In other words, relatively low macroeconomic volatility yields the same result as high macroeconomic transparency ($\kappa \to 1$), which is an intuitive finding.

3.4.2 Welfare Analysis

The analysis so far has shown that the effect of economic transparency on the volatility of inflation and output tends to be nonmonotonic. Even the effect of perfect economic transparency ($\kappa = 1$) appears ambiguous, as the variance is lower for π_1, π_2, and y_2, but may be higher for y_1. Thus, it is essential to conduct a welfare analysis. Assume that the social welfare function is the same as the central bank's objective function: (3.1) and (3.2). This is a useful benchmark because it means that monetary policy is not affected by a principal-agent problem, but only by transparency issues.

Substituting (3.32) into (3.10) yields

$$
E[W_2] = -\frac{1}{2}\frac{\alpha}{1+\alpha}\left\{\mu^2\left(1+\frac{\alpha}{1+\alpha}u_i\right)^2\sigma_\tau^2 + u_i^2\mu^2(1-\kappa_d)\sigma_d^2 \right.
$$
$$
\left. + \left[\frac{\alpha^2}{(1+\alpha)^2}u_i^2\mu^2(1-\kappa_s)+1\right]\sigma_s^2\right\}.
$$

(3.34)

Under perfect economic transparency $u_i = -(1+\alpha)/\alpha$ and $\kappa_d = \kappa_s = 1$, so $E[W_2^T] = -\frac{1}{2}\frac{\alpha}{(1+\alpha)}\sigma_s^2 > E[W_2]$. Not surprisingly, opacity is socially detrimental in period two as it makes private sector inflation expectations π_2^e more noisy and thereby increases the volatility of macroeconomic outcomes in the second period.

Substituting (3.27) and (3.28) into (3.1) produces, after some rearranging,[9]

$$
E[W_1] = -\frac{1}{2}\frac{\alpha}{1+\alpha}\left\{1+\alpha(1-\mu)^2\left(\frac{1+\alpha}{\alpha u_i}+1\right)^2\right\}\sigma_\tau^2
$$
$$
-\frac{1}{2}(1+\alpha)(1-\mu)^2(1-\kappa_d)\sigma_d^2 - \frac{1}{2}\frac{\alpha}{1+\alpha}\left\{1+\alpha(1-\mu)^2(1-\kappa_s)\right\}\sigma_s^2.
$$

(3.35)

Under perfect economic transparency, $u_i = -(1+\alpha)/\alpha$ and $\kappa_d = \kappa_s = 1$, so $E[W_1^T] = -\frac{1}{2}\frac{\alpha}{(1+\alpha)}\sigma_\tau^2 - \frac{1}{2}\frac{\alpha}{(1+\alpha)}\sigma_s^2 > E[W_1]$. Intuitively, economic transparency reduces the variance of inflation and output due to demand shocks. Although there is greater output volatility due to supply shocks, this actually allows the central bank to achieve a more desirable tradeoff between inflation and output volatility. Hence, perfect economic transparency is socially beneficial in period one.

Substituting (3.35) and (3.34) into (3.2) yields

$$E[U] = -\frac{1}{2}A_\tau \sigma_\tau^2 - \frac{1}{2}A_d \sigma_d^2 - \frac{1}{2}A_s \sigma_s^2, \tag{3.36}$$

where

$$A_\tau = \frac{\alpha}{1+\alpha}\left\{1 + \delta\mu\left(1 + \frac{\alpha}{1+\alpha}u_i\right)^2\right\}, \tag{3.37}$$

$$A_d = (1+\alpha)(1-\mu)(1-\kappa_d), \tag{3.38}$$

$$A_s = \frac{\alpha}{1+\alpha}\{1 + \delta + \alpha(1-\mu)(1-\kappa_s)\}. \tag{3.39}$$

Note that $A_\tau > 0$, $A_d > 0$, and $A_s > 0$, so greater uncertainty about the inflation target τ and a higher volatility of demand and supply disturbances all increase social welfare losses. In the special case of perfect economic transparency, $u_i = -(1+\alpha)/\alpha$ and $\kappa_d = \kappa_s = 1$, so $A_\tau^T = \alpha/(1+\alpha)$, $A_d^T = 0$, and $A_s^T = \frac{\alpha}{1+\alpha}(1+\delta)$. Clearly, $A_\tau^T \le A_\tau$, $A_d^T \le A_d$, and $A_s^T \le A_s$, with a strict inequality if $\kappa_m \ne 1$. Thus, perfect economic transparency is socially optimal, as could already have been inferred immediately from the welfare effects for periods one and two.

Concerning intermediate degrees of economic transparency, it is straightforward to show that $dA_\tau/d\kappa_m \le 0$ using the fact that $d\mu/d\kappa_m < 0$ and $du_i/d\kappa_m < 0$. However, A_d and A_s are generally nonmonotonic in κ_d and κ_s, respectively. Assuming again that $\kappa_d = \kappa_s = \kappa$, figure 3.5 shows that the net effect of κ on $E[U]$ is unambiguously positive for the baseline parameter configuration with $\alpha = \delta = 1$ and $\sigma_\tau^2 = \sigma_d^2 = \sigma_s^2 = 1$. Moving from complete economic opacity ($\kappa = 0$) to full transparency ($\kappa = 1$) reduces expected social welfare losses stemming from macroeconomic volatility by over 20%.

The result that greater economic transparency is welfare-improving holds more generally. In particular, it can be shown that $E[U]$ is monotonically increasing in κ:

$$\frac{dE[U]}{d\kappa} = \frac{1}{2}\frac{1-\mu}{1+\alpha}[(1+\alpha)^2 \sigma_d^2 + \alpha^2 \sigma_s^2] > 0. \tag{3.40}$$

As a result, the net effect of greater economic transparency on expected social welfare is always positive. Intuitively, it gives the central bank more flexibility to offset demand shocks without worrying

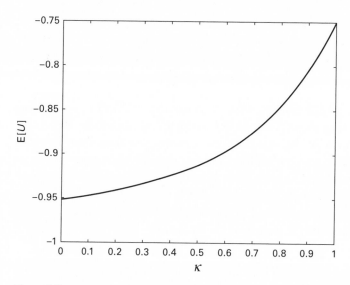

Figure 3.5
The effect of economic transparency κ on expected social welfare, for parameter values $\alpha = \delta = 1$ and $\sigma_\tau^2 = \sigma_d^2 = \sigma_s^2 = 1$.

about perturbing private sector inflation expectations. For the same reason, the central bank is able to achieve a more desirable tradeoff between inflation and output volatility due to supply shocks.

3.5 Discussion

The model shows how macroeconomic transparency gives the central bank greater flexibility to stabilize aggregate demand and supply shocks. In fact, central banks that are opaque about macroeconomic shocks optimally decide to mute their interest rate response to prevent undesired effects on private sector inflation expectations. As a result, opaque central banks effectively become less conservative in their reaction to supply shocks and no longer fully offset aggregate demand shocks that they anticipate.

Nevertheless, more macroeconomic transparency could lead to greater volatility of inflation (expectations) and output, in particular when the degree of macroeconomic transparency is low and preference transparency is high. This finding is similar to Morris and Shin (2002), who show that greater transparency about economic fundamentals increases economic volatility when public signals are noisy compared to private signals (i.e., when economic transparency is low). But their result relies on a coordination motive of private agents that induces them to put greater weight on the public signal, whereas this paper considers a signal extraction problem that is not distorted by other motives.

Although greater macroeconomic transparency could increase volatility, it is always welfare-improving in the model. Of course, this result may be sensitive to the assumptions of the model. Since high levels of economic transparency make the interest rate more volatile, they may no longer be desirable if the central bank directly cares about interest rate volatility because of financial stability considerations. In addition, in an economy with capital formation, volatile interest rates are likely to negatively affect investment. Furthermore, if the central bank's objective does not coincide with social welfare because there is a principal-agent problem, opacity may be beneficial because it leads to a level of inflation that is closer to the public's prior and slows down the updating of inflation expectations. So, economic opacity could be advantageous, similar to the finding in Geraats (2007), which considers a model in which political pressures make monetary mystique desirable.

The finding that greater transparency about macroeconomic shocks is beneficial is also in contrast to Jensen (2000, 2002) and Walsh (2007a, 2007b, 2008), who assume a New Keynesian Phillips curve rather than the plain expectations-augmented Phillips curve in the present paper. However, the latter is not driving the results, because one could substitute $E_t[\pi_{t+1}]$ for π_t^e without affecting the key results (although auxiliary assumptions would then be needed to determine expectations in the final period). Instead, what matters more is the timing of the formation of expectations relative to the communication of macroeconomic shocks. This is also the reason Cukierman (2001) and Gersbach (2003) find that transparency about aggregate supply shocks is detrimental in a simple static model. They assume that supply shocks s_t are observed before inflation expectations π_t^e are formed. However, long lags in the transmission of monetary policy mean that in practice, the effect of inflation expectations π_t^e on macroeconomic outcomes y_t and π_t is delayed and very little information is available about supply shocks so far in advance. In contrast, in the present paper the public signal ξ_t^m of macroeconomic shocks is observed only after inflation expectations π_t^e have been formed. Nevertheless, it helps the private sector to infer the central bank's intentions τ from its policy rate i_t, which makes private sector inflation expectations π_{t+1}^e less sensitive to the policy action i_t and gives the central bank greater flexibility to stabilize macroeconomic disturbances in period t.

Another issue is the extent to which the results depend on the assumption of rational expectations. In particular, it may be unrealistic to presume that the public is able to perform the nontrivial computation of the rational updating coefficient u_i for its inflation expectations. In chapter 2 in this volume, De Grauwe abandons rational expectations by assuming that private sector agents have cognitive limitations and use simple rules for forecasting. In this spirit, assume that agents use the heuristic $u_i^H = -\kappa \, (1 + \alpha)/\alpha$ rather than (3.22). This simple yet reasonable rule has similar properties to (3.22)—in particular, $0 \leq u_i^H \leq u_i^T$, $\lim_{\kappa \to 1} u_i^H = u_i^T$, and $du_i^H/d\kappa < 0$. So, inflation expectations π_2^e still respond negatively to the interest rate i_1, and the strength of the response is increasing in the degree of macroeconomic transparency κ as the interest rate becomes a more informative signal of the central bank's intentions.

Using this heuristic, the algebraic expressions for the macroeconomic outcomes are still given by (3.26), (3.27), (3.28), and (3.32), and expected social welfare by (3.36), (3.37), (3.38), and (3.39), but with u_i replaced by u_i^H (also in μ). It is straightforward to show that perfect economic transparency ($\kappa = 1$) continues to be socially optimal in this case. To assess the robustness of the monotonicity of the welfare results, a grid search was conducted using the same parameter configurations as in section 3.4.1. Expected welfare E[U] continues to be monotonically increasing in κ when $\kappa > 0.65$ for all 16,954,566 parameter configurations, and even over the entire range of $\kappa \in [0, 1]$ for 63.42% of the parameter space. But for sufficiently small levels of macroeconomic transparency κ, E[U] is sometimes decreasing in κ. The range for κ over which E[U] is downward-sloping was on average 0.1569 over all parameter configurations. This provides some support for the argument by De Grauwe that cognitive limitations could affect the impact of central bank communications. More transparency could even be detrimental, but only in economies that are relatively opaque.

The result that economic opacity causes the central bank to mute its interest rate response to macroeconomic shocks, which continues to hold when using the heuristic u_i^H, could be interpreted as a form of interest rate "smoothing." However, interest rate smoothing is usually associated with monetary policy inertia, whereas in this paper the interest rate response is only attenuated but not delayed. This effect would be even stronger if the central bank were uncertain about the response u_i of private sector inflation expectations (in line with the uncertainty generated by De Grauwe's "bottom-up" approach in chapter 2). In particular, suppose that u_i is stochastic with $E[u_i] = \bar{u}_i$ and $Var[u_i] = \sigma_u^2$; then it is straightforward to show that this leads to multiplicative uncertainty for the central bank with $\mu = \dfrac{(1+\alpha)^2}{(1+\alpha)^2 + \delta\alpha(\bar{u}_i^2 + \sigma_u^2)}$. So the central bank's policy response to macroeconomic shocks that are not anticipated by the public would be further reduced by the uncertainty σ_u^2 about the adjustment of private sector expectations. Some empirical evidence of the effect of uncertainty (derived from central bank minutes and the dispersion of votes) on the policy rate is provided by Mayes and Montagnoli in chapter 11.

A key feature of the model is that the central bank has private information that is reflected in the interest rate decision and is relevant for future monetary policy. In chapter 12, Horváth, Šmídková, and Zápal apply this idea to a monetary policy committee and provide empirical evidence from six countries that voting records (which reflect private information by central bankers) help to predict future policy rates. The present model also implies that private sector expectations are affected by the policy rate decision and central bank communications (through the public signals ξ_t^d and ξ_t^s. There is ample empirical evidence for this (see Blinder et al. 2008 for a survey), including Lamla and Sturm in chapter 5, who focus on the ECB and expectations transmitted by the media, and Chirinko and Curran in chapter 8, who examine the effect of Federal Reserve policy actions and communications on bond market futures.

The model derives some interesting effects of transparency on macroeconomic volatility, which in principle would be testable. However, an assessment of the empirical implications of the model is greatly complicated by the predicted nonmonotonic effects of transparency on the variability of the policy rate, output, and inflation (expectations). Thus, the effects depend on the initial level of transparency. Although data on information disclosure practices by central banks, such as the publication of central bank forecasts, could be used, this is hard to translate into the degree of economic transparency κ that is required to evaluate the testable implications. In addition, the critical points at which the effect of transparency on volatility reverses differ across the variables and are sensitive to the parameter values, including the degree of central bank conservativeness α, the initial preference uncertainty σ_τ^2, and the variance of aggregate demand and supply shocks σ_d^2 and σ_s^2. As a result, a rigorous empirical evaluation of the model appears practically infeasible.

More informally, there is some evidence in favor of the key result of the paper that greater economic transparency is welfare-improving. There has been a worldwide trend toward greater information disclosure about monetary policymaking. As shown by Geraats (2009), some of the greatest advances have been in economic transparency. In particular, the publication of numerical macroeconomic forecasts has spread from 18% of central banks in 1998 to 57% in 2006, for a sample of 98 central banks. Since these increases in information disclosure tend to go far beyond formal accountability requirements, they could be interpreted as the revealed preference of central banks, which suggests that the rise in transparency has been beneficial.

3.6   Conclusion

Central banks have increasingly become transparent about macroeconomic prospects, often far beyond any formal disclosure requirements. This paper shows that such macroeconomic transparency may be beneficial to the central bank because it allows the central bank to stabilize macroeconomic shocks without disturbing private sector inflation expectations. This makes it easier for the central bank to reach its macroeconomic objectives of inflation and output gap stabilization. But when there is opacity about the shocks to which the central bank responds, the policy rate becomes a noisier signal of the central bank's inflationary intentions, which induces greater volatility of private sector inflation expectations. To mitigate this problem, the central bank mutes the stabilization of macroeconomic shocks under opacity. In particular, an opaque central bank no longer fully offsets aggregate demand shocks it anticipates to avoid upsetting inflation expectations. As a result, opacity leads to undesirable macroeconomic volatility. This paper shows that expected social welfare is monotonically increasing in the degree of macroeconomic transparency. This result helps to explain why so many central banks have become more transparent about the macroeconomic shocks they aim to stabilize.

Appendix 3.1　Perfect Economic Transparency

This appendix derives equations (3.13), (3.14), (3.15) and (3.16). In the special case of perfect economic transparency, $\kappa_d = \kappa_s = 1$ so that $d_t = \xi_t^d$ and $s_t = \xi_t^s$. Use this to solve (3.12) for τ:

$$\tau = \frac{1}{\alpha(1+\alpha) - \delta\alpha u_i}\{-[((1+\alpha)^2 + \delta\alpha u_i^2)]i_1 + (1+\alpha)^2\bar{r} + [(1+\alpha)^2$$
$$+ \alpha(1+\alpha)]\pi_1^e - \delta\alpha u_i u_0 + [-\delta\alpha u_i u_d + (1+\alpha)^2]\xi_1^d - [\delta\alpha u_i u_s + \alpha(1+\alpha)]\xi_1^s\}.$$

Then, use $(\pi_2^e)^T = E_1^T[\tau \mid i_1] = \tau$ and match coefficients with (3.11):

$$u_0 = \frac{1}{\alpha(1+\alpha) - \delta\alpha u_i}\{(1+\alpha)^2\bar{r} + [(1+\alpha)^2 + \alpha(1+\alpha)]\pi_1^e - \delta\alpha u_i u_0\},$$

$$u_i = -\frac{(1+\alpha)^2 + \delta\alpha u_i^2}{\alpha(1+\alpha) - \delta\alpha u_i},$$

$$u_d = \frac{1}{\alpha(1+\alpha) - \delta\alpha u_i}[-\delta\alpha u_i u_d + (1+\alpha)^2],$$

$$u_s = -\frac{1}{\alpha(1+\alpha) - \delta\alpha u_i}[\delta\alpha u_i u_s + \alpha(1+\alpha)].$$

Solving these equations yields (3.13), (3.14), (3.15), and (3.16):

$$u_0^T = \frac{1}{\alpha(1+\alpha)}\{(1+\alpha)^2\bar{r} + [(1+\alpha)^2 + \alpha(1+\alpha)](\pi_1^e)^T\}$$
$$= (\pi_1^e)^T + \frac{1+\alpha}{\alpha}(\bar{r} + (\pi_1^e)^T),$$

$$u_i^T = -\frac{1+\alpha}{\alpha},$$

$$u_d^T = \frac{1+\alpha}{\alpha},$$

$$u_s = -1.$$

Appendix 3.2　General Case

To derive the updating coefficients (3.22), (3.23), (3.24), and (3.25) for the general case, first substitute (3.5) and (3.6) into (3.12):

$$i_1 = \frac{1}{(1+\alpha)^2 + \delta\alpha u_i^2} \{(1+\alpha)^2(\bar{r} + \pi_1^e) - \alpha(1+\alpha)(\tau - \pi_1^e) + \delta\alpha u_i(\tau - u_0)$$
$$+ [-\delta\alpha u_i u_d + (1+\alpha)^2]\xi_1^d - [\delta\alpha u_i u_s + \alpha(1+\alpha)]\xi_1^s$$
$$+ (1+\alpha)^2 \eta_1^d - \alpha(1+\alpha)\eta_1^s\}. \tag{3.41}$$

As a result,

$$\mathrm{Cov}_1\{i_1, \tau\} = -\frac{1}{(1+\alpha)^2 + \delta\alpha u_i^2}[\alpha(1+\alpha) - \delta\alpha u_i]\sigma_\tau^2,$$

$$\mathrm{Var}_1[i_1] = \frac{1}{[(1+\alpha)^2 + \delta\alpha u_i^2]^2}\{[\alpha(1+\alpha) - \delta\alpha u_i]^2 \sigma_\tau^2$$
$$+ (1+\alpha)^4(1-\kappa_d)\sigma_d^2 + \alpha^2(1+\alpha)^2(1-\kappa_s)\sigma_s^2\},$$

recalling that $\mathrm{Var}[\eta_t^d] = (1-\kappa_d)\sigma_d^2$ and $\mathrm{Var}[\eta_t^s] = (1-\kappa_s)\sigma_s^2$. So, matching coefficients between (3.21) and (3.11) yields

$$u_i = -\frac{[(1+\alpha)^2 + \delta\alpha u_i^2][\alpha(1+\alpha) - \delta\alpha u_i]\sigma_\tau^2}{[\alpha(1+\alpha) - \delta\alpha u_i]^2 \sigma_\tau^2 + (1+\alpha)^4(1-\kappa_d)\sigma_d^2 + \alpha^2(1+\alpha)^2(1-\kappa_s)\sigma_s^2}.$$

Rearranging gives

$$[\alpha(1+\alpha) - \delta\alpha u_i]^2 u_i \sigma_\tau^2 + \{(1+\alpha)^4(1-\kappa_d)\sigma_d^2 + \alpha^2(1+\alpha)^2(1-\kappa_s)\sigma_s^2\} u_i$$
$$= -[(1+\alpha)^2 + \delta\alpha u_i^2]\alpha(1+\alpha)\sigma_\tau^2 + [(1+\alpha)^2 + \delta\alpha u_i^2]\delta\alpha u_i \sigma_\tau^2.$$

Note that $\delta^2\alpha^2 u_i^3 \sigma_\tau^2$ drops out from both sides, leaving the quadratic equation

$$-\delta\alpha^2\sigma_\tau^2 u_i^2 + (1+\alpha)[\alpha(\alpha-\delta)\sigma_\tau^2 + (1+\alpha)^2(1-\kappa_d)\sigma_d^2 + \alpha^2(1-\kappa_s)\sigma_s^2] u_i$$
$$+ \alpha(1+\alpha)^2\sigma_\tau^2 = 0. \tag{3.42}$$

This equation has two real roots, $u_i^+ > 0$ and $u_i^- < 0$:

$$u_i = \frac{1+\alpha}{2\delta\alpha^2\sigma_\tau^2}\{\alpha(\alpha-\delta)\sigma_\tau^2 + (1+\alpha)^2(1-\kappa_d)\sigma_d^2 + \alpha^2(1-\kappa_s)\sigma_s^2$$
$$\pm \sqrt{[\alpha(\alpha-\delta)\sigma_\tau^2 + (1+\alpha)^2(1-\kappa_d)\sigma_d^2 + \alpha^2(1-\kappa_s)\sigma_s^2]^2 + 4\delta\alpha^2\sigma_\tau^2\alpha\sigma_\tau^2}\}.$$

The argument of the square root can be rearranged as follows:

$$[\alpha(\alpha-\delta)\sigma_\tau^2 + (1+\alpha)^2(1-\kappa_d)\sigma_d^2 + \alpha^2(1-\kappa_s)\sigma_s^2]^2 + 4\delta\alpha^2\sigma_\tau^2\alpha\sigma_\tau^2$$
$$= [\alpha(\alpha+\delta)\sigma_\tau^2 + (1+\alpha)^2(1-\kappa_d)\sigma_d^2 + \alpha^2(1-\kappa_s)\sigma_s^2]^2$$
$$- 4\delta\alpha[(1+\alpha)^2(1-\kappa_d)\sigma_d^2 + \alpha^2(1-\kappa_s)\sigma_s^2]\sigma_\tau^2.$$

Substitute this into u_i^- to obtain (3.22):

$$u_i = \frac{1+\alpha}{2\delta\alpha^2\sigma_\tau^2}\left\{\alpha(\alpha-\delta)\sigma_\tau^2 + (1+\alpha)^2(1-\kappa_d)\sigma_d^2 + \alpha^2(1-\kappa_s)\sigma_s^2\right.$$

$$\left. - \sqrt{\begin{array}{l}[\alpha(\alpha+\delta)\sigma_\tau^2 + (1+\alpha)^2(1-\kappa_d)\sigma_d^2 + \alpha^2(1-\kappa_s)\sigma_s^2]^2 \\ -4\delta\alpha[(1+\alpha)^2(1-\kappa_d)\sigma_d^2 + \alpha^2(1-\kappa_s)\sigma_s^2]\sigma_\tau^2\end{array}}\right\}.$$

Note that

$$u_i \geq \frac{1+\alpha}{2\delta\alpha^2\sigma_\tau^2}\{\alpha(\alpha-\delta)\sigma_\tau^2 + (1+\alpha)^2(1-\kappa_d)\sigma_d^2 + \alpha^2(1-\kappa_s)\sigma_s^2$$

$$- [\alpha(\alpha+\delta)\sigma_\tau^2 + (1+\alpha)^2(1-\kappa_d)\sigma_d^2 + \alpha^2(1-\kappa_s)\sigma_s^2]\}$$

$$= -\frac{1+\alpha}{\alpha},$$

where the lower bound is reached if $\sigma_d^2 \to 0$ and $\sigma_s^2 \to 0$ or if $\kappa_d = \kappa_s = 1$.
Hence, $-\dfrac{1+\alpha}{\alpha} = u_i^T \leq u_i < 0$.

Using (3.42), it follows from the implicit function theorem that

$$\frac{du_i}{d\kappa_d} = \frac{(1+\alpha)^3\sigma_d^2 u_i}{-2\delta\alpha^2\sigma_\tau^2 u_i + (1+\alpha)[\alpha(\alpha-\delta)\sigma_\tau^2 + (1+\alpha)^2(1-\kappa_d)\sigma_d^2 + \alpha^2(1-\kappa_s)\sigma_s^2]},$$

$$\frac{du_i}{d\kappa_s} = \frac{(1+\alpha)\alpha^2\sigma_s^2 u_i}{-2\delta\alpha^2\sigma_\tau^2 u_i + (1+\alpha)[\alpha(\alpha-\delta)\sigma_\tau^2 + (1+\alpha)^2(1-\kappa_d)\sigma_d^2 + \alpha^2(1-\kappa_s)\sigma_s^2]}.$$

Substituting for the term in square brackets using (3.42) and simplifying yields

$$\frac{du_i}{d\kappa_d} = \frac{(1+\alpha)^3\sigma_d^2 u_i^2}{-2\delta\alpha^2\sigma_\tau^2 u_i^2 + \delta\alpha^2\sigma_\tau^2 u_i^2 - \alpha(1+\alpha)^2\sigma_\tau^2} = -\frac{(1+\alpha)^3\sigma_d^2 u_i^2}{\delta\alpha^2\sigma_\tau^2 u_i^2 + \alpha(1+\alpha)^2\sigma_\tau^2},$$

$$\frac{du_i}{d\kappa_s} = \frac{(1+\alpha)\alpha^2\sigma_s^2 u_i^2}{-2\delta\alpha^2\sigma_\tau^2 u_i^2 + \delta\alpha^2\sigma_\tau^2 u_i^2 - \alpha(1+\alpha)^2\sigma_\tau^2} = -\frac{(1+\alpha)\alpha^2\sigma_s^2 u_i^2}{\delta\alpha^2\sigma_\tau^2 u_i^2 + \alpha(1+\alpha)^2\sigma_\tau^2}.$$

Hence, $\dfrac{du_i}{d\kappa_d} < 0$ and $\dfrac{du_i}{d\kappa_s} < 0$. When the degree of economic transparency
is the same for demand and supply shocks, i.e., $\kappa_d = \kappa_s = \kappa$, then

$$\frac{du_i}{d\kappa} = -\frac{(1+\alpha)^2\sigma_d^2 + \alpha^2\sigma_s^2}{[\delta\alpha u_i^2 + (1+\alpha)^2]\alpha\sigma_\tau^2}(1+\alpha)u_i^2 = -\frac{(1+\alpha)^2\sigma_d^2 + \alpha^2\sigma_s^2}{(1+\alpha)\alpha\sigma_\tau^2}\mu u_i^2 < 0, \quad (3.43)$$

using the fact that $\mu \equiv \dfrac{(1+\alpha)^2}{(1+\alpha)^2 + \delta\alpha u_i^2} > 0$.

To derive the other updating coefficients, write (3.21) as $\pi_2^e = \overline{\tau} + u_i i_1 - u_i E_1[i_1]$ and use (3.41) to substitute for $E_1[i_1]$. Then, matching coefficients between (3.21) and (3.11) yields

$$u_0 = \overline{\tau} - \frac{u_i}{(1+\alpha)^2 + \delta\alpha u_i^2}\{(1+\alpha)^2(\overline{r} + \pi_1^e) - \alpha(1+\alpha)(\overline{\tau} - \pi_1^e) + \delta\alpha u_i(\overline{\tau} - u_0)\},$$

$$u_d = -\frac{u_i}{(1+\alpha)^2 + \delta\alpha u_i^2}[-\delta\alpha u_i u_d + (1+\alpha)^2],$$

$$u_s = \frac{u_i}{(1+\alpha)^2 + \delta\alpha u_i^2}[\delta\alpha u_i u_s + \alpha(1+\alpha)].$$

Rearranging each equation gives (3.23), (3.24), and (3.25):

$$u_0 = \overline{\tau} + u_i\frac{\alpha}{1+\alpha}(\overline{\tau} - \pi_1^e) - u_i(\overline{r} + \pi_1^e)$$

$$= -\frac{\alpha}{1+\alpha}u_i\pi_1^e + \left(1 + \frac{\alpha}{1+\alpha}u_i\right)\overline{\tau} - u_i(\overline{r} + \pi_1^e),$$

$$u_d = -u_i,$$

$$u_s = \frac{\alpha}{1+\alpha}u_i.$$

Substituting these updating coefficients into (3.12) and using (3.5) and (3.6) yields (3.26):

$$i_1 = \frac{1}{(1+\alpha)^2 + \delta\alpha u_i^2}\left\{(1+\alpha)^2(\overline{r} + \pi_1^e) - \alpha(1+\alpha)(\tau - \pi_1^e)\right.$$

$$+ \delta\alpha u_i(\tau - \overline{\tau} - u_i\frac{\alpha}{1+\alpha}(\overline{\tau} - \pi_1^e) + u_i(\overline{r} + \pi_1^e)) + \delta\alpha u_i^2\xi_1^d$$

$$\left. - \delta\alpha u_i^2\frac{\alpha}{1+\alpha}\xi_1^s + (1+\alpha)^2 d_1 - \alpha(1+\alpha)s_1\right\}$$

$$= \frac{(1+\alpha)^2}{(1+\alpha)^2 + \delta\alpha u_i^2}\left\{\left[1 + \frac{\delta\alpha u_i^2}{(1+\alpha)^2}\right](\overline{r} + \pi_1^e) - \frac{\alpha}{1+\alpha}(\tau - \pi_1^e)\right.$$

$$+ \frac{\delta\alpha u_i}{(1+\alpha)^2}\left[(1 + u_i\frac{\alpha}{1+\alpha})(\tau - \overline{\tau}) - u_i\frac{\alpha}{1+\alpha}(\tau - \pi_1^e)\right]\right\}$$

$$+ (1-\mu)\left(\xi_1^d - \frac{\alpha}{1+\alpha}\xi_1^s\right) + \mu d_1 - \mu\frac{\alpha}{1+\alpha}s_1$$

$$= \bar{r} + \pi_1^e - \frac{\alpha}{1+\alpha}(\tau - \pi_1^e) + (1-\mu)\left(\frac{1}{u_i} + \frac{\alpha}{1+\alpha}\right)(\tau - \bar{\tau})$$

$$+ (\xi_1^d + \mu\eta_1^d) - \frac{\alpha}{1+\alpha}(\xi_1^s + \mu\eta_1^s),$$

where $\mu \equiv \dfrac{(1+\alpha)^2}{(1+\alpha)^2 + \delta\alpha u_i^2}$ $(0 < \mu < 1)$.

Substituting (3.26) into (3.3) and (3.4), and using (3.24) and (3.25) produces

$$y_1 = \bar{y} + \frac{\alpha}{1+\alpha}(\tau - \pi_1^e) - (1-\mu)\left(\frac{1}{u_i} + \frac{\alpha}{1+\alpha}\right)(\tau - \bar{\tau})$$

$$+ (1-\mu)\eta_1^d + \frac{\alpha}{1+\alpha}\xi_1^s + \mu\frac{\alpha}{1+\alpha}\eta_1^s,$$

$$\pi_1 = \pi_1^e + \frac{\alpha}{1+\alpha}(\tau - \pi_1^e) - (1-\mu)\left(\frac{1}{u_i} + \frac{\alpha}{1+\alpha}\right)(\tau - \bar{\tau})$$

$$+ (1-\mu)\eta_1^d - \frac{1}{1+\alpha}\xi_1^s - \left(1 - \mu\frac{\alpha}{1+\alpha}\right)\eta_1^s.$$

Use the latter equation and impose rational expectations (i.e., $\pi_1^e = \mathrm{E}[\pi_1]$) to get $\pi_1^e = \bar{\tau}$.

As a result, (3.27) and (3.28) follow:

$$y_1 = \bar{y} + \left[\frac{\alpha}{1+\alpha} - (1-\mu)\left(\frac{1}{u_i} + \frac{\alpha}{1+\alpha}\right)\right](\tau - \bar{\tau}) + (1-\mu)\eta_1^d + \frac{\alpha}{1+\alpha}(\xi_1^s + \mu\eta_1^s),$$

$$\pi_1 = \bar{\tau} + \left[\frac{\alpha}{1+\alpha} - (1-\mu)\left(\frac{1}{u_i} + \frac{\alpha}{1+\alpha}\right)\right](\tau - \bar{\tau})$$

$$+ (1-\mu)\eta_1^d - \frac{1}{1+\alpha}(\xi_1^s + (1+(1-\mu)\alpha)\eta_1^s).$$

To find second-period inflation expectations, substitute (3.23), (3.24), and (3.25) into (3.11) to get

$$\pi_2^e = \bar{\tau} + u_i\frac{\alpha}{1+\alpha}(\bar{\tau} - \pi_1^e) + u_i[i_1 - (\bar{r} + \pi_1^e)] - u_i\xi_1^d + \frac{\alpha}{1+\alpha}u_i\xi_1^s.$$

Substituting (3.26) then yields (3.32):

$$\pi_2^e = \tau - \mu\left(1 + \frac{\alpha}{1+\alpha}u_i\right)(\tau - \bar{\tau}) + u_i\mu\eta_1^d - \frac{\alpha}{1+\alpha}u_i\mu\eta_1^s.$$

This reduces to $(\pi_2^e)^T = \tau$ in the case of perfect economic transparency as $u_i = -(1+\alpha)/\alpha$ and $\eta_1^d = \eta_1^s = 0$.

Appendix 3.3 Welfare Analysis

Substituting (3.32) into (3.10) yields (3.34):

$$E[W_2] = -\frac{1}{2}\frac{\alpha}{1+\alpha}\left\{\mu^2\left(1+\frac{\alpha}{1+\alpha}u_i\right)^2\sigma_\tau^2 + u_i^2\mu^2(1-\kappa_d)\sigma_d^2\right.$$
$$\left. + \left[\frac{\alpha^2}{(1+\alpha)^2}u_i^2\mu^2(1-\kappa_s)+1\right]\sigma_s^2\right\}.$$

Substituting (3.27) and (3.28) into (3.1) produces (3.35) after some rearranging:

$$E[W_1] = -\frac{1}{2}\alpha\left\{\left[\frac{1}{1+\alpha}+(1-\mu)\left(\frac{1}{u_i}+\frac{\alpha}{1+\alpha}\right)\right]^2\sigma_\tau^2+(1-\mu)^2(1-\kappa_d)\sigma_d^2\right.$$
$$\left. + \frac{1}{(1+\alpha)^2}[\kappa_s+(1+(1-\mu)\alpha)^2(1-\kappa_s)]\sigma_s^2\right\}$$
$$-\frac{1}{2}\left\{\left[\frac{\alpha}{1+\alpha}-(1-\mu)\left(\frac{1}{u_i}+\frac{\alpha}{1+\alpha}\right)\right]^2\sigma_\tau^2+(1-\mu)^2(1-\kappa_d)\sigma_d^2\right.$$
$$\left. + \frac{\alpha^2}{(1+\alpha)^2}[\kappa_s+\mu^2(1-\kappa_s)]\sigma_s^2\right\}$$
$$= -\frac{1}{2}\left\{\frac{\alpha}{1+\alpha}+(\alpha+1)(1-\mu)^2\left(\frac{1}{u_i}+\frac{\alpha}{1+\alpha}\right)^2\right\}\sigma_\tau^2-\frac{1}{2}(1+\alpha)(1-\mu)^2(1-\kappa_d)\sigma_d^2$$
$$-\frac{1}{2}\frac{\alpha}{(1+\alpha)^2}\{(1+\alpha)\kappa_s+[(1+\alpha-\alpha\mu)^2+\alpha\mu^2](1-\kappa_s)\}\sigma_s^2$$
$$= -\frac{1}{2}\frac{\alpha}{1+\alpha}\left\{1+\alpha(1-\mu)^2\left(\frac{1+\alpha}{\alpha u_i}+1\right)^2\right\}\sigma_\tau^2-\frac{1}{2}(1+\alpha)(1-\mu)^2(1-\kappa_d)\sigma_d^2$$
$$-\frac{1}{2}\frac{\alpha}{1+\alpha}\{1+\alpha(1-\mu)^2(1-\kappa_s)\}\sigma_s^2.$$

Substituting (3.35) and (3.34) into (3.2) yields

$$E[U] = -\frac{1}{2}A_\tau\sigma_\tau^2-\frac{1}{2}A_d\sigma_d^2-\frac{1}{2}A_s\sigma_s^2,$$

where

$$A_\tau = \frac{\alpha}{1+\alpha}\left\{1+\left[(1-\mu)^2\frac{(1+\alpha)^2}{\alpha u_i^2}+\delta\mu^2\right]\left(1+\frac{\alpha}{1+\alpha}u_i\right)^2\right\},$$

$$A_d = (1+\alpha)(1-\mu)^2(1-\kappa_d)+\frac{\alpha}{1+\alpha}\delta u_i^2\mu^2(1-\kappa_d),$$

$$A_s = \frac{\alpha}{1+\alpha}\left\{1+\alpha(1-\mu)^2(1-\kappa_s)+\delta\left[\frac{\alpha^2}{(1+\alpha)^2}u_i^2\mu^2(1-\kappa_s)+1\right]\right\}.$$

Using the fact that $\mu \equiv \dfrac{(1+\alpha)^2}{(1+\alpha)^2+\delta\alpha u_i^2}$ implies $\dfrac{\delta\alpha u_i^2}{(1+\alpha)^2}=\dfrac{1-\mu}{\mu}$, rearranging gives (3.37), (3.38), and (3.39):

$$A_\tau = \frac{\alpha}{1+\alpha}\left[1+\delta\mu\left(1+\frac{\alpha}{1+\alpha}u_i\right)^2\right],$$

$$A_d = (1+\alpha)(1-\mu)(1-\kappa_d),$$

$$A_s = \frac{\alpha}{1+\alpha}[1+\delta+\alpha(1-\mu)(1-\kappa_s)].$$

It is straightforward to show that

$$\frac{dA_\tau}{du_i} = \frac{\alpha}{1+\alpha}\left[\delta\left(1+\frac{\alpha}{1+\alpha}u_i\right)^2\frac{d\mu}{du_i}+2\frac{\alpha}{1+\alpha}\delta\mu\left(1+\frac{\alpha}{1+\alpha}u_i\right)\right]\geq 0,$$

using $\dfrac{d\mu}{du_i}=-\mu^2\dfrac{2\delta\alpha u_i}{(1+\alpha)^2}>0$ and $u_i\geq -\dfrac{1+\alpha}{\alpha}$, with a strict inequality if $\kappa\neq 1$. Since $\dfrac{du_i}{d\kappa_m}<0$, it follows that $\dfrac{dA_\tau}{d\kappa_m}\leq 0$, with a strict inequality if $\kappa_m\neq 1$. However, A_d and A_s are generally nonmonotonic in κ_d and κ_s, respectively. So it is important to investigate the net effect of κ on $E[U]$. Using (3.36), (3.37), (3.38), and (3.39) and substituting (3.43) gives

$$\frac{dE[U]}{d\kappa} = -\frac{1}{2}\left\{\frac{\alpha}{1+\alpha}\left[\delta\left(1+\frac{\alpha}{1+\alpha}u_i\right)^2\frac{d\mu}{du_i}+2\frac{\alpha}{1+\alpha}\delta\mu\left(1+\frac{\alpha}{1+\alpha}u_i\right)\right]\frac{du_i}{d\kappa}\sigma_\tau^2\right.$$

$$\left.-\frac{1}{1+\alpha}\left[(1-\kappa)\frac{d\mu}{d\kappa}+(1-\mu)\right][(1+\alpha)^2\sigma_d^2+\alpha^2\sigma_s^2]\right\}$$

$$=\frac{1}{2}\frac{1}{1+\alpha}\left\{\left[-\delta\left(1+\frac{\alpha}{1+\alpha}u_i\right)^2\mu^2\frac{2\delta\alpha u_i}{(1+\alpha)^2}+\frac{2\alpha}{1+\alpha}\delta\mu\left(1+\frac{\alpha}{1+\alpha}u_i\right)\right]\frac{\mu u_i^2}{1+\alpha}\right.$$

$$\left.+\left[(1-\kappa)\mu^2\frac{2\delta\alpha u_i}{(1+\alpha)^2}\frac{(1+\alpha)^2\sigma_d^2+\alpha^2\sigma_s^2}{(1+\alpha)\alpha\sigma_\tau^2}\mu u_i^2+(1-\mu)\right]\right\}[(1+\alpha)^2\sigma_d^2+\alpha^2\sigma_s^2]$$

$$
= \frac{1}{2}\frac{1-\mu}{1+\alpha}\left\{-\delta\left(1+\frac{\alpha}{1+\alpha}u_i\right)^2\mu^2\frac{2u_i}{1+\alpha}+2\mu\left(1+\frac{\alpha}{1+\alpha}u_i\right)\right.
$$
$$
\left.+\left[2\mu^2\frac{\delta\alpha u_i^2-(1+\alpha)^2-(1+\alpha)(\alpha-\delta)u_i}{(1+\alpha)^2}+1\right]\right\}[(1+\alpha)^2\sigma_d^2+\alpha^2\sigma_s^2],
$$

where the last equality uses the fact that $\dfrac{\delta\alpha u_i^2}{(1+\alpha)^2}=\dfrac{1-\mu}{\mu}$ and substitutes

for $(1-\kappa)[(1+\alpha)^2\sigma_d^2+\alpha^2\sigma_s^2]u_i$ using (3.42). The term in curly brackets can be further simplified to

$$
\left[-\delta\left(1+\frac{\alpha}{1+\alpha}u_i\right)\mu^2\frac{2u_i}{1+\alpha}+2\mu-2\mu^2\right]\left(1+\frac{\alpha}{1+\alpha}u_i\right)
$$
$$
+2\mu(1-\mu)+2\mu^2\frac{\delta u_i}{1+\alpha}+1
$$
$$
=-\delta\mu^2\frac{2u_i}{1+\alpha}\left(1+\frac{\alpha}{1+\alpha}u_i\right)+2\mu(1-\mu)+2\mu^2\frac{\delta u_i}{1+\alpha}+1=1.
$$

Therefore, the effect of greater economic transparency on expected social welfare is unambiguously positive:

$$
\frac{dE[U]}{d\kappa}=\frac{1}{2}\frac{1-\mu}{1+\alpha}[(1+\alpha)^2\sigma_d^2+\alpha^2\sigma_s^2]>0.
$$

Notes

Acknowledgments: I thank Bob Chirinko and seminar participants at the University of Athens and the CESifo Venice Summer Institute on Central Bank Communication, Decision-Making, and Governance for helpful comments. A previous version of this paper circulated under the title "Transparency, Stabilization, and Interest Rate Smoothing."

1. Although multiple rational expectations equilibria may exist, this specification precludes sunspots and satisfies McCallum's (1983) minimum-state-variable criterion.

2. The derivation is available in appendix 3.1.

3. The derivations for this section are in appendix 3.2.

4. Note that $1-(1-\mu^2)(1-\kappa_m)=\kappa_m+\mu^2(1-\kappa_m)$.

5. To see this, note that $\kappa_s+[1+(1-\mu)\alpha]^2(1-\kappa_s)=1+[2+(1-\mu)\alpha](1-\mu)\alpha(1-\kappa_s)]$.

6. Recall that $\mu\equiv(1+\alpha)^2/[(1+\alpha)^2+\delta\alpha u_i^2]$ and $u_i<0$.

7. Values of α, σ_d^2, σ_τ^2, or σ_s^2 closer to zero are not used, as they regularly give rise to numerical problems when computing (3.22).

8. This follows from (3.43).

9. The derivations for this section are in appendix 3.3.

References

Barro, R. J., and D. B. Gordon. 1983. A Positive Theory of Monetary Policy in a Natural Rate Model. *Journal of Political Economy* 91 (1):589–610.

Bernanke, B. S., and M. Woodford. 1997. Inflation Forecasts and Monetary Policy. *Journal of Money, Credit and Banking* 29 (4):653–686.

Blinder, A. S., M. Ehrmann, M. Fratzscher, J. D. Haan, and D.-J. Jansen. 2008. Central Bank Communication and Monetary Policy: A Survey of Theory and Evidence. *Journal of Economic Literature* 46 (4):910–945.

Cukierman, A. 2001. Accountability, Credibility, Transparency and Stabilization Policy in the Eurosystem. In *The Impact of EMU on Europe and the Developing Countries*, ed. C. Wyplosz, 40–75. Oxford: Oxford University Press.

Geraats, P. M. 2002. Central Bank Transparency. *Economic Journal* 112 (483):F532–F565.

Geraats, P. M. 2005. Transparency and Reputation: The Publication of Central Bank Forecasts. *Topics in Macroeconomics* 5(1.1): 1–26.

Geraats, P. M. 2007. Political Pressures and Monetary Mystique. CESifo Working Paper 1999.

Geraats, P. M. 2009. Trends in Monetary Policy Transparency. *International Finance* 12 (2):235–268.

Gersbach, H. 2003. On the Negative Social Value of Central Banks' Knowledge Transparency. *Economics of Governance* 4 (2):91–102.

Jensen, H. 2000. Optimal Degrees of Transparency in Monetary Policymaking: The Case of Imperfect Information about the Cost-Push Shock. Mimeo, University of Copenhagen.

Jensen, H. 2002. Optimal Degrees of Transparency in Monetary Policymaking. *Scandinavian Journal of Economics* 104 (3):399–422.

Kydland, F. E., and E. C. Prescott. 1977. Rules Rather Than Discretion: The Inconsistency of Optimal Plans. *Journal of Political Economy* 85 (3):473–491.

McCallum, B. T. 1983. On Non-uniqueness in Rational Expectations Models: An Attempt at Perspective. *Journal of Monetary Economics* 11 (2):139–168.

Morris, S., and H. S. Shin. 2002. Social Value of Public Information. *American Economic Review* 92 (5):1521–1534.

Peek, J., E. S. Rosengren, and G. M. B. Tootell. 1999. Is Bank Supervision Central to Central Banking? *Quarterly Journal of Economics* 114 (2):629–653.

Romer, C. D., and D. H. Romer. 2000. Federal Reserve Information and the Behavior of Interest Rates. *American Economic Review* 90 (3):429–457.

Walsh, C. E. 2007a. Optimal Economic Transparency. *International Journal of Central Banking* 3 (1):5–36.

Walsh, C. E. 2007b. Transparency, Flexibility, and Inflation Targeting. In *Monetary Policy under Inflation Targeting*, ed. F. S. Mishkin and K. Schmidt-Hebbel, 227–263. Santiago: Banco Central de Chile.

Walsh, C. E. 2008. Transparency, the Opacity Bias, and Optimal Flexible Inflation Targeting. Paper presented at Allied Social Science Association meetings, January.

II Empirical Methods in Central Bank Communication Research

4 Central Bank Communication and Financial Stress

Marianna Blix Grimaldi

4.1 Introduction

In this chapter we exploit the information contained in central bank communication to measure the level of stress in financial markets. Communication from central banks is not only a matter of giving out information on key rates but has increasingly become one of the banks' key instruments for managing market expectations about future policy rates. Notably, any information that gives forward guidance is scrutinized by the markets.

One implication is that central bank communication has become much more multidimensional—and is aimed at the markets, the public, and sometimes also politicians and governments. Minutes, speeches, and other publications contain a large amount of information. The challenge in a particular context is to extract the useful information in a systematic way. Moreover, to be helpful, the results need to be assessed alongside the level of uncertainty they reflect. This means that, after central bank communication has been quantified, all the classic tools of signal-to-noise extraction techniques can be applied. A key step is to make a valid and informative quantification of central bank communication, something we address in this chapter.

Quantifying central bank communication lends itself to several potential areas of interest—for academics as well as for market participants. One strand of the literature quantifies its effect on the predictability of asset prices; see, for example, Andersson et al. (2006), Rosa and Verga (2008), Heinemann and Ullrich (2007), Lucca and Trebbi (2009), De Haan and Sturm (2011), and Ehrmann and Fratzscher (2009). Another strand of the literature addresses transparency issues; see, for example, Bligh and Hess (2009) and Bulíř et al. (2012). But here we will focus on only one element: detecting the level of financial stress in the economy.

Since stress is not a well-defined concept, there are some conceptual as well as methodological issues to confront. It is important to note that financial stress is related to—but is not identical to—market volatility. For example, there can be a lot of volatility in the market when new, unexpected information arrives, but this need not imply that there is stress in the market.

Our work is related to the literature on financial stress indicators, or FSI (see, for example, Nelson and Perli 2006; Illing and Liu 2006; Cardarelli, Elekdag, and Lall 2009), but takes a novel approach in extracting the information in central bank communication in a systematic way. There are no other papers so far that have used central bank communication to measure stress. Our focus is on the euro area and we draw on information contained in the European Central Bank's (ECB) *Monthly Bulletin*.

The FSI derived from central bank communication has a number of potential uses. For example, it can help assess the state of the economy. Data from the real economy and information from financial markets rarely provide a clear-cut picture of where the economy stands and much less where it might be headed; see, for example, Orphanides and van Norden (2002). Individual signals contain varying degrees of noise; the available data taken together typically contains a lot of conflicting signals. Using quantitative techniques, the FSI provides a way to weigh a lot of information together that is more informative about the state of the economy than the individual raw data, thereby implicitly taking a stand on how to resolve conflicting information. The FSI can never be a substitute for analyzing raw data, but it can provide a complement. For example, it can provide a starting point for asking further questions on which signals may, in fact, be due to noise and which are informative.

One possible drawback of constructing a single indicator is that it may discard information. While this is undoubtedly the case, it should be weighed against the problem of information overload. In an environment where information is complex, interpreting the signals from a variety of sources is a challenge in its own right and may at times be overwhelming; see Thaler and Mullainathan (2001) and De Grauwe and Grimaldi (2006).

While the challenge of interpreting information is always considerable, during times of stress when the environment is volatile it is particularly difficult but, arguably, most important. It is well documented that agents may tend to overreact and in so doing further contribute to the complexity of the information and to uncertainty about the direction of the market. The onset of the financial crisis in 2007 contained all these elements, providing a mixture of mild and strong signals from raw data. Contingent indicators such as the FSI together with other information can function as a barometer and aid in assessing the severity and intensity of stress.

The rest of this chapter is organized as follows: section 4.2 describes the rationale for the FSI and how we construct it by aggregating market-based variables and extracting information from the ECB *Monthly Bulletin* as well as selected financial press; section 4.3 discusses how to compute the FSI and robustness properties; section 4.4 concludes.

4.2   Constructing the Financial Stress Indicator (FSI)

4.2.1   Using Words to Define Stress
The financial literature does not provide a precise definition of financial stress, but at a conceptual level it is arguably the interaction of vulnerable markets and shocks. For the purposes of this paper, we can think of the *level* of stress as being determined by the interaction between financial vulnerabilities and the size of shocks. The more fragile financial conditions are—i.e., the more vulnerable markets are—the more likely a shock is to result in stress. In extreme cases, either when the shock is very large or when financial conditions are very weak, a shock can result in a crisis and extreme stress.

We derive a measure of financial stress in the form of an indicator (FSI) with several attractive features. First, it is based on real-time, high-frequency data. Second, it takes a broad perspective, as the aim is the assessment of the level of stress of the overall financial system at any point in time. Third, it belongs to a very small group of indicators constructed for developed economies. Related papers are Illing and Liu (2006), who develop a financial stress index for the Canadian economy; Nelson and Perli (2006), who construct one for the US economy; and more recently Cardarelli, Elekdag, and Lall (2009), who analyze episodes of financial stress and economic cycles among 17 advanced economies over the past three decades. Another example is the Kansas City Financial Stress Index, a measure constructed by the Federal Reserve Bank of Kansas City that uses 11 financial market variables at monthly frequency.

A few measures of stress, or more generally of market conditions, are also available from private market data providers and private research institutions. For example, Bloomberg has its own financial conditions index which is based on yield spreads and measures of money, bond, and stock markets.

We use a three-step procedure to compute the FSI. First, we select a list of "stressful" events, then we construct a measure of stress, and finally we connect the previous two by using a logit model.

4.2.2   First Step: Constructing a List of Stress Events

We build a list of stress events for the euro area by using one of the more common methods in context analysis that is based on a word count; see Manning and Schütze (2003) and Loughran and McDonald (2011). The idea is that the frequency of words tends to be correlated with market conditions. Thus, if negative words are overrepresented in a certain period, then that period is likely to be a "negative" period, i.e., a period of increased stress. We construct and run an algorithm to count preselected negative and positive words from the entire text of each ECB *Monthly Bulletin*.

The text in the *Monthly Bulletin* reflects market developments, of course, and would—if represented as simultaneous equations in an econometric model—contain tricky identification issues. However, just as econometric identification is a problem only insofar as parameters of interest cannot be uniquely determined without further assumptions, it does not directly pose a problem for us. For our purposes, we are interested not in the "parameters" of the model but only in the "fitted model" and the goodness of fit.

More practically, Lucca and Trebbi (2009), Bligh and Hess (2009), and De Haan and Sturm (2011) show that information from central banks is indeed relevant for the movements and the volatility of financial markets (see also De Haan and Berger 2010; Berger, De Haan, and Sturm 2011). In addition, Rosa and Verga (2008) have shown that the *Monthly Bulletins* contain information complementary to that of the markets that has a value in its own right. Ultimately the performance of the FSI should be measured on how well it extracts information and how much it helps us to clarify the often conflicting signals from different sources.

Table 4.1 shows the complete list of selected words.[1] We have selected negative words whose meaning is commonly associated with stress, tension, vulnerability, or general weakness in the financial markets as well as in the overall economy. We have also included words with positive meanings, such as "recovery," "robust," and "favorable." To

Table 4.1
List of Selected Words

slowdown	stabilis*
uncertain*	improv*
weak*	eas*
deceler*	expan*
advers*	sound
risk*	robust*
deterior*	favour*
difficul*	recover*
vigilant	upturn
tensio*	optim*
imbalanc*	
downturn	
contract*	
turmoil	
crisis	
pessim*	

* Denotes a wildcard used in the search algorithm to capture variations of the chosen words.

capture variations of the chosen words, we use a wildcard in the search algorithm, which in table 4.1 is denoted by a "*."

The list of positive words, without including inflections, consists of 10 words, fewer than the 16 in the list of negative words. The greater prevalence of negative words is in part a reflection of the text. In addition, there tend to be more negative words that are unambiguously negative compared to positive words. For example, the noun "risk," depending on the context, could have a positive nuance if "risks were lower" or negative if "risks were higher." Nonetheless, when the word "risk" appears, it means that "there are risks," and therefore that there is (at least some) stress in the economy. While it is certainly possible to write about negative developments with words such as "favorable," "optimistic," "upturn," or "recovery," such use often becomes convoluted or overly categorical ("no evidence for an upturn"; "recovery is not in sight"). For this reason, we deem the problem of negation to be of a lower order of magnitude compared to our main extraction problem.[2]

To set a benchmark for the stress signal, for each month we compute the average number of negative (positive) words. The difference

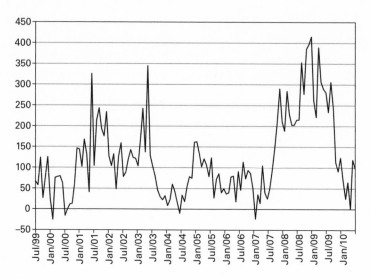

Figure 4.1
The *net* variable. Note: *net* is computed as the difference between the words of negative and positive meaning.

between the average number of negative and positive words can be thought of as a measure of net negativity/positivity.[3] We call this variable *net*. When the *net* variable is above (below) its long-term average, it signals stress (no stress) and translates as a binary variable with value 1 (0) in a logistic model that we explain in section 4.2.4.[4]

Financial tensions were clearly higher in the markets from summer 2007 till the end of 2009 and, as can be seen from figure 4.1 which plots the *net* measure, these are also the months in which *net* signals elevated stress in the markets. The pattern in figure 4.1 is broadly consistent with anecdotal evidence from other points in time. Using as an example the dot.com episode, the effects from the sharp decline in the NASDAQ composite index from its peak in March 2000 were beginning to be more widely felt on the European markets only starting in mid-spring. In fact, despite the sharp decline in the NASDAQ, the mood on the European markets remained fairly positive; for example, the *Economist*, referring to the dot.com bubble, focuses on the mergers and acquisitions activities of several European stock exchanges (Economist 2000). The editorial of the March *Monthly Bulletin* in 2000 (last paragraph on page 6) reports: "In conclusion, economic conditions and prospects for the euro area appear to be better at present than at any time in the past decade. Growth is strong, employment is expected to increase further and the still high level of unemployment should continue to fall. Remaining vigilant to counter upside risks to price stability and pursuing structural reform are the foundation for a sustained period of strong economic expansion and a lasting process of job creation."

4.2.3   Second Step: (a) Selecting Individual Market-Based Variables

We select market-based variables as basic financial measures. In order to have data with a small noise component, we choose only data that are of high quality, are available at daily frequency, have economic relevance, and are able to reflect agents' behavior. Most of the series are based on euro-area data, but to guard against possible oversensitivity in the choice of selected variables, we also include variables outside the euro area. Altogether we have a set of 24 underlying indicators, with 6 indicators representing US data; see table 4.2.

Table 4.2
List of Financial Variables

Euro-area data, weekly data, July 1999–June 2010	
• AA risk spreads	• Equity risk premium
• BBB risk spreads	• DJEuroSTOXX
• High-yield risk spread	• Actual earnings per share (EPS)
• Sovereign bond spreads (Austria, Belgium, Finland, France, Greece, Ireland, Italy, Netherlands, Portugal, Spain versus Germany)	• 1m Euribor-EONIA spread
	• 3m Euribor-EONIA spread
	• Main refinancing rate—2-year bond yield
• Difference between the euro-area 10-year and 2-year bond yield	
• DJ EUROSTOXX Financial	• Long implied bond volatility
	• Implied stock volatility
	• Euribor futures implied volatility
	• 1-year swaption on 1-year swap implied volatility
	• 1-year swaption on 10-year swap implied volatility
	• VSTOXX

US data, weekly data, July 1999–June 2010	
• AA risk spreads	• Difference between the 10-year and 2-year bond yield
• BBB risk spreads	• S&P 500
• High-yield risk spread	• VIX

The choice of the variables reflects to some extent the choice of variables in related studies, including Kaminsky (1999) and Illing and Liu (2006). The corporate bond yield spreads are used as measures of stress for the corporate sector; see Illing and Liu (2006).

For the sovereign bond markets we use the spreads between euro-area countries' long-term bonds (10 years) vis-à-vis Germany's long-term (10 years) bond.[5] In the literature, sovereign spreads are often related to "fundamentals," i.e., liquidity and credit risk premiums, as well as to market uncertainty. While liquidity and country creditworthiness usually play a role, market uncertainty is commonly found to play a not trivial role, especially at times of stress when market uncertainty increases.

For the banking sector, we use bank share prices to proxy for banking market stress. As in the literature on stock market bubbles, an increase in bank share prices may be indicative of the building up of imbalances (a bubble) and therefore might be interpreted as a signal of *impending* stress, while a sudden and protracted decrease in bank share prices (a crash) is interpreted as a sign of stress.

For the equity markets we use share prices, actual earnings per share, and equity risk premium to proxy for stress. High equity risk premiums are (often) indicative of stress. A decline in earnings per share (EPS) may signify trouble and is often interpreted as a sign of stress.

We use the spreads between interbank market rates at different maturities as measures of liquidity premium, which may contain information about stress in the money markets. In addition, we include the spread between the main refinancing rate and the 2-year bond yield. This spread is indicative of monetary liquidity, with a downtrend suggesting a worsening of liquidity; see Nelson and Perli (2006).

Finally, we use several measures of risk aversion like the implied stock volatility, which is computed through option prices and therefore contains information about expectations. We also include in our dataset several measures of uncertainty about the future level of interest rates, which may also reflect expectations about future monetary policy. An increase in such measures is interpreted as a sign of stress.

4.2.4 Second Step: (b) Aggregating Information from the Underlying Variables

Following Nelson and Perli (2006), the information contained in these basic individual measures is summarized into three summary indices that capture their *level, rate of change,* and *comovement.* Together these three indices contain much of what characterizes periods of stress that each one on their own might not detect.

The first index, the *level index,* is a simple arithmetic average of the values of the individual variables. The individual variables have been weighted by the inverse of their variances so that higher values of the index are associated with greater market stress.

The *speed* with which the underlying market variables change may also give valuable information. For example, one would expect that when liquidity premiums, risk spreads, and measures of uncertainty move higher, markets are becoming more vulnerable and stress is building up. Conversely, when they move down rapidly, this might indicate that the period of (acute) stress may be passed even if the index remains at elevated levels. In order to capture this feature, we construct the second index, the *rate of change* of the level index computed over a rolling window (over 18 weeks).[6]

Finally, we compute the *comovement index,* which is the percentage of the total variation of the individual variables explained by a common component.[7] The idea behind such an index is that periods of financial stress are the periods in which we observe an elevated correlation of the underlying individual financial variables.

4.2.5 Third Step: Combining the Underlying Variables into a Single Indicator

In the third step, the information contained in all three indices is combined into a single financial stress indicator obtained by using a logit model to extract the information contained in the indices in an efficient way. Specifically, the index is constructed by including the three indices on the right-hand side and a binary variable (i.e., $S_t = 0$ or 1) on the left-hand side of the equation. The binary variable S_t identifies periods of financial stress, as we have explained in section 4.2:

$$S_t = L(\beta_0 + \beta_1\lambda_t + \beta_2\delta_t + \beta_3\rho_t), \tag{4.1}$$

where λ is the level index, δ the rate of change, ρ the comovement index, β_i ($i = 1, \ldots, 3$) are the coefficients, and L denotes the logit probability distribution function. The model is estimated using weekly data from July 1999 to June 2010.[8] The fitted probability from the estimation of equation (4.1) is the FSI. Appendix 4.1 shows the estimation table.

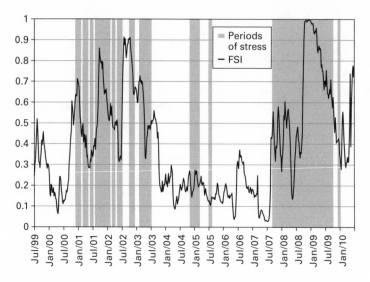

Figure 4.2
The FSI.

4.3   The FSI: A Contingent Indicator

The model in equation (4.1) is a model of a contingent indicator, and therefore the FSI gives information about vulnerabilities and stress in the economy and their magnitude as they transpire.

Figure 4.2 shows the FSI, i.e., the fitted probability of being in a period of stress at each point in time as computed in equation (4.1) in the chosen sample period. The shaded areas represent the stressful periods as described in section 4.2. As can be seen from figure 4.2, the indicator captures reasonably well well-known periods of financial stress.

Not surprisingly, the period of August 2007 onward emerges as the most acute episode of financial stress of recent history. Interestingly, the indicator also captures the switch in sentiment that the market experienced during the turmoil. For example, at times when major central banks temporarily succeeded in calming the markets by injections of liquidity, the indicator decreases, only to increase again soon afterward.

In spring 2010, markets were greatly affected by a new wave of stress due to worries and uncertainties about the sustainability of public finances in several euro-area countries. The indicator mirrors the mood of the markets both on the ups and the downs when rescue measures were put in place and (temporarily) succeeded in calming the markets.

Notably, the indicator also shows an increase in the probability of stress at other points in time. For example, there is a significant increase in 2000 in the wake of the dot.com bust. In 2002, financial markets experienced uneasiness originating from a string of defaults from large companies in telecommunications that was accompanied by the World-com implosion, and the Enron and Vivendi-Universal accounting irregularities.[9]

4.4   The FSI Performance

One way to assess the performance of the FSI is to measure its signal/ noise content by considering a threshold level when the markets go from signaling a tranquil period to signaling a period of stress. The critical threshold level is calculated so as to strike a balance between "bad" and "good" signals. A "bad" signal is a signal not followed by an actual period of stress within a certain horizon, and a "good" signal is one followed by an actual period of stress within the chosen horizon, similar to Kaminsky, Lizondo, and Reinhart (1998).

There are four possible cases to consider. A first possible outcome is that a signal is followed by a stress period in the current period.[10] A second possible outcome is that the signal is not followed by a stress period. A third is that the signal has not been issued and yet a stress period occurs within the chosen window. The final possible outcome is that a signal was not issued and stress did not occur. Following Kaminsky, Lizondo, and Reinhart (1998), this information can be sum-marized in the matrix in table 4.3.

Here, A is the number of periods that a good signal was issued, B is the number of periods that a bad signal was issued, C the number of periods that a signal should have been issued (a *missing* signal), and D is the number of periods that a signal was, rightly, not issued. The ratio C/(A+C) represents the share of missed periods of stress when stress occurred (A + C). It can also be interpreted as the share of type I errors. Similarly, the ratio B/(B + D) represents the share of false alarms when

Table 4.3
Noise/Signal Matrix

	Stress	No stress
Signal	A	B
No Signal	C	D

Table 4.4
The Success Ratio (July 1999–June 2010)

T	Right signal		False signal		Number of no-stress periods	Number of stress periods
	S = 0	S = 1	S = 0	S = 1		
0.1	0.09	1.00	0.91	0.00	347	227
0.2	0.44	0.93	0.56	0.07	347	227
0.3	0.62	0.87	0.38	0.13	347	227
0.4	0.74	0.71	0.26	0.29	347	227
0.5	0.83	0.52	0.17	0.48	347	227
0.6	0.92	0.41	0.08	0.59	347	227
0.7	0.95	0.27	0.05	0.73	347	227
0.8	0.97	0.17	0.03	0.83	347	227
0.9	0.99	0.11	0.01	0.89	347	227

stress did not occur (B + D), and therefore it also can be thought of as the share of type II errors. By using these ratios, a so-called success ratio can be obtained. In table 4.4 we show the success ratio for different threshold values. The first column shows the threshold values, while column 2 shows as a percentage of the total number of periods with no stress the number of weeks the FSI was below the threshold within a tranquil period (right signal). Column 3 shows the number of weeks the FSI was above the threshold within a stress period (right signal). Columns 4 and 5 show the false signal, when the FSI was below the threshold within a stress period and when it was above within a tranquil period, respectively. For reasonable values of the threshold, such as those close to the median, the percentage of right signals is relatively large and above that of false signals, indicating that the overall performance of the FSI is good.

The FSI can also be evaluated by looking at its out-of-sample performance. In order to do this, we estimate the parameters of the FSI up to July 2006 (thus excluding the financial crisis of 2007–2009 as well as the period of the European sovereign crisis). We then estimate the FSI out-of-sample based on these parameters.[11]

Figure 4.3 shows the resulting estimates in the sample in the solid line, and out-of-sample estimates in the dotted line. The solid line is the FSI as estimated in the previous section, and it can be thought of as the "actual" FSI, while the dotted line is the (out-of-sample) fitted FSI.

As the figure shows, the out-of-sample FSI mirror the "actual" FSI well; it picks up the surge in stress around August 2007 and remains

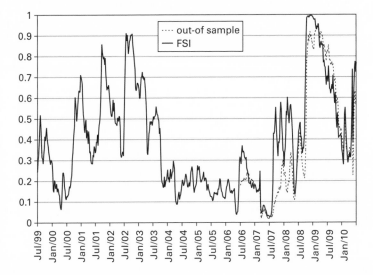

Figure 4.3
The FSI and the FSI out-of-sample.

at elevated levels throughout the entire 2007–2009 crisis period and also during the European debt crisis in 2010.[12] As shown in table 4.5, the performance of the FSI based on more formal tests, such as the Theil's inequality coefficient, is also good.

4.5   Conclusions

In this paper we used central bank communication to extract information about financial stress in the euro area in the form of a Financial Stress Indicator (FSI). By using statistical techniques on central bank communication, in particular the ECB *Monthly Bulletin*, together with relatively high-frequency financial market data, we are able to extract a signal of financial stress that has a good performance.

By quantifying central bank communication, we extract a lot of useful information that otherwise might be lost. Using automated content analysis techniques, we can detect and interpret patterns that the human eye would probably be unable to discern. We have shown that the FSI is well able to capture the advent of financial stress. It performs well in terms of the signal-to-noise ratio, and in particular it yields few false positives. We show that the results are robust in various dimensions including out-of-sample performance.

Table 4.5
Evaluation of Fit

RMSE	0.47
Theil Inequality Coefficient	0.38
Bias	0.09
Variance	0.19
Covariance	0.72

Table 4.6
Logit Estimation Results

Level	0.59
	(0.000)
Change	0.01
	(0.001)
Comovement	(0.06)
	(0.000)

Note: p-values in parenthesis.

Appendix 4.1   Logit Model Estimation

The dependent variable S_t in equation (4.1) is a binary variable where 0 denotes no stress and 1 stress.

Following the usual notation in a logit model, it is assumed that S_t is an indirect observation of the continuous latent variable S_t^*, where

$$S_t^* = \alpha + \beta' X_t + \varepsilon_t. \tag{4.2}$$

$T = 1, \dots, T$, and X_t is the set of explanatory variables. Under the logistic distribution for ε_t, the probability of being in stress can be written:

$$P\langle S_t = 1 | X_t, \alpha, \beta \rangle = \frac{\exp(\alpha + \beta' X_t)}{1 + \exp(\alpha + \beta' X_t)}$$

$$P\langle S_t = 0 | X_t, \alpha, \beta \rangle = \frac{1}{1 + \exp(\alpha + \beta' X_t)}. \tag{4.3}$$

In the text, the set of variables X consist of the *level*, the *change*, and the *comovement* indicators. The estimation results are presented in table 4.6.[13]

Notes

1. We ran a preselection on a larger pool of words. One of the preselection criteria is that selected words appear at least once in the *Monthly Bulletin* for each year. In addition, in the case of synonyms, we choose the word that appears more often. One alternative would have been to use Harvard's General Inquirer, but it is not specific to the discipline of finance. Loughran and McDonald (2011) have shown that word lists developed for other disciplines significantly misclassify common words in financial texts.

2. Negation of negative words ("there are no risks") to express positive meaning is not appealing either.

3. In order to avoid distortions due to the different lengths of the *Monthly Bulletins*, the average of negative (positive) words is weighted by the number of pages.

4. The long-term average is computed on the entire sample. Different thresholds computed over shorter samples such as 1999–2007 give the same qualitative results.

5. The long-term German bond, Bund, is commonly used as the benchmark, as it features both low liquidity and credit risk premiums.

6. The length of the window is chosen as it gives the highest R-squared in the logit model of equation (4.1).

7. This variable is extracted through a principal component analysis.

8. All three variables—level, rate of change, and comovement—are significant at least at 5% significance level.

9. Among others, for example, the Adelphia, one of the largest US broadcasting companies, defaulted. In Europe, ABB, a Swiss-Swedish engineering firm, and Elan, an Irish biotech firm, were also caught in a string of severe accounting irregularities.

10. Results are robust to different lengths of the chosen window, such as three periods before and after the current period.

11. More precisely, we perform a conditional out-of-sample forecast based on the observed value for the out-of-sample period of the independent variables.

12. The results are robust to different starting point of the out-of-sample period.

13. We use a robust HAC covariance matrix when we estimate the model.

References

Andersson, M., H. Dillen, and P. Sellin. 2006. Monetary Policy Signaling and Movements in the Term Structure of Interest Rates. *Journal of Monetary Economics* 53:1815–1855.

Berger, H., J. De Haan, and J.-E. Sturm. 2011. Does Money Matter in the ECB Strategy? New Evidence Based on ECB Communication. *International Journal of Finance and Economics* 16 (1):16–31.

Bligh, M., and G. Hess. 2009. A Quantitative Assessment of the Qualitative Aspects of Chairman Greenspan's Communications. http://www.wlu.ca/viessmann/CBCOM/Hess.pdf.

Bulíř, A., M. Čihák, and K. Šmídková. 2012. Writing Clearly: ECB's Monetary Policy Communication. *German Economic Review*, doi:10.1111/j.1468-0475.2011.00562.x.

Cardarelli, R., S. Elekdag, and S. Lall. 2009. Financial Stress, Downturns and Recoveries. IMF Working Papers Series 100.

De Grauwe, P., and M. Grimaldi. 2006. *The Exchange Rate in a Behavioral Finance Framework*. Princeton: Princeton University Press.

De Haan, J., and H. Berger. 2010. *The European Central Bank at Ten*. Berlin: Springer.

De Haan, J., and J.-E. Sturm. 2011. Does Central Bank Communication Really Lead to Better Forecasts of Policy Decisions? *Weltwirtschaftliches Archiv / Review of World Economics* 147 (1):41–58.

Economist. 2000. Frankfurt's Dot.com Dreams. *The Economist*, March 30.

Ehrmann, M., and M. Fratzscher. 2009. Explaining Monetary Policy in Press Conferences. *International Journal of Central Banking* 5 (2):42–84.

Heinemann, F., and K. Ullrich. 2007. Does It Pay to Watch Central Bankers' Lips? The Information Content of the ECB Wording. *Swiss Journal of Economics* 143 (2):155–185.

Illing, M., and Y. Liu. 2006. Measuring Financial Stress in a Developed Country: An Application to Canada. *Journal of Financial Stability* 2 (3):243–265.

Kaminsky, G. 1999. Currency and Banking Crises: The Early Warnings of Distress. IMF Working Papers 178.

Kaminsky, G., S. Lizondo, and C. Reinhart. 1998. Leading Indicators of Currency Crisis. IMF Staff Papers 145.

Loughran, T., and B. McDonald. 2011. When Is Liability Not a Liability? Textual Analysis, Dictionaries and 10-Ks. *Journal of Finance* 66:35–65.

Lucca, D. O., and F. Trebbi. 2009. Measuring Central Bank Communication: An Automated Approach with Application to FOMC Statements. NBER Working Paper w15367.

Manning, C. D., and H. Schütze. 2003. *Foundations of Statistical Natural Language Processing*. Cambridge, Mass.: MIT Press.

Nelson, W., and R. Perli. 2006. Selected Indicators of Financial Stability. http://www.ecb.int/events/pdf/conferences/jcbrconf4/Perli.pdf.

Orphanides, A., and S. van Norden. 2002. The Unreliability of Output-Gap Estimates in Real Time. *Review of Economics and Statistics* 84 (4):569–583.

Rosa, C., and G. Verga. 2008. The Impact of Central Bank Announcements on Asset Prices in Real Time. *International Journal of Central Banking* 4 (2):175–217.

Thaler, R., and S. Mullainathan. 2001. Behavioral Economics. In *International Encyclopedia of the Social and Behavioral Sciences*, ed. N. J. Smelser and P. B. Baltes. Amsterdam: Elsevier.

5   Interest Rate Expectations in the Media and Central Bank Communication

Michael J. Lamla and Jan-Egbert Sturm

5.1   Introduction

Market participants use interest rate decisions as well as communications of the central bank to infer the future path of monetary policy. In chapter 13 of this volume, Karagedikli and Siklos estimate the impact of central bank written statements and interest rate announcements on the New Zealand–US dollar and the New Zealand–Australian dollar exchange rates, and in chapter 8 Chirinko and Curran investigate the transmission of formal pronouncements of US Fed officials on Treasury bond futures. Other studies, like Ehrmann and Fratzscher (2009) and Brand, Buncic, and Turunen (2006), also explore the importance of the press conference relative to the announced interest rate decision for guiding money markets. While monitoring market interest rates, they find that additional information provided by the press conference is at least as relevant as the announced interest rate decision.

This study extends this line of research by employing a different way of measuring expectations. Commonly, changes in interest rates or exchange rates or derivatives thereof have been utilized to track the impact of central bank actions and to infer the future path of policymaking. However, measuring expectations that way often implies focusing on intraday or even tick-by-tick responses of financial markets. Central bank communication is arguably intended to also shape the expectations of households and firms which go beyond that focus.

The ECB is most likely to reach the general public via the media. In a survey of a random sample of the US population, Blinder and Krueger (2004) identify television and newspapers as the two most important sources of economic information. Berger, Ehrman, and Fratscher (2011) also show that the ECB receives great attention from the media.[1] Instead of reading the press releases and attending the media conferences of the ECB, it appears rational for the general public to assimilate this kind of information via a generally reliable and cheap source: the media.[2] Hence, to infer the expectations of the general public, we survey media releases printed one and two days after the ECB's press conference. In those two days, journalists are likely to write about the consequences that the ECB interest rate decision and its press statement hold for future monetary policy. This paper analyzes to what extent the ECB's announcements as communicated during their monthly press conferences are affecting media coverage and content about future monetary policy.

The paper is structured in the following way. Section 5.2 describes the data and the econometric methodology, section 5.3 presents the results, and section 5.4 concludes.

5.2   Data and Methodology

Our measure of interest rate expectations is based on data provided by Media Tenor, a media research institute. Media Tenor has coded all media articles that contain statements by the ECB regarding its upcoming decision on the main refinancing rate in the aftermath of the governing council meeting. They capture whether a statement in the media says the ECB will increase, sustain, or cut the main refinancing rate. The statements are extracted from articles printed in the *Financial Times Europe* (FTE) one and two days after the governing council meeting and are coded based on the method of content analysis. Media content analysis is a scientific method to capture the content of text passages. Several trained persons, called coders, read the news items and code them according to several characteristics, such as the topic, the tone, or the visibility of a news item. The characteristics coded are discussed in the main text below. Inter-coder reliability tests guarantee the high quality of the data. One main advantage of these tests is that the coding is done by at least two different coders, after which the tests check whether the coders came up with the same results. If not, unequally coded passages are recoded. This allows the capturing of the objective content of each statement and ensures reproducibility.[3]

We are only interested in statements on the future interest rate decision by the ECB in the aftermath of the previous decision. Figure 5.1 should clarify the timing. Thus, we get information on the amount of statements, whether the writer expects a tightening or a loosening monetary policy, and a broad definition of the type of writer (ECB

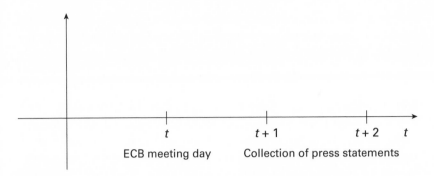

Figure 5.1
Timeline.

official, journalist, or other). The following paragraph should exemplify how a statement is coded.

Coding Example: "The upshot is that we do not expect the ECB to raise rates at all in 2005."

Direction: Sustain

Rating: Neutral

Source: Journalist

Time: Present and future

On average we capture roughly 10 statements dealing with the ECB monetary policy in the aftermath (1–2 days) of a governing council meeting. Overall our database consists of roughly 700 statements on the expected path of the main refinancing rate of the ECB. The resulting dependent variable is calculated as the difference between the total amount of statements expecting a monetary tightening (increasing the main refinancing rate) and the total amount of statements expecting a looser monetary policy (a cut in the main refinancing rate) divided by the total amount of statements on the future path of the monetary policy:

$$Exp_t = \frac{Expect\ increase_t - Expect\ cut_t}{Expect\ increase_t + Expect\ sustain_t + Expect\ cut_t}. \tag{5.1}$$

We label this balance variable "media expectations."

The expectations transmitted or generated by the media should be explained by the ECB's past interest rate decision and communication. For the interest rate decision, we take the main refinancing rate.

Moreover, we control for interest rate surprise by deducting the main refinancing rate from the rate average from the survey poll conducted by Reuters. Regarding the communication indicator, we apply a battery of communication indicators. Specifically, we use the same set of indicators also applied in Sturm and De Haan (2011), Berger, De Haan, and Sturm (2011), Heinemann and Ullrich (2007), the KOF Monetary Policy Communicator (KOF MPC)[4] (Conrad and Lamla 2010), and Rosa and Verga (2007). Our main communication indicator, however, will be Berger, De Haan, and Sturm (2011), because it also allows us to disentangle the wording of the ECB among its topics. That indicator monitors the risk to price stability, e.g., an increase means that the ECB's assessment of the economic situation implies a higher risk to price stability. The advantage of this communication indicator is that it can be disaggregated into three policy-relevant topics. Hence, it is able to capture the risk to price stability stemming from the real sector, the monetary sector, as well as developments related to prices.

Figure 5.2 shows the shares of media reports that expect rising, sustained, or falling rates together with the ECB's main refinancing rate. Except for 2002, during which expectations quite suddenly switched from falling to rising rates and back again, the overall comovement of the two series is quite strong. Whereas the actual interest rate did not follow media expectations in 2002, the communication indicator of Berger, De Haan, and Sturm (2011) shows a pattern similar to our media expectations (see figure 5.3). This sharp rise and fall might therefore be seen as a successful (mis-)guidance by the central bank, especially because no interest move happened.

Regarding the econometric analysis, we employ the following setup:

$$Exp_t = \alpha + \beta_1 Exp_{t-1} + \beta_2 \Delta ci_t + \Gamma \Delta c_t^j + \varepsilon_t, \tag{5.2}$$

where Exp_t is our media expectations variable. Exp_{t-1} is the last value of the expectations measure; ci_t is the announced interest rate decision, and c_t^j with $j = a, p, m, r$ represents the communication of the central bank with respect to prices (p), monetary aggregates (m), the real sector (r), and an overall assessment (a) in the introductory statement. Note that t relates to the meeting in each month. To make the coefficients comparable, we normalize each of the explanatory variables. ε_t is a well-behaved i.i.d. error term.

As we are dealing with a dependent variable that is bounded between [−1, 1], ordinary least squares (OLS) might be inappropriate. It has to be taken into account that if Exp_t is bounded, the marginal

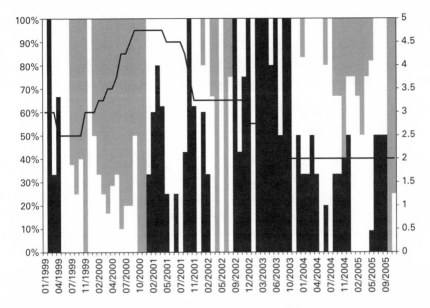

Figure 5.2
Media expectations in the aftermath of the introductory statement. The solid line equals
the ECB main refinancing rate (right-hand scale). Bars denote shares of expected interest
rate changes in the media (left-hand scale). Dark gray bars denote shares of statements
expecting rising rates, while light gray bars represent shares of statements expecting
falling rates. White bars reflect shares of statements indicating no expected change in the
main refinancing rate.

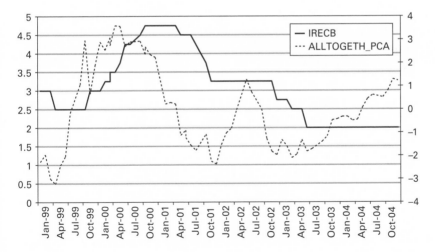

Figure 5.3
Interest rate changes, ECB communication, and expectations. IRECB = interest rate of the
ECB; ALLTOGETH_PCA= Berger, De Haan, and Sturm indicator.

effect of any particular explanatory variable cannot be constant through-out its range. Furthermore, the predicted values of OLS regressions cannot be guaranteed to lie within the unit interval. The problem becomes severe if a substantial mass of the distribution is located close to the bounds.

If we could transform our dependent variable to be $y \in (0, 1)$, we could simply use log-odd ratios and apply

$$E\left(\log\left[\frac{y}{1-y}\right]\bigg|X\right) = X\beta.$$

However, as our dependent variable takes on values at the bounds, i.e., $y \in [-1, 1]$, this is not a realistic option. In order to circumvent inference problems, we follow Papke and Wooldridge (1996). First, we rescale our variable to fit into the interval $[0, 1]$ using the formula $\hat{y} = (y - \bar{y})/(\bar{y} - \underline{y})$, where $y \in [\underline{y}, \bar{y}]$. Subsequently, we estimate the equation using the Bernoulli log-likelihood function given by

$$l_i(b) = \hat{y}_i\log[G(x_ib)] + (1 - \hat{y}_i)\log[1 - G(x_ib)],$$

where $G(x_ib)$ is the logistic function $G(x_ib) = \exp(x_ib)/[1 + \exp(x_ib)]$. β will be obtained by maximizing

$$\max_b \sum_{t=1}^{N} l_i(b).$$

The Bernoulli quasi-maximum likelihood estimator (QMLE) is a con-sistent and asymptotically normal estimator regardless of the distribu-tion of y. To test for the necessity of using the QMLE method, Papke and Wooldridge (1996) propose the Ramsey (1969) RESET test. While using our main communication indicator as well as the interest rate decision as explanatory variables, the RESET test applied to a standard OLS regression rejects the null hypothesis that the powers of the fitted dependent variable are zero at the 5 percent level.[5] Thus, using the QMLE estimation is recommended.

5.3   Results

First, we investigate the impact of central bank communication and the interest rate announcement on the created media expectation measure when applying a battery of different communication indicators. In table 5.1 we report the estimation results using the indicators of Berger,

Table 5.1
Results of Different Communication Indicators

	Berger, De Haan, and Sturm	Rosa and Verga	Rosa and Verga	KOF MPC	Heinemann and Ullrich
Media Exp $(t-1)$	2.13***	2.379***	2.008***	2.173***	2.365***
	(0.534)	(0.537)	(0.632)	(0.546)	(0.519)
Δi	4.217***	3.883***	3.664***	3.854***	3.709***
	(1.160)	(0.862)	(1.091)	(0.816)	(0.947)
ΔComm All	0.373*				
	(0.205)				
ΔRosa and Verga index $(-2,-1,0,1,2)$		0.792***			
		(0.240)			
ΔRosa and Verga index $(-1,0,1)$			0.344		
			(0.484)		
Cummulative version of the KOF MPC				0.320**	
				(0.141)	
ΔDuisenberg wording indicator of H&U					0.240*
					(0.131)
Constant	−1.190***	−1.351***	−1.310***	−1.128***	−1.261***
	(0.256)	(0.256)	(0.294)	(0.270)	(0.257)
Observations	61	55	44	61	61

De Haan, and Sturm (2011), Rosa and Verga (2007), Heinemann and Ullrich (2007), and the KOF MPC. While all indicators measure the content of central bank communication, their constructions differ. For instance, Berger, De Haan, and Sturm capture the subjective content, whereas Rosa and Verga concentrate on certain code words.

Despite their different constructions, the estimation results point in the same direction. Taking expectations from media sources as the dependent variable, both interest rate changes as well as central bank communication are important. In this horse race of indicators on the impact on the media, it seems that the Berger-De Haan-Sturm indicator, the finer-grained Rosa and Verga indicator, and the Heineman and Ullrich indicator are significant. The KOF MPC indicator is only significant when included in levels.

In a next step we estimate the Berger-De Haan-Sturm indicator and its different subdimensions in conjunction with the interest rate movements. Table 5.2 depicts the results. Column 1 reveals that both instruments affect the expectations of the future interest-rate path as

Table 5.2
Results Using Different Topics of Communication and Surprises

	1	2	3	4	5	6	7
Media Exp ($t-1$)	2.130***	2.234***	2.275***	2.290***	2.220***	2.083***	1.848***
	(0.534)	(0.522)	(0.555)	(0.538)	(0.548)	(0.541)	(0.537)
Δi	4.217***	3.869***	4.079***	3.876***	3.926***	5.665***	6.678***
	(1.160)	(0.862)	(1.165)	(0.921)	(1.243)	(1.129)	(1.830)
ΔComm All	0.373*					0.363*	0.390***
	(0.205)					(0.189)	(0.182)
ΔPrices		0.232***			0.213		
		(0.136)			(0.144)		
ΔMoney			0.099		0.018		
			(0.156)		(0.170)		
ΔReal				0.128	0.031		
				(0.151)	(0.159)		
Median surprise						-4.018**	
						(1.985)	
Mean surprise							-5.572**
							(2.550)
Constant	-1.190***	-1.216***	-1.226***	-1.132***	-1.217***	-1.136***	-1.01***
	(0.256)	(0.253)	(0.265)	(0.258)	(0.262)	(0.261)	(0.261)
Observations	61	61	59	61	59	61	61

communicated by the media to the public. In terms of a shock by one standard deviation, the interest rate decision has higher power to guide markets compared to the communication signal. In that respect, deeds matter more than words. While monitoring and interpreting intraday movements in the EUR-US$ exchange rate, Ehrmann and Fratzscher (2009), Brand, Buncic, and Turunen (2006), as well as Conrad and Lamla (2010) find similar results. Columns 2, 3, and 4 investigate the relevance of the topic communicated. In line with recent studies like Lamla and Lein (2011), Conrad and Lamla (2010), as well as Ehrmann and Fratzscher (2009), we confirm that the ECB's assessment of price developments matters most. Moreover, congruent with Berger, De Haan, and Sturm (2011), we show that communication on the monetary aggregates is, relative to statements on prices, of minor importance.[6] Romer and Romer (2000) provide evidence in favor of the Federal Reserve's information advantage in forecasting real output growth and inflation. This type of asymmetric information may also likely be present for the ECB. In column 5 we include all indicators into the regression. While none of them is significant at standard levels of confidence due to multicollinearity, the coefficient measuring price developments dominates in terms of size and statistical significance.

Columns 6 and 7 investigate whether the interest rate signal is mainly driven by market surprises (news). We can report that there is a significant response to surprises. A positive interest rate surprise substantially lowers the expectations for another future rise in the main refinancing rate. The explanation might be that the interest rate response may come earlier than expected and thus, on average, no further move is expected to be necessary.

5.4 Conclusions

Using media reports we try to capture how the decisions and actions of the ECB are perceived by journalists and afterward how they are conveyed to the public. Because it is not straightforward for the general public to evaluate the monetary policy decision by themselves, the public are most likely to update their expectations by reading newspapers. As the public gets most of their information from the media, the journalists' assessments may to a large extent shape their perceptions and expectations of ECB monetary policy. Hence, it is of key importance to examine how the ECB is perceived by the press.

We generate a novel expectations measure and focus on how ECB communication (words), as compared to actual interest rate decisions (deeds), affect expectations. We conclude that both deeds and words are important tools for guiding expectations as transmitted by the media. Nevertheless, deeds clearly outperform the words that are delivered by the introductory statement after each governing council meeting. The interest rate signal is significant in all specifications and its impact is always bigger than that of the communication signal. With respect to communication, information regarding price developments in particular seems to be of major importance. Overall, we can confirm results of previous studies, but we do so by using a very different and novel way to capture expectations formed and transmitted by the media.

Notes

1. Notably, the ECB itself maintains a database of press articles investigating how it is perceived by the media in terms of favorableness. In chapter 6 of this book, the information in this database is exploited by Berger, Ehrmann, and Fratzscher.

2. Sims (2003) argues that face capacity constraints and thus agents are temporarily rationally inattentive. The importance of media for the quality of inflation expectations has been convincingly demonstrated by Carroll (2003) and Lamla and Lein (2008).

3. Media Tenor's homepage provides more details on media content analysis. See http://www.mediatenor.com.

4. Available at: http://www.kof.ethz.ch/en/indicators/ monetary-policy-communicator/.

5. F-test $(3,58) = 3.19$; Prob $> F = 0.03$.

6. While this result may not be surprising, it is certainly remarkable. The ECB honored the heritage of the German Bundesbank by extensively discussing the developments of monetary aggregates in their communication. Given that, it is interesting to see that the public did not react to statements regarding monetary aggregates.

References

Berger, H., J. De Haan, and J.-E. Sturm. 2011. Does Money Matter in the ECB Strategy? New Evidence Based on ECB Communication. *International Journal of Finance and Economics* 16 (1):16–31.

Berger, H., M. Ehrmann, and M. Fratzscher. 2011. Monetary Policy in the Media. *Journal of Money, Credit and Banking* 43 (4):689–709.

Blinder, A. S., and A. B. Krueger. 2004. What Does the Public Know about Economic Policy, and How Does It Know It? NBER Working Papers 10787 (September), National Bureau of Economic Research.

Brand, C., D. Buncic, and J. Turunen. 2006. The Impact of ECB Monetary Policy Decisions and Communication on the Yield Curve. Working Paper Series 657, European Central Bank.

Carroll, C. D. 2003. Macroeconomic Expectations of Households and Professional Forecasters. *Quarterly Journal of Economics* 118 (1):269–298.

Conrad, C., and M. J. Lamla. 2010. The High-Frequency Response of the EUR-US Dollar Exchange Rate to ECB Monetary Policy Announcements. *Journal of Money, Credit and Banking* 72 (7):1391–1417.

Ehrmann, M., and M. Fratzscher. 2009. Explaining Monetary Policy in Press Conferences. *International Journal of Central Banking* 5 (2):42–84.

Heinemann, F., and K. Ullrich. 2007. Does It Pay to Watch Central Bankers' Lips? The Information Content of ECB Wording. *Swiss Journal of Economics and Statistics* 127 (2):155–185.

Lamla, M. J., and S. M. Lein. 2008. The Role of Media for Consumers' Inflation Expectation Formation. KOF Working Paper 201, KOF ETH Zurich.

Lamla, M. J., and S. M. Lein. 2011. What Matters When? The Impact of ECB Communication on Financial Market Expectations. *Applied Economics* 43 (28):4289–4309.

Papke, L. E., and J. M. Wooldridge. 1996. Econometric Methods for Fractional Response Variables with an Application to 401(K) Plan Participation Rates. *Journal of Applied Econometrics* 11 (6):619–632.

Ramsey, J. 1969. Tests for Specification Errors in Classical Linear Least Squares Regression Analysis. *Journal of the Royal Statistical Society, Series A (General)* 31 (2):350–371.

Romer, C. D., and D. H. Romer. 2000. Federal Reserve Information and the Behavior of Interest Rates. *American Economic Review* 90 (3):429–457.

Rosa, C., and G. Verga. 2007. On the Consistency and Effectiveness of Central Bank Communication: Evidence from the ECB. *European Journal of Political Economy* 23 (1):146–175.

Sims, C. 2003. Implications of Rational Inattention. *Journal of Monetary Economics* 50 (3):665–690.

Sturm, J.-E., and J. De Haan. 2011. Does Central Bank Communication Really Lead to Better Forecasts of Policy Decisions? *Review of World Economics* 147 (1):41–58.

6 Extreme Views Make News

Helge Berger, Michael Ehrmann, and Marcel Fratzscher

6.1 Introduction

Economists have long embraced the notion that the processing of information and the production of news is best understood as an outcome of market mechanisms (e.g., Coase 1974). News can be characterized as public goods, as experience goods, or as a product with multiple dimensions, and its production process is best described as one of high fixed costs and low variable costs. Hamilton (2004) shows that these market features can explain the positioning of news outlets in their coverage of soft and hard news. And George and Waldfogel (2003) show that high fixed costs and heterogeneous product preferences among consumers determine the mix of products available in the market; the larger a group of consumers with similar product preferences, the more suppliers will target that group.

Recently, Mullainathan and Shleifer (2005) have modeled the market for news under the assumptions that readers hold beliefs which they like to see confirmed, and that newspapers can slant stories toward these views. They show that in such a case, even in a competitive market, slanting toward reader biases will indeed result. Moreover, if reader beliefs are heterogeneous, newspapers are likely to segment the market and slant toward extreme positions. An indirect conclusion from this model is that extreme views should receive more coverage, or more prominent coverage, in the media.

This paper tests this prediction in an analysis of newspaper reports about the monetary policy decisions of the European Central Bank (ECB), using a novel data set that contains information both on the intensity and on the favorableness of media reporting of ECB monetary policy decisions since 1999. The paper also addresses the common argument that the news media generally overemphasize negative views (Fogarty 2005). The empirical results show that, indeed, extreme views receive more coverage, and that in particular negative views are reported upon more extensively. These intriguing asymmetries in the media coverage have important implications for the conduct and communication of economic policy decisions. This paper adds to a small but growing literature focusing on the interaction of monetary policy and the media (see, e.g., Lamla and Sturm in this volume; Berger, Ehrmann, and Fratzscher 2011) and, more generally, the role of the media as a source of information for economic agents (Carroll 2003; Lamla and Lein 2008).

6.2   Data on Press Coverage

The data set employed in this paper has been created by specialized media experts in the ECB for the purpose of internal reporting. The ECB's monetary policy decisions are typically announced and explained in a press conference on the first Thursday of each month. Following these press conferences, the media experts evaluate the reports in the Friday and weekend editions of 57 newspapers, 18 of which can be categorized as financial press.[1]

Coverage of each newspaper is measured in a qualitative index and a quantitative index. The qualitative index measures the *favorableness* with which the ECB's monetary policy decision is discussed on a scale ranging from –2 (very negative) to 2 (very favorable). For the quantitative index, each newspaper is allocated a ranking between 0 and 4 as follows:

0 Poor: minor news item based possibly on a news agency report, a couple of sentences added to another story, or no coverage at all;

1 Moderate: one-column headline or a small news item, report written by the newspaper's staff, the issue mentioned;

2 Average: no front-page news, medium importance elsewhere in the paper, two- to three-column headline;

3 Extensive: a minor hint on the first page, one of the leading news items elsewhere;

4 Very extensive: major news, headlines of four to six columns on the front page.

Finally, a national index is constructed by taking a simple arithmetic average of the different newspapers in a given country and rounding it to the nearest half-point, and an international index is similarly constructed for the international press. The indices are available to us from October 1999 until January 2005.

Table 6.1 provides a number of summary statistics for the indices. Our sample consists of 54 policy decisions. The summary statistics suggest that the favorableness of reporting is broadly balanced and that news about the ECB typically generate two- to three-column headlines, albeit not on the front page. There is substantial variation in the indices across countries and even more over time.

6.3 Determinants of Press Media Coverage

Table 6.2 reports results from a number of ordered probit models that relate the amount of press coverage to favorableness.[2] Model (1) shows that there is no linear relationship between favorableness and press coverage. However, Model (2) provides evidence of a nonlinear relationship using the squared value of favorableness, with more extreme opinions leading to more extensive coverage. Model (3) adds a dummy variable that is equal to 1 if the favorableness index is negative, to capture the idea of negativity bias (Fogarty 2005). While not necessarily establishing causation, these results suggest that more extreme opinions and negative opinions get more extensive coverage.

Models (1) to (3) do not control for the context of the decision or its newsworthiness. As shown in Model (4), such factors are highly relevant for explaining press coverage: policy rate changes receive substantially more coverage than decisions to leave rates unchanged. Furthermore, the surrounding communication is important. Using the market reaction to the press conferences as a proxy for its informational content, we find that more news content in the press conference is reflected in more reporting. Another interesting dimension is the location of meetings: if the ECB's Governing Council convenes outside Frankfurt twice a year, visiting a different euro-area country each time, national media in the host country tend to report more extensively. At the same time, the ECB's decisions seem to be discussed in an international context, as there is a marked increase in coverage if the US Federal Reserve has changed its policy rates in the two weeks preceding the ECB decision.

Other factors relate to the performance of the ECB and the economic environment. For instance, media coverage intensifies if inflation exceeds the ECB's objective, as well as in countries where national

Table 6.1
Summary Statistics of the Favorableness and Press Coverage Indices

Country	Favorableness of press coverage					Extent of press coverage				
	Observations	Mean	Standard deviation	Minimum	Maximum	Observations	Mean	Standard deviation	Minimum	Maximum
International	53	0.028	0.532	-1.5	1.5	52	2.625	0.656	1.0	4.0
Austria	49	0.071	0.433	-1.0	1.5	48	1.958	1.071	0.0	4.0
Belgium	52	0.067	0.505	-1.0	1.0	51	2.500	0.707	1.0	4.0
Finland	53	-0.009	0.410	-1.0	1.0	52	2.269	0.668	0.5	3.5
France	54	-0.009	0.440	-1.0	1.0	53	2.792	0.639	1.5	4.0
Germany	53	0.066	0.555	-1.0	1.0	52	2.971	0.546	2.0	4.0
Greece	46	-0.076	0.537	-1.5	1.0	45	2.733	0.580	1.5	4.0
Ireland	49	-0.041	0.443	-1.0	1.5	48	2.479	0.857	1.0	4.0
Italy	50	-0.010	0.371	-1.0	1.5	48	2.875	0.541	2.0	4.0
Luxembourg	52	0.163	0.417	-0.5	1.5	51	1.922	0.796	0.0	4.0
Netherlands	53	0.028	0.523	-1.5	1.0	51	2.157	0.919	0.5	4.0
Portugal	53	0.085	0.389	-1.0	1.5	52	2.154	0.814	0.5	4.0
Spain	54	0.148	0.501	-1.0	1.5	53	2.425	0.890	1.0	4.0
Total	671	0.041	0.470	-1.5	1.5	656	2.450	0.822	0.0	4.0

inflation rates deviate more from the euro-area average (in either direction). This is intuitive, as a given ECB policy will require more explanation in relation to the national context.

Importantly, the addition of these controls does not affect the main variables of interest: extreme views and negative views continue to receive more coverage in the newspapers. Our results also prove robust when replacing squared favorableness by the absolute values of favorableness, or when dropping the international press. Column 5 in table 6.2 reports results from an OLS estimation, with basically unchanged statistical significance.

The OLS estimates also allow a straightforward interpretation of the magnitude of the coefficients: moving from a neutral view to a favorableness index of 1.5 implies that the coverage index increases by 0.56. In case of a negative view, coverage increases additionally by 0.23 points, thus bringing the overall increase to 0.79, i.e., in the range of one standard deviation of the coverage index (which amounts to 0.82).

6.4   Conclusions

This paper has assessed the international and national press coverage that the ECB receives in response to its monetary policy decisions. The context and newsworthiness of ECB monetary policy decisions matter, as does the economic environment. Furthermore, there is a significant link between the tone and the extent of reporting: extreme views occupy substantially more space or get more prominence in newspapers. Finally, negative news receives more coverage.

These findings are in line with the model by Mullainathan and Shleifer (2005). One implication is that—from a central bank's perspective—communication efforts to shape the favorableness of media coverage and to avoid extensive negative coverage are particularly important.

Table 6.2
Favorableness as Determinant for the Extent of Press Coverage

	(1)		(2)		
	Coefficient	Std. err.	Coefficient		Std. err.
Favorableness factors					
Favorableness	0.010	0.108	—	—	—
Squared favorableness	—	—	0.877	***	0.150
Negative favorableness	—	—	—	—	—
Context of ECB policy decisions					
ECB rate change	—	—	—	—	—
Market reaction to press conference	—	—	—	—	—
Meeting outside Frankfurt	—	—	—	—	—
Fed rate change	—	—	—	—	—
Economic environment					
Euro-area inflation above 2%	—	—	—	—	—
Euro-area industrial production above average	—	—	—	—	—
Absolute national inflation differential	—	—	—	—	—
Special events and changes					
Presidency of J-C. Trichet	—	—	—	—	—
Press conference after summer break	—	—	—	—	—
Duisenberg's departure	—	—	—	—	—
Trichet's first press conference	—	—	—	—	—
Number of observations	656		656		
McFadden's adjusted R^2	0.04		0.07		
Cragg-Uhler (Nagelkerke) adjusted R^2	0.25		0.33		
McKelvey and Zavoina's R^2	0.37		0.43		
Adjusted R^2	—		—		
BIC	−1748.92		−1816.55		

Notes: ***, **, and * indicate significance at the 99%, 95%, and 90% levels, respectively. Robust standard errors are in italics. Columns 1 to 4: Ordered probit. Column 5: OLS. All models control for newspaper coverage, expert fixed effects, and country fixed effects. Dependent variable: Extent of press coverage. *Favorableness factors:* based on the favorableness indices. *ECB rate change:* Dummy variable; 1 for policy rate changes. *Market reaction to press conference:* Absolute return in German long-term bund futures contracts during the course of the press conference; *Meeting outside Frankfurt:* Dummy variable; 1 for the country in which the meeting takes place, 0 for all other countries, 0 for all countries for meetings in Frankfurt; *Fed rate change:* Dummy variable; 1 if US policy rates have been changed in the two preceding weeks; *Euro-area inflation above 2%:* Dummy variable; 1 if the latest figure for euro-area HICP inflation exceeds 2%, the ECB's definition of price stability; *Euro-area industrial production above average:* Dummy variable; 1 if the latest figure for euro-area industrial production exceeds the sample average; *Absolute national inflation differential:* Absolute difference between national and euro-area HICP inflation; *Special events and changes:* Dummy variables for Trichet's ECB presidency, for the press conferences after the summer break, for the press conference in which former ECB president Duisenberg announced his departure, and for president Trichet's first press conference.

(3)			(4)			(5)		
Coefficient		Std. err.	Coefficient		Std. err.	Coefficient		Std. err.
—	—	—	—	—	—	—	—	—
0.732	***	0.154	0.559	***	0.154	0.250	***	0.077
0.508	***	0.122	0.469	***	0.139	0.233	***	0.070
—	—	—	1.523	***	0.136	0.733	***	0.061
—	—	—	0.728	**	0.352	0.364	**	0.184
—	—	—	3.428	***	0.442	1.533	***	0.171
—	—	—	0.644	***	0.143	0.300	***	0.071
—	—	—	0.443	***	0.103	0.244	***	0.058
—	—	—	0.307	***	0.090	0.164	***	0.049
—	—	—	25.803	***	7.637	13.342	***	4.050
—	—	—	0.099		0.112	0.070		0.064
—	—	—	0.333	**	0.168	0.148	*	0.088
—	—	—	3.478	***	0.477	1.509	***	0.163
—	—	—	0.282		0.287	0.166		0.153
656			656			656		
0.08			0.19			—		
0.34			0.58			—		
0.44			0.65			—		
—			—			0.51		
−1826.95			−2091.64			−2903.29		

Notes

We would like to thank the ECB's Press and Information Division for providing us with the press indices. These have been used for regular internal ECB reporting; the underlying concept has been developed by Jukka Ahonen. We are also grateful to Ann-Kristin Koch for her able research assistance, and to Heli-Kirsti Airisniemi, Jukka Ahonen, Rainer Böhme, Frank Smets, and seminar participants at the ECB, ETH Zurich, Erasmus University Rotterdam, and University of Milan-Bicocca for comments and discussions. Berger thanks the ECB's Research Department for its hospitality. This paper presents the authors' personal opinions and does not necessarily reflect the views of the European Central Bank or of the IMF, its Executive Board, or its management.

1. A more detailed description of the data, as well as an overview of the newspapers that are covered, is provided in Berger, Ehrmann, and Fratzscher (2011).

2. The models contain a number of controls, namely, country fixed effects, fixed-effect variables for each of the experts producing the press indices, and three controls for differences in newspaper coverage: first, a dummy variable for countries with one or no specialized newspaper in the sample; second, the number of newspapers sampled within each country for each press conference; third, an equivalent variable for the coverage of specialized newspapers for each country and press conference.

References

Berger, H., M. Ehrmann, and M. Fratzscher. 2011. Monetary Policy in the Media. *Journal of Money, Credit and Banking* 43 (4):689–709.

Carroll, C. 2003. Macroeconomic Expectations of Households and Professional Forecasters. *Quarterly Journal of Economics* 118 (1):269–298.

Coase, R. H. 1974. The Market for Goods and the Market for Ideas. *American Economic Review* 64 (2):384–391.

Fogarty, B. 2005. Determining Economic News Coverage. *International Journal of Public Opinion Research* 17 (2):149–172.

George, L., and G. Waldfogel. 2003. Who Affects Whom in Daily Newspaper Markets? *Journal of Political Economy* 111 (4):765–784.

Hamilton, J. 2004. *All the News That's Fit to Sell: How the Market Transforms Information into News*. Princeton: Princeton University Press.

Lamla, M., and S. Lein. 2008. The Role of Media for Consumers' Inflation Expectation Formation. KOF Working Paper 201, KOF ETH Zurich.

Mullainathan, S., and A. Shleifer. 2005. The Market for News. *American Economic Review* 95 (4):1031–1053.

III The Fed's Experience

7 Deconstructing Alan: A Quantitative Assessment of the Qualitative Aspects of Chairman Greenspan's Communication

Michelle Bligh and Gregory Hess

7.1 Introduction

There can be no doubt that for a considerable period of time the Federal Open Market Committee (FOMC) has articulated its message at a measured pace.[1] This has not always been the case. Indeed, for much of its history the FOMC has been largely uncommunicative, preferring to surround itself with mystery as it has implemented monetary policy.

Alan Greenspan's tenure as the chairman of the Federal Reserve Board is associated with a fundamental change in the practice of both the conduct and communication of US monetary policy. Historically, transparency had not been high on any monetary authority's list of priorities. For example, Rockoff (1990) sees *The Wizard of Oz* as focused on the debates over a bimetallic currency standard at the end of the nineteenth century, with those who conduct monetary policy portrayed as grandiose wizards who hide behind smoke and mirrors and are ultimately filled with hot air. In a widely read book, William Greider (1987) describes the Fed's level of transparency in equally unpleasant terms:

The central bank, notwithstanding its claims to rational method, enfolded itself in the same protective trappings that adorned the temple—secrecy, mystique, and an awesome authority that was neither visible nor legible to mere mortals. Like the temple, the Fed did not answer to the people, it spoke for them. Its decrees were cast in a mysterious language people could not understand, but its voice, they knew, was powerful and important.

The FOMC, however, has made some recent demonstrated progress in articulating its decisions. For example, it actually started announcing decisions in 1994 (prior to that, it had allowed market participants to infer its actions from the conduct of open market operations). From the middle of 1999, it has provided an approximately 150-word statement after the conclusion of each and every meeting, regularly scheduled or not. Moreover, FOMC members routinely make speeches that are placed on the Federal Reserve Board's website, as are their prepared testimonies to the House and Senate. FOMC minutes are provided in a timely manner, and Federal Reserve forecasts for key macroeconomic variables are now made available to the public.

There are two important questions about Federal Reserve communications: What are the goals of the Federal Reserve's communication? And what are the best ways to accomplish these goals? We will defer discussion of the second question to the end of this paper and concentrate for now on the first one.

William Poole (2005), former president of the Federal Reserve Bank of St. Louis, points to several necessary preconditions for an appropriate FOMC communication strategy in an environment where it does not have private information about the economy.[2] The first is that the central bank must be clear about its objectives. The second is that the market and the central bank must have a correct understanding of how the economy works. The third is that unexpected economic outcomes are to be understood as news, that is, information that cannot currently be forecasted.

Consequently, monetary policy communication should lead to an understanding of the strategy for future monetary policy actions. As such, it should be as informative about future policy as possible, making this policy as predictable as possible within the confines of Poole's three necessary conditions: that the FOMC stick to its objectives, that the FOMC and the market understand the workings of the economy, and that it be understood that the actual path of future monetary policy may be affected by events that cannot currently be forecasted.

In the evidence below, we undertake a positive analysis that investigates whether Federal Reserve Board Chairman Greenspan's communications generally accomplished this goal of providing relevant information as well as making policy more predictable. In section 7.2 we discuss the recent empirical literature on central bank communication. In section 7.3 we introduce the empirical data we use in our study and discuss our empirical methodology. We present summary statistics and the empirical results in section 7.4 and conclude in section 7.5.

7.2 Literature Review

There have been a number of papers that analyzed Federal Reserve communications from an empirical standpoint.[3] Kohn and Sack (2004) estimate a standard baseline model, as shown below in equation (7.1), whereby unexpected movements in monetary policy (i.e., the one-month federal funds futures rate) and unexpected movements in macroeconomic variables lead to movements in financial variables.

Accordingly, they posit that if Federal Reserve communications provide information to the market, then the residual market volatility should be higher on days when there is a communication by the Fed. Indeed, they find strong evidence for this in statements and testimony. They also provide results from a variance decomposition, from which they conclude that such communications convey information on near-term policy moves but also information on the economic outlook. In complementary work, Gürkaynak, Sack, and Swanson (2005) provide evidence that FOMC statements also have a strong impact on longer-term Treasury yields.

While Federal Reserve communications, if informative, should move markets, a test of the usefulness of this information is whether it can help predict future movements of these financial variables. As such, our paper and important work by Ehrmann and Fratzscher (2007a, 2007b) investigate the language of Federal Reserve communications as they help to predict movements in financial markets variables. For instance, Ehrmann and Fratzscher (2007b) compare how markets forecasted future financial markets during periods when the Fed was less transparent as compared to its more recent period of greater transparency. In addition, Ehrmann and Fratzscher (2007a) compare the more individualistic style of communication in the Federal Reserve System as compared to the more collegial communication strategy of the Bank of England.[4]

Importantly, the work by Ehrmann and Fratzscher summarizes the language of the communications by examining press releases by Reuters just minutes after each communication; then, "based on our own judgment and reading of the newswire reports," they classify the communications into measures of stronger, unchanged, or weaker economic outlooks as well as tighter, no change, or easing monetary policy inclinations. While they acknowledge that they cannot "rule out a wrong classification in individual cases," these judgments are a useful starting point for reducing the dimensionality of communication.

Our paper's arm's-length ahistoric real-time analysis of Federal Reserve communication can be thought of as at the opposite end of the spectrum from the earlier "market response" approach. Of course, both approaches are useful for understanding the role of communication. In our approach, rather than use our own judgment to interpret the Federal Reserve's intent from its communications, as do Ehrmann and Fratzscher, we allow content analysis to ascertain the following three characteristics of each communication: certainty, pessimism, and macroeconomic language.[5,6] Below, we explain both our empirical strategy and content analysis, and demonstrate that these qualitative aspects of Chairman Greenspan's communications are statistically and economically important predictive factors of financial market variables.

As a final matter, and consistent with the literature cited above, we investigate a broad range of Federal Reserve communication outlets, for several reasons. First of all, the chairman's speeches are obviously prominent because of their timeliness and placement in prominent venues. Hence one may take the view that speeches should be important, and perhaps uniquely so, as a means of the Fed's communication. However, the chairman is not the only voice that communicating or interprets monetary policy actions. Indeed, Federal Reserve presidents, governors, and professional economists provide both reinforcing and contradictory views on the economy's outlook, sometimes in direct response to the chairman's message. This cacophony of communication can potentially drown out or lessen the value of the chairman's speeches, since, while he is an important voice on policy, he is not the only voice.

Second, other types of communications such as statements and testimonies are additional opportunities for the chairman to communicate important ideas and news pertaining to policy, the economic outlook, and potential risk factors. Unlike speeches, these statements and testimonies have the added appeal that they also bear the imprimatur of the broader membership of the Federal Open Market Committee, the Federal Reserve governors, and/or the Federal Reserve Board. As such, statements and testimonies may suffer from fewer issues of "noise," since presumably they speak on behalf of the Fed's consensus. Taken in total, it is an empirical question as to whether the chairman speeches, statements, or testimonies matter more to markets.

7.3 Data and Methods

In the following two subsections, we describe the data and methodology used in our analysis of the quantitative impact of the qualitative factors of official communications by Chairman Greenspan. First we describe the economic data and a baseline specification for predicting movements in standard financial market data. Then we describe our use of content analysis to help quantify the effect of Chairman Greenspan's language on financial markets, also presenting some summary statistics from the data.

7.3.1 Economic Data

Recent research has examined the role that FOMC communications (speeches, statements, and testimonies by Chairman Greenspan) have played in moving markets. Kohn and Sack (2004) investigate the role of communications in raising or lowering the volatility of markets, the former being evidence according to the authors that there is "news" in the communications that is driving the market. Their evidence involves results from the following regression:

$$\Delta r_t = \alpha_0 + \alpha_1 \Delta FF_t^u + \sum_{i=1}^{12} \beta_i NEWS_{it} + v_t, \qquad (7.1)$$

where Δr_t is the change in one of the financial market return variables under consideration, ΔFF_{it} is the unexpected change in the federal funds rate as measured by Kuttner (2001), and $NEWS_{it}$ refers to macroeconomic news. This standard baseline specification indicates that financial variables change in response to unexpected and actual moves in monetary policy as proxied by the federal funds rate, as well as news about the macroeconomy.

Implicitly, the level of financial variables should price in the expected path of monetary policy and macroeconomic activity so that changes in financial variables represent unexpected changes or news to these same variables. The residual term, v_t, allows for omitted factors that move financial market variables.

For the dependent variables, we use the daily changes in various financial variables, as done in Kohn and Sack (2004).[7] We use many of the same variables, including the changes in the federal funds futures rate three and six months ahead, FF(3M) and FF(6M), Treasury forward rates zero to one year ahead, TF(0|1), one to two years ahead, TF(1|2), and four to five years ahead, TF(4|5), as well as growth of the S&P 500 and the dollar (US$). All the interest rate data are reported in basis points (that is, 100 times the percentage), while the data for the US dollar and the S&P 500 are reported in percentages (i.e., 100 times the change in the natural log levels of the data). The data in the analysis are similar to those in Kohn and Sack.[8] Descriptive statistics for these variables, and others, are provided in table 7.3 and are discussed below.

As we discussed above, the analysis uses a proxy variable for the unexpected component of monetary policy developed in Kuttner (2001) and used in Kohn and Sack (2004). The federal funds futures rates are a market-based predictor of future policy, though they must be adjusted in order to adequately measure the expected and unexpected component of monetary policy. Two problems must be resolved. First, the settlement price of the contract is the average of the month's overnight federal funds futures rates, not the rate on the last day of the month. Second, futures contracts are based on the market rate rather than the target federal funds rate. The difference of the two can be significant on a day-to-day basis. To correct for these problems, Kuttner (2001) derives the unexpected change in the federal funds target rate for date t as:

$$\Delta FF_t^u = \left[\frac{m}{m-t}\right](F_{s,t}^0 - F_{s,t-1}^0),$$

where the left side is the unexpected change in monetary policy (change in the federal funds target rate), m is the total number of days in the month, t is the day of the month, and F is the spot futures rate on a given day t in month s. If the target rate change is in the last three days of the month, the daily change in the one-month spot futures rate is used to correct the targeting error of day t and the change in the expectation of future targeting errors. A complete description of this variable is available in Kuttner (2001).

The macroeconomic news variables were taken from the Money Market Services report. These 12 data series are constructed from the median of the survey of forecasts in the Friday before the data are reported for the first time. The surprise is constructed by subtracting the actual reported number from the most recent survey.[9] The 12 surprise variables are for the advanced estimate of GDP, capacity utilization, consumer confidence, core consumer index, durable goods orders, Institute of Supply Management Index, nonfarm payrolls, new home sales, core producer price index, retail sales, unemployment rate, and initial claims for unemployment. To avoid cluttering the paper, individual results on these macroeconomic surprises will not be presented, though we collectively report results for NEWS as a p-value for the F-test that all the coefficients on the macroeconomic news variables are jointly equal to zero.

7.3.2 Content Analysis

To further explore the role of the qualitative factors of Greenspan's language and their quantitative impact on financial markets, we augment equation (7.1) with language variables constructed from linguistic content analysis:

$$
\Delta cq_t = \alpha_0 + \alpha_1 \Delta FF_t^u + \alpha_2 \Delta r_{t-1} + \sum_{t=1}^{12} \beta_t NEWS_{it}
$$
$$
+ \sum_{j=3}^{3} \gamma_j COM_{jt} + \sum_{j=1}^{3} \sum_{k=1}^{3} \phi_{jk} [COM \times LANG_{kt}] + v_t. \tag{7.2}
$$

There are four sets of terms that we include on the right side of expression (7.2). The first two are unrelated to communication, but provide a richer empirical structure. The first is to include a measure of the unexpected change of monetary policy as measured by the unexpected change in the federal funds rate, ΔFF_t^u. The second is an autoregressive term for the market return variable, namely Δr_{t-1}. The third is a set of three dummy variables for the presence of a communication on day t, COM_t. Such communications are FOMC statements (STATE), and speeches (SPEECH) and testimonies (TEST) by Chairman Greenspan.

The second additional set of regressors in equation (7.2) allows for the quantification of the qualitative factors of these communications using content analysis. As a methodology, content analysis allows the investigator insight into the often symbol-laden connotations employed by leaders in context, making it a valuable tool for researchers specifically interested in leadership as the management of meaning; e.g., see Smircich and Morgan (1982). Given the focus on Chairman Greenspan's language, this suggests that Greenspan's specific choice of words can be particularly telling about his motives, intentions, and underlying assumptions, and may have significant effects on financial markets; see Bligh and Hess (2007). Due to the highly visible and politicized nature of Greenspan's position, computerized content analysis has the additional advantage of providing a completely impartial analysis of his leadership based solely on his public policy communications.

For each form of communication, the entire text was read into the Diction program, which is a content analysis program that keeps track of a number of key features of language that conform to key lists of words constructed by linguists.[10] There are 251 communications in our sample, including 58 FOMC statements, 58 testimonies before the

House or the Senate, and 135 speeches during the time period May 18, 1999 to January 31, 2006. This period was chosen because May 18, 1999 is the date from which all FOMC meetings were followed with a statement. We then perform content analysis on all these communications and score the messages based on the following criteria: CERTAINTY, PESSIMISM, and MACRO (these criteria are detailed below). Each of these 3 characteristics of speech, for each of the 3 types of communications, is treated separately in the regression, so that there are 9 additional explanatory variables that quantify the content of Chairman Greenspan's communications.[11]

We chose Diction 5.0 (Hart 2000) for our analysis, a computerized content analysis program specifically designed for public policy discourse. Diction has been used to study semantics in a variety of social discourse arenas such as politics and communication, and more recently has been used in business applications such as evaluating annual reports and press releases about earnings forecasts—see Bligh, Kohles, and Meindl (2004), Davis, Piger, and Sedor (2007), and the references therein. Because we wanted the measure of the chairman's speech to be generic and impartial, Diction was a natural choice due to its explicit development for political discourse and careful attention to linguistic theory.[12] To our knowledge, Diction is the only existing content analysis program that has been specifically designed for public policy dialog, and that is expressly concerned with the types of words frequently encountered in American public discourse. Thus, it seemed particularly appropriate for the analysis of policy communications made by Chairman Greenspan.

There are obvious advantages and disadvantages to using computerized content analysis. Let's start with some drawbacks. First, the sterility of analysis may preclude creative insights or innovative breakthroughs (e.g., the recent use by the FOMC of the expression "a considerable period"); second, it is based on the assumption that more frequent use of a word or phrase means that the latter is more meaningful or important than infrequently used words or phrases; and finally, it does not account for the fact that words in this analysis are divorced from their original contexts—again, see Bligh, Kohles, and Meindl (2004).

With respect to the advantages, first and foremost, content analysis is highly systematic and reliable. One particular aspect of the analysis should not be undervalued: at some level, language for monetary policy purposes does not live in a context separate from all other types of language. Explicitly, the term "a considerable period" actually may mean what it says. As such, one can argue that it should conform to the same standards of analysis as other types of communication. In addition, due to its microscopic nature, Diction is ideal for uncovering aspects of language that may be missed by the human eye. Third, all of Diction's dictionaries contain individual words only, and homographs are explicitly treated by the program through statistical weighting procedures to partially correct for context; see Hart (2000).

By default, Diction uses numerous dictionaries, containing over 10,000 search words, to analyze a given communication. In order to keep our analysis as simple as possible, we construct three composite variables from seven of these dictionaries that are likely to be of interest with respect to monetary policymaking: these composite variables are CERTAINTY, PESSIMISM, and MACRO. Table 7.1 provides a formal definition of these variables, and table 7.2 provides a few examples. Briefly, CERTAINTY refers to words that indicate resoluteness, inflexibility, and completeness. PESSIMISM refers to language that endorses or highlights blame or hardship.

We also made two important adjustments to the data. First, a problem with examining individual words is that they can be preceded by a negation that completely reverses the meaning of the individual word. For instance, Chairman Greenspan's oft-used expression "There can be no doubt" is clearly affected by the presence of a negation. To deal with this, we remove any words from CERTAINTY and PESSIMISM that are preceded by the word "no" or "not."[13] Second, we created an additional composite variable to more closely follow the extent to which macroeconomic terms are present in the chairman's communications. We constructed this list of words by accumulating the dictionary of terms provided at the end of the popular intermediate macroeconomic textbooks Abel and Bernanke (2005), Delong (2002), and Mankiw (2003). We label this variable MACRO.

While expression (7.2) provides an empirical relationship that allows us to see whether the qualitative components of Chairman Greenspan's communications help to predict market returns, it is also important to see whether monetary policy language systematically predicts changes in credit quality spreads and market volatility. To be more precise, in expression (7.3) we estimate the relationship between changes in credit quality spreads, Δcq_t, and monetary policy language as follows:

Table 7.1
Diction Dictionaries and Composite Dictionaries

Dictionary	Description	Sample words
Certainty =	**Language indicating resoluteness, inflexibility, and completeness as well as a tendency to speak ex cathedra.**	**Tenacity + Leveling + Concreteness + Insistence − Ambivalence**
Tenacity	Includes all uses of the verb "to be", definitive verb forms and their variants, and associated contractions. These verbs connote confidence and totality.	Is, am, will, shall, has, must do, he'll, they've, ain't
+ Leveling	Words used to ignore individual differences and to build a sense of completeness and assurance.	Everybody, anyone, each, fully, always, completely, inevitably, consistently, unconditional, consummate, absolute
+ Concreteness	A dictionary of words denoting tangibility and materiality, including physical structures, modes of transportation, articles of clothing, household animals, etc.	Airplane, ship, bicycle, stomach, eyes, lips, slacks, pants, shirt, cat, insects, horse, wine, grain, sugar, oil, silk, sand, courthouse, temple, store
− Ambivalence	Words expressing hesitation or uncertainty, implying an inability or unwillingness to commit to what is being said.	Allegedly, perhaps, might, almost, approximate, vague, baffled, puzzling, hesitate, could, would, guess, suppose, seems
Pessimism =	**Language endorsing or highlighting the negative entailments of some person, group, concept, or event.**	**Blame + Hardship**
Blame	Terms designating social inappropriateness and evil, as well as unfortunate circumstances.	Mean, naïve, sloppy, stupid, fascist, repugnant, malicious, bankrupt, rash, morbid, weary, nervous, painful, detrimental, cruel
+ Hardship	Natural disasters, hostile actions, censurable human behavior, unsavory political outcomes, and human fears.	Earthquake, starvation, killers, bankruptcy, enemies, vices, infidelity, despots, betrayal, injustices, exploitation, grief, death
Macroeconomics	The dictionary of terms provided at the end of the popular intermediate macroeconomic textbooks by Professors Abel and Bernanke (2005), Delong (2002), and Mankiw (2003).	Unemployment, inflation, natural rate, aggregate demand, cash flow, competition, depreciation, dividends, exports, foreign trade, gross national product, interest, leading indicators, microeconomics, nominal appreciation, price index

Note: To offset the potential problem of negation affecting the meaning of a CERTAINTY or PESSIMISM word, such words that were preceded by "no" or "not" were subtracted from each of these dictionary's word totals.

Table 7.2
Computerized Coding of Sample Statement Passages

Construct	Computerized coding
Certainty	"The <u>evidence</u> <u>accumulated</u> over the intermeeting <u>period</u> <u>indicates</u> that output is continuing to expand at a solid pace and labor market conditions have improved." (06/30/04)
Pessimism	"Heightened <u>uncertainty</u> and <u>concerns</u> about a <u>deterioration</u> in business conditions both here and abroad are damping economic activity." (11/06/01)
Macro	"<u>Consumer</u> and <u>business</u> <u>confidence</u> has eroded further, exacerbated by rising energy costs that continue to drain consumer purchasing power and press on business profit margins." (01/31/01)

$$\Delta cq_t = \alpha_0 + \alpha_1 \Delta FF_t^u + \alpha_2 \Delta r_{t-1} + \sum_{t=1}^{12} \beta_t NEWS_{it}$$
$$+ \sum_{j=3}^{3} \gamma_j COM_{jt} + \sum_{j=1}^{3} \sum_{k=1}^{3} \phi_{jk}[COM \times LANG_{kt}] + v_t. \tag{7.3}$$

Specification (7.3) is identical to expression (7.2) with the exception that the dependent variable is now the change in a standard credit quality spread. We measure credit quality using four interest rate spreads: first, the *TED(1M)* spread, which is the difference between the one-month LIBOR rate less the one-month Treasury bill rate; second, the spread between the one-month commercial paper rate for financial firms and the one-month Treasury bill rate, *CPTB-F(1M)*; third, the spread between the one-month commercial paper rate for nonfinancial firms and the one-month Treasury bill rate, *CPTB-NF(1M)*; lastly, the spread between the corporate bond rate for debt rated BAA and that for AAA-rated debt, *BOND(10Y)*.

Finally, our specification relating financial market volatility, ΔV_t, and monetary policy language adopts the following specifications:

$$\Delta V_t = \alpha_0 + \alpha_1 (\Delta FF_t^u)^2 + \alpha_2 \Delta V_{t-1} + \sum_{t=1}^{12} \beta_t NEWS_{it} + \sum_{t=1}^{12} \delta_t NEWS_{it}^2$$
$$+ \sum_{j=3}^{3} \gamma_j COM_{jt} + \sum_{j=1}^{3} \sum_{k=1}^{3} \phi_{jk}[COM \times LANG_{kt}] + v_t. \tag{7.4}$$

Specification (7.4) is similar to that in expressions (7.2) and (7.3), except that financial market volatility is affected by the volatility of unexpected federal funds rate changes and the level and volatility of macroeconomic news.[14] We measure financial market volatility using options-based market measures of volatility for equities and government securities: *VIX(1M)*, *MOVE(1M)*, *MOVE(3M)*, and *MOVE(6M)*. *VIX(1M)* is the Chicago Board of Options's volatility index conveyed by S&P 500 stock index option prices over a one-month period, while *MOVE(1M)* (Merrill Lynch's Option Volatility Estimate) is an index that tracks how much traders expect Treasuries maturing in two to 30 years to fluctuate in a month. Correspondingly, we also define *MOVE(3M)* and *MOVE(6M)* for implied volatility at the three- and six-month horizons.

7.4 Empirical Results

This section is separated into two subsections, the first of which examines the stylized facts of our data, while the second provides estimates of the effect of monetary policy language on financial market returns and financial market volatility, as described in empirical equations (7.2) and (7.4).

7.4.1 Empirical Regularities

The top part of table 7.3 provides summary statistics for the dependent and language variables that we will be investigating. Again the interest rate variables are reported as daily basis point changes. There are a few items worth noting in this table. First, interest rate variables were flat or declined during this period—recall that the FOMC's first experiment with an extended policy of near-zero interest rates took place during this time period. Second, generally speaking, longer-term interest rates demonstrate more volatility than shorter-term interest rates. Third, credit quality spreads also declined during this period, in part owing to the Federal Reserve's expansionary policy and the economy's strong economic performance throughout all but the first part of the sample. Finally, the dollar and the stock market were relatively flat during this period, with the stock market showing substantial volatility.[15]

The bottom part of table 7.3 provides some summary statistics for the content analysis data of Chairman Greenspan's communications.[16] Note that the data are presented so that they indicate the number of words per 100 in a particular communication.[17] If a communication does not take place for that day, then its language components are all equal to zero. Each row indicates a particular component of language, e.g., *CERTAINTY* for a particular form of communication (*SPEECH*).

Table 7.3
Sample Statistics (May 18, 1999 to January 31, 2006)

Variable		Mean	Standard deviation	Minimum	Median	Maximum	NOBS
ΔFF_t^u		−0.067	1.812	−42.500	0	15	1682
$\Delta FF(3M)$		−0.021	3.496	−35.000	0	26	1682
$\Delta FF(6M)$		−0.011	4.536	−37.000	0	30	1682
$\Delta TFW(0\,\vert\,1)$		−0.029	5.010	−53.520	0.105	22.54	1682
$\Delta TFW(1\,\vert\,2)$		−0.066	7.798	−50.030	−0.140	36.8	1682
$\Delta TFW(4\,\vert\,5)$		−0.087	6.858	−24.030	−0.535	31.03	1682
$\Delta\ln(US\$)$		−0.013	0.462	−3.716	−0.002	5.032	1682
$\Delta\ln(S\&P)$		−0.003	1.181	−6.005	0.018	5.574	1682
$\Delta TED(1M)$		−0.017	7.107	−81.725	0.088	63.675	1682
$\Delta CPTB\text{-}F(1M)$		−0.014	7.396	−87.600	0	49.3	1682
$\Delta CPTB\text{-}NF(1M)$		−0.017	7.486	−77.600	0	50.321	1682
$\Delta BOND(10Y)$		0.009	1.895	−9.999	0	41.002	1682
$\Delta VIX(1M)$		−0.009	1.239	−5.570	−0.060	9.92	1682
$\Delta MOVE(1M)$		−0.016	4.256	−17.570	−0.085	34.64	1682
$\Delta MOVE(3M)$		0.004	2.465	−11.750	0	13.82	1682
$\Delta MOVE(6M)$		0.004	1.940	−11.880	0	15.98	1682
CERTAINTY	ST	8.188	1.618	3.808	8.443	11.416	58
PESSIMISM	ST	1.289	0.686	0	1.122	3.686	58
MACRO	ST	5.053	1.039	1.974	5.122	7.051	58
CERTAINTY	SP	8.028	2.064	3.388	7.666	15.46	135
PESSIMISM	SP	1.167	0.790	0	0.994	3.374	135
MACRO	SP	2.651	1.222	0.225	2.516	5.723	135
CERTAINTY	TE	8.104	3.238	2.618	7.744	27.733	58
PESSIMISM	TE	1.149	0.653	0.148	1.076	2.9	58
MACRO	TE	3.013	0.946	0.606	3.116	5.211	58

Notes: Data are for business days from May 18, 1999, to January 31, 2006. There are 251 communications samples made up of 58 FOMC statements, 58 testimonies before the House or Senate, and 135 speeches during this time period. $\Delta FF(3M)$ and $\Delta FF(6M)$ are the change in the federal funds futures rate three and six months ahead, respectively, $\Delta TFWD(0\,\vert\,1)$, $\Delta TFWD(1\,\vert\,2)$, and $\Delta TFWD(4\,\vert\,5)$ are the change in Treasury forward rates (zero to one years ahead, one to two years ahead, and four to five years ahead), $\Delta\ln(US\$)$ is the log growth rate of trade-weighted dollar, and $\Delta\ln(S\&P)$ is the log growth rate of the S&P 500. Following the same convention, $TED(1M)$ is the difference between the one-month LIBOR rate and the one-month Treasury bill rate; $CPTB\text{-}F(1M)$ and $CPTB\text{-}NF(1M)$ are the spread between the one-month commercial paper rate, financial and nonfinancial, and the one-month Treasury bill rate; and $BOND(10Y)$ is the spread between the corporate bond rate for debt rated BAA less that for AAA-rated 10-year debt. $VIX(1M)$ is the Chicago Board of Option's volatility index conveyed by S&P 500 stock index option prices, while $MOVE(1M)$ (Merrill Option Volatility Estimate) is an index that tracks how much traders expect Treasuries maturing in two to 30 years to fluctuate in a month. $MOVE(3M)$ and $MOVE(6M)$ are similarly defined for three- and six-month fluctuations. All the interest rate data are reported in basis points (that is, 100 times the percentage), while the data for the dollar and the S&P 500 are in percentages. Language variables CERTAINTY, PESSIMISM, and MACRO are discussed in the text. ST, SP, and TE refer to STATEMENT, SPEECH, and TESTIMONY. NOBS is the number of observations.

There are two important factors worth noting in table 7.3. First, statements have, on average, more *MACRO* language than speeches and testimonies. This may in fact be due to the fact that since statements are so short, *MACRO* language can be a useful way to parsimoniously convey information. Second, there is more heterogeneity about *CERTAINTY* in testimonies. Of course, because testimonies are less constrained by time and provide more background materials, this may allow for the greater variety of information that they communicate about the level of certainty in the environment.

Table 7.4 also demonstrates a number of key features of the volatility of the underlying financial data series when there is either macroeconomic news on a given day or some form of communication by the chairman. Each row represents a financial data series, while each column presents the standard deviation of the data over alternative subsamples of the data. Test results are also presented to answer whether one can reject the null hypothesis that the standard deviation of the data subsample differs from that when there is neither news nor communication (i.e., *NO_COM_NO_NEWS*). Note that for the financial market returns, we measure volatility by the standard deviation of the series. By contrast, for market volatility measures such as *VIX* and *MOVE*, we measure volatility by the change in the level of the variable.

There are four interesting results demonstrated in table 7.4. First, on days when macroeconomic news is released, financial markets are generally more volatile for the shorter-term interest rate data: days of macroeconomic news typically have significantly higher interest rate volatility in the federal funds and Treasury forward markets as well as the credit quality spreads as compared to days when there is neither news nor communication. Second, there is one strong exception to the preceding observation: namely, direct measures of financial market volatility derived from options markets—*VIX*, *MOVE(1M)*, *MOVE(3M)*, and *MOVE(6M)*—actually are unchanged or decline on days of economic news or communication. Third, days when there was a communication by Federal Reserve Chairman Greenspan show an almost identical pattern of volatility changes as compared to that for days of *NEWS* (i.e., the columns labeled *NEWS* and *COM* have similar patterns of statistical significance), with the exception of the credit quality spread variables. As such, one can infer that *NEWS* and communication each embody similar attributes as evidenced by their effect in a wide variety of financial markets. Fourth, the different modes of

Table 7.4
Market Movement of Financial Variables across News and Communications

Variable	Measure of volatility	ALL	NO_NEWS_NO_COM	NEWS	COM	STATE	SPEECH	TEST
$\Delta FF(3M)$	σ	3.496	1.872	4.284[c]	4.182[c]	7.451[c]	2.263[c]	2.752[c]
$\Delta FF(6M)$	σ	4.536	3.305	5.355[c]	5.150[c]	7.391[c]	3.891[c]	4.952[c]
$\Delta TFW(0\|1)$	σ	5.010	4.275	5.637[c]	5.227[c]	6.496[c]	4.513	5.371[c]
$\Delta TFW(1\|2)$	σ	7.798	6.716	8.786[c]	8.014[c]	8.778[c]	7.078	9.308[c]
$\Delta TFW(4\|5)$	σ	6.858	6.229	7.503[c]	6.908[b]	6.799	6.281	8.384[c]
$\Delta \ln(US\$)$	σ	0.462	0.478	0.462	0.381[c]	0.322[c]	0.379[c]	0.427
$\Delta \ln(S\&P)$	σ	1.181	1.192	1.175	1.217	1.443[b]	1.204	0.941[b]
$\Delta TED(1M)$	σ	7.107	6.903	7.285	6.254[b]	7.560	6.086[a]	5.200[c]
$\Delta CPTB\text{-}F(1M)$	σ	7.397	6.662	7.906[c]	6.929	9.519[c]	6.226	5.259[b]
$\Delta CPTB\text{-}NF(1M)$	σ	7.487	7.028	7.742[c]	7.192	9.530[c]	6.542	5.741[a]
$\Delta BOND(10Y)$	σ	1.895	1.598	2.107[c]	1.938[c]	2.493[c]	1.732	1.734
$\Delta VIX(1M)$	μ	-0.009	0.122	-0.113[c]	-0.081[b]	-0.340[c]	-0.076[a]	0.165
$\Delta MOVE(1M)$	μ	-0.016	0.265	-0.084	-0.860	-2.584[c]	-0.445[a]	-0.100
$\Delta MOVE(3M)$	μ	0.004	0.003	0.033	-0.085	0.074	-0.051	-0.326
$\Delta MOVE(6M)$	μ	0.004	-0.017	0.042	-0.062	0.009	-0.079	-0.093

Notes: See definitions in table 7.3. The measures of volatility are standard deviation (σ) and mean (μ). The standard deviations and means are of the actual data. ALL, NO_COM_NO_NEWS, NEWS, and COM refer to whether the statistic is calculated over the full sample, only for days when there is neither communication nor news, for days when one of the 12 news variables were reported, or only for days when there was a speech or testimony by Greenspan or an FOMC statement. STATE, SPEECH, and TEST refer to days when there was either an FOMC statement, a speech, or a testimony by Greenspan, respectively. The superscripts a, b, and c indicate respectively the .10, .05, and .01 levels of statistical significance at which one can reject the null hypothesis that the standard deviation of the data sample differs from that when there is neither news nor communication. The p-values are derived from tests that are robust to heteroskedasticity of unknown form.

communication—that is statements, speeches, and testimonies—each have wide-ranging effects on financial markets.

7.4.2 Regression Analysis

The key results from our estimates of expression (7.2) are presented in table 7.5, where we report the estimated parameters of the key language variables for each of the seven dependent variables that measure financial market returns. In the bottom panel of this and the following two tables, there is a list of variables where we report the associated p-value from the F-test when the coefficients on the collection of variables are jointly equal to zero. We report evidence on the collective impact of *NEWS*, all *LANGUAGE*, as well as the separate testimonies, speeches, and statements.

There are a number of key findings in table 7.5.[18] First, controlling for unexpected movements in the federal funds rate is important, as they are predictors of changes in federal funds futures rates at the 3-month and 6-month horizon. Moreover, *NEWS* is statistically significant across all the financial markets considered in table 7.5. Second, the qualitative aspects of language are statistically significant at or below the 0.1 level for 3- and 6-month changes in the federal funds futures market, and the growth of the value of the dollar. Third, the language in statements appears to have a broad amount of predictive ability for financial market variables. In particular, statements with more *CERTAINTY* language are consistent with increases in federal funds futures rates, while statements with more *MACRO* language are associated with a rise in the value of the US dollar. Fourth, speeches with more *PESSIMISM* are associated with declines in the S&P 500 and the 3-month federal funds futures market. Fifth, testimonies have no statistically significant impact on same-day movements in financial variables except that of the US dollar. Overall, then, *CERTAINTY* language seems to have the greatest statistical impact on raising shorter-term interest rates futures, while *PESSIMISM* language tends to lower the value of the dollar, the stock market, and near-term federal funds futures.

The findings in table 7.5 that point to the role of enhanced levels of *CERTAINTY* in FOMC statements and speeches during Alan Greenspan's tenure are consistent with our earlier findings in Bligh and Hess (2007).[19] Indeed, in our prior work we find strong evidence that in periods of economic strength (weakness) the language from the Federal Reserve has higher (lower) levels of certainty. Based on these combined

Table 7.5
Regression Results for Market-Based Rates of Return

		$\Delta FF(3M)$	$\Delta FF(6M)$	$\Delta TF(0\|1)$	$\Delta TF(1\|2)$	$\Delta TF(4\|5)$	$\Delta\ln(US\$)$	$\Delta\ln(S\&P)$
ΔFF_t^u		.756^c	.569^c	.494^b	0.301	0.056	−.008	−.090
		[.111]	[.161]	[.216]	[.340]	[.171]	[.013]	[.042]
Δr_{t-1}		.118^c	.094^c	0.034	0.016	.056^b	−.019	−.023
		[.035]	[.027]	[.027]	[.026]	[.025]	[.026]	[.033]
CERTAINTY	ST	.817^c	1.34^c	.940^a	0.603	0.457	0.024	0.003
		[.311]	[.510]	[.537]	[.890]	[.661]	[.030]	[.132]
PESSIMISM	ST	−.463	−1.21	−1.12	−1.95	−1.80	−.073	−.484
		[.775]	[1.16]	[1.09]	[1.62]	[1.27]	[.066]	[.345]
MACRO	ST	0.362	0.973	0.831	0.519	0.199	.078^a	−.120
		[.323]	[.676]	[0.800]	[1.10]	[.832]	[.041]	[.120]
CERTAINTY	SP	.156^b	0.200	.312^b	0.244	0.030	−.029	−.016
		[.069]	[.134]	[.158]	[.262]	[.215]	[.015]	[.039]
PESSIMISM	SP	−.433^a	−.358	−.481	−.226	0.187	−.003	−.321^b
		[.236]	[.412]	[.517]	[.815]	[.711]	[.039]	[.155]
MACRO	SP	0.155	0.147	0.113	−.152	−.220	−.033	−.002
		[.139]	[.224]	[.313]	[.514]	[.473]	[.029]	[.078]
CERTAINTY	TE	0.029	0.129	−.014	−.269	−.342	−.030	0.073
		[.207]	[.314]	[.370]	[.707]	[.845]	[.028]	[.068]
PESSIMISM	TE	−.768	−1.35	−1.62	−1.94	−.614	−.227^c	−.105
		[.569]	[1.09]	[1.06]	[1.83]	[1.69]	[.083]	[.161]
MACRO	TE	0.183	−.046	−.017	0.35	−.350	−.014	0.140
		[.394]	[.666]	[.755]	[1.29]	[1.38]	[.052]	[.137]
NOBS		1682	1682	1682	1682	1682	1682	1682
R^2		0.249	0.262	0.111	0.094	0.061	0.031	0.036
NEWS		0	0	0	0	0	0	0.028
LANG		0.012	0.017	0.103	0.795	0.932	0.003	0.261
ST		0.007	0.001	0.052	0.400	0.436	0.017	0.261
SP		0.051	0.418	0.174	0.807	0.968	0.128	0.179
TE		0.567	0.671	0.427	0.645	0.895	0.032	0.478
CERTAINTY		0.007	0.023	0.072	0.671	0.880	0.155	0.730
PESSIMISM		0.147	0.346	0.282	0.457	0.540	0.041	0.075
MACRO		0.450	0.462	0.762	0.939	0.951	0.182	0.575

Notes: See definitions in tables 7.3 and 7.4. Regressions also include a constant, lagged dependent variable and macroeconomic news variables. R^2 is adjusted R-squared. There are 12 macroeconomic surprise variables, 3 communication variables, and 3 language variables per type of communication. The bottom panel presents p-values for the F-tests when the collection of variables indicated in each row are jointly equal to zero.

findings, it appears that in times of strength (weakness) in US economic activity, the FOMC under Greenspan spoke with a voice that connoted more (less) certainty, which the markets took to be a sign that future FOMC moves would lead to future tightening (loosening) of monetary policy. Moreover, when the Fed speaks more pessimistically, this tends to suggest a more challenging economic environment, which appears to be priced into some assets.[20]

Table 7.6 provides estimates for the change in credit quality spreads, cq_t, as modeled in equation (7.3). The results from this specification suggest that the change in credit quality spreads is much less responsive to news and Chairman Greenspan's communication as compared to the results for change in interest rates provided in table 7.5. Indeed, all the results for p-values listed at the bottom of table 7.6 indicate that neither individually nor collectively do macroeconomic news or Greenspan's communications predictably move these credit quality spreads. For sake of comparison, the R^2 in table 7.6 is approximately 0.035, as compared to over 0.25 for several specifications in table 7.5. One interesting finding, however, is that an increase in the CERTAINTY language in the STATEMENT tends to lower the credit quality spread, as measured by the TED spread and both commercial paper spreads. Overall, this indicates that a rise in certainty in the language of the FOMC statements could provide some reassurance to the private sector, and this in turn gets priced into different asset classes.

As a final component in our analysis, the results in table 7.7 provide a broader understanding of how Chairman Greenspan's communication and language predict the volatility in the movements in financial variables.[21] Recall from the regression specification (7.4) that ΔV_t is a measure of volatility measured using volatility indices from market-based options.

The results in table 7.7 provide a number of interesting findings. First, measures of the squared unexpected federal funds rate changes and NEWS measures are not significantly associated with the measures of financial market volatility.[22] Second, as demonstrated by the p-values reported in the bottom panel of the table, the language variables are significant predictors of volatility in the Treasury forward rates for less than one year—i.e., MOVE(1M), MOVE(3M), and MOVE(6M). Third, MACRO language is consistently a significant variable in explaining changes in the MOVE volatility indices. Typically, for the MOVE indices, MACRO language in speeches and statements is significant. Hence, broadly speaking, the chairman's testimonies appear to be

Table 7.6
Regression Results for Market-Based Credit Quality Spreads

	Type	ΔTED(1M)	ΔCPTB-F(1M)	ΔCPTB-NF(1M)	ΔBOND(10Y)
ΔFF_t^u		−0.545[a]	−0.652[a]	−0.424	−0.045
		[0.297]	[0.362]	[0.383]	[0.055]
Δcp_{t-1}		0.053	−0.007	−0.003	−0.019
		[0.052]	[0.052]	[0.048]	[0.036]
CERTAINTY	ST	−1.273[b]	−1.428[a]	−1.774[b]	−0.068
		[0.643]	[0.868]	[0.837]	[0.281]
PESSIMISM	ST	−1.368	−2.734	−3.319[a]	0.602
		[1.513]	[1.984]	[1.988]	[0.367]
MACRO	ST	0.021	−0.004	−0.138	−0.290
		[0.879]	[1.043]	[1.009]	[0.215]
CERTAINTY	SP	−0.262	−0.287	−0.265	−0.065
		[0.218]	[0.224]	[0.237]	[0.065]
PESSIMISM	SP	0.190	0.258	0.268	0.020
		[0.542]	[0.611]	[0.626]	[0.246]
MACRO	SP	−0.248	−0.317	−0.749	−0.083
		[0.424]	[0.454]	[0.475]	[0.113]
CERTAINTY	TE	0.213	0.120	0.082	0.014
		[0.308]	[0.322]	[0.353]	[0.092]
PESSIMISM	TE	0.802	0.338	−0.167	−0.592
		[1.406]	[1.345]	[1.566]	[0.378]
MACRO	TE	−0.637	−0.950	−0.665	−0.092
		[0.672]	[0.693]	[0.851]	[0.219]
NOBS		1682	1682	1682	1682
R^2		0.037	0.033	0.038	0.026
NEWS		0.774	0.559	0.962	0.119
LANGUAGE		0.557	0.523	0.269	0.256
ST		0.262	0.351	0.159	0.264
SP		0.483	0.423	0.196	0.532
TE		0.732	0.574	0.847	0.212
CERTAINTY		0.116	0.217	0.113	0.788
PESSIMISM		0.738	0.524	0.399	0.160
MACRO		0.740	0.487	0.359	0.464

Notes: See definitions in tables 7.3–7.5. Dependent variables are the volatility measures labeled at the top of each column.

Table 7.7
Regression Results for Options-Based Measures of Financial Market Volatility

		$\Delta VIX(1M)$	$\Delta MOVE(1M)$	$\Delta MOVE(3M)$	$\Delta MOVE(6M)$
$(\Delta FF_t^u)^2$		−0.010	0.007	0.007	0.008
		[0.007]	[0.013]	[0.011]	[0.008]
ΔV_{t-1}		−0.027	0.031	0.108[c]	0.111[b]
		[0.035]	[0.030]	[0.035]	[0.043]
CERTAINTY	ST	−0.131	0.094	0.307	0.207
		[0.104]	[0.425]	[0.231]	[0.154]
PESSIMISM	ST	0.104	−0.875	0.144	0.293
		[0.208]	[0.965]	[0.438]	[0.311]
MACRO	ST	0.183[a]	−0.728	−0.692[b]	−0.363[a]
		[0.109]	[0.706]	[0.297]	[0.213]
CERTAINTY	SP	−0.005	−0.028	−0.007	−0.049
		[0.043]	[0.143]	[0.083]	[0.066]
PESSIMISM	SP	0.113	0.559	0.485[a]	0.347[a]
		[0.137]	[0.469]	[0.257]	[0.195]
MACRO	SP	0.047	−0.570[b]	−0.356[b]	−0.314[b]
		[0.081]	[0.267]	[0.169]	[0.125]
CERTAINTY	TE	−0.077	−0.452	−0.187	−0.281[a]
		[0.068]	[0.331]	[0.181]	[0.169]
PESSIMISM	TE	0.127	−0.448	0.934	0.535
		[0.191]	[0.957]	[0.653]	[0.440]
MACRO	TE	−0.123	−1.583[b]	0.257	0.201
		[0.137]	[0.664]	[0.367]	[0.238]
NOBS		1682	1682	1682	1682
R^2		0.103	0.102	0.035	0.035
NEWS		0.288	0.002	0.749	0.961
LANGUAGE		0.586	0.103	0.015	0.012
ST		0.260	0.499	0.040	0.081
SP		0.715	0.140	0.098	0.034
TE		0.557	0.067	0.127	0.129
CERTAINTY		0.415	0.585	0.430	0.152
PESSIMISM		0.712	0.496	0.126	0.137
MACRO		0.253	0.012	0.014	0.025

Notes: See definitions in tables 7.3–7.6. Dependent variables are the volatility measures labeled at the top of each column.

unusually influential in forecasting movement in the financial market volatility, and this is primarily due to the significance of *MACRO* language.

7.5 Conclusion

The positive evidence suggests that the language in monetary policy communications by Chairman Greenspan was informative and aided in the improved predictability of financial market variables. These effects have been demonstrated to be statistically significant. In all, we find that macroeconomic news and macroeconomic language in the chairman's speeches and statements moved financial markets. Given our analysis of text on a word-by-word basis, our language components mostly address the tone of the communication, rather than the specific topic of the conversation.

An important question remains, however, as to whether the Federal Reserve System has fully exploited the net gains from communication. Generally speaking, an argument can be put forth that the Federal Reserve System under Chairman Greenspan may have improved upon yet still underutilized its ability to beneficially communicate to the markets and broader public. For example, as indicated by the evidence, FOMC statements and speeches by Chairman Greenspan appear to have had an important impact on the direction of short-term expectations about policy as well as on options-based measures of financial volatility. Macroeconomic language, in particular, also appeared to be important for lowering the volatility in financial markets, which suggests that the markets turn to the Federal Reserve for macroeconomic explanations and analysis. In all, the Federal Reserve's attempts post-Greenspan to improve the range and contents of its language and communications affirm that it felt that communications in earlier periods, such as the one examined in this study, were both useful and could be improved upon.

Finally, though complex and at times difficult to put in context, one should not trivialize the FOMC's or the chairman's language of communication (tempting though it may be). As discussed in Bligh and Hess (2007), monetary policy communication requires an outsized level of subtlety. The economic terrain is best described by tradeoffs and uncertainty, which necessitates that a successful communication policy be nuanced. But nuanced information need not be limited information. One legacy of Alan Greenspan's chairmanship has been to firmly remind us that communication matters. The follow-up for the Federal Reserve to consider is how to make communication matter even more.

Notes

1. Corresponding author: Gregory D. Hess, Robert Day School of Economics and Finance, Claremont McKenna College, Claremont, CA 91711. E-mail: ghess@cmc.edu, tel: (909) 607-686, fax: (909)621-8249. We thank seminar participants at the Bank of Japan, the Federal Reserve Banks of Kansas City, San Francisco, and St. Louis, the Cass Business School at the City University of London, Oxford University, the Society for Computational Economics Conference in Limassol, Cyprus, and the Central Bank Communication, Decision-Making and Governance Conferences at Wilfrid Laurier University and CESifo's Venice Summer Institute for their helpful comments. Justin Eskind and Paul VanDeventer provided superb research assistance, and we also thank Ken Kuttner and the Federal Reserve Bank of San Francisco for data assistance. We would also like to thank Michael Ehrmann, David-Jan Jansen, Alberto Montagnoli, and Pierre Siklos for their detailed comments. We gratefully acknowledge the Kravis Leadership Institute, the Financial Economics Institute, and the Fletcher Jones Foundation for partially funding our research.

2. See Amato, Morris, and Shin (2002) for an analysis of central bank communication when the central bank has private information. They point to the problems of providing public information in these types of environments, as it may diminish the range of expectations in the market and force the coordination of market expectations on the incorrect outcome.

3. Note that Jansen and De Haan (2006) investigate the role of the contradictory nature of statements by national central bank presidents and the European Central Bank. Also see the recent survey by Blinder et al. (2008).

4. Interestingly, they also note and contrast the collegial decision-making process of the FOMC and the individualistic decision-making style of the Bank of England.

5. Boukus and Rosenberg (2006) also take a more automated approach to extracting information from the FOMC minutes for the time period 1987–2005. Their approach uncovers latent characteristic themes across the minutes based on the observed sample, much like in atheoretical principal-components analysis. By contrast, our approach scores communications based on ex ante constructed components explicitly developed for public policy discourse and based on linguistic theory.

6. In addition, work by Blix Grimaldi and Mayes and Montagnoli (in this volume) construct their own lists of words for content analysis in order to capture specific aspects of central bank language.

7. In an interesting paper in this volume, Chirinko and Curran analyze the change in long-term Treasury excess returns and trading volumes every five minutes around the time of Federal Reserve communications. They present interesting findings with regard to market movements immediately before and immediately after these communications. Their results are limited, however, to a sample of data from 1997 to 1999.

8. Indeed, the Treasury forward rate data were obtained from the Federal Reserve Board's Treasury forward rate curves.

9. The data were purchased from Haver Analytics.

10. Diction 5.0 also includes content analysis for Realism, Commonality, and Activity. When we evaluated Federal Reserve communications for these linguistic characteristics and included these terms in our analysis, we did not find statistical significance. Hence, rather than include these variables in our empirical tables, we decided to concentrate on variables where there was some empirical and statistical significance. Also, *PESSIMISM* is a negative part of a broader term on *OPTIMISM*: however, the non-*PESSIMISM* part of *OPTIMISM* was also a poor empirical predictor and so it was dropped from the analysis.

11. While a few words exist on more than one list—e.g., unemployment is both a *PESSIMISM* word and a *MACRO* word—these speech variables are not significantly correlated with one another at conventional levels on days of communication.

12. See Hart (2000) for a more thorough discussion of the development of Diction.

13. Our method can be explained as follows: if a *PESSIMISM* or *CERTAINTY* word is preceded by a "not" or a "no," we reduce the overall count of this category by one, as it connotes the opposite meaning to the word and it does not have a neutral meaning. Of course, other two-word combinations could be important, such as "considerable period." This is a broader shortcoming of the literature to date that will need to be addressed in future work.

14. Our findings are not affected by the inclusion of both these linear and squared *NEWS* variables. In addition to the variables included in (7.2), specification (7.4) also includes dummy variables for whether the FOMC meeting was scheduled or not, and effects stemming from whether it was held on a Monday, Friday, or first day of the month. Again, the inclusion of these additional variables does not affect the results.

15. Note that the time period covered in this analysis includes the aftermath of the terrorist attack on the United States on September 11, 2001. Removing from the data sample the time period from this incident until the end of the 2001 does not affect the results presented below.

16. We have looked at subsamples of the data and find broad consistency in the findings reported below (not shown in table 7.3). In an interesting new paper in this volume, Jansen and De Haan linguistically evaluate the communication consistency of the ECB.

17. For example, if there are 10 *MACRO* words out of a 500 word communication, *MACRO* would be coded as 2.0 $(100 \times (10/500))$ for that particular day for that particular form of communication.

18. The estimated standard errors have been bootstrapped using 1,000 replications. The results are similar using clustering methods and other robust estimation methods.

19. To gauge the size of this effect, let's consider the effect from moving to the highest to the lowest level of *CERTAINTY* in an FOMC statement on movements in the short-term federal funds futures markets. Note that table 7.3 indicates that the movement from the lowest to the highest level of *CERTAINTY* in a statement is approximately 8, while the effect of this variable on short-term federal funds futures is about 1. Hence, the effect of enhanced *CERTAINTY* could move this market by at most 8 basis points, which is about one-third the value of a 25-basis-point move.

20. Note that our classification of communications addresses the tone of the communication—e.g., does the chairman's communication generically seem more pessimistic, even if we do not know the exact topic that he is being pessimistic about?

21. Note that volatility is useful for another reason. For example, let's say that Greenspan's comments were either pessimistic about inflation or output. Depending on what he was pessimistic about, this would push interest rate expectations and futures and forward rates in different directions. These would be difficult to capture in a simple regression. However, articulated pessimism by Greenspan, regardless of what he was pessimistic about, would increase movement in financial variables, which would increase observed volatility. Hence, volatility may be better at capturing the effects of monetary policy language on financial market variables.

22. Note that if we remove the linear terms for NEWS in the regressions, the remaining variables for NEWS do become significant.

References

Abel, A. B., and B. S. Bernanke. 2005. *Macroeconomics*. 5th ed. Boston: Addison Wesley.

Amato, J., S. Morris, and H. S. Shin. 2002. Communication and Monetary Policy. *Oxford Review of Economic Policy* 18 (4):495–503.

Bligh, M. C., and G. D. Hess. 2007. Leading Cautiously: Alan Greenspan, Rhetorical Leadership, and Monetary Policy. *Leadership Quarterly* 18 (2):87–104.

Bligh, M. C., J. C. Kohles, and J. R. Meindl. 2004. Charisma under Crisis: Presidential Leadership, Rhetoric, and Media Responses before and after the September 11th Terrorist Attacks. *Leadership Quarterly* 15 (2):211–239.

Blinder, A. S., M. Ehrmann, M. Fratzscher, J. De Haan, and D.-J. Jansen. 2008. Central Bank Communication and Monetary Policy: A Survey of Theory and Evidence. *Journal of Economic Literature* 46 (4):910–945.

Boukus, E, and J. V. Rosenberg. 2006. The Information Content of FOMC Minutes. Mimeo, Federal Reserve Bank of New York.

Davis, A. K., J. Piger, and L. M. Sedor. 2007. Beyond the Numbers: Managers' Use of Optimistic and Pessimistic Tone in Earnings Press Releases. Mimeo, University of Oregon.

Delong, J. B. 2002. *Macroeconomics*. Rev. ed. New York: McGraw-Hill.

Ehrmann, M., and M. Fratzscher. 2007a. Communication and Decision-Making by Central Bank Committees: Different Strategies, Same Effectiveness? *Journal of Money, Credit and Banking* 39 (2–3):509–541.

Ehrmann, M., and M. Fratzscher. 2007b. Transparency, Disclosure and the Federal Reserve. *International Journal of Central Banking* 3 (1):179–225.

Greider, W. 1987. *Secrets of the Temple: How the Federal Reserve Runs the Country*. New York: Simon and Schuster.

Gürkaynak, R. S., B. Sack, and E. T. Swanson. 2005. Do Actions Speak Louder Than Words? The Response of Asset Prices to Monetary Policy Actions and Statements. *International Journal of Central Banking* 1 (1):55–93.

Hart, R. P. 2000. *DICTION 5.0: The Text-Analysis Program*. Thousand Oaks, CA: Scolari/ Sage Publications.

Jansen, D-J., and J. De Haan. 2006. Look Who's Talking: ECB Communications During the First Years of EMU. *International Journal of Finance and Economics* 11 (3):219–228.

Kohn, D. L., and B. P. Sack. 2004. Central Bank Talk: Does It Matter and Why? In *Macroecnomics, Monetary Policy, and Financial Stability*, 175–206. Ottawa: Bank of Canada.

Kuttner, K. 2001. Monetary Policy Surprises and Interest Rates: Evidence from the Fed Funds Futures Market. *Journal of Monetary Economics* 47:523–544.

Mankiw, N. G. 2003. *Macroeconomics*. 5th ed. New York: Worth Publishers.

Poole, W. 2005. How Should the Fed Communicate? Speech given to the Center for Economic Policy Studies, Princeton University, April 2. Available at: http://fraser.stlouisfed.org/historicaldocs/1101/download/41097/20050402.pdf.

Rockoff, H. 1990. The "Wizard of Oz" as a Monetary Allegory. *Journal of Political Economy* 98 (4):739–760.

Smircich, L., and G. Morgan. 1982. Leadership: The Management of Meaning. *Journal of Applied Behavioral Science* 18:257–273.

8 Greenspan Shrugs: Central Bank Communication, Formal Pronouncements, and Bond Market Volatility

Robert S. Chirinko and Christopher Curran

The verdict among most, if not all, our "watchers" seems to be that—broadly speaking—the ECB has done a good job but has not been very effective in presenting and explaining itself.
—Otmar Issing, Chief Economist, ECB (2001)

I used to think if there was reincarnation, I wanted to come back as the president or the pope or a .400 baseball hitter. But now I want to come back as the bond market. You can intimidate everybody.
—James Carville, advisor to President Clinton (1993)

In such circumstances, certain types of central bank talk might actually impinge on welfare-enhancing market pricing by being misunderstood and receiving too much weight relative to private judgments.
—Donald Kohn, Vice Chair, Board of Governors of the Federal Reserve System (2005)

8.1 Introduction

There is a broad consensus among central bankers and monetary policy scholars that transparency enhances economic performance. Expectations about the future course of the economy have a substantial impact on economic decisions, and monetary policy has a substantial role in influencing these expectations.[1] The lifting of the veil on central banking operations lowers the level of uncertainty confronting firms, households, and investors, and thus enhances incentives for risk-averse agents to undertake long-term commitments. A more transparent monetary policy informs and anchors expectations. With fewer monetary surprises, economic activity becomes less volatile. Moreover, transparency is consistent with the democratic principles of accountability of public institutions to their citizens.[2]

While transparency is a widely held goal, how do central banks communicate?[3] As indicated by the above quotation from Otmar Issing, communication is an essential element in the conduct of monetary policy.[4] Blinder et al. (2001) suggest that, in principle, the central bank should talk about its objectives, its methods for attaining these objectives, and its process of deliberations. There is an extensive literature on the specifics of how central banks should and do communicate—explicit announcement of targets, immediate notification of policy decisions, prompt publication of the transcripts of central bank meetings, and detailed documentation of economic forecasts and the underlying models (see the survey by Blinder et al. 2008). One communication channel that has received much less attention is the formal pronouncements made by central bankers. This paper examines this aspect of communication policy and assesses the impact and nature of the formal pronouncements made by Alan Greenspan.

Focusing on "Greenspan's shrugs" affords several advantages.[5] The chair of the Board of Governors of the Federal Reserve System is one of the most important economic policymakers in the world. For the period we study, Greenspan's influence had been substantially enhanced by the exceptional performance of the US economy during his long tenure and the perception that the Federal Reserve played a prominent role in generating this "Long Boom." Greenspan communicated frequently in three different ways—in speeches to industry groups, academic audiences, and professional associations; in testimony before Congressional committees; and in Federal Open Market Committee (FOMC) decisions. Given the institutional structure and norms of the Board of Governors and his chairing of the FOMC, Greenspan exerted substantial control over monetary policy. Thus, financial markets were particularly interested in his speeches (S) and testimonies (T) and the outcomes of the FOMC meetings (F). We refer to these formal pronouncements collectively as STFs. Studying the reaction of financial markets to STFs allows us to assess several interesting aspects of the nature of central bank communication policy.

We begin in section 8.2 with a description of the data. We focus on the 30-year Treasury bond futures market because of its important role in connecting real and financial activity (per the above quotation from Carville) and for a variety of additional reasons discussed in that section. Our data are based on a proprietary algorithm that determines the cheapest-to-deliver issue and its price for a given futures contract. The reaction of the bond market to STFs is evaluated in terms of two measures of information flows: price volatility (measured by the absolute value of the excess return) and quantity volatility (measured by trading volume). The data set consists of the 56,937 five-minute trading intervals from the beginning of January 1997 through the end of December 1999, and it includes 49 speeches, 40 testimonies, and 24 FOMC meetings.

The next three sections explore the three questions concerning communication policy summarized in figure 8.1. We begin by asking what impact, if any, the STFs have on the bond market. If this aspect of communication policy is redundant or if the bond market is strong form efficient, we would expect the effects to be nil. In contrast to these predictions, section 8.3 reports that bond market volatility is positively affected by STFs and, somewhat surprisingly, that the effects are stronger before the release. We then evaluate the separate effect of each STF and find that testimonies and FOMC meetings have the most impact.

There are two competing explanations of why STFs affect the bond market: they transmit substantive information relevant for economic

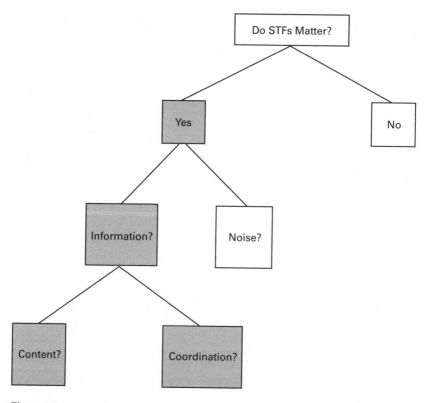

Figure 8.1
Do STFs matter?

decisions, or they just create noise that agitates markets. Section 8.4 distinguishes between these two explanations by examining how much volatility increases since the prior STF. We define a waiting-time (or duration) variable that captures unresolved uncertainty and is measured by the distance (measured in terms of the number of trading periods) between the current period and the release date for the most recent prior STF. If Greenspan's pronouncements merely introduce noise, we would not expect to find any systematic impact of the waiting-time variable. However, if the STFs transmit information and resolve uncertainty about monetary policy, we would expect that the waiting-time variable will be positively associated with volatility in the bond market. The latter implication is confirmed in our empirical work.

Section 8.5 examines the nature of the information documented in the prior section and tests whether it contains substantive content or just provides a widely observed costless signal that coordinates activity. In the latter case, STFs are coordinating devices for private agents operating with imperfect common knowledge.[6] Understanding the relevance of the coordination role is important because, in "global games" or "herding" models, rational agents may underweight private information, thus reducing welfare and suggesting that the STFs may be counterproductive. If the information is substantive in providing information about the stance of policy or the state of the economy, then the response of bond prices should occur immediately after the pronouncement. Any response before the announcement suggests a role for coordination. We examine the impact of STFs at five-minute intervals one hour before and one hour after the release of the pronouncement and find evidence in favor of both roles that differ across STFs.

Section 8.6 discusses our results in light of some of the literature on central bank transparency and communication, and section 8.7 concludes.

8.2 Data and the Estimating Equation

The impacts of "Greenspan's shrugs" on financial markets are assessed by examining the relation between Greenspan's formal pronouncements and volatility in the 30-year Treasury bond futures market. Formal pronouncements include all original speeches and testimonies made by Alan Greenspan during the period January 1, 1997 through December 31, 1999, as well as the statements (or non-statements) that follow FOMC meetings. Our dataset contains 49 speeches (S) to business, economic, social, and educational groups, 40 testimonies (T) to Congress, and 24 FOMC meetings (F). We refer to these formal pronouncements collectively as STFs. The source of the STF data and the time at which they were released to the public (not necessarily when Greenspan begins to speak) is the website of the Board of Governors (see the Web appendix for a detailed listing).[7] The dates for the STFs are set far in advance, and thus they can be viewed as exogenous and widely known. This three-year period of study is selected for several reasons. First, in choosing the period length, we face a tradeoff between the number of STFs and a reasonably stable environment.[8] We believe that a three-year period is long enough to provide sufficient STFs for our econometric analysis and short enough to attenuate the incidence of major shocks or structural shifts. (One important shift involved a change in the release of the FOMC policy directives about the balance of risks in May 1999; the impact of this shift is explored in section 8.5 and table 8.5.) Second, during this particular period, the macroeconomy and domestic financial markets were relatively stable. Third, at the beginning of our sample period, Greenspan had been chair of the FOMC and the 30-year US Treasury bond had been the benchmark long-run security for many years, and thus instabilities due to learning effects were absent from financial markets. Lastly, near the end of our sample period, auctions of new 30-year Treasury bonds were suspended (in 2001), and the inflation measure formally discussed by the FOMC in its semiannual Humphrey-Hawkins report to Congress changed (in February 2000) from the consumer price index to the personal consumption expenditure deflator.

We focus on the 30-year Treasury bond futures market for several reasons: its sensitivity to monetary policy pronouncements, its substantial effects on real spending, its long-standing role (at that time) as the benchmark long-term Treasury security, its depth, and the availability of market prices at five-minute intervals. The dataset consists of the 56,937 five-minute trading intervals from the beginning of January 1997 through the end of December 1999. Futures prices are anchored to bond prices that are specified for delivery. In order to insure the liquidity of the 30-year Treasury bond futures market, several Treasury bonds with different maturities and coupons can be used to settle a futures contract. Given the bond conversion factors (provided by the exchange) and a possibly sloping yield curve, one of these securities will dominate as the least expensive way to satisfy the futures contract. The price of this bond is the cheapest-to-deliver price. Our price data are based on a proprietary algorithm that determines the cheapest-to-deliver bond price for a given futures contract. There is an important difference between converted futures prices and the cheapest-to-deliver price. The analysis by Sihvonen (2008, section II.1) of 10-year German government bonds shows that, between May 2001 and December 2006, the difference between the cheapest-to-deliver bond and the next cheapest bond ranged from about 15 to 125 basis points (comparable figures for the 30-year Treasury market were not available).

The reaction of the bond market to STFs is evaluated in terms of information flow measured in terms of prices (IFP_t, price volatility measured as the absolute value of excess returns) and quantities (IFQ_t, trading volume).[9] These two measures are related to information flows in several asset pricing models, but they may have differential sensitivities to information (Ross 1989; Campbell, Grossman, and Wang 1993; Beber, Brandt, and Kavajecz 2011),

$$\text{Information Flow, Price Measure} \equiv IFP_t \equiv ABS[XR_t] \tag{8.1}$$

$$\text{Excess Return} \equiv XR_t \equiv [(P_t - P_{t-1}) \, / \, P_{t-1}] - [(1+RF_t)^{(1/360)} - 1.0] \tag{8.2}$$

$$\text{Information Flow, Quantity Measure} \equiv IFQ_t \equiv Volume_t, \tag{8.3}$$

where P_t is the cheapest-to-deliver price for the closing contract over a five-minute interval for the period January 1, 1997 to December 31, 1999, and RF_t is the risk-free rate (90-day Treasury bills) for that day. The use of five-minute intervals is a compromise between understating the impact of the STF by using lower-frequency data and microstructure noise by using higher-frequency data (see Aït-Sahalia, Mykland, and Zhang 2005 and Andersen et al. 2003 for further discussion). An advantage of focusing on volatility—either price volatility or quantity volatility qua trading volume—is that we do not have to undertake the very challenging and historic path-dependent task of deciding whether a certain pronouncement is expected to raise or lower bond prices.[10] Since price volatility is computed with excess returns, we are controlling for the impact of an STF on the short-term risk-free rate, and thus our estimates capture medium-term and long-term policy effects for this measure of volatility.

These series have three interesting characteristics. First, price volatility is more variable in our sample than trading volume, where variability is measured by the coefficients of variation (CV): $CV_{Volatility} = 3.8922 \, / \, 3.8643 = 1.01$ and $CV_{Volume} = 14.4648 \, / \, 20.7767 = 0.70$. Second, the excess return series is unrelated to any day-of-week or time-of-day effects. A regression of XR_t on indicator variables for days of the week and the time periods within a day yields an R^2 of 0.00009. Third, by contrast, price volatility and trading volume vary systematically over the week. For example, volume peaks during the opening half hour on Friday (128% higher than average weekly volume). Monday during the 12:00 to 1:00 hour is the most tranquil period, with volume that is 47% lower than average weekly volume.

These patterns may present a problem for our analysis if certain STFs tend to be released during the same time period and if this period has abnormal volatility.[11] In this case, the STF would be reflecting the effects of release time independent of any additional impact of the pronouncement. To avoid this ambiguity, we compute the means for each day of the week and, within that day, for each of the time-of-day periods (7:30 to 8:00, 8:00 to 9:00, ... , 1:00 to 2:00). We subtract these means from the IFP_t and IFQ_t series. These adjusted series are mean zero, and they are used in our subsequent analysis.

We measure the effect of the STFs on bond market volatility with three measures of increasing refinement. Note that increasing refinement of the STF indicator variables does not necessarily lead to better estimates, as the finer measures may be more sensitive to measurement error. The first measure is defined broadly for the day of an STF,

$$DAY_t = 1 \text{ if an STF occurs on that day,} \tag{8.4}$$

$$0 \text{ otherwise.}$$

A more refined measure assesses the effects one hour before and after the STF,

$$BEFORE_t = 1 \text{ if } t^* - 60 \le t < t^*, \tag{8.5a}$$

$$0 \text{ otherwise,}$$

$$AFTER_t = 1 \text{ if } t^* \le t < t^* + 60, \tag{8.5b}$$

$$0 \text{ otherwise,}$$

where t^* is the five-minute interval during which the STF is released. Given our large dataset, we can use a third and even more refined set of indicator variables defined for each five-minute interval 60 minutes before and after the STF,[12]

$$BEFORE60_t = 1 \text{ if } t^* - 60 \le t < t^* - 55; 0 \text{ otherwise,} \tag{8.6a}$$

$$BEFORE55_t = 1 \text{ if } t^* - 55 \le t < t^* - 50; 0 \text{ otherwise,} \tag{8.6b}$$

...

$BEFORE5_t = 1$ if $t^* - 5 \le t < t^*$; 0 otherwise,   (8.6l)

$AFTER5_t = 1$ if $t^* \le t < t^* + 5$; 0 otherwise,   (8.6m)

...

$AFTER60_t = 1$ if $t^* + 55 \le t < t^* + 60$; 0 otherwise.   (8.6x)

These 24 indicator variables are referred to collectively as Z_t, defined in equation (8.7),

$$Z_t \equiv \{BEFORE60_t, BEFORE55_t, \dots, AFTER60_t\}.$$ (8.7)

Note that the interval during which the STF is released (t^*) is included in the $AFTER5_t$ indicator variable, which might more accurately be referred to as $ON\text{-}or\text{-}AFTER5_t$.

The waiting time (or duration) variable will be discussed in section 8.5.

8.3   Do STFs Matter?

This section assesses the first of our three questions (cf. figure 8.1), asking what impact, if any, the STFs have on the bond market. The null hypothesis of no impact is consistent with this aspect of communication policy being redundant relative to the other ways that the Federal Reserve communicates. Moreover, if the bond market is strong-form efficient, then the STFs will not represent any new information, and we would again expect the effects to be nil.

We begin by estimating the following three regressions to determine if there is an effect on the day an STF is released:

$IFP_t = G[DAY_t],$ (8.8a)

$IFQ_t = G[DAY_t],$ (8.8b)

$IFQ_t = G[DAY_t, IFQ_{t-1}],$ (8.8c)

where $G[.]$ represents a linear operator. Equations (8.8) are estimated by OLS because it is the efficient estimator under the plausible assumption that the STFs, whose release dates are determined well in advance, are exogenous.[13] Moreover, the regression framework permits the convenient computation of standard errors. As we shall see, there is a great deal of positive autocorrelation in the residuals from equation (8.8b), and we include a lagged dependent variable in equation (8.8c) to address this problem and its impact on standard errors.

The null hypothesis is evaluated by the coefficient on DAY_t, and the results are reported in table 8.1, where columns 1, 2, and 3 correspond to equations (8.8a), (8.8b), and (8.8c), respectively. For all three equations, the coefficient on DAY_t in the first row is positive and statistically significant at conventional levels. Autocorrelation in the residuals is assessed by ρ, the first-order autocorrelation coefficient for the residuals, and the Durbin m-statistic.[14] As shown in column 2, the residuals in the trading volume equation are highly autocorrelated. The inclusion of the lagged dependent variable in column 3 leads to a substantial reduction in ρ and the m-statistic. In all three models, the formal test for the absence of autocorrelation is rejected, though this result is influenced by the very large sample size. The evidence in table 8.1 clearly indicates that STFs are statistically significant.

Table 8.1
OLS Estimates on the Day of an STF and One Hour Before/After an STF

	DAY			*BEFORE/AFTER*		
	(1)	(2)	(3)	(4)	(5)	(6)
	IFP	*IFQ*	*IFQ*	*IFP*	*IFQ*	*IFQ*
DAY	0.1382	0.7104	0.2957	—	—	—
	(0.0496)	(0.1442)	(0.1111)			
BEFORE	—	—	—	1.4453	6.4337	3.3153
				(0.1785)	(0.4576)	(0.3325)
AFTER	—	—	—	0.2244	2.0315	0.2258
				(0.1216)	(0.4031)	(0.3243)
LDV	—	—	0.5984	—	—	0.5958
			(0.0051)			(0.0051)
R^2	0.0002	0.0005	0.3585	0.0037	0.0071	0.3601
SER	3.8141	12.6599	10.1420	3.8076	12.6182	10.1292
ρ	0.1668	0.5984	−0.0605	0.1636	0.5950	−0.0607
Durbin m	17.5579	117.3333	−9.4531	17.4043	116.6667	−9.4844

Note: Estimates are based on equations (8.8a), (8.8b), and (8.8c) for columns 1 to 3 respectively, and equation (8.9) for columns 4 to 6. The dependent variables—IFP_t and IFQ_t—are defined in equations (8.1) and (8.2) and equation (8.3), respectively. The indicator variables DAY_t, $BEFORE_t$, and $AFTER_t$ are defined in equations (8.4), (8.5a), and (8.5b), respectively. The indicator variables S, T, and F equal 1 for the occurrence of a speech, testimony, or FOMC meeting, respectively. LDV is a lagged dependent variable. Standard errors are heteroskedasticity-consistent using the White correction and are displayed in parentheses. R^2 is the customary goodness-of-fit measure. SER is the standard error of the regression. The ρ parameter and the Durbin m-statistic measure first-order autocorrelation in the residuals; see note 14 for details. The sample period extends from January 1997 to December 1999 and contains 56,936 observations.

To evaluate economic significance, we compare the coefficient on DAY_t to the sample standard deviation of the dependent variable. (In the case of column 3 with a lagged dependent variable, the appropriate comparison is the coefficient on DAY_t divided by one minus the coefficient on the lagged dependent variable.) The ratios of the estimated DAY_t coefficients to the sample standard deviation are 3.55%, 4.91%, and 5.09% for columns 1 to 3, respectively.[15] Relative to the average variation in volatility, the STFs appear to have a modest impact on the bond market.

Columns 4 to 6 in table 8.1 extend the analysis by examining bond market activity one hour before and after the release of an STF. Rather than writing out each equation, we use the following concise notation to describe the estimating equations:

$$Y_t = G[BEFORE_t, AFTER_t: IFQ_{t-1}]$$

$$Y_t = \{IFP_t, IFQ_t\}, \tag{8.9}$$

where the lagged dependent variable only enters the equation containing IFQ_t as the dependent variable. (Our subsequent discussions of IFQ_t will emphasize the results based on the model with the lagged dependent variable, though we will also present results for IFQ_t without this additional variable.) A surprising result is that the effects of the STF are much larger before than after the release. For example, for the IFP_t results in column 4, the ratio of the estimated $BEFORE_t$ and $AFTER_t$ coefficients is 6.44; comparable statistics for the IFQ_t results in columns 5 and 6 are 3.17 and 14.68, respectively. These results generally support the importance of STFs for bond markets, and they further suggest that care must be taken to differentiate between the impacts before and after the release. Thus, the DAY_t regressor is omitted in subsequent models.

Table 8.2 provides an even finer breakdown by examining the separate impacts of speeches, testimonies, and FOMC meetings one hour before and after the release:

$$Y_t = G[S_t^*BEFORE_t, S_t^*AFTER_t, T_t^*BEFORE_t, T_t^*AFTER_t,$$
$$F_t^*BEFORE_t, F_t^*AFTER_t: IFQ_{t-1}]$$

$$Y_t = \{IFP_t, IFQ_t\}. \tag{8.10}$$

Two interesting results emerge from this decomposition of the STFs. First, speeches have a statistically significant impact on information flow only for the IFQ_t regression for the before period. By contrast,

Table 8.2
OLS Estimates One Hour Before/After an S, T, or F

	(1)	(2)	(3)
	IFP	IFQ	IFQ
S*BEFORE	0.2053	0.7115	1.0270
	(0.1598)	(0.5217)	(0.4079)
S*AFTER	0.2426	1.1556	−0.0081
	(0.2093)	(0.6533)	(0.5244)
T*BEFORE	2.1062	9.6534	4.0227
	(0.3652)	(0.7996)	(0.6028)
T*AFTER	0.1275	2.1779	0.6315
	(0.1432)	(0.5177)	(0.4090)
F*BEFORE	3.2573	14.6555	7.7900
	(0.5014)	(1.2059)	(0.8762)
F*AFTER	0.3936	3.9922	0.0987
	(0.2996)	(1.0575)	(0.8832)
LDV	—	—	0.5939
			(0.0051)
R^2	0.0062	0.0122	0.3611
SER	3.8028	12.5860	10.1216
ρ	0.1614	0.5927	−0.0601
Durbin m	17.3548	116.2157	−9.3906

Note: Estimates are based on equation (8.10). The dependent variables—IFP_t and IFQ_t—are defined in equations (8.1) and (8.2) and equation (8.3), respectively. The indicator variables $BEFORE_t$ and $AFTER_t$ are defined in equations (8.5a) and (8.5b), respectively. The indicator variables S, T, and F equal 1 for the occurrence of a speech, testimony, or FOMC meeting, respectively. LDV is a lagged dependent variable. Standard errors are heteroskedasticity-consistent using the White correction and are displayed in parentheses. R^2 is the customary goodness-of-fit measure. SER is the standard error of the regression. The ρ parameter and the Durbin m-statistic measure first-order autocorrelation in the residuals; see note 14 for details. The sample period extends from January 1997 to December 1999 and contains 56,936 observations.

testimonies and FOMC meetings generate statistically and economically significant effects before the release for all three regressions. Price volatility (column 1) before the release of testimony or FOMC meetings is higher by 54% and 84%, respectively, relative to the average price volatility. Comparable statistics for trading volume (column 3) are 69% and 133%. Second, no effects are found after the release of STFs, though, as we will see in section 8.5, this result reflects the coarseness of the $AFTER_t$ measure of STF influence used in this section. Table 8.2

suggests two general results concerning impact hierarchies: (i) F (FOMC meetings) > T (testimonies) > S (speeches) and (ii) $BEFORE$ > $AFTER$.

8.4   Information or Noise?

There are two plausible explanations as to why STFs matter: (1) they communicate information relevant to bond prices or (2) they merely create noise that agitates markets. If STFs provide information to the markets either directly or indirectly, then we would expect our IFP_t and IFQ_t variables, which reflect information flows, to respond positively. Regarding case (2), Mendel and Shleifer (2012, pp. 303–304) analyze noise in a model where there are three types of investors: "a small number of investors, called insiders, who possess valuable information and trade completely rationally, a small number of noise traders who are vulnerable to sentiment shocks and trade on those, and the vast majority of outside investors, who possess no information but learn from prices and trade rationally." Their simulations document that outside investors can get confused and chase noise. Thus, a small amount of noise can have a substantial effect on volatility. The information and noise channels are observationally equivalent.

To isolate the effects of information from noise, we examine whether the volatility associated with STFs increases since the time of the last STF. With the passage of time, questions arise and accumulate about the state of the economy and the stance of policy, and, from the perspective of bond market participants, uncertainty rises. This uncertainty will be resolved if STFs provide information relevant to the bond market either directly or indirectly. The longer the length of time since the last STF, the greater will be the information flow from the release of an STF and hence the greater the impact on volatility. We define a waiting-time (or duration) variable, $WAIT_t$, as the distance between the current period and the most recent STF measured in terms of the number of trading periods, and then apply this value (defined at t^*) to the one-hour intervals before and after the STF,

$WAIT$ = number of five-minute trading periods since the last STF
(or since the beginning of 1997 for the first STF). This
value is applied to the one-hour intervals before and
after the STF.   (8.11)

If Greenspan's pronouncements merely introduce noise or have very little impact on volatility, we would expect the coefficients on $WAIT_t$ to be close to zero. However, the alternative hypothesis that STFs are informative and resolve uncertainty about monetary policy or the economy suggests a positive effect of the waiting time variable on bond market volatility.

We introduce $WAIT_t$ into the following OLS regression equation:

$$Y_t = G[WAIT_t*BEFORE_t, WAIT_t*AFTER_t, BEFORE_t, AFTER_t: IFQ_{t-1}]$$

$$Y_t = \{IFP_t, IFQ_t\}. \tag{8.12}$$

The results presented in table 8.3 differ before and after the release of the STF. The coefficients for the interaction between the W_t and $BEFORE_t$ in the first row are positive and statistically significant at conventional levels in all three regressions. These results reject the null hypothesis of noise in favor of the information alternative. A different conclusion is obtained from the interaction between W_t and $AFTER_t$ in

Table 8.3
OLS Estimates One Hour Before/After an STF Interacted with the WAIT Variable

	(1)	(2)	(3)
	IFP	IFQ	IFQ
WAIT*BEFORE	0.0019	0.0070	0.0033
	(0.0006)	(0.0011)	(0.0008)
WAIT*AFTER	−0.0917	−0.7008	−0.1340
	(0.0383)	(0.1267)	(0.1083)
BEFORE	0.5414	3.0690	1.7252
	(0.3060)	(0.6711)	(0.4994)
AFTER	0.7296	5.8788	0.9680
	(0.2912)	(0.9543)	(0.8135)
LDV	—	—	0.5950
			(0.0051)
R^2	0.0049	0.0094	0.3604
SER	3.8052	12.6039	10.1267
ρ	0.1624	0.5945	−0.0602
Durbin m	17.6522	116.5686	−9.4063

Note: Estimates are based on equation (8.12). The dependent variables—IFP_t and IFQ_t—are defined in equations (8.1) and (8.2) and equation (8.3), respectively. The indicator variables $BEFORE_t$ and $AFTER_t$ are defined in equations (8.5a) and (8.5b), respectively. The indicator variable $WAIT_t$ is the number of trading periods since the last STF and is defined in equation (8.11). LDV is a lagged dependent variable. Standard errors are heteroskedasticity-consistent using the White correction and are displayed in parentheses. R^2 is the customary goodness-of-fit measure. SER is the standard error of the regression. The ρ parameter and the Durbin m-statistic measure first-order autocorrelation in the residuals; see note 14 for details. The sample period extends from January 1997 to December 1999 and contains 56,936 observations.

the second row. These coefficients are negative, and here the noise hypothesis is sustained against the information alternative.

We further investigate whether STFs transmit information or noise by decomposing each STF into one of its three components (per table 8.2) and interacting each component with $WAIT_t$:

$$Y_t = G[WAIT_t{}^*S_t{}^*BEFORE_t, WAIT_t{}^*T_t{}^*BEFORE_t, WAIT_t{}^*F_t{}^*BEFORE_t,$$
$$WAIT_t{}^*S_t{}^*AFTER_t, WAIT_t{}^*T_t{}^*AFTER_t,$$
$$WAIT_t{}^*F_t{}^*AFTER_t: IFQ_{t-1}]$$

$$Y_t = \{IFP_t, IFQ_t\}. \tag{8.13}$$

The results presented in table 8.4 are broadly consistent with the prior results. For the $BEFORE_t$ variable, the interaction coefficients are significant for speeches and testimonies, but negative for FOMC meetings. The interaction coefficients for the $AFTER_t$ variable are either negative or very close to zero.

The weight of the evidence presented in tables 8.3 and 8.4 suggests that formal pronouncements by Chairman Greenspan generally contain information.

8.5 Content or Coordination?

While the evidence suggests that STFs are an effective part of the Federal Reserve's communication policy, the nature of the information being transmitted remains unclear. A communication that has content—information that relates to insights about future policy decisions or the state of the economy—is different from information that serves to coordinate the actions of private agents operating with imperfect public common knowledge. This coordination channel can arise in at least two types of theoretical models. In recent work, Allen, Morris, and Shin (2006), Amato, Morris, and Shin (2002), and Morris and Shin (2002, 2003) develop "global games" models in which rational investors coordinate their activities on a common public signal. Investors are imperfectly informed, and each observes public and private signals (the latter unobservable to all other investors) that are used to infer the true but unobservable state. In a straightforward adaptation of Morris and Shin (2002), we can assume that investors' utility depends on a weighted average of two terms: the difference between the trading price and the true value and the difference between the trading price and the trading prices of all other investors. These two differences reflect long-run and short-run considerations, respectively. The STFs serve as a public signal

Table 8.4
OLS Estimates One Hour Before/After an S, T, or F Interacted with a *WAIT* Variable

	(1)	(2)	(3)
	IFP	*IFQ*	*IFQ*
*WAIT*S*BEFORE*	0.0015	0.0070	0.0032
	(0.0006)	(0.0016)	(0.0013)
*WAIT*S*AFTER*	−0.0521	−0.3247	0.0659
	(0.0678)	(0.2111)	(0.1797)
*WAIT*T*BEFORE*	0.0039	0.0133	0.0062
	(0.0019)	(0.0018)	(0.0017)
*WAIT*T*AFTER*	−0.0871	−0.7829	−0.3772
	(0.0439)	(0.1505)	(0.1246)
*WAIT*F*BEFORE*	−0.0010	−0.0059	−0.0032
	(0.0010)	(0.0021)	(0.0016)
*WAIT*F*AFTER*	−0.1812	−1.3393	−0.1540
	(0.0862)	(0.3120)	(0.2876)
*S*BEFORE*	−0.4442	−2.2360	−0.3124
	(0.2452)	(0.7755)	(0.6318)
*S*AFTER*	0.5360	2.9747	−0.3572
	(0.5159)	(1.5773)	(1.3461)
*T*BEFORE*	0.4746	4.1355	1.4782
	(0.7337)	(1.0975)	(0.9011)
*T*AFTER*	0.6085	6.5024	2.7180
	(0.3199)	(1.1037)	(0.9030)
*F*BEFORE*	4.0722	19.2721	10.3025
	(0.9216)	(2.1382)	(1.6147)
*F*AFTER*	1.3451	11.0233	0.9144
	(0.6852)	(2.4435)	(2.2152)
LDV	—	—	0.5927
			(0.0051)
R^2	0.0080	0.0154	0.3617
SER	3.7996	12.5663	10.1177
ρ	0.1597	0.5922	−0.0596
Durbin *m*	17.5495	116.1176	−9.3125

Note: Estimates are based on equation (8.13). The dependent variables—IFP_t and IFQ_t—
are defined in equations (8.1) and (8.2) and equation (8.3), respectively. The indicator
variables $BEFORE_t$ and $AFTER_t$ are defined in equations (8.5a) and (8.5b), respectively.
The indicator variable $WAIT_t$ is the number of trading periods since the last STF and is
defined in equation (8.11). LDV is a lagged dependent variable. The indicator variables
S, T, and F equal 1 for the occurrence of a speech, testimony, or FOMC meeting, respectively. Standard errors are heteroskedasticity-consistent using the White correction and
are displayed in parentheses. R^2 is the customary goodness of fit measure. SER is the
standard error of the regression. The ρ parameter and the Durbin *m*-statistic measure
first-order autocorrelation in the residuals; see note 14 for details. The sample period
extends from January 1997 to December 1999 and contains 56,936 observations.

that transmits substantive information about the unobserved true state of the economy and serves as a focal point. In some cases, the public signal will overwhelm private information, and the resulting equilibrium will be socially inefficient.

Herding models are also based on imperfectly informed investors and provide a second theoretical framework highlighting the potentially deleterious effects of public information. In the herding model of Banerjee (1992), trades are observed by other investors, who base their inferences on prior trades. An impending STF (with a release date known well in advance) is the event that initiates the sequential decision problem facing investors. The resulting equilibrium is inefficient because investors will rely too little on their own information. This "herd externality" can lead to an equilibrium in which "society may actually be better off by constraining some of the people to use only their own information" (p. 798). Avery and Zemsky (1998) introduce several dimensions of uncertainty into a herding model and show that at least three dimensions of uncertainty are required to lead to substantial mispricing and volatility in the short run.

The important policy implication from either the global games or herding models is that private information may be underweighted relative to the optimum. Welfare is thus reduced, and STFs, which may coordinate this inefficient activity, can be counterproductive.

To differentiate between content and coordination, we observe that, if the communication has substantive content, the response of bond prices should occur immediately after the pronouncement. Any response before the announcement suggests that the STF is serving as a coordination device. We thus examine the impact of STFs at five-minute intervals one hour before and one hour after the pronouncement based on estimates of the following OLS model:

$Y_t = G[Z_t: IFQ_{t-1}]$

$$Y_t = \{IFP_t, IFQ_t\}, \tag{8.14}$$

where Z_t is defined in equation (8.7). Results are reported in figure 8.2 for IFP_t and IFQ_t. The horizontal axis represents "event time," the time (stated in five-minute periods) one hour before and one hour after the release of the STF. In order to ensure comparability, the two mean-zero series are divided by the standard deviation over the sample of price volatility and trading volume, respectively. Thus, an entry in figure 8.2

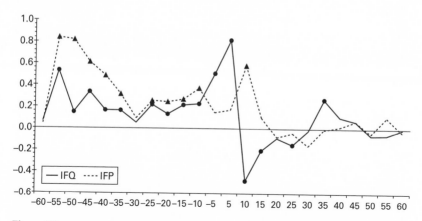

Figure 8.2
IFP and IFQ point estimates before and after an STF (● and ▲ denote significance at the 5% level).

of 0.50 implies that price volatility (IFP_t) or trading volume (IFQ_t) is 50% higher than the average variability for these series.

Figure 8.2 provides evidence in favor of both information and coordination roles. There is a large jump 5 to 10 minutes after the announcement, a result consistent with new information being incorporated into asset prices. The response of IFP_t is for one period and disappears quickly. For IFQ_t, the response at the release time is larger and lingers below the average trading volume for several periods after the release. Both measures of information flow also show a substantial response before the release of the STF. Beginning 55 minutes before the release, most of the coefficients are statistically different from zero and many are economically important.

We extend this analysis by differentiating by the type of STF and run the following OLS regression:

$$Y_t = G[S_t^*Z_t, T_t^*Z_t, F_t^*Z_t: IFQ_{t-1}]$$

$$Y_t = \{IFP_t, IFQ_t\}. \tag{8.15}$$

These results are reported in figures 8.3, 8.4, and 8.5 for speeches, testimonies, and FOMC meetings, respectively. Each figure contains estimates based on IFP_t and IFQ_t normalized by the standard deviations over the sample.

The impacts of the STFs are heterogenous across types. Speeches (figure 8.3) have an impact upon release that quickly disappears. For

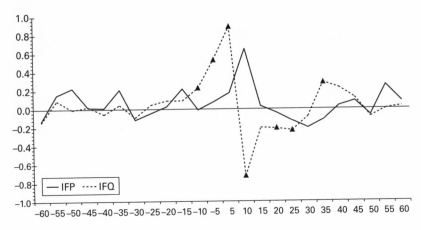

Figure 8.3
IFP and IFQ point estimates before and after a speech (• and ▲ denote significance at the 5% level).

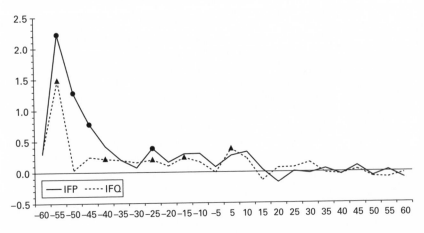

Figure 8.4
IFP and IFQ point estimates before and after a testimony (• and ▲ denote significance at the 5% level).

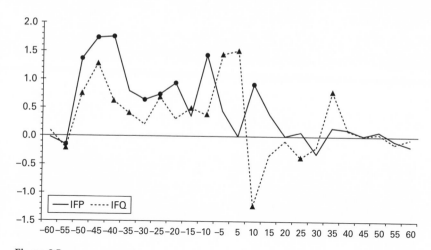

Figure 8.5
IFP and IFQ point estimates before and after an FOMC meeting (● and ▲ denote significance at the 5% level).

IFQ_t, there are substantial effects 5 and 10 minutes prior to the release. These significant results may indicate some imprecision in recording the release time of the speech or a systematic prerelease leakage of the impending speech. The largest impact is in the five-minute interval immediately after the release time. This result strongly suggests that speeches impact the bond market by providing content and that the prior conclusion about the weaknesses of the speech communication channel is traceable to using too coarse a measure. The response of IFP_t is relatively muted, though there is a notable (but statistically insignificant) uptick 10 minutes after the release time.

Testimonies (figure 8.4), by contrast, have a substantial impact before release on both IFP_t and IFQ_t. This statistically and economically significant pattern of coefficients suggests that testimonies largely impact the bond market through coordination.

FOMC meetings (figure 8.5) reflect both content and coordination. During the five minutes before and after a release, trading volume is about 1.40 times larger than on a typical day. Price volatility is also elevated during this period. These are the largest effects reported for any of the three STFs, and they clearly indicate that the FOMC meetings deliver valuable news to the bond market. FOMC meetings also serve as a coordination device, as most of the coefficients prior to the release are statistically significant and large relative to a typical day.[16]

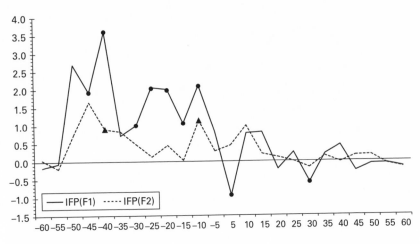

Figure 8.6
IFP point estimates before and after an FOMC meeting with (F1) or without (F2) a change in the target federal funds rate (● and ▲ denote significance at the 5% level).

Two additional tests are performed. The FOMC meeting dates represent a mixture of pronouncement effects and, on some occasions, actual changes in interest rates. We disentangle these two effects by decomposing the F_t variable into one variable that identifies FOMC meetings accompanied by a change in the target federal funds rate ($F1_t$) and another for FOMC meetings not accompanied by a change in the rate ($F2_t$):

$$Y_t = G[S_t^*Z_t, T_t^*Z_t, F1_t^*Z_t, F2_t^*Z_t: IFQ_{t-1}]$$

$$Y_t = \{IFP_t, IFQ_t\}. \tag{8.16}$$

Figure 8.6 contains the plots for IFP_t for the $F1_t$ and $F2_t$ pronouncements. The response of IFP_t to $F1_t$ is larger than to $F2_t$. More information seems to be transmitted by FOMC pronouncements when rates are not altered. However, this pattern is not sustained with trading volume. In Figure 8.7, the relative response of IFQ_t to $F1_t$ and $F2_t$ is reversed, though the differences are not as large as those for IFP_t.

Our second additional test examines the importance of a key change in communication policy on the information flows associated with STFs. Beginning in May 1999, the FOMC policy directives about the balance of risks were released. Prior to this date, this information was not shared with the public. This communication policy change increases the information contained in the FOMC statements, and we would

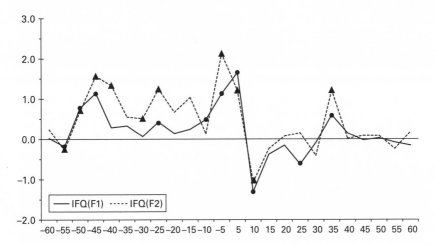

Figure 8.7
IFQ point estimates before and after an FOMC meeting with (F1) or without (F2) a change in the target federal funds rate (● and ▲ denote significance at the 5% level).

expect volatility to be more sensitive to these particular pronouncements beginning in May 1999. This increased information flow decreases uncertainty about monetary policy, and we would expect speeches and testimonies to have less impact on the bond market after the change. Table 8.5 examines the impact of this change on volatility by comparing results for the full sample (columns 1 to 3) to results from the sample truncated in April 1999 (columns 4 to 6). For the truncated period, the *AFTER* results continue to be estimated imprecisely, and no discernible pattern emerges. The *BEFORE* results are statistically significant for *T* and *F* for both the full and truncated samples. Testimonies did not become appreciably more important (3.88 vs. 4.02), but the impact of FOMC meetings rose from 5.75 prior to May 1999 to 7.79 for the full sample, a large movement relative to standard errors. These results are consistent with those reported by Ehrmann and Fratzscher (2007a), who conclude that markets have extracted more information from FOMC statements since the communication policy change.

8.6   Discussion

Perhaps the most interesting findings from our empirical analysis are the substantial effects of STFs before the release and the need to examine responses at high frequencies (five-minute time periods in our

Table 8.5

OLS Estimates One Hour Before/After an S, T, or F with Split Samples

| | January 1997 to December 1999 | | | January 1997 to April 1999 | | |
| | (1) | (2) | (3) | (4) | (5) | (6) |
	IFP	IFQ	IFQ	IFP	IFQ	IFQ
S*BEFORE	0.2053	0.7115	1.0270	0.1316	0.3291	0.8893
	(0.1598)	(0.5217)	(0.4079)	(0.1773)	(0.6043)	(0.4692)
S*AFTER	0.2426	1.1556	−0.0081	0.2265	1.0269	−0.1395
	(0.2093)	(0.6533)	(0.5244	(0.1773)	(0.7780)	(0.6236)
T*BEFORE	2.1062	9.6534	4.0227	1.9408	9.3255	3.8833
	(0.3652)	(0.7996)	(0.6028)	(0.1797)	(0.8373)	(0.6264)
T*AFTER	0.1275	2.1779	0.6315	0.0717	1.6154	0.3591
	(0.1432)	(0.5177)	(0.4090)	(0.1797)	(0.5350)	(0.4198)
F*BEFORE	3.2573	14.6555	7.7900	1.9926	10.0815	5.7486
	(0.5014)	(1.2059)	(0.8762)	(0.2651)	(1.2159)	(0.8944)
F*AFTER	0.3936	3.9922	0.0987	0.3151	3.8715	0.3632
	(0.2996)	(1.0575)	(0.8832)	(0.2651)	(1.2200)	(1.0394)
LDV	—	—	0.5939	—	—	0.5974
			(0.0051)			(0.0057)
R^2	0.0062	0.0122	0.3611	0.0040	0.0094	0.3632
SER	3.8028	12.5860	10.1216	3.7860	12.3901	9.9332
ρ	0.1614	0.5927	−0.0601	0.1634	0.5965	−0.0643
Durbin m	17.3548	116.2157	−9.3906	15.8641	104.6491	−9.0563

Note: Estimates are based on equation (8.10). The dependent variables—IFP_t and IFQ_t—are defined in equations (8.1) and (8.2) and equation (8.3), respectively. The indicator variables $BEFORE_t$ and $AFTER_t$ are defined in equations (8.5a) and (8.5b), respectively. The indicator variables S, T, and F equal 1 for the occurrence of a speech, testimony, or FOMC meeting, respectively. LDV is a lagged dependent variable. Standard errors are heteroskedasticity-consistent using the White correction and are displayed in parentheses. R^2 is the customary goodness-of-fit measure. SER is the standard error of the regression. The ρ parameter and the Durbin m-statistic measure first-order autocorrelation in the residuals; see note 14 for details. For columns 1 to 3, the sample period extends from January 1997 to December 1999 and contains 56,936 observations; for columns 4 to 6, the sample period extends from January 1997 to April 1999 and contains 42,823 observations.

analysis). While several studies have examined the impact of macro-economic announcements on the Treasury bond market, they either use daily data (Jones, Lamont, and Lumsdaine 1998) or do not examine responses many periods before the release (Ederington and Lee 1993; Fleming and Remolona 1999a, 1999b). The one exception is Balduzzi, Elton, and Green (2001), who examine the impact of announcements on trading volume in two prerelease intervals, 30 to 5 minutes before the release and 5 minutes after the release. Interestingly, they too find statistically significant impacts on the 10-year note for 8 of 23 announcements for the 30-to-5-minute interval; the monetary policy announcement is one of the 8 announcements. These results were not discussed by Balduzzi et al. and are similar to those presented in figures 8.2 to 8.7.

There are several interpretations of significant prerelease effects. One explanation is that the impending STF exposes traders carrying long or short positions to additional risk, and they hedge prior to the STF. After release, trading books are rebalanced. This account implies that trading volume should be both high and of nearly the same magnitude before and after the release (to rebalance positions) and that this heightened trading activity should occur close to the release time (to minimize risk exposure). Our figures contain little evidence of a rebalancing effect after the release.

A second interpretation is that the impending STF initiates a flow of reports from companies supporting the trading community (e.g., investment banks, forecasting firms) that stimulates trading. This flow of reports resembles a focal point in a global games model. Whether the processing of stale information leads to new information in markets is unclear, though the resolution of this question has important welfare implications.

Our preferred interpretation of significant prerelease effects is that STFs affect markets through coordination in global games or herding models. The global games model developed by Morris and Shin (2002) has the particularly striking implication that central bank communication can be excessive and can lower welfare. That is, central bankers can talk too much. Given this controversial conclusion, the model has received much attention. Woodford (2005, pp. 414–421) raises several concerns with the Morris and Shin model, including the appropriate specification of the social welfare function. Svensson (2006) carefully examines the original Morris and Shin model and raises an important question about the plausibility of the precisions of the public and private signals. (Other studies challenging the Morris and Shin finding are listed in Svensson's footnotes 1 and 2.) Morris, Shin, and Tong (2006) acknowledge Svensson's concern, but note that the model in question is one that assumes that the public and private signals (conditional on the true state) are independent. In more general models where these two signals are correlated (as might arise if there is a flawed conventional wisdom; for example, that housing prices do not fall) or where the informativeness of the aggregate price level is endogenous (Amador and Weill 2009), the original Morris and Shin finding holds.

While rigorous examinations and critiques are always welcome, we believe that the criticism of Morris and Shin's specific model is somewhat beside the central point. The key insight from their model is that public information can crowd out private information when investors care about the opinions of other investors, regardless of the accuracy of those opinions. This point is nicely summarized by Donald Kohn, vice chair of the Board of Governors (Kohn 2005, pp. 1–2):

One consideration involves the nature of information and its relationship to market pricing. In fact, economists do not fully understand how markets incorporate information. Herding behavior, information cascades, multiple equilibria, and the amount of investment in financial research all pose puzzles about markets and information. The situation is complicated still more when an important participant is seen as having superior information owing to its investment in research or its understanding of its own behavior.

In such circumstances, certain types of central bank talk might actually impinge on welfare-enhancing market pricing by being misunderstood and receiving too much weight relative to private judgments.

There is a very large literature examining the effects of policymakers' pronouncements on a variety of economic activity. Blinder et al. (2008) have surveyed part of this literature and placed the studies into two broad categories depending on whether pronouncements affect financial markets or inflation performance. Here we largely discuss studies in the former category and focus on those that relate to our findings with government bond markets.

Some early studies examine the impact of various forms of communication on the level and volatility of bond market rates. Guthrie and Wright (2000) study the effects of news articles containing phrases linked to New Zealand monetary policy, and they report a substantial effect of this form of communication on the level of interest rates. Most of their results are with daily data. One of their analyses is based on hourly data for 13 months (their figure 8.2, p. 507) and, in contrast to our results, they do not find any impact before the release. Kohn and Sack (2004) examine the impact of STFs on the volatility of Treasury securities with maturities up to and including four years. Based on daily data and conditioning on unanticipated information in the pronouncements and macroeconomic announcements (using the technique of Kuttner 2001), they report the following impact hierarchy for maturities up to two years: FOMC meetings > testimonies > speeches. For maturities of two to four years ahead, testimonies are the only STF that has a significant impact. Bligh and Hess (this volume, chapter 7) introduce their measures of certainty, pessimism, and macroeconomic language (derived by content analysis of STFs); among other results, they find that macroeconomic language has the largest impact on financial market variables. While these and other studies with daily data are very informative, they do not permit an examination of effects before and after the release on the same day and of hypotheses contrasting coordination versus content.

The study by Reeves and Sawicki (2007) sheds some additional light on the relevance of using higher-frequency data. They present results with data at both daily and higher frequencies (5-, 15-, and 60-minute time periods). They examine data for the response of 10-year spot yields on futures contracts of UK government securities of different maturities to minutes of the Monetary Policy Committee (MPC) meetings, the inflation report, speeches by MPC members, and testimonies by MPC members. For daily data, the volatility of the 3-month, 6-month, and 12-month short sterling futures and a 10-year security are increased by the release of the MPC minutes relative to the five working days before the release. These increases are statistically significant. (In contrast to the results by Kohn and Sack (2004) and in our paper, testimonies were found to have no significant impact.) For higher-frequency data, the releases of the MPC minutes, as well as of the inflation report, have statistically significant impacts on the same four government securities relative to the five working days before the release. Gürkaynak, Sack, and Swanson (2005, section 1.3 and table 1) document the different results obtained from using daily data, intraday data with a wide window, and intraday data with a narrow window when assessing the effects of monetary policy actions and statements. Higher-frequency data appear to be more powerful in capturing the impacts of pronouncements.

Some results suggest that communication channels depend on the current and past macroeconomic and policy environments. Clare and Courtenay (2001) find that, since the independence of the Bank of England in May 1997, the sensitivity of UK long gilt futures (among other assets) has fallen and the speed of reaction has risen. The latter development is attributed to increased transparency by the Bank of England. Joyce and Read (2002) find that the sensitivity of UK bond prices to unexpected movements in the retail price index (RPI) increased after inflation targets were announced, suggesting that the information contained in RPI releases increased in the inflation-targeting environment. Ehrmann and Fratzscher (2007b) document that the effects of Federal Reserve pronouncements are state-dependent. Andersen et al. (2007) show that the response of asset prices to macroeconomic announcements is sensitive to the state of the business cycle. Shifts in the macroeconomic and policy environments can affect communication channels, and hence estimates of the effects of pronouncements over long sample periods may be unreliable.

The above studies generally find that pronouncements matter for financial markets. This conclusion is confirmed by studies that directly examine the impact of pronouncements on monetary policy variables. Siklos and Bohl (2007) study the behavior of the Bundesbank in a VAR framework. While actions speak louder than words, they find that communication does also play a role and serves as a substitute for interest rate smoothing (see Geraats, this volume, for a related theoretical model). Sturm and De Haan (2011) examine the incremental information introduced by ECB pronouncements above that contained in a Taylor rule. They find that ECB pronouncements add information useful in predicting policy decisions. There are dissenting opinions. Bomfim and Reinhart (2000) study the impact of FOMC decisions on financial markets, and Berger, De Haan, and Sturm (2011) examine the impact of the monetary pillar (as expressed in the ECB's monthly press conferences) on monetary policy. Both studies report that pronouncements are not effective relative to actions. These disparate results suggest that the effects of pronouncements may depend on the nature of the pronouncement, the macroeconomic and policy environments, and the history of past policies.

8.7 Summary

This paper has explored one aspect of central bank communication policy—formal pronouncements by central bankers—to obtain a better understanding of whether this channel matters and, if so, the nature of the information being transmitted. We examine the relationship between Chairman Alan Greenspan's speeches and testimonies and the FOMC meetings and volatility in the 30-year bond market at five-minute intervals. The pattern of hypothesis tests and our results are summarized in figure 8.1. We find that STFs matter for bond market volatility, that this impact depends on the transmission of information (rather than just noise), and that this information reflects both substantive content and a coordination signal. We further find that speeches only deliver content, that testimonies are largely a coordination device, and that FOMC meetings play both roles. These findings of a quantitatively important coordination channel document the relevance of the "global games" model of Morris and Shin and the herding model of Banerjee.

Our results have several important policy implications, including the possibility that one or more aspects of the STFs may be counterproductive by crowding out private information. More generally, they raise questions about the optimal communication policy, how a central bank becomes transparent, and the tradeoff between releasing information to the public and amplifying volatility in financial markets.

Notes

We are grateful for the comments and suggestions offered by seminar participants at the American Economic Association (in particular our discussant, Ken Kuttner), Bank of England, CESifo Venice Summer Institute (in particular our discussant, Greg Hess, and the conference organizers, Pierre Siklos and Jan-Egbert Sturm), Deutsche Bundesbank, Emory University, Ente Einaudi, Illinois Economic Association, Midwest Finance Association (in particular, our discussant Stephen Figlewski), Sveriges Riksbank, and the University of Illinois at Chicago, and by Torben Andersen, John Curran, Hashem Dezhbakhsh, Amir Kia, Kai Konrad, Jeff Moore, Rose Pianalto, Peter Postl, Andrea Prat, Arkalgud Ramaprasad, Huntley Schaller, Jukka Sihvonen, Alfons Weichenrieder, and especially by Helge Berger and Hugo Mialon. We thank Kelli Lanier for her timely research support. This paper grew out of Ben Carter's undergraduate honors thesis; we regret that Ben's private-sector job commitments precluded his continuing on this project. A substantial amount of the work on this project was completed while Chirinko was a Visiting Scholar at the Center for Economic Studies, whose research support and hospitality are gratefully acknowledged. Additional critical financial support has been provided by the Bank of England's Houblon-Norman/George Senior Fellows Program, Emory University's Institute for Comparative and International Studies, and two centers at the University of Illinois at Chicago: the International Center for Futures and Derivatives, and the Center for Quantitative Finance and Risk Management. All errors and omissions remain the sole responsibility of the authors, and the conclusions do not necessarily reflect the views of the organizations with which they are associated.

1. The connection between monetary policy transparency and expectations has been analyzed by Blinder et al. (2008, especially sections 1 and 2), Rudebusch and Williams (2008), and Woodford (2005). Mishkin (2010) lists this channel as one of the nine basic scientific principles that guide thinking by monetary economists and policymakers.

2. See the lively discussion of transparency, communication, and related issues and references to the literature in Blinder et al. (2001) and the comprehensive survey by Geraats (2002).

3. The case for transparency in the face of supply shocks has been questioned recently. See Geraats (this volume, chapter 3) for citations and a model in which full transparency remains beneficial even when supply shocks proliferate.

4. Bulíř, Čihák, and Šmídková (this volume, chapter 11) evaluate the clarity of the ECB's monetary policy communications and find that the ECB's communications are on a par with or better than those of most other central banks. These results suggest that Issing may have been a bit too hard on himself and the ECB.

5. The title of the paper is not only an informal description of monetary policy pronouncements by Chairman Greenspan, but also a reference to the Ayn Rand novel *Atlas Shrugged* and Greenspan's embrace of her free market philosophy.

6. Relevant theoretical models will be discussed in section 8.5.

7. The appendix is available from the authors or at http://www.cesifo-group.de/ifoHome.

8. See the studies discussed in section 8.6 suggesting that communication channels depend on the current and past macroeconomic and policy environments.

9. An alternative measurement of price volatility, squared returns, is adversely affected by measurement error relative to absolute returns (Forsberg and Ghysels 2007).

10. Several of the papers in this volume (Bligh and Hess; Jansen and De Haan; Lamla) highlight the challenges in interpreting central bank communications.

11. We thank Torben Andersen for making us aware of this possible problem.

12. The models based on the one-hour-*BEFORE/AFTER* indicator variables and the 24 five-minute intervals defining the indicator variables in Z can be thought of as nested models. The latter model is the most general. The *BEFORE/AFTER* model is a restricted version where the first 12 *BEFORE* coefficients and the latter 12 *AFTER* coefficients are constrained to be the same. The *DAY* variable is not nested because it contains time periods for the entire day, as opposed to just the one hour before and after the release of the STF. In the latter case where this indicator variable is defined only over a two-hour interval, it would be a restricted version of the *BEFORE/AFTER* model.

13. Endogeneity might arise because of a relation between current conditions and the content of an STF. This possible channel does not affect our results, which are based only on the occurrence of an STF, not its content.

14. The Durbin m-statistic is the t-statistic on the ρ coefficient from the following auxiliary regression: $u_t = \rho^* u_{t-1} + W_t' \Gamma + v_t$, where W_t represents the regressors appearing in a given equation, Γ is an incidental parameter vector, and v_t is an error term. The Monte Carlo evidence in Dezhbakhsh (1990) favors the Durbin m-statistic over several other tests for autocorrelation.

15. The sample standard deviations are 3.8922 and 14.4648 for IFP_t and IFQ_t, respectively.

16. The result for the one-hour period before the release is somewhat in contrast to that of Bomfim (2003), who finds that, on the day before the release, the stock market is less volatile.

References

Aït-Sahalia, Y., P. A. Mykland, and L. Zhang. 2005. How Often to Sample a Continuous-Time Process in the Presence of Market Microstructure Noise. *Review of Financial Studies* 18:351–416.

Allen, F., S. Morris, and H. S. Shin. 2006. Beauty Contests, Bubbles and Iterated Expectations in Asset Prices. *Review of Financial Studies* 19:719–752.

Amador, M., and P.-O. Weill. 2009. Learning from Prices: Public Communication and Welfare. Mimeo, Stanford and UCLA.

Amato, J. D., S. Morris, and H. S. Shin. 2002. Communication and Monetary Policy. *Oxford Review of Economic Policy* 18:495–503.

Andersen, T. G., T. Bollerslev, F. X. Diebold, and C. Vega. 2003. Micro Effects of Macro Announcements: Real-Time Price Discovery in Foreign Exchange. *American Economic Review* 93:38–62.

Andersen, T. G., T. Bollerslev, F. X. Diebold, and C. Vega. 2007. Real-Time Price Discovery in Global Stock, Bond and Foreign Exchange Markets. *Journal of International Economics* 73:251–277.

Avery, C., and P. Zemsky. 1998. Multidimensional Uncertainty and Herd Behavior in Financial Markets. *American Economic Review* 88:724–748.

Balduzzi, P., E. J. Elton, and C. Green. 2001. Economic News and the Yield Curve: Evidence from the US Treasury Market. *Journal of Financial and Quantitative Analysis* 36:523–543.

Banerjee, A. V. 1992. A Simple Model of Herd Behavior. *Quarterly Journal of Economics* 107:797–817.

Beber, A., M. W. Brandt, and K. A. Kavajecz. 2011. What Can Equity Orderflow Tell Us about the Economy? *Review of Financial Studies* 24:3688–3730.

Berger, H., J. De Haan, and J.-E. Sturm. 2011. Does Money Matter in the ECB Strategy? New Evidence Based on ECB Communication. *International Journal of Finance and Economics* 16:16–31.

Blinder, A., M. Ehrmann, M. Fratzscher, J. De Haan, and D.-J. Jansen. 2008. Central Bank Communication and Monetary Policy: A Survey of Theory and Evidence. *Journal of Economic Literature* 46:910–945.

Blinder, A., C. Goodhart, P. Hildebrand, D. Lipton, and C. Wyplosz. 2001. *How Do Central Banks Talk?* Geneva Reports on the World Economy 3. Oxford: Information Press for the International Center for Monetary and Banking Studies and CEPR.

Bomfim, A. N. 2003. Pre-announcement Effects, News Effects, and Volatility: Monetary Policy and the Stock Market. *Journal of Banking and Finance* 27:133–151.

Bomfim, A. N., and V. R. Reinhart. 2000. Making News: Financial Market Effects of Federal Reserve Disclosure Practices. Board of Governors of the Federal Reserve System, March.

Campbell, J. Y., S. J. Grossman, and J. Wang. 1993. Trading Volume and Serial Correlation in Stock Returns. *Quarterly Journal of Economics* 108:905–939.

Carville, J. 1993. *Wall Street Journal*, February 25, p. A1.

Clare, A., and R. Courtenay. 2001. Assessing the Impact of Macroeconomic News Announcements on Securities Prices under Different Monetary Policy Regimes. Bank of England.

Dezhbakhsh, H. 1990. The Inappropriate Use of Serial Correlation Tests in Dynamic Linear Models. *Review of Economics and Statistics* 72 (1):126–132.

Ederington, L. H., and J. H. Lee. 1993. How Markets Process Information: New Releases and Volatility. *Journal of Finance* 48:161–191.

Ehrmann, M., and M. Fratzscher. 2007a. Transparency, Disclosure, and the Federal Reserve. *International Journal of Central Banking* 3:179–225.

Ehrmann, M., and M. Fratzscher. 2007b. Social Value of Public Information: Testing the Limits to Transparency. European Central Bank, Working Paper No. 821.

Fleming, M. J, and E. M. Remolona. 1999a. What Moves Bond Prices? *Journal of Portfolio Management* 25 (Summer):28–37.

Fleming, M. J, and E. M. Remolona. 1999b. Price Formation and Liquidity in the U.S. Treasury Market: The Response to Public Information. *Journal of Finance* 54:1901–1916.

Forsberg, L., and E. Ghysels. 2007. Why Do Absolute Returns Predict Volatility So Well? *Journal of Financial Econometrics* 5:31–67.

Geraats, P. 2002. Central Bank Transparency. *Economic Journal* 112:F532–F565.

Gürkaynak, R. S., B. Sack, and E. Swanson. 2005. Do Actions Speak Louder Than Words? The Response of Asset Prices to Monetary Policy Actions and Statements. *International Journal of Central Banking* 1:55–93.

Guthrie, G., and J. Wright. 2000. Open Mouth Operations. *Journal of Monetary Economics* 46:489–516.

Issing, O. 2004. Should Central Banks Burst Bubbles? *Wall Street Journal*, February 18.

Jones, C. M., O. Lamont, and R. L. Lumsdaine. 1998. Macroeconomic News and Bond Market Volatility. *Journal of Financial Economics* 47:315–337.

Joyce, M. A. S., and V. Read. 2002. Asset Price Reactions to RPI Announcements. *Applied Financial Economics* 12:253–270.

Kohn, D. L. 2005. Central Bank Communication. Speech at the Annual Meeting of the American Economic Association, January 9.

Kohn, D. L., and B. P. Sack. 2004. Central Bank Talk: Does It Matter and Why? In *Macroeconomics, Monetary Policy, and Financial Stability: A Festschrift in Honour of Charles Freedman*, 175–206. Ottawa: Bank of Canada.

Kuttner, K. N. 2001. Monetary Policy Surprises and Interest Rates: Evidence from the Fed Funds Futures Market. *Journal of Monetary Economics* 47:523–544.

Mendel, B., and A. Shleifer. 2012. Chasing Noise. *Journal of Financial Economics* 104:303–320.

Mishkin, F. S. 2010. Will Monetary Policy Become More of a Science? In Volker Wieland, *The Science and Practice of Monetary Policy Today*, 81–103.

Morris, S., and H. S. Shin. 2002. Social Value of Public Information. *American Economic Review* 92:1521–1534.

Morris, S., and H. S. Shin. 2003. Global Games: Theory and Applications. In *Advances in Economics and Econometrics: Theory and Applications, Eighth World Congress*, ed. M. Dewatripont, L. P. Hansen, and S. J. Turnovsky, 1:56–116. Cambridge: Cambridge University Press.

Morris, S., H. S. Shin, and H. Tong. 2006. Social Value of Public Information: Morris and Shin (2002) Is Actually Pro-Transparency, Not Con. [Reply.] *American Economic Review* 96:453–455.

Reeves, R., and M. Sawicki. 2007. Do Financial Markets React to Bank of England Communication? *European Journal of Political Economy* 23:207–227.

Ross, S. 1989. Information and Volatility: The No-Arbitrage Martingale Approach to Timing and Resolution Irrelevancy. *Journal of Finance* 44:1–17.

Rudebusch, G. D., and J. C. Williams. 2008. Revealing the Secrets of the Temple: The Value of Publishing Central Bank Interest Rate Projections. In *Asset Prices and Monetary Policy*, ed. John Y. Campbell, 247–284. Chicago: University of Chicago Press.

Sihvonen, J. 2008. The Cheapest-to-Deliver Premium in German Bund Prices. University of Vaasa, May.

Siklos, P. L., and M. T. Bohl. 2007. Do Words Speak Louder Than Actions? Communication as an Instrument of Monetary Policy. Wilfred Laurier University and European University Viadrina Frankfurt (Oder).

Sturm, J.-E., and J. De Haan. 2011. Does Central Bank Communication Really Lead to Better Forecasts of Policy Decisions? *Weltwirtschaftliches Archiv / Review of World Economics* 147 (1):41–58.

Svensson, L. E. O. 2006. Social Value of Public Information: Comment: Morris and Shin (2002) Is Actually Pro-Transparency, Not Con. *American Economic Review* 96:448–452.

Woodford, M. 2005. Central Bank Communication and Policy Effectiveness. In *The Greenspan Era: Lessons for the Future*, ed. Federal Reserve Bank of Kansas City, 399–474. Kansas City: Federal Reserve Bank of Kansas City.

IV   The ECB's Experience

9 An Assessment of the Consistency of ECB Communication

David-Jan Jansen and Jakob de Haan

9.1 Introduction

Over the past two decades, communication has become an important instrument for monetary policymakers. In line with this development, there has been a surge in empirical studies on central bank communication (Blinder et al. 2008). Many of these studies refer to the communication policy of the European Central Bank (ECB). There is substantive evidence that ECB communications move financial markets in the intended direction (see, for instance, Ehrmann and Fratzscher 2007). Likewise, there are clear indications that ECB communications increase the predictability of interest decisions (see, for instance, Sturm and De Haan 2011).

Still, especially during the ECB's first years of operation, many observers were critical of ECB communication. Looking back, Cecchetti and Schoenholtz (2008, p. 12) note that "the . . . record is filled with outside complaints about ECB communication with financial markets." Referring to public statements by ECB officials, Gros et al. (2000, p. 27) describe how "such comments have often expressed conflicting views of the policy outlook and of policy priorities, making it harder to understand collective decisions inside the ECB." Artis (2002, p. 26) mentions how the ECB has been "roundly criticized by several authorities and institutions . . . for weaknesses in its communication strategy," before going on to note that "it is certainly possible to identify a number of occasions when communication has been less than perfect." ECB officials themselves have also acknowledged the challenges of communicating their policies. In a speech in 2001, Executive Board member Sirkka Hämäläinen (2001) noted: "It is true that we have not always been very successful in our communication despite ambitious intentions. But communication is not easy in a pan-European context in which differing cultures, languages, traditions and motives affect how messages are interpreted by the different counter-parties involved."

With these critiques of ECB communication in mind, we should perhaps not expect positive results when we investigate consistency. Still, consistency is an important requirement for communication to be effective. If central bankers too frequently change their vocabulary, it will be difficult for observers to properly infer the message that the central bankers are trying to convey. So, on the one hand we have evidence that ECB communication has been effective (Ehrmann and Fratzscher 2007; Sturm and De Haan 2011), while on the other hand there have been various critiques. To investigate this contradiction further, this chapter assesses the internal consistency of ECB communication. Put differently, we assess the similarities in the ECB's vocabulary over time. How alike, for instance, was the way in which the ECB communicated about its monetary policy stance in 1999 and in 2009? Did the ECB often change its mode of communication, or were observers able to learn the way in which it communicated regarding its policies? It is important to note that this concept of consistency differs from the one used in previous studies, which usually focus on the match between words and subsequent policy decisions (Berger, De Haan, and Sturm 2011). Another prominent take on consistency has been the degree of dispersion in communications by various officials from the same central bank (Jansen and De Haan 2006; Ehrmann and Fratzscher 2007).

Although consistency is important, some flexibility may be necessary when communicating monetary policy. As circumstances change, communication is bound to look for new ways to express the motivations underlying policy decisions. From that perspective, too much emphasis on providing consistency may mean too much rigor with respect to communication. Therefore, we also study potential changes in communication.

With respect to the ECB, there are a number of occasions on which changes in wording may have occurred. Some would argue that, as a new organization, the ECB perhaps had to learn how to communicate effectively with the outside world. The first years of the Economic and Monetary Union (EMU) may, therefore, have constituted a learning period for the ECB. Second, after an internal assessment, the ECB clarified its monetary policy strategy in May 2003. Although this was not supposed to reflect a change in strategy, many observers interpreted the clarification as downplaying the importance of the role of money in the ECB's strategy (Berger et al. 2011). In any case, the terms "economic analysis" and "monetary analysis" were introduced as new elements in the introductory statements. Third, in order to provide additional relevant information in a timely matter, the ECB started to discuss the quarterly macroeconomic projections by ECB or Eurosystem staff in June 2004. Four times a year, therefore, the introductory statements now contained a type of information which they had not before mid-2004. Finally, the financial turmoil may have led communication to adapt since mid-2007. The turbulence in financial markets, followed by a severe economic downturn, may have led the ECB to find new words to describe the considerations underlying its monetary policy in this changed environment.

In this chapter, we examine whether ECB communications have remained consistent over time, and whether possible changes in vocabulary have increased our understanding of monetary policy. We investigate these two issues by conducting the following thought experiment. Suppose someone had closely followed and analyzed ECB communications during the early years of the EMU. How well would this person have been able to understand monetary policy during subsequent years, *without heavily investing in any further kind of analysis*?

To conduct our thought experiment, we use the Wordscores methodology introduced by Laver, Benoît, and Garry (2003). The underlying idea is the following: From texts of which the policy position is known (the so-called reference texts), Wordscores extracts information using word frequencies, and this information is employed to estimate the policy positions of subsequent texts about which nothing is known (the so-called virgin texts). All that is used to infer the policy positions of virgin texts are the words contained in these texts, which are compared with the words observed in reference texts with a known policy position.

We apply the Wordscores methodology to the introductory statements by the president of the ECB at the press conference following the ECB's monetary policy meetings, as that is the ECB's most important communication device (Blinder et al. 2008). We start by using the introductory statements between 1999 and 2001 as reference texts and statements in subsequent years (2002–July 2009) as virgin texts. Wordscores requires that the reference texts are coded. To do so, we use two coding schemes. First, we rely on various indicators of ECB communication developed by different authors. As an alternative, we use the ECB's actual policy decisions. To investigate changes in wording, we subsequently expand the time frame for the reference texts by one year. Thus, we are able to determine whether this enhances the ability of Wordscores to identify the policy positions of the virgin texts.

Given the reasons to expect that the ECB's communications may have changed over time, one might suppose that the mechanical approach underlying Wordscores would have difficulty in generating an accurate representation of ECB monetary policy. However, we find that solely on the basis of the introductory statements during the first three years of the EMU, the Wordscores method is able to present a fairly accurate picture of the ECB's policy decisions in subsequent years. From that perspective, the ECB's communication as laid down in the introductory statements can be considered quite consistent over the last decade. With the various critiques of ECB communication in mind, our findings may be seen as surprising.

At the same time, the evidence also suggests that ECB communications have changed: adding more years of introductory statements to the set of reference texts generally improves our understanding of ECB monetary policy decisions. From that perspective, it seems the introductory statements continued to provide new relevant information for central bank watchers. Overall, we conclude that ECB communication during the first decade of the EMU was characterized by consistency as well as flexibility.

This chapter proceeds as follows. Section 9.2 outlines the Wordscores methodology and discusses our particular application to ECB communication. Section 9.3 presents the results, and section 9.4 provides a concluding discussion.

9.2   Using Wordscores to Analyze ECB Communication

Laver et al. (2003) introduced the Wordscores methodology to estimate policy positions of political parties in the United Kingdom. In a nutshell, the underlying idea is to estimate policy positions by comparing two sets of texts using the relative frequency of words. Prior knowledge concerning the first set of texts, called reference texts, is used to infer the policy positions of the texts in the second set, which are labeled virgin texts. All that is needed to infer the positions of the virgin texts are the words contained in these texts, which are compared with the words observed in reference texts holding "known" policy positions.

The Wordscores method has a particular take on analyzing texts. Laver et al. (2003, p. 312) note how the method treats "texts not as discourses to be read, understood and interpreted for meaning—either by a human coder or a computer program applying a dictionary—but as collections of word data containing information about the position of the texts' authors on predefined policy dimensions." The method we use in this paper, therefore, differs from that of the related papers in this volume, as those contributions use the timing of communication (Chirinko and Curran), devise their own coding schemes to analyze communications (Bulíř, Čihák and Šmídková), or use methods for automated content analysis (Bligh and Hess).

Laver et al. (2003) identify several benefits of the Wordscores methodology. First, it can be used for texts written in any language. Second, because it treats words unequivocally as data, Wordscores is also able to calculate confidence intervals for the estimated scores. Finally, there is no need for heavy human intervention, and Wordscores can be implemented efficiently using programs that the authors have made available on the Internet.[1]

To use Wordscores properly, the selection of appropriate reference texts is crucial. The reference texts are required to provide sufficient information on the policy dimension for which one would like to evaluate the virgin texts. Laver et al. (2003) identify three guidelines for the selection of reference texts. Most importantly, the reference texts should be used in the same context as the virgin texts. It is precisely this key requirement that we use as the basis for studying consistency. In a sense, we are reversing the direction of the analysis. Wordscores requires similarity between reference texts and virgin texts in order to be effective. We will argue that, if it turns out that reference texts are useful for interpreting virgin texts, this shows that the two set of texts are internally consistent.

The other two guidelines are also intuitive. The reference texts should contain enough variation in policy positions to cover the complete spectrum of positions. Finally, the reference texts should contain as many different words as possible. The more words the reference texts contain, the more likely it is that words from the virgin texts can be assigned scores.

We focus on the ECB's most important communication device: the president's introductory statement at the monthly press conference in which he reports on the decisions taken by the ECB's Governing Council. Following meetings of the Council, which typically take place on the first Thursday of each month, the ECB announces the monetary policy decisions at 13:45 (CET). Some 45 minutes later, at around 14:30, the ECB president and vice-president hold a press conference that comprises two elements: a prepared introductory statement that contains the background considerations for the monetary policy decision, and a question-and-answer part during which the president and the vice-president are available to answer questions by the attending journalists. The introductory statement is understood to reflect the position and views of the Council, agreed upon word-by-word by its members (Ehrmann and Fratzscher 2009; Berger et al. 2011).

We use the ECB president's introductory statements from the early years of the EMU in order to understand introductory statements in later years. To be more precise, as a first step we consider the period between January 1999 and December 2001 as the reference period, and use the introductory statements from that period to understand monetary policy between January 2002 and July 2009. As the ECB's monetary policy showed sufficient variation—in terms of the number of rate changes and their direction—between 1999 and 2001, there is enough relevant information in the reference texts, which can then be used to identify the policy positions of the virgin texts. Finally, we are able to use a respectable number of words as references. The introductory statements are of course much shorter than the party manifestos used by Laver et al. (2003), but our number of reference texts is larger. Our baseline set of reference texts (1999–2001) contains well over 45,000 words. Therefore, the third requirement for applying Wordscores is also met.

Wordscores requires that the reference texts be coded. So, although Wordscores offers the ability to process a large body of communication quickly, there is still a need for an initial phase of content analysis. In that sense, the method differs somewhat from other methods that offer automated content analysis, such as Alceste (see, for instance, Bailey and Schonhardt-Bailey 2008) or Diction (see, for example, Bligh and Hess in this volume). Because we wanted to focus on the specific use of Wordscores, we chose to use four indicators of ECB communication from the existing literature. These indicators are all based on the ECB president's introductory statements. We use the aggregate indicator of Berger et al. (2011), the updated indicator of Rosa and Verga (2007), the indicator of Ullrich (2008), and the KOF MPC Communicator index.[2] These indicators code ECB communications on a numerical scale. Negative (positive) values are assigned to communications that are perceived as dovish (hawkish), and zero to those that appear to be neutral. Whereas some researchers restrict the coding to directional indications by using a scale between −1 and +1, others assign a finer grid that is at least suggestive of magnitude, e.g., by coding statements on a scale from −2 to +2.[3] As an alternative to these four indicators, we employ the actual policy decisions by the ECB Governing Council. In doing so, we define the policy dimension ranging between monetary easing (which we assign a score of −1) and tightening (which we assign a score of +1).[4]

The four indicators have been used previously for various purposes. Berger et al. (2011) examine the role of money in the policies of the ECB, using introductory statements of the ECB president at the monthly press conferences during 1999–2004. They construct an aggregate indicator as well as indicators of the economic and monetary analysis. We use their aggregate indicator, as we want to include all possibly relevant statements. Rosa and Verga (2007) use the introductory statements to show that the predictive ability of these statements is similar to that implied by market-based measures of monetary policy expectations. To do so, they provide a glossary that translates the qualitative information of the press conferences into an ordered scale. Ullrich (2008) shows how the indicator measuring ECB rhetoric contributes to explaining the formation of inflation expectations. Finally, the KOF MPC offers a quantification of the statements of the ECB president made during the monthly press conference. The indicator is based on those parts of the introductory statements that reveal the Governing Council's assessment of developments which directly affect future price stability. As the indicators use different scales, we standardize each index and then take the average of the standardized indicators. This average is the score for the reference texts. The policy dimension is defined as the number of standard deviations from a neutral policy stance.

We also use the Wordscores methodology to make inferences about changes in the ECB's vocabulary. As noted, Wordscores assumes that reference texts contain useful information for understanding virgin texts published at a later date. However, as Laver et al. (2003, p. 314) acknowledge with respect to the party manifestos that they analyze, this "assumption is unlikely to be 100 percent correct, since the meaning and usage of words in party manifestos changes over time, even over the time period between two elections in one country." As we have argued, the same may be true for ECB communications. To identify whether this is the case, we therefore gradually expand the window of introductory statements that we consider as reference texts. If ECB communication changes over time, the positioning of the virgin texts will then also change. As more information becomes available through the wording of the statements, we expect that the method will be better able to match actual interest rate policy. We check this by confronting the estimated policy positions of the virgin text with the actual developments in the ECB's monetary policy stance.

9.3   Results

First, we discuss how well the estimated policy positions obtained using Wordscores match with actual developments in ECB monetary policy. For clarity, we note that we evaluate the match between the score for each introductory statement and the *contemporaneous* policy decision.[5] Figure 9.1 shows the results when we use the introductory statements between January 1999 and December 2001 as reference texts

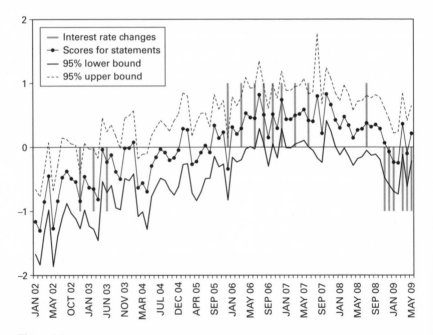

Figure 9.1
Results for 2002–2009 using actual policy decisions as anchors. The dots denote the scores for the ECB president's introductory statements between January 2002 and July 2009, with the 95% confidence interval around these estimates. The bars denote the change in the ECB policy rate, where positive values indicate monetary policy tightening and nega-tive values denote easing. If there are no bars for a certain date, policy rates remained unchanged. The reference texts are taken for the period 1999–2001 and coded using actual ECB policy decisions.

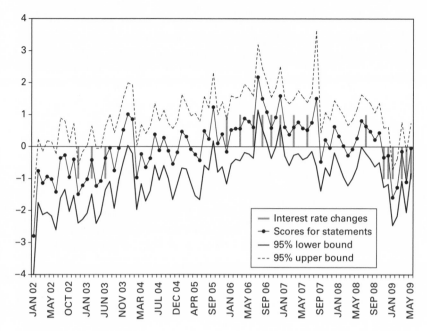

Figure 9.2
Results for 2002–2009 using communication indicators as anchors. The dots denote the scores for the ECB president's introductory statements between January 2002 and July 2009, with the 95% confidence interval around these estimates. The bars denote the change in the ECB policy rate, where positive values indicate monetary policy tightening and negative values denote easing. If there are no bars for a certain date, policy rates remained unchanged. The reference texts are taken for the period 1999–2001 and coded using four ECB communication indicators from the literature.

and code them using the actual policy decisions. The solid line with dots shows the scores for the virgin texts, i.e., the introductory statements spanning the period January 2002 to July 2009. The figure also shows the 95% confidence interval around the scores. The bars indicate the timing and direction of changes in the ECB main refinancing rate. Figure 9.2 shows the results when the reference texts are coded using the ECB communication indicators.

At first glance, it is striking how the estimated scores for the introductory statements broadly follow the actual developments in ECB monetary policy. As such, the scores obtained from Wordscores are helpful in obtaining an indication of the ECB monetary policy stance over the years. Admittedly, the correlation is not perfect, which indicates that the scores may not be the best possible forecasts. Nevertheless, using only information from introductory statements for the first three years of the EMU as reference texts goes a long way in understanding monetary policy in subsequent years. From this perspective, we conclude that ECB communication over the last decade may be considered quite consistent.

Next, we address the possibility of changes over time. Tables 9.1 and 9.2 provide various metrics of how well the estimated policy positions match the contemporaneous policy decisions. The window for the reference texts is expanded by one year in subsequent steps. For instance, the last column shows results when we use the introductory statements between 1999 and 2006 as reference texts. Again, we relate the scores to the contemporaneous decisions.[6] The first row of each table shows the correlation between the scores of the virgin texts and the actual policy decisions. The remaining rows of the tables show indicators for the ability of the scores for the virgin texts to match policy decisions taken between January 2007 and July 2009. This sample includes the period when one of the changes in communication may have occurred. In table 9.1 the reference texts are coded using actual policy decisions, while in table 9.2 these texts are coded using the ECB communication indicators.

Although there is some variation, the overall impression is that adding additional introductory statements to the set of reference texts

Table 9.1
Accuracy When Using Actual Policy Decisions to Code Statements

	Reference period ends in:					
	2001	2002	2003	2004	2005	2006
Correlation	0.26	0.33	0.21	0.43	0.65	0.52
% correct easing	0.0	0.0	16.7	50.0	50.0	33.3
% correct tightening	0.0	33.3	0.0	0.0	0.0	66.7
% correct no change	75.0	80.0	75.0	80.0	85.0	70.0
% incorrect easing	NA	NA	0.0	40.0	50.0	50.0
% incorrect tightening	100.0	80.0	100.0	100.0	NA	66.7
% incorrect no change	37.5	33.3	34.8	27.3	26.1	26.3

Note: The correlation is measured between an indicator (measured on a scale of –1, 0, 1) of actual decisions and the Wordscores for the introductory statements. The correlation is computed over the entire sample of virgin texts. All other measures are based on an evaluation for the period January 2007 to July 2009. The percentage of correct classifications is conditional on the actual decisions, while the percentage of incorrect classifications is conditional on classifications. The classification is determined by checking the scores for the texts. When the score is higher (lower) than +0.5 (–0.5), the predicted value is equal to +1 (–1), whereas in between the predicted value is 0.

Table 9.2
Accuracy When Using the Average of Four ECB Communication Indicators to Code
Statements

	Reference period ends in:					
	2001	2002	2003	2004	2005	2006
Correlation	0.38	0.34	0.28	0.56	0.65	0.62
% correct easing	33.3	16.7	16.7	50.0	50.0	33.3
% correct tightening	0.0	0.0	0.0	0.0	0.0	66.7
% correct no change	90.0	90.0	85.0	95.0	95.0	75.0
% incorrect easing	33.3	0.0	0.0	25.0	25.0	0.0
% incorrect tightening	100.0	100.0	100.0	NA	NA	71.4
% incorrect no change	28.0	30.8	32.0	24.0	24.0	25.0

Note: The correlation is measured between an indicator (measured on a scale of $-1, 0, 1$)
of actual decisions and the Wordscores for the introductory statements. The correlation
is computed over the entire sample of virgin texts. All other measures are based on an
evaluation for the period January 2007 to July 2009. The percentage of correct classifications is conditional on the actual decisions, while the percentage of incorrect classifications is conditional on classifications. The classification is determined by checking the
scores for the texts. When the score is higher (lower) than $+1.0$ (-1.0), the predicted value
is equal to $+1$ (-1), whereas in between the predicted value is 0.

leads to a better correspondence between the scores and the actual
development in the monetary policy stance. For instance, the correlation increases, although not monotonically. Also, the percentages of
correct classifications, in most cases, increases over time, while the
number of incorrect classifications decreases.

The last columns of tables 9.1 and 9.2 provide interesting results.
Adding the introductory statements from the year 2006 to the reference
texts does not uniformly improve the correspondence between estimated positions and actual policy.[7] The correlations between the scores
and actual interest rate policy decrease compared with when the reference period ends in 2005. Also, the percentage of correct "no change"
decisions is lower. In contrast, decisions to tighten monetary policy are
better matched. For the first time, we are able to correctly match two
of the three decisions to tighten monetary policy in 2007 and 2008.
Figures 9.3 and 9.4 further illustrate this point. The figures show the
match between scores for the virgin texts and the actual policy decisions, using the introductory statements of the ECB president from
1999 to 2006 as reference texts. Compared to figures 9.1 and 9.2,
the estimated policy positions are more closely linked in the case of

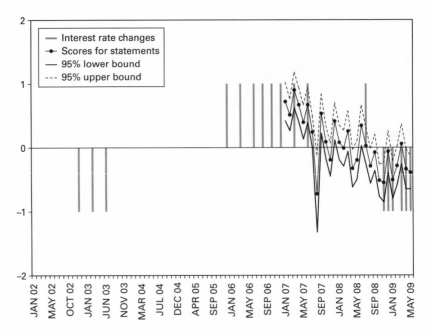

Figure 9.3
Results for 2007–2009 using actual policy decisions as anchors. The dots denote the scores for the ECB president's introductory statements between January 2007 and July 2009, with the 95% confidence interval around these estimates. The bars denote the change in the ECB policy rate, where positive values indicate monetary policy tightening and negative values denote easing. If there are no bars for a certain date, policy rates remained unchanged. The reference texts are taken for the period 1999–2006 and coded using actual ECB policy decisions.

decisions to tighten monetary policy, especially when the references texts are coded using the ECB communication indicators.

Table 9.3 presents another piece of evidence with respect to this finding. These results are based on a moving-window experiment in which we keep the reference period constant at three years: the first reference period is 1999 to 2001, the next is 2000 to 2002, and so forth. The last reference period begins in 2004 and ends in 2006. This period is the only one that includes 2006.[8] The results are based on using actual policy decisions to code the reference texts. The results from the earlier exercise are clearly supported. Once we include the introductory statements from 2006 among the reference texts, we find that the scores better match the actual policy decisions.

What could account for the specific results for 2006? The role of keywords such as "vigilance" is one plausible explanation for the better

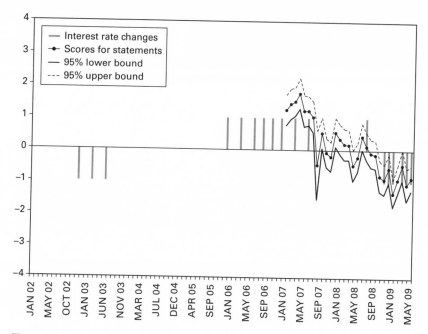

Figure 9.4
Results for 2007–2009 using communication indicators as anchors. The dots denote the scores for the introductory statements between January 2007 and July 2009, with the 95% confidence interval around these estimates. The bars denote the change in the ECB policy rate, where positive values indicate monetary policy tightening and negative values denote easing. If there are no bars for a certain date, policy rates remained unchanged. The reference texts are taken for the period 1999–2006 and coded using four ECB communication indicators from the literature.

match with respect to tightening decisions. In earlier work (Jansen and De Haan 2007), we discussed how this term (and variations thereof) was often used to signal the ECB's worry on rising euro area inflation expectations from early 2004 onward. However, after December 2005, the use of "vigilance" was increasingly seen as an indication of upcoming tightening of ECB monetary policy.[9] It seems plausible that adding 2006 to the set of reference texts changes the relative occurrence of "vigilance" in the introductory statements, enabling us to better match tightening decisions in 2007 and 2008.

9.4   Conclusions

In this chapter, we apply Wordscores—a method of textual analysis based on word frequencies—to the introductory statements by the ECB

Table 9.3
Accuracy When Using a Moving Window of Three Years

	Reference period					
	99–01	00–02	01–03	02–04	03–05	04–06
Correlation	0.50	0.59	0.64	0.42	0.61	0.44
% correct easing	50.0	33.3	83.3	50.0	33.3	0.0
% correct tightening	0.0	0.0	0.0	0.0	0.0	66.7
% correct no change	80.0	90.0	100.0	100.0	95.0	75.0
% incorrect easing	25.0	33.3	0.0	0.0	0.0	100.0
% incorrect tightening	100.0	100.0	NA	NA	100.0	66.7
% incorrect no change	27.3	28.0	16.7	23.1	26.9	31.8

Note: The correlation is measured between an indicator (measured on a scale of −1, 0, 1) of actual decisions and the Wordscores for the introductory statements. All measures are based on an evaluation for the period January 2007 to July 2009. The percentage of correct classifications is conditional on the actual decisions, while the percentage of incorrect classifications is conditional on classifications. The classification is determined by checking the scores for the texts. When the score is higher (lower) than +1.0 (−1.0), the predicted value is equal to +1 (−1), whereas in between the predicted value is 0. The coding for reference texts is based on actual policy decisions.

president at the press conference following monetary policy meetings. To use Wordscores, we code introductory statements from the early years of the Economic and Monetary Union using various indicators of ECB communication as well as actual policy decisions.

We see two contributions from our analysis. First, we introduce Wordscores to the literature on central bank communication. From a purely methodological viewpoint, Wordscores may be an interesting addition to the researcher's toolkit. The underlying algorithm incorporated in Wordscores may help researchers in more efficiently analyzing vast amounts of communications by central banks. At the same time, Wordscores still requires some a priori coding for the reference texts, which could be time-intensive. Therefore, Wordscores is more likely a complement to, rather than a substitute for, other methods of automated content analysis.

We also introduce Wordscores as we think it can be used to analyze consistency. Therefore, this chapter's second contribution is an assessment of the consistency of ECB communication during the first ten years of its operations. In contrast to much of the existing literature, we focus on the internal consistency of ECB communication over the years. There are two main conclusions. First, by combining a thorough analysis of ECB communication from the early years of the EMU with Wordscores, we are able to present a fairly accurate picture of ECB monetary policy in subsequent years. From that perspective, the ECB's communication as laid down in the president's introductory statements can be seen as quite consistent over the last decade. This point becomes especially clear if we again consider the simplicity of the Wordscores methodology. We only use information on the number of times particular words appear in ECB statements. Using more sophisticated methods would probably only increase the matching between estimated and actual policy decisions.

Given the various critiques of ECB communication (for a discussion, see, e.g., Cecchetti and Schoenholtz 2008), and the occasional changes in emphasis in communication strategy, our finding that ECB communication was reasonably consistent over the years can be seen as surprising. At the same time, this finding is in line with papers that argue that ECB communication has been effective (Ehrmann and Fratzscher 2007; Sturm and De Haan 2011).

Although consistency is important in communication, in all likelihood there is also a need for flexibility. Therefore, we also try to assess the role of possible changes in communication. Adding more introductory statements to the set of reference texts helps, in general, to improve our understanding of monetary policy in subsequent years. From that perspective, the introductory statements seem to have provided new relevant information for central bank watchers. Overall, we conclude that ECB communication during the first decade of the EMU was characterized by consistency as well as flexibility.

Appendix 9.1

This appendix provides technical details on the Wordscores methodology. Wordscores proceeds in three steps:[10]

Treatment of reference texts:

1. There is a set R of reference texts, each of which has a position on the policy dimension d.

2. The position on this dimension of individual texts—denoted by r—is denoted by A_{rd}.

3. The relative frequency, as a proportion of the total number of words in a text, of each unique word w in text r is denoted by F_{wr}.

4. Wordscores uses the matrix of F for all unique words in a text to estimate the conditional probability that one is reading text r given that one is reading word w.

5. This probability is calculated as:

$$P_{wr} = F_{wr} / \sum_r F_{wr}.$$ (9.1)

6. The matrix of the conditional probabilities for all unique words is then used to produce a score S_{wd} for each word on dimension d. This score is the expected position on dimension d, given that one is reading w.

7. This score is the average of a priori scores for the reference texts weighted by the probabilities P. It is calculated as:

$$S_{wd} = \sum_r (P_{wr} * A_{rd}).$$ (9.2)

Treatment of virgin texts

1. First, the relative frequency of each word in the virgin texts is calculated. This frequency is denoted by F_{wv}.

2. The score of any virgin text v on dimension d is the mean dimension score of the scored words weighted by the frequency of the scored words. It is computed as:

$$S_{vd} = \sum_w (F_{wv} * S_{wd}).$$ (9.3)

Transformation of raw virgin scores

1. A final technical issue is the fact that common words in the reference texts tend to be assigned the mean overall scores of the reference texts.

2. Therefore, raw virgin text scores tend to be more clustered than those for the reference texts.

3. To deal with this issue, Laver et al. (2003) propose a transformation to guarantee that the scores of the virgin texts have the same dispersion metric as those of the reference texts. The results presented throughout this chapter are the transformed scores.

4. The transformation is done by computing

$$S_{vd}^* = (S_{vd} - S_{\bar{v}d})(SD_{rd}/SD_{vd}) + S_{\bar{v}d},$$ (9.4)

where $S_{\bar{v}d}$ is the average score of virgin texts, and SD_{rd} and SD_{vd} are the sample standard deviations for reference and virgin text scores.

Notes

We thank Michael Ehrmann, Roman Horváth, Michael Lamla, Pierre Siklos, and Jan-Egbert Sturm and participants in the 2010 CESifo Venice Summer Institute Workshop on "Central Bank Communication, Decision-Making and Governance" for useful comments. Joanna Slawatyniec provided excellent research assistance. Jansen thanks the Monetary Policy Research Division of the European Central Bank for its generous hospitality. This chapter presents the authors' personal opinions. Views expressed in this chapter do not necessarily coincide with those of de Nederlandsche Bank, the European Central Bank, or the Eurosystem.

1. Wordscores is implemented as a set of Stata programs, which can be downloaded at http://www.tcd.ie/Political_Science/wordscores/software.html. A version in R is available at http://www.williamlowe.net/software/. We present the technical details underlying Wordscores in appendix 9.1. See also Lowe (2008) for a further discussion.

2. We downloaded the KOF MPC data from http://www.kof.ethz.ch/publications/indicators/communicator/en (last accessed March 25, 2010). We thank Carlo Rosa, Giovanni Verga, and Katrin Ullrich for making their data available.

3. Using these indicators, Sturm and De Haan (2011) examine whether ECB communication adds information compared to the information provided by a Taylor rule model in which expected inflation and output are used. They find that even though the indicators are sometimes quite different from one another, they add information that helps predicting the next policy decision of the ECB compared to the information provided by expected inflation and expected output growth.

4. An interesting extension would be to use the *size* of the interest rate change as the policy dimension.

5. Therefore, our results do not so much address the issue of predictability of policy decisions. We did evaluate how well the scores of the statements matched *next month's* decisions; in general, the match was not as good as in the contemporaneous case.

6. Also for this moving-window analysis, the results are similar to the contemporaneous case if we relate today's statements to next month's decisions. Results are available upon request.

7. It would be interesting, therefore, to expand the set of reference texts further. Momentarily, this would leave us with too few interest rate changes to evaluate the estimated policy positions.

8. For this exercise, one of the conditions for Wordscores to be effective is no longer automatically valid. Between the reference periods, there are now differences in the number of occasions on which interest rates change as well as in the distribution between decisions to ease and tighten. For instance, the reference period between 2002 and 2004 only contains three occasions on which policy was changed. In each case, rates were eased.

9. According to Bloomberg, "ECB president Jean-Claude Trichet has used the word 'vigilant' to flag each of the six rate increases since late 2005" (Bloomberg News, February 15, 2007). Likewise, according to UBS, "Trichet has made a practice of effectively pre-announcing hikes at the prior meeting with the use of the key 'vigilant' phrase" (UBS FX Trade and Research, January 9, 2007).

10. This appendix is based on Laver et al. (2003), pp. 315–316.

References

Artis, M. 2002. The Performance of the European Central Bank. *International Review of Applied Economics* 16 (1):19–29.

Bailey, A., and C. Schonhardt-Bailey. 2008. Does Deliberation Matter in FOMC Monetary Policymaking? The Volcker Revolution. *Political Analysis* 16 (4):404–427.

Berger, H., J. De Haan, and J.-E. Sturm. 2011. Does Money Matter in the ECB Strategy? New Evidence Based on ECB Communication. *International Journal of Finance and Economics* 16 (1):16–41.

Blinder, A. S., M. Ehrmann, M. Fratzscher, J. De Haan, and D. Jansen. 2008. Central Bank Communication and Monetary Policy: A Survey of Theory and Evidence. *Journal of Economic Literature* 46 (4):908–943.

Cecchetti, S. C., and K. L. Schoenholtz. 2008. How Central Bankers See It: The First Decade of ECB Policy and Beyond. NBER Working Paper 14489.

Ehrmann, M., and M. Fratzscher. 2007. Communication by Central Bank Committee Members: Different Strategies, Same Effectiveness? *Journal of Money, Credit and Banking* 39 (2–3):509–541.

Ehrmann, M., and M. Fratzscher. 2009. Explaining Monetary Policy Decisions in Press Conferences. *International Journal of Central Banking* 5 (2):41–84.

Gros, D., O. Davanne, M. Emerson, T. Mayer, G. Tabellini, and N. Thygesen. 2000. *Quo Vadis Euro? The Cost of Muddling Through. Second Report of the CEPS Macroeconomic Policy Group.* Brussels: Centre for European Policy Studies.

Hämäläinen, S. 2001. The ECB's Monetary Policy: Accountability, Transparency and Communication. Speech at the conference "Old Age, New Economy and Central Banking," organized by CEPR/ESI and Suomen Pankki. Available at http://www.ecb.int/press/key/date/2001/html/sp010914.en.html (last accessed December 23, 2011).

Jansen, D., and J. De Haan. 2006. Look Who's Talking: ECB Communication During the First Years of EMU. *International Journal of Finance and Economics* 11 (3):219–228.

Jansen, D., and J. De Haan. 2007. The Importance of Being Vigilant: Has ECB Communication Influenced Euro Area Inflation Expectations? De Nederlandsche Bank Working Paper No. 148.

Laver, M., K. Benoît, and J. Garry. 2003. Extracting Policy Positions from Political Texts Using Words as Data. *American Political Science Review* 97 (2):311–331.

Lowe, W. 2008. Understanding Wordscores. *Political Analysis* 16(4): 356–371.

Rosa, C., and G. Verga. 2007. On the Consistency and Effectiveness of Central Bank Communication: Evidence from the ECB. *European Journal of Political Economy* 23 (1):146–175.

Sturm, J.-E., and J. De Haan. 2011. Does Central Bank Communication Really Lead to Better Forecasts of Policy Decisions? New Evidence Based on a Taylor Rule Model for the ECB. *Weltwirtschaftliches Archiv/Review of World Economy* 147(1): 41–58.

Ullrich, K. 2008. Inflation Expectations of Experts and ECB Communication. *North American Journal of Economics and Finance* 19 (1):93–108.

10 Are You Clear Now? The ECB's Written Communication on Monetary Policy

Aleš Bulíř, Martin Čihák, and Kateřina Šmídková

10.1 Introduction

This paper presents a novel approach to measuring the clarity of monetary policy messages, using the European Central Bank (ECB) as an example. The dramatic increase in monetary policy communication in the past two decades or so has been justified by benefits of policy transparency (Geraats 2002; Čihák 2007; Geraats, Giavazzi, and Wyplosz 2008). Most of the empirical literature on central bank communication has focused either on quantitative measures of monetary policy transparency (such as the volume of information provided) or on short-term effects of central bank announcements (for instance, on market prices and spreads), with much less attention paid to the overall clarity of the communication. In practice, however, voluminous and frequent disclosures are not necessarily a good thing. They can be of little use or even damaging if they have the potential to confuse the intended recipients.

The core contribution of the paper is to emphasize clarity as a crucial dimension of central banks' communication, and to illustrate the concept of communication clarity using the example of one of the world's premier central banks, the ECB. Clear communication ensures that the public understands monetary policy decisions, even if the direction of the policy rate adjustment contradicts the expected direction of the adjustment implied by a policy rule. For example, a central bank needs to communicate its reason for a policy rate cut when inflation is above the target. A failure to communicate reasons for departures from policy rules will ultimately damage credibility of the central bank. An additional contribution is that we extend the analysis of ECB communication beyond the previously researched press releases, to cover the more analytical *Monthly Bulletin*.

The ECB's monetary policy has been subject to considerable scrutiny, and "ECB watching" has become an industry in itself.[1] The ECB sees communication as an important part of its toolkit (European Central Bank 2004), providing fertile ground for empirical analysis (e.g., De Haan 2008; Winkler 2000). While the ECB discloses a considerable volume of information, several authors (e.g., European Commission 2008; Geraats, Giavazzi, and Wyplosz 2008; Geraats 2010) have suggested that the ECB has been falling behind state-of-the-art transparency, and that this explains at least partly why, during the ECB's first decade, euro area inflation was above the ECB's own criterion of "below but close to 2% over the medium term." These authors therefore call on the ECB to communicate better. What has been missing so far in this stream of literature is a rigorous measurement of the degree of clarity, based on content analysis of the ECB's written communication.

To provide such a rigorous analysis of clarity of monetary policy communication, we build on previous authors, in particular Bernanke and Woodford (1997) and Svensson (1997), in assuming that inflation projections and the monetary policy (inflation) target are the main explanatory variables of policy interest rates. To this end, we use the methodology introduced by Guthrie and Wright (2000), Šmídková and Bulíř (2007), and Bulíř et al. (2008) that analyzes the various measures of risks attached to the central inflation projection (the projection risk) that the public can derive from central bank communication. The projection risk measure provides additional information to the public, improving the understanding of monetary policy decisions.[2]

The information on the projection risk is necessary when the monetary policy decisions are complex and a policy rule fails to fully explain the moves in the policy rate. The public can understand monetary policy if the central bank's key policy documents send a coordinated message identifying the projection risk that explains why the chosen interest rate path deviates from that identified by the policy rule. In such a case, we would call monetary policy communication *clear*. In the opposite case, when the messages are uncoordinated, we would call monetary policy communication *confusing*. If monetary policy communication is confusing, it hampers transparency, even if large amounts of information are being disclosed.

To adequately analyze monetary policy in the context of the ECB, we take into account the special features of the ECB's monetary policy regime. In particular, an important feature of the regime is that it relies on a so-called two-pillar approach to monetary policy setting: the first ("economic analysis") pillar monitors a range of data and uses various models to produce short- to medium-term inflation projections for the euro area; the second ("monetary") pillar pays attention to monetary developments, which are assumed to play a role in determining medium- to long-term inflation (European Central Bank 2000, 2004).

One way to extract projection risk measures from the key documents is to count words typically associated with upward or downward projection risk (Heinemann and Ullrich 2007; Rosa and Verga 2007). Our approach incorporates this but goes further by encompassing additional resources: we analyze all verbal assessments of inflation factors (both in ECB press releases and *Monthly Bulletin*), including those coming from the second, monetary pillar. We also analyze the explicitly mentioned overall projection risk and transform these assessments into numerical representation of the inflation projection risk. Clear policy communication is achieved when the various communication tools (the inflation projections, monetary policy target, and verbal assessments contained in the key documents) are consistent with the policy rate changes.

Our main finding is that during 1999–2007,[3] the ECB's communication was clear in about 90% of cases and that the clarity has improved over time.[4] The 90% clarity is comparable with that of other industrial-country central banks and better than in emerging-country central banks for which an assessment using the same methodology was carried out (Šmídková and Bulíř 2007; Bulíř et al. 2008). Our analysis suggests that some of the additional information contained in the ECB's *Monthly Bulletin* improves clarity as compared to the press releases. In particular the *Bulletin*'s explicit description of the projection risk helps to improve clarity. On the other hand, the *Bulletin*'s discussion of monetary developments seems to reduce clarity. In this regard, the ECB's communication policy has been appropriately putting an increased emphasis on the explicit description of the projection risk and a decreased emphasis on the monetary pillar, improving the understanding of monetary policy decisions.

In what follows, section 10.2 provides a short overview of the literature, section 10.3 explains the methodology and data, section 10.4 presents the results, and section 10.5 concludes.

10.2   Literature on Monetary Policy Communication

The impetus for increased central bank communication is that "transparency is not only an obligation for a public entity, but also a real benefit to the institution and its policies" (Issing 2005), and that transparent central banks tend to achieve lower inflation (Geraats 2009). However, simply providing a greater volume of information is not always helpful, because much of the information communicated by central banks is either noisy or imperfect (Morris and Shin 2002; Woodford 2005), and the value of communicating detailed yet imperfect information is ambiguous (Dale, Orphanides, and Österholm 2008). Conveying a "more certain" information may improve the public's understanding of monetary policy to the extent that clear communication crowds out noise generated by imperfect information.

There is a substantial body of empirical literature on the *quantity and timeliness* of the ECB's communication (see Blinder et al. 2008 for a survey). The ECB staff evaluations of the ECB's monetary policy strategy indicated that communication was "an area where the institutional and multilingual context of the euro area poses particular challenges," and noted that one of the main purposes was to address "certain misunderstandings that had emerged in [the ECB's] communication with the public" (European Central Bank 2003). A subsequent review of the ECB's communications to the financial markets found a high degree of predictability for its monetary policy decisions, comparable with other major central banks (European Central Bank 2006). Geraats, Giavazzi, and Wyplosz (2008) criticized the ECB, however, for several communication "sins," such as failure to explain policy further ahead, inconsistent communication of uncertainty, and occasional policy decisions that could not be reconciled with real-time evidence. In particular, these authors claim that the ECB failed to explain convincingly why inflation during the 1999–2007 period was on average above the ECB's own criterion of "below but close to 2% over the medium term."

In contrast to the literature on quantity and timeliness of communication, the literature on *quality* of central bank communication is still only at a nascent stage. Several studies tried to approach the issue indirectly by asking whether the central bank's communication helps in predicting future monetary policy moves. In particular, Brand, Buncic, and Turunen (2006) have found that the ECB's communication results in significant changes in the euro area money market yield curve, that is, market expectations of future monetary policy, and that these changes affect medium- to long-term rates. Jansen and De Haan (2007) have found some evidence of a negative relationship between the ECB's communication of risks to price stability (measured by the use of the keyword "vigilance") and changes in euro area inflation. Rosa and Verga (2007) focused on the ECB president's press conferences, finding that the public generally understands and believes the ECB's signals. European Central Bank (2007) cited a trend toward lower market volatility on the short-term money market as an indication that the ECB's communication has improved over time. Jansen and De Haan (2009) studied the link between the ECB's communication and predictions of its interest rate decisions, finding that communication-based models of policy rate changes do not outperform models based on macroeconomic data. However, Sturm and De Haan (2011) reversed that result by finding that the ECB president's press conference introductory statement adds information that helps predict the next policy decision.

The focus of the ECB's communication is still evolving as the ECB transitions from an institution stressing the information content of monetary aggregates to one that focuses on inflation projections. Gerlach (2007) has concluded that the ECB's Governing Council reacts to M3 growth, but that the impact of monetary developments is non-linear. Berger, De Haan, and Sturm (2006) concluded that the ECB has paid diminishing attention to monetary analysis and that its statements have become more correlated with the inflation projection analyses. Lamla and Rupprecht (2006) argued—based on the analysis of high-frequency interest rate data—that financial markets have stopped paying attention to Governing Council communication regarding the monetary pillar altogether and react either to price news or economic analyses. Conrad and Lamla (2007) showed that, based on the high-frequency response of the euro-US dollar exchange rate, the ECB's information on price developments is considered news by foreign exchange market participants, but that the ECB's assessments of monetary developments are not. Lamla and Sturm (in this volume) attempted to infer how much weight the public places on the interest rate signal relative to the communication signal (newspapers coded by Mediatenor) when it comes to predicting the next interest rate decision of the ECB. While both instruments were found to be important tools to guide market expectations, the interest rate signal seemed to outperform the communication signal. However, the impact of the interest rate signal is not necessarily bigger than that of the communication signal. Coffinet and Gouteron (2007) reported that long-term market rates react to M3 growth surprises but short-term rates do not. Still, even if the short-term impact of monetary aggregates is limited, it may affect medium-term inflation (Roffia and Zaghini 2007; Hofmann 2008).

A more direct approach to assessing the quality of central bank communication has been pioneered by Fracasso, Genberg, and Wyplosz (2003), who proposed the following three criteria for good central bank communication: clarity, consistency, and coverage of key issues (policy objectives, decision making, analytical framework, input data, presentation of forecasts, evaluation of past forecasts and policies). The authors examined 19 inflation-targeting central banks other than the ECB, finding a positive link between report quality and policy predictability. Closely aligned with this approach are the papers by Šmídková and Bulíř (2007) and Bulíř et al. (2008) that assess clarity of monetary policy communication by analyzing numerical measures of projection risk that the public can obtain from various sources of central bank communication.

10.3 Methodology and Data

10.3.1 Communicating Clearly

Clear communication requires that the various communication tools send signals that are mutually consistent, and our methodology measures such consistency. For example, the public could become confused if (i) the central bank did not change the policy rate, while (ii) presenting an official inflation projection that is (substantially) below the central bank's target, and (iii) emphasizing downward inflation projection risk in its press release. This confusion could be averted if the central bank emphasized in its press release either pro-inflation factors or projection risks, because these would explain why the policymakers decided to deviate from the policy rule. In reality, the complicating factor is that actual inflation deviates from its projection because of unforeseen shocks that hit the economy in the interim. The following three situations can then occur with regard to clarity of monetary policy communication:

1. *Clarity, no shocks.* The central bank consistently communicates its policy response, inflation projection, and projection risk. No significant shocks occur afterward. This is the most favorable situation: the public

understands well the policy response and forms inflation expectations accordingly, anticipating correctly the eventual inflation outturn.

2. *Clarity under shocks.* The central bank provides the same consistent communication as in the first case; however, post-projection, unanticipated shock(s) push inflation above or below the projection. These shocks may even push inflation in the opposite direction to that indicated in the projection risk communication. This is a less favorable situation, because the public is surprised by the inflation outturn. However, owing to the central bank's consistent communication, the public is still able to form meaningful inflation expectations, and it can understand that inflation deviated from the projection because of some unanticipated, temporary shocks.

3. *Confusion.* The central bank's inflation projection and policy rate point in different directions, while the policy documents send an inconsistent message vis-à-vis the projection risk. This is the least favorable outturn, because the public may become confused and fail to form meaningful inflation expectations.

10.3.2 Measuring Clarity: Four-Step Methodology

Based on this general approach, we analyze the clarity of the ECB's communication. Specifically, we compare the ECB's inflation projections, monetary policy (inflation) target, policy rate changes, and projection risk, all readily available variables. The ECB regularly publishes inflation projections,[5] and its monetary policy target is well known. It regularly communicates the projection risk via its two key policy documents, the press release and *Monthly Bulletin*. We use these two publications to construct the projection risk variable encompassing verbally described inflation factors, monetary developments, and the ECB's assessment of the inflation projection risk.

First step: the inflation projection and target When assessing communication clarity, it is reasonable to assume that the public will try to understand monetary policy with as little effort as possible. The ECB let it be known that it would follow a forward-looking strategy of monitoring inflation, output gap, and so on (Gerlach and Smets 1999), and therefore we expect the public to measure the ECB's actions against a policy rule approximating such a strategy (King 2005).[6] Unfortunately, variables such as the output gap are not readily available (Orphanides 2001), and the public is likely to rely on a simpler rule, such as that in which the policymaker reacts only to the inflation projection deviating from the target, both of which are real-time, readily available variables (Batini and Haldane 1999). We therefore assume that, initially at least, the public relies on the three main economic variables that are readily observable: the inflation target, the inflation projection, and the policy rate. If the values of these variables suggest that the ECB is following a policy rule, the public would form its inflation expectations using the ECB's inflation projection as follows:

$$i_t = \gamma i_{t-1} + (1 - \gamma)\left[\delta\left(\pi_{t+j}^{F,ECB} - \pi^*\right) + i^n\right],$$ (10.1)

where i_t is the policy instrument (the short-term nominal interest rate); $\pi_{t+j}^{F,ECB}$ denotes the ECB's inflation projection published at time t (we use a projection for 12 months ahead); π^* is the publicly announced price stability target of about 2% ("below but close to 2% over the medium term");[7] and i^n is a policy-neutral interest rate, equal to the sum of an equilibrium real interest rate and the policy target. The equilibrium real rate is assumed to be 2%, a typical number used in the literature on the euro area (Bernhardsen 2005; European Commission 2008).

In our framework, the public tries to extract the policy rate-smoothing and inflation aversion coefficients (γ and δ, respectively) from ECB decisions. In principle, one can try estimating the policy rule using a regression based on past data. Indeed, a number of papers have tried to come up with regression estimates of policy rules. However, using such estimates to define γ and δ is problematic for a number of reasons (for a critical review of the literature on empirical policy rules, see for instance Carare and Tchaidze 2005). First, regression-based estimates for the ECB have found implausibly strong policy rate smoothing, implying extremely gradual reaction to inflation news. It has been shown, however, that policy rules with interest rate smoothing reflect persistence in inflation factors rather than policymakers' slow reaction to inflation shocks (Rudebusch 2006; Carare and Tchaidze 2005). Second, the regression estimates are almost exclusively done for backward-looking rules, even though central banks base their policy decisions on forward-looking ones. Third, the estimates typically include variables such as the output gap or exchange rate gap, which are pieces of information that the public does not possess, making it difficult to relate this to the observed policy decisions. Moreover, on a practical level, coming up with robust estimates of policy rules is rather difficult due to the limited number of observed changes in the policy

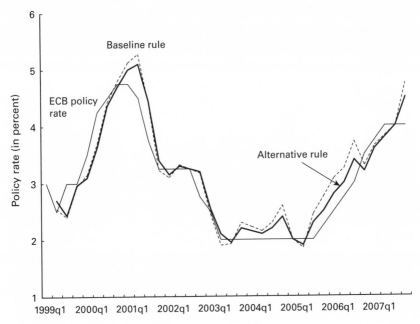

Figure 10.1
Actual ECB policy rate and fitted rates using two rules. The calibration of the baseline rule assumes $\gamma = 0.7$ and $\delta = 5$, $\pi^* = 2.0$; the calibration of the alternative rule assumes $\gamma = 0.8$. Source: ECB; authors' calculations.

rate and the frequency of inflation projection changes during the sample period.

For all these reasons, our approach is based on calibrating the rule and examining how results change if benchmark calibration is replaced by a range of alternative calibrations. After considering the available evidence, we set $\gamma = 0.7$ and $\delta = 5.0$ in the benchmark calibration of the rule. The benchmark values of γ and δ reflect the ECB's interest rate setting reasonably well (figure 10.1). While the smoothing parameter is close to what most empirical studies have found, the inflation aversion coefficient is higher, capturing the effect of the omitted output gap. The baseline calibration is such as to jointly minimize the statistical bias and mean square forecast error of the policy rate—lower values of δ quickly increase the statistical bias.

Second step: an implied projection update   If the policy rate decision corresponds to that implied by rule (10.1), the public will not examine any additional information sources. If the policy rate decision contradicts the one suggested by the policy rule, the public will look for clarification. In other words, a rule-contradicting rate change implies a different inflation projection. The rule-based inflation projection, $\pi_{t+j}^{F,\text{RULE}}$, can be obtained by rearranging (10.1):

$$\pi_{t+j}^{F,\text{RULE}} = \frac{\Delta i_t}{(1-\gamma)\delta} + \frac{i_{t-1} - i^n}{\delta} + \pi^*, \tag{10.2}$$

where $\pi_{t+j}^{F,\text{RULE}}$ measures what the public thinks inflation will be given the rule and the policy rate change effected by the ECB, Δi_t. The need for clarification is proportional to the difference between the above rule-based inflation projection and the official ECB inflation projection, $\pi_{t+j}^{F,\text{ECB}}$. We call this difference the *implied projection update*:

$$\pi_{t+j}^{F,\text{RULE}} - \pi_{t+j}^{F,\text{ECB}} = \frac{\Delta i_t}{(1-\gamma)\delta} + \frac{i_{t-1} - i^n}{\delta} - \left(\pi_{t+j}^{F,\text{ECB}} - \pi^* \right). \tag{10.3}$$

The public knows, of course, that the rule is an approximation of policymaking and is concerned only about large implied projection updates that indicate that the policymakers have revised the original inflation projection with some additional information.

When to call the implied projection update "substantial"? One approach is to consider the ex-ante admitted uncertainty of monetary policy decision making, and assume that the public will perceive a change in projections as substantial if it exceeds this previously communicated uncertainty (Šmídková 2005). The ECB's publicly communicated uncertainty of inflation projections in the one-year projection horizon is ±0.5 percentage points,[8] so in principle it could be argued that the public could focus on deviations larger than ±0.5 percentage points and ignore those that are below this threshold. At the same time, the typical ECB policy rate change in the period under observation was 25 basis points. According to (10.3), a 0.25-percentage-point change in policy interest rates is associated with roughly 0.17 percentage points in terms of the implied projection update (using the benchmark values for the γ and δ parameters). It could be argued that if the implied projection update is comparable with the typical ECB rate change of 0.25 percentage points, the public would choose to examine the related communication.[9] On balance, in the benchmark calibration, we assume that the public would pay attention to implied projection updates that exceed (in absolute terms) 0.25 percentage points, and would ignore

Table 10.1
Key Parameters: Benchmark Calibration and Robustness Analysis

	Policy rule parameters		When are the implied projection updates "substantial"?	
	Smoothing (γ)	Inflation aversion (δ)	Shocks	Deviations from the target
Benchmark calibration	0.7	5.0	0.25	0.25
Higher inflation aversion	0.7	7.0	0.25	0.25
Higher rate smoothing	0.8	5.0	0.25	0.25
Lower sensitivity to shocks	0.7	5.0	0.50	0.25
Less emphasis on target	0.7	5.0	0.25	0.50

those below this threshold. Also in the benchmark calibration, the ECB is assumed to react only to inflation projections higher or lower than the target by 0.25 percentage points.

To assess the robustness of our calculations, we examine the results not only for the baseline calibration but also for several alternative parameterizations of the rule (table 10.1). These include a higher inflation aversion parameter ($\delta = 7.0$ instead of 5.0), a higher policy rate smoothing parameter ($\gamma = 0.8$ instead of 0.7), lower sensitivity to shocks (i.e., the public considers the implied projection update "substantial" only if it exceeds 0.50 percentage points instead of 0.25 percentage points), and lower emphasis on the inflation target (the ECB is assumed to react only to inflation projections deviating from the target by 0.50 percentage points instead of by 0.25 percentage points). Given the asymmetric and partly unspecified nature of the ECB's inflation target ("inflation below but close to 2%"), we also examine how the results would change if the "true" inflation target were 1.8% rather than 2.0%. Finally, as an additional robustness test, we examine how the results change if we replace the ECB's inflation forecast by corresponding (12-months-ahead) market expectations.

Third step: reading what the ECB says about the inflation projection risk   Substantial implied projection updates are to be explained verbally in monetary policy documents as descriptions of the projection risk (Bernanke and Woodford 1997). To this end, we constructed a numerical approximation of the ECB's projection risk, ρ_t, from the verbal assessments of the inflation factors, monetary developments, and projection risk, relying on two key policy documents: the introductory statement at the ECB's monthly press conference and the ECB's *Monthly Bulletin*.[10] Overall, we used 108 press releases and *Bulletins* from January 1999 to December 2007.

The introductory statement—known as "the principal vehicle of the ECB's communication" (European Central Bank 2007)—conveys the collective monetary policy decision of the ECB's Governing Council, and reaches out to a wide audience through the media. The *Monthly Bulletin*—published monthly one week after the first meeting of the Governing Council—provides a more comprehensive explanation and analysis than the press releases, especially with respect to supply-side developments.

While the verbal assessments from the press releases have been used in previous studies (Rosa and Verga 2007; Heinemann and Ullrich 2007), the *Bulletin* has been mostly ignored. To our best knowledge, the only other paper analyzing the *Bulletin* is Gerlach (2007), who scrutinized the ECB's views on economic activity, realized inflation, and M3 growth on inflation.

Classifying the inflation factors in the ECB documents is labor-intensive, requiring that each be cataloged into supply, demand, or external environment factors (corresponding to the "economic analysis" pillar), and then classified as pushing the rate of inflation either higher (+1), lower (–1), or neither (0); see figure 10.2 for summary indicators. We gave each inflation factor an equal weight, because neither document provides information on the factors' quantitative importance, and because we wanted to avoid subjective judgments of the type made by Rosa and Verga (2007). Monthly observations were then aggregated to obtain the desired indexlike measure of the projection risk. Two observations are worth noting. The balance of the factors has been clearly positive for most of the sample period, except for 2001–2003 (figure 10.2), indicating a pro-inflation projection risk. The inflation factors—with the exception of aggregate supply factors—have been serially correlated (table 10.2).

Second, the interpretation of the monetary pillar is less straightforward. Although the short-run implications of M3 growth should not be taken mechanically, ECB documents restated the usefulness of this indicator in understanding ECB's monetary policy (European Central Bank 2003, 2004). Until the 2003 review of the ECB monetary policy framework (European Central Bank 2003) it was understood that the rate of growth of M3 above/below the reference rate of 4.5% annually

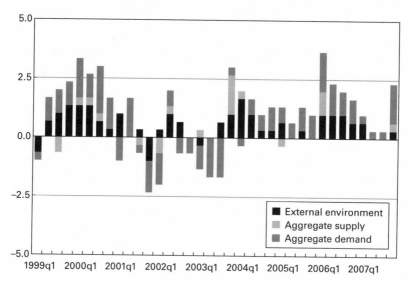

Figure 10.2
ECB *Monthly Bulletins*: inflation factors. The height of each bar indicates quarterly frequency of demand, supply, or external factors, as identified in the *Monthly Bulletin*, that were expected to affect future inflation. Source: European Central Bank; authors' calculations.

Table 10.2
Components of the Projection Risk and Their Serial Correlation

Components	One lag	Two lags
Aggregate demand	0.41	0.05
Aggregate supply	0.06	−0.02
External environment	0.49	0.42
All factors combined	0.49	0.21
Explicit projection risk	0.89	0.77

Source: European Central Bank; authors' calculations.

implies loose/tight monetary conditions in the medium to long run.[11] Starting with that of May 2003, the *Bulletins* include a verbal statement of the following sort: "the monetary analysis confirms the prevailing upside risks to price stability at medium to longer horizons." However, these statements have remained highly correlated with the M3 growth indicator, and we therefore continue to use the M3 growth relative to the reference rate.

Third, explicit verbal assessments of downward or upward projection risk are summarized in the *Bulletin*'s editorial, presumably encompassing both the economic and monetary pillars. A typical assessment reads: "the outlook for price developments remains . . . subject to upside risks." The correlation between the projection risk and inflation factors (the economic pillar) was high, between 0.5 and 0.8, breaking only during the low-inflation period of 2001–2003, when the ECB communication did not mention downward risks to the inflation projection, despite the economic pillar signaling strong deflationary pressures.

Our estimates of the projection risk, ρ_t, are comparable to the alternative estimates. Our summary index is highly correlated, at 0.77 and 0.82, respectively, with the KOF Monetary Policy Communicator published by the Swiss Federal Institute of Technology in Zurich and the Rosa-Verga index of ECB president announcements (table 10.3). These correlations also highlight the value added of the bulletins: the press releases, and therefore also the KOF and Rosa-Verga indexes, largely ignore the supply-side factors of inflation as they focus almost exclusively on demand factors.

Fourth step: does the projection risk explain the implied projection update? The public views monetary policy communication as clear if the projection risk, ρ_t, matches the inflation projection update $\left(\pi_{t+j}^{F,RULE} - \pi_{t+j}^{F,ECB} \right)$. For example, a positive inflation projection update is explained away by upward inflation factors or upward risks to the inflation projection, or both. If, however, the projection update and projection risk point in opposite directions, the ECB communication is not clear, no matter how much information is disclosed in the process. As a result, the public may get confused and not know which inflation projection is relevant for expectation formation.

Clarity in communication ensures that the public understands the actions of the ECB and that it can form its inflation expectations effectively; however, it does not guarantee that the ECB is going to fulfill

Table 10.3
Correlation of the Alternative Indexes with Our Indexes (Spearman's rank correlation coefficient; the corresponding *p*-level in parentheses)

	KOF MPC	RV	Press release	Aggregate demand	Aggregate supply
RV	0.76				
	(0.00)				
Press release	0.83	0.77			
	(0.00)	(0.00)			
Our summary index	0.77	0.82	0.76		
	(0.00)	(0.00)	(0.00)		
Of which	0.58	0.60	0.48		
Aggregate demand	(0.00)	(0.00)	(0.02)		
Aggregate supply	0.02	0.19	0.24	0.36	
	(0.92)	(0.36)	(0.26)	(0.09)	
External environment	0.61	0.72	0.60	0.36	0.23
	(0.00)	(0.00)	(0.00)	(0.09)	(0.28)

Sources: Authors' calculations; KOF MPC index was kindly provided by the KOF; Rosa and Verga (2007).
Notes: KOF is the Monetary Policy Communicator based on the ECB president's statements on risks to price stability made during the monthly press conferences; RV is the Rosa-Verga index of ECB president's announcements about future monetary policy moves. Press releases and the remaining entries are based on our coding of the ECB documents.

either the inflation target or the inflation projection. Other things being equal, inflation will differ from the projection by the cumulative shocks hitting the economy during the *j* projection periods:

$$\left(\pi_{t+j} = \pi_{t+j}^{F,\text{RULE}} + \sum_{t=1}^{j} \varepsilon_t \right). \tag{10.4}$$

10.3.3 Stylized Facts

To apply our methodology empirically, we use the publicly available harmonized consumer price index from the ECB and Eurostat. While the headline inflation frequently exceeded the 2% target, core inflation was subdued and inflation expectations remained stable (figure 10.3). The ECB inflation projections are constructed from the published mid-points of the projection range. The policy interest rate is the repo rate, measured at end of month.

The inputs for our methodology are summarized in figure 10.4. The public is assumed to use the ECB's 12-months-ahead inflation

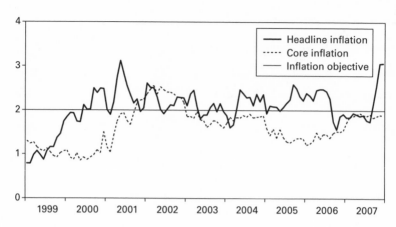

Figure 10.3
Euro area: inflation developments, 1999–2007. Core inflation excludes energy, food, alcohol, and tobacco. Sources: Eurostat, ECB; Haver Analytics.

projections (Chart I in figure 10.4) and policy rate changes (Chart II) to derive an implied projection update (Chart III). Positive values of the update indicate that the public's expectations of inflation—conditional on the policy rule—are above the official ECB projection, $\left(\pi_{t+j}^{F,\mathrm{RULE}} > \pi_{t+j}^{F,ECB}\right)$. If the deviation is sizable, say ±0.5, the public tries to match the projection update with corresponding inflation factors (Chart IV).

10.4   Results

We present our results in several steps, gradually adding more components to the estimate of the projection risk. We start with the press release; add inflation factors contained in the *Monthly Bulletin*, then the explicit verbal description of projection risk; and finally the monetary pillar. To assess the robustness of our findings, we present the results of each of these steps for different calibrations as defined in table 10.1. The main results ("benchmark calibration") and the robustness checks are summarized in figures 10.5–7.

10.4.1   Press Statements
Assuming that the public forms a view on the ECB's policy based on the press releases only and under the benchmark calibration, the ECB communication is found clear in 80% of all cases and potentially confusing in the remaining 20%. In the four alternative calibrations, the frequency of clear communication varies from 70% to 95%, with

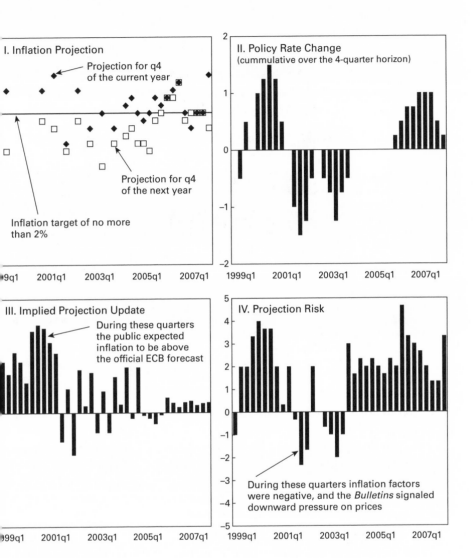

Figure 10.4
The ECB: inflation projection, the implied projection update, and projection risk. The ECB's projections were initially published annually, semiannually from 2001, and quarterly from 2004q3. Source: European Central Bank; authors' calculations.

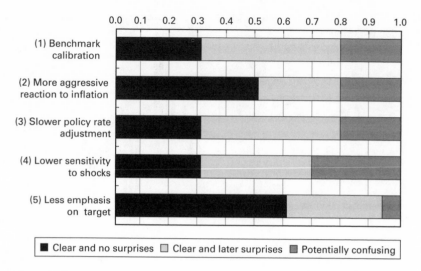

Figure 10.5
The clarity of communication with press releases only. (In figures 10.5 to 10.7, the black bars indicate the share of observations where the projection risk matched the implied projection update and the actual inflation was within ±0.25 percentage points; the white bars indicate the share of observations with a projection error of more than ±0.25 percentage points; the gray bars indicate the share of observations where the projection risk did not match the implied projection update. Source: authors' calculations.)

the frequency of potentially confusing cases varying from 5% to 30% (figure 10.5).

The ECB communication appears clearest when one puts less emphasis on the inflation target. This result holds for all calibrations (5) in figures 10.5 to 10.7. Narrowing down the sample period to after mid-2003 (that is, following the 2003 clarification of the communication framework), the share of potentially confusing communication declines to 5% in the benchmark specification and 0% to 5% in the alternative specifications. This result too holds across the whole exercise, i.e., the share of potentially confusing information declines for the post-2003 period if we look at the *Bulletin* and include the monetary pillar information. As an additional robustness test, we have examined how the results change if the ECB's inflation forecast is replaced by the corresponding (12-months-ahead) market expectations. The results were not materially different from those presented in figures 10.5 to 10.7, and are therefore not presented here separately (but are available upon request).

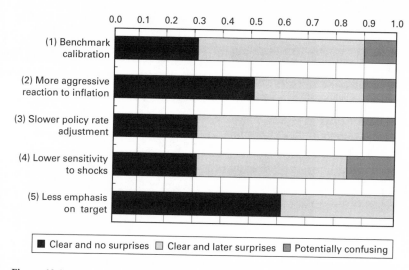

Figure 10.6
The clarity of communication with the *Bulletins*: inflation factors, but no projection risk description. Source: authors' calculations.

10.4.2 *Monthly Bulletins*

What if the public, in addition to the press releases, also extracts information about the inflation factors from the explicit description of the projection risk in the *Bulletin*? We find substantial information gains, and our analysis suggests that it is not the additional details about inflation factors by themselves but the combination of this additional information with the information on projection risk that improves the understanding of the ECB's monetary policy vis-à-vis the press releases. The results are summarized in figure 10.6.

We find that the *Bulletin*'s additional information about the inflation factors and the projection risk substantially improves communication clarity relative to a situation where the public only relies on the press releases. In the benchmark specification, the ECB's communication is clear in 90% of all cases and potentially confusing in 10% of cases. In the alternative specifications, the communication is clear in 85–100% of all cases. That is a clear and significant improvement over the results for press releases only. The results suggest that a big part of monetary policy ambiguity can be eliminated by saying explicitly "we don't know." By communicating explicitly its degree uncertainty about the future (its "projection risk"), the ECB can make the public understand and tolerate bigger departures from the rule than it would do otherwise.

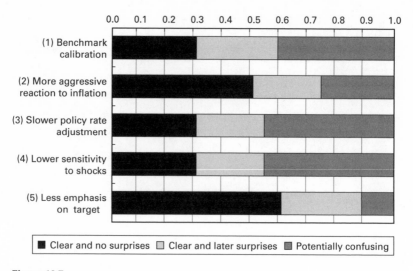

Figure 10.7
The clarity of communication with the *Bulletins*: adding the monetary pillar. Source: authors' calculations.

10.4.3 *Monthly Bulletins*: Adding the Monetary Pillar

Lastly, what if the public also takes into account the *Bulletin*'s information on the monetary pillar? We find that adding information on the monetary pillar does little to improve the understanding of the ECB's policymaking, and may in fact confuse the public (figure 10.7). In the benchmark calibration, only 60% of communication can be characterized as clear, while 40% has potential for confusion, a significantly worse outcome than in the benchmark calibrations presented in figures 10.5 and 10.6. Also, the results for most of the robustness calibrations are worse than those without the monetary pillar, with the communication being clear in only 55–90% of cases and potentially confusing in 10–45% of cases, depending on the specification.

Examples of the periods of potentially confusing communication include the period following the 2001q3 above-target projection, $\left(\pi_{t+j}^{F,ECB} - \pi^* = 0.3\right)$, when the policy rate was lowered by 1 percentage point during the next 12 months, while our indicator of the projection risk was close to zero (−0.33). Thus, the verbal assessments failed to explain the case for the rate cut. Another example occurred in 2004q3, when the ECB kept the rate unchanged despite the negative implied projection update and the verbal assessments that were strongly biased toward pro-inflation factors.

10.5   Conclusions

The ECB's press releases and *Monthly Bulletins* help in understanding its monetary policy. Based on our analysis of the ECB's inflation projections, policy target, and verbal descriptions of the inflation factors and projection risk, and the monetary pillar, we conclude that the ECB's written communication has been fairly clear during 1999–2007, and instances of potential confusion have been rare and unlikely to damage the credibility of the ECB's communication. The overall clarity is comparable with that of other industrial-country central banks for which similar analysis has been carried out, and better than clarity in emerging-country central banks.

An important corollary of our findings is that the ECB's flagship publication, the *Monthly Bulletin*, contains some additional information that helps improve clarity compared to ECB's press releases. In particular, the assessment of the projection risk improves clarity measurably. In contrast, however, the *Bulletin*'s discussion of monetary developments seems to somewhat reduce communication clarity and increase the risk of confusion relative to the press releases.

The policy implication of our paper is that although ECB's overall communication is mostly clear, some scope remains for improvement. Additional emphasis on explicit description of the projection risk in the press releases and the *Bulletins* could improve understanding, and so could less emphasis on the monetary pillar. More generally, the paper illustrates that while the provision of greater volumes of information tends to be useful for monetary policy purposes, there is a risk that in some cases the additional information could lead to inconsistent messages and to confusion among the public about the direction of monetary policy.

Notes

The views presented in this paper are those of the authors and do not necessarily represent those of the IMF or the CNB. Authors' e-mail addresses: abulir@imf.org; mcihak@imf.org; katerina.smidkova@cnb.cz.

1. The annual "ECB Watchers' Conference" organized by the Center for Financial Studies in Frankfurt brings together academics, analysts, and policymakers to discuss euro area monetary policy (to https://www.ifk-cfs.de/).

2. An alternative, narrower approach to approximating clarity is to focus on readability of the documents. For example, in a related piece of research, Bulíř, Čihák, and Jansen (2013) examine readability of the ECB's (and six other central banks') written

communication, using the Flesch-Kincaid grade level as a proxy for readability. An important advantage of readability proxies such as the above is that they are easy to calculate. The drawback is that they are based purely on the complexity of words and sentences in the written text, not on what the report says on the relevant issues such as inflation outlook, i.e., not on its contents.

3. To keep the analysis contained, we focus on the period preceding the global financial crisis. During the crisis, the core part of the ECB's policy framework remained unchanged but important enhancements were made, placing an increased premium on clear communication (e.g., to distinguish liquidity management and monetary policy stance). For an analysis of ECB policies in the crisis, see Čihák, Harjes, and Stavrev (2009).

4. In a related paper, Jansen and De Haan (in this volume) found that the ECB's communication has been both internally consistent and flexible.

5. The ECB's inflation projections are based on some important assumptions. In particular, they are conditional on bilateral exchange rates remaining unchanged, fiscal policy following the national budget plans, and future interest rates following the existing market expectations (earlier ECB forecasts assumed constant policy rates going forward). For further information, see http://www.ecb.int/mopo/strategy/html/index.en.html.

6. De Grauwe (in this volume) argues that agents have a limited understanding of the underlying model of the economy and therefore use simple rules to forecast its evolution.

7. To examine the robustness of the results with respect to the (unspecified) exact value of the target, we have carried out the calculations not only for $\pi^* = 2.0\%$ but also for $\pi^* = 1.8$, the average of the ECB's 2-years-ahead inflation projections, with largely similar results.

8. For example, the ECB's December 2007 *Monthly Bulletin* said that "staff projections foresee annual inflation . . . to rise between 2.0% and 3.0% in 2008," implying a ±0.5-percentage-point confidence interval.

9. Financial analysts and ECB watchers of course tend to dissect even smaller deviations. Berger, Ehrmann, and Fratzscher (2006) found that for a sample of professional "ECB watchers," the average forecasting error in terms of policy rates varied from 0.02 percentage points to 0.10 percentage points.

10. We exclude from our analysis interviews (as well as Q&A sessions) and speeches by the members of the Governing Council. Such exclusion may bias our results toward higher clarity, since previous research has suggested that such releases lower the market's ability to anticipate the future path of interest rates (Ehrmann and Fratzscher 2005).

11. From January 1999 to April 2003 the actual M3 rate of growth always exceeded the reference rate.

References

Batini, N., and A. Haldane. 1999. Forward-Looking Rules for Monetary Policy. In *Monetary Policy Rules*, ed. J. B. Taylor. Chicago: University of Chicago Press.

Berger, H., J. De Haan, and J.-E. Sturm. 2006. Does Money Matter in the ECB Strategy? New Evidence Based on ECB Communication. CESifo Working Paper No. 1652.

Berger, H., M. Ehrmann, and M. Fratzscher. 2006. Forecasting ECB Monetary Policy: Accuracy Is (Still) a Matter of Geography. IMF Working Paper No. 06/41.

Bernanke, B., and M. Woodford. 1997. Inflation Forecasts and Monetary Policy. *Journal of Money, Credit and Banking* 29:653–684.

Bernhardsen, T. 2005. The Neutral Interest Rate. Norges Bank staff memo, 2005/1.

Blinder, A., M. Ehrmann, M. Fratzscher, J. De Haan, and D.-J. Jansen. 2008. Central Bank Communication and Monetary Policy: A Survey of Theory and Evidence. *Journal of Economic Literature* 46:910–945.

Brand, C., D. Buncic, and J. Turunen. 2006. The Impact of ECB Monetary Policy Decisions and Communication on the Yield Curve. ECB Working Paper No. 657.

Bulíř, A., M. Čihák, and D.-J. Jansen. 2013. What Drives Clarity of Central Bank Communication about Inflation? *Open Economies Review* 24:125–145.

Bulíř, A., K. Šmídková, V. Kotlán, and D. Navrátil. 2008. Inflation Targeting and Communication: It Pays Off to Read Inflation Reports. IMF Working Paper No. 08/234.

Carare, A., and R. Tchaidze. 2005. The Use and Abuse of Taylor Rules: How Precisely Can We Estimate Them? IMF Working Paper No. 05/148.

Čihák, M. 2007. The Art and Science of Monetary Policy Communication. *Czech Journal of Economics and Finance* 57:490–498.

Čihák, M., T. Harjes, and E. Stavrev. 2009. Euro Area Monetary Policy in Unchartered Waters. IMF Working Paper No. 09/185.

Coffinet, J., and S. Gouteron. 2007. Euro Area Market Reactions to the Monetary Policy Developments Press Release. ECB Working Paper No. 792.

Conrad, C., and M. Lamla. 2007. The High-Frequency Response of the EU-US Dollar Exchange Rate to ECB Monetary Policy Announcements. KOF Swiss Economic Institute ETH Zurich Working Paper, 07-174.

Dale, S., A. Orphanides, and P. Österholm. 2008. Imperfect Central Bank Communication— Information versus Distraction. IMF Working Paper No. 08/60.

De Haan, J. 2008. The Effect of ECB Communication on Interest Rates: An Assessment. *Review of International Organizations* 3:375–398.

Ehrmann, M., and M. Fratzscher. 2005. How Should Central Banks Communicate? ECB Working Paper No. 557.

European Central Bank. 2000. The Two Pillars of the ECB's Monetary Policy Strategy. *ECB Monthly Bulletin*, November.

European Central Bank. 2003. The Outcome of the ECB's Evaluation of Its Monetary Policy Strategy. *ECB Monthly Bulletin*, June.

European Central Bank. 2004. *The Monetary Policy of the ECB*. Frankfurt: ECB.

European Central Bank. 2006. The Predictability of the ECB's Monetary Policy. *ECB Monthly Bulletin*, January.

European Central Bank. 2007. Communicating Monetary Policy to Financial Markets. *ECB Monthly Bulletin*, April.

European Commission. 2008. *EMU@10: Successes and Challenges after 10 Years of Economic and Monetary Union.* Luxembourg: Office for Official Publications of the European Communities.

Fracasso, A., H. Genberg, and C. Wyplosz. 2003. *How Do Central Banks Write?* Geneva: Center for Economic Policy Research.

Geraats, P. 2002. Central Bank Transparency. *Economic Journal* 112:F532–F565.

Geraats, P. 2009. Trends in Monetary Policy Transparency. CESifo Working Paper No. 2584.

Geraats, P. 2010. ECB Credibility and Transparency. In *The Euro: The First Decade*, ed. Marco Buti et al. Cambridge: Cambridge University Press.

Geraats, P., F. Giavazzi, and C. Wyplosz. 2008. *Transparency and Governance.* London: Centre for Economic Policy Research.

Gerlach, S. 2007. Interest Rate Setting by the ECB, 1999–2006: Words and Deeds. *International Journal of Central Banking* 3:1–45.

Gerlach, S., and F. Smets. 1999. Output Gaps and Monetary Policy in the EMU Area. *European Economic Review* 43:801–812.

Guthrie, G., and J. Wright. 2000. Open Mouth Operations. *Journal of Monetary Economics* 46:489–516.

Heinemann, F., and L. Ullrich. 2007. Does It Pay to Watch Central Bankers Lips? The Information Content of ECB Wording. *Swiss Journal of Economics* 143:155–185.

Hofmann, B. 2008. Do Monetary Indicators Lead Euro Area Inflation? ECB Working Paper No. 867.

Issing, O. 2005. Communication, Transparency, Accountability: Monetary Policy in the Twenty-First Century. *Federal Reserve Bank of St. Louis Review* 87:65–83.

Jansen, D.-J., and J. De Haan. 2007. The Importance of Being Vigilant: Has ECB Communication Influenced Euro Area Inflation Expectations? CESifo Working Paper No. 2134.

Jansen, D.-J., and J. De Haan. 2009. Has ECB Communication Been Helpful in Predicting Interest Rate Decisions? An Evaluation of the Early Years of the Economic and Monetary Union. *Applied Economics* 41:1995–2003.

King, M. 2005. Monetary Policy: Practice ahead of Theory. Mais Lecture delivered at the Cass Business School, City University, London, May 17.

Lamla, M., and S. Rupprecht. 2006. The Impact of ECB Communication on Financial Market Expectations. ETH Zurich Working Paper, 06-135.

Morris, S., and H. Shin. 2002. Social Value of Public Information. *American Economic Review* 92:1521–1534.

Orphanides, A. 2001. Monetary Policy Rules Based on Real-Time Data. *American Economic Review* 91:964–985.

Roffia, B., and A. Zaghini. 2007. Excess Money Growth and Inflation Dynamics. ECB Working Paper No. 749.

Rosa, C., and G. Verga. 2007. On the Consistency and Effectiveness of Central Bank Communication: Evidence from the ECB. *European Journal of Political Economy* 23:146–175.

Rudebusch, G. 2006. Monetary Policy Inertia: Fact or Fiction? *International Journal of Central Banking* 2:85–136.

Šmídková, K. 2005. How Inflation Targeters (Can) Deal with Uncertainty. *Czech Journal of Economics and Finance* 55:316–332.

Šmídková, K., and A. Bulíř. 2007. Striving to Be "Clearly Open" and "Crystal Clear": Monetary Policy Communication of the CNB. *Czech Journal of Economics and Finance* 57:540–557.

Sturm, J.-E., and J. De Haan. 2011. Does Central Bank Communication Really Lead to Better Forecasts of Policy Decisions? *Weltwirtschaftliches Archiv / Review of World Economics* 147 (1):41–58.

Svensson, L. 1997. Inflation Forecast Targeting: Implementing and Monitoring Inflation Targets. *European Economic Review* 41:1111–1146.

Winkler, B. 2000. Which Kind of Transparency? On the Need for Clarity in Monetary Policy-Making. ECB Working Paper No. 26.

Woodford, M. 2005. Central Bank Communication and Policy Effectiveness. NBER Working Paper No. 11898.

V The International Experience

11 Uncertainty and Monetary Policy

David Mayes and Alberto Montagnoli

11.1 Introduction

There has been growing interest in uncertainty in monetary policymaking, and in the communication of monetary policy. There are many sides to the problem, starting simply with the fact that the future is uncertain. Also central banks in particular (notably the ECB, the Bank of England, and the US Federal Reserve) have sponsored research into model uncertainty.[1] Attention has also been paid to the uncertainty faced by markets, to which central banks can contribute by erratic or unclear decision making. This has raised the importance of transparency on the part of the central bank (e.g., Eusepi 2005). The main conclusion in the literature is that central bank transparency renders "the optimal policy rule robust to expectational mistakes, even in the plausible case where the economic agents face other sources of uncertainty about the economic environment. On the other end, lack of transparency can lead to a welfare-reducing outcome where self-fulfilling expectations destabilize the economic system" (Eusepi 2005, p. 22). Similarly Mishkin (2004) argues that inflation targeting in particular is made more effective by transparency. Thus the message is that, whatever the sources of uncertainty, the central bank should not add to them.

Yet there have been dissenting voices regarding the unambiguous benefits of transparency, as Geraats (2002) shows in her survey article. Where the central bank is itself uncertain over the appropriate action, transparency which communicates that uncertainty could make monetary policy less effective. This issue is most relevant where this uncertainty is understood as being distinct from quantifiable risk, i.e., as reflecting the need for decision makers to go beyond any one model and exercise judgment (Dow 2004).

A large body of research has sought to derive models of optimal monetary policy (e.g., to derive optimal Taylor-type rules) in the presence of uncertainty. The majority of the results adhere to the Brainard (1967) principle of *conservatism* or *gradualism*, that is, that when a central bank is unsure about the magnitude and the nature of the economic effect on change in its instrument, it should change that instrument less than it would were it sure.[2] Within a Taylor rule context, the theoretical literature[3] has suggested two ways in which uncertainty should be handled: First, uncertainty lowers the weights on the output gap and inflation but does not have a direct effect on the interest rate. Second, uncertainty regarding one variable (e.g., inflation) should increase the weight put on the other (e.g., output gap).[4] Using data for the US, Martin and Milas (2009) find support for these theoretical predictions.

Matching the work on uncertainty, a new literature has been emerging that takes the issue of central bank communication seriously.[5] This literature is based on the view that monetary policy consists not just of an interest rate decision and its communication, but also of the analysis of the central bank, its expectations, and the confidence with which these are held, all of which are also to be communicated. This wider communication is effected through press conferences and published documents, as well as different measures such as the central banks' fan charts that try to make the concepts and judgments clear. Thus Cobham (2003) and Dow, Klaes, and Montagnoli (2009) have provided a textual analysis of UK monetary policy committee minutes, while Rosa and Verga (2005a, 2005b) have analyzed ECB press conference transcripts, to explain how such communication is used.

The methodology that we apply in this article builds on Dow, Klaes, and Montagnoli (2009) and Rosa and Verga (2005a) in particular. We analyze the semantic context of the minutes of the Monetary Policy Committee (MPC) of the Bank of England, the Executive Board (EB) of the Riksbank, and the Bank Board (BB) of the Czech National Bank; more specifically we contextualize the use of the word "uncertainty" so that we can build a glossary to translate the language used in the minutes into quantitative variables.[6] This allows us to capture the degree of uncertainty surrounding the meetings. Moreover, the index should capture the weight and the context in which the policymakers refer to the concept of uncertainty.

Our analysis allows comparison with previous research on other central banks, by studying the language used by central banks with respect to uncertainty in a common manner. Hence our aim is twofold. First we aim to derive indicators reflecting the uncertainty faced by the policymakers in their considerations.[7] More specifically, after having constructed the uncertainty indexes, we investigate whether they have any particular role in the setting of monetary policy. Then, we link the textual analysis to the actual policy implementation; we estimate a Taylor rule model in which the coefficients on inflation and output gap are functions of our measures of uncertainty. Additionally we explore the possibility that the direction of voting can be used as a measure of uncertainty faced by the monetary policy committees. Since the policy decisions are taken collegially, it is possible that each individual member has his/her own model; even when a single model prevails, the uncertainty surrounding it may be subjective for each member.

Hence we test whether this manifestation of uncertainty can explain the setting of the interest rate.

The remainder of the chapter is structured as follows. The next section presents the context of uncertainty in which central banks operate, section 11.3 presents the methodology used to construct the uncertainty indexes, section 11.4 contains the econometric methodology, section 11.5 discusses the results, section 11.6 presents a discussion of uncertainty and committee dispersion, and section 11.7 concludes.

11.2   The Nature of Uncertainty in Monetary Policy

Monetary policy operates in conditions of uncertainty about the future and also of a potential asymmetry between the knowledge of the monetary authority and that of market participants. Dow, Klaes, and Montagnoli (2007, 2009) define three sources of uncertainty. The first of these is global uncertainty, which is a consequence of the stochastic nature of the economic environment. This also comprises uncertainty about the state of the economy, since there is imperfect information derived from the availability of data and the quality of the data themselves; some economic indicators are unobservable (e.g., the NAIRU, the potential output, and the equilibrium rate of interest). Moreover, the nature and the persistence of shocks are frequently unknown.

The second type of uncertainty is model uncertainty; even in a deterministic world, our limited knowledge might not allow us to reach a single trusted model. While it would ease analysis of the problem if somehow the knowledge base of the central bank could be represented by a single definable and describable entity, policy decisions are usually taken by a committee whose members have diverse backgrounds, each with their own views on how the economy works and what may happen. Even though in a formal context central banks may have a formal model that they use in forecasting and explanation, at the very least they augment it with a range of other models, so there can be no exact exposition of the opinion-forming process.[8]

A third type of uncertainty is signal uncertainty. Monetary policy is conducted not only via a change in the short-term interest rate, but also by communicating the analysis and the motivation behind that particular value. This component is, probably, of central importance for a successful monetary policy, since the interest rate change itself appears to have little impact on future inflation and economic activity. This is largely because, as Svensson (2007) highlights, a successful policymaker is able to influence private-sector inflation expectations. These expectations have a direct impact on the yield curve and on the long-term interest rate, which in turn will determine the path of current and future consumption and investment. In this framework, central bank communication leaves room for interpretation. Agents therefore have to make judgments about the implications, thereby adding uncertainty which may also be asymmetric in nature. This could make central bank transparency a two-edged sword. If the private sector understands the uncertainty facing the central bank better, this may lead to less well anchored inflation expectations in the private sector (if it had previously thought there was less uncertainty). While anchoring expectations on the central bank's target is beneficial for effective policy, anchoring them on a spuriously based certainty is a potential threat to future stability and effectiveness of policy should the weakness be realized—something that is most likely to happen when the economy and monetary policy are under stress.

Central banks are likely to have better resources by which to form a view about likely inflation developments and how they might be influenced than most others in either the public or private sectors, since this is their primary focus while others have broader concerns. While they will have a good understanding of the limitations of their knowledge, outsiders will neither know what that knowledge is nor the degree of certainty with which it is held. The ability to communicate is also imperfect, and there is hence a clear incentive to be clear rather than complete in one's messages in the event of difficulty. There is further interdependence between the monetary authority's knowledge and uncertainty and those of the private sector, in that each forms expectations of what the other is likely to do both in the light of their own knowledge and their understanding of the other. As Issing (2005) reminds us, "data are often not self-explanatory, as their information content changes depending on the way they are communicated by the sender" (p. 67).

Moreover, since the information provided by the central bank on its decision-making process is both quantitative and discursive, information uncertainty has both quantifiable and nonquantifiable aspects.

Although institutionalized procedures ultimately result in specific interest rate decisions, they are nevertheless open to different interpretations by market participants. It is this context that sets the scene for current debates on the transparency of central bank policies (e.g., Geraats 2002). The challenge for a policy committed to transparency consists in ensuring adequate transparency of the form and content of decision procedures to reveal the collective judgment of the decision-making body, as well as sometimes revealing difference of opinion.[9] This form of transparency should make it more likely that market behavior will be conditioned by the same expectations as the Central Bank, helping to improve the policymakers' ability to predict. It also facilitates a closer anticipation of future decisions if the past decision process is well understood and procedures clearly follow a consistent pattern. Hence, these signals play a central role in monetary policy. The channels through which these signals are formed are therefore of key importance in the success of the enterprise.

Our primary aim is to investigate whether uncertainty enters the reaction function of the policymakers. Key to our analysis is the ability to study the discussion that takes place when monetary policy is set. The central banks under investigation here follow an inflation-targeting strategy; they all make decisions by committee and publish minutes that reveal internal differences of opinion. This comparative study allows some assessment of uncertainty emerging from the minutes and how the voting dispersion on the committee shapes monetary policy. This precludes using most other central banks (including the European Central Bank) in our study, as their policy committee's minutes or voting records are not available.[10]

Many central banks, including those in this study, make a very clear distinction between uncertainty and risk, very much along the lines of Knight (1921) and Keynes (1921), namely between sources of variation that can be quantified and those that cannot. The use of fan charts typifies the view that it is the distribution of possible outcomes that is more valuable to the reader and more realistic for the forecaster—point estimates are always highly likely to be wrong and convey only limited information. The distribution of possible outcomes is a function of the probability distribution of shocks that can strike the economy over the forecast period.[11]

If the central bank had no view at all about the factors that might impinge on the economy, then fan charts would always be symmetric and risk and uncertainty would be lumped together in the probability distribution. In practice, however, there is a list of possible events that may occur that are obvious from recent developments. These may relate to policy changes, for example. In these circumstances, the distribution of likely outcomes may no longer be simply normal; hence central banks produce a skewed distribution for forecasts depending on the balance of risk.[12] In these circumstances the usual procedure is simply to add a third moment to the forecast distribution in order to describe the skew. This is a highly simplified procedure, reflecting the softness of the information and how it can be handled. It is, however, noteworthy that in many other circumstances, such as the mainstream finance literature, risk is usually described by variance. When central banks discuss risk, they are normally discussing whether there are grounds for being able to talk about higher moments. In the face of crises, for example, kurtosis may also enter the discussion, as the chance of a "fat tail" on the downside increases, although the word itself is not likely to be used in describing the problem.

The idea that risk can be quantified and that many forces affecting the economy can be translated into a skew is common (Britton, Fisher, and Whitley 1998); even the ECB signals the imprecision of point estimates by quoting a range rather than a point estimate. Nevertheless, in the same way that assuming a normal distribution measures the likely distribution of outcomes, it is simplistic to suppose that adding the third moment captures risks.

Risks are therefore normally discussed in an explicit section of monetary policy reports and may be either explicitly incorporated into the forecast or expressed in terms of scenarios. In the former case this represents a judgment on the balance of risks, whereas in the latter case it is an illustration of the impact of specific alternative sets of assumptions that reflect the materialization of a specific risk or set of risks. Uncertainty, on the other hand, tends to be treated much more generally and relates to the confidence with which the various statements made in the text can be substantiated. This may relate even to the discussion of risks.

11.3 Methodology

Our basic premise here is that while uncertainty as such is unquantifiable in any direct way, it is still possible to identify evidence of more or less uncertainty on the part of central bank decision makers, even if such uncertainty can at best be partially ranked. This suggests broadening the range of economic data to include semantic information as well, and recent literature on central bank communication has done just that, by seeking to translate discursive information such as minutes of central bank committees and press releases into indicators of economic risk and uncertainty. Rosa and Verga (2005a, 2005b), analyzing the ECB president's monthly conference, build an index that gives "summary statistics of the ECB Governing Council view about both the future prospect of inflation and real activity in the euro area." On the most basic level, a simple count of uses of the terms "uncertain" and "uncertainty" can be taken as an ordinal indicator of how much uncertainty the central bank was experiencing.[13]

Our hypothesis is that perceived uncertainty has an impact on decision making in monetary policy. If so, adding measures of the perceived uncertainty to the explanation of how monetary policy has been set, say through an empirical Taylor rule, should improve that explanation.

Our focus is on the language of uncertainty in the three studied banks (Bank of England, Czech National Bank, and Sveriges Riksbank) in such a way as to allow some comparison with previous studies of how monetary policy is determined. This should shed some light on the implications of the framework differences among the monetary authorities for communication about uncertainty, and how that relates to monetary policy decisions. Initially we treat the committee as a single entity (i.e., a single voice) rather than a plurality. In this way we can develop measures that represent the views of the committee as a whole, drawing on how they themselves communicate uncertainty.

More specifically, we analyze the frequencies of the term "uncertainty," studying how it is used in the minutes of the monetary policy committees without imposing our own interpretations. Since our focus is on how the committee communicates its uncertainty, we follow Dow,

Klaes, and Montagnoli (2009) and consider all word forms arising from
the word stem "uncertain." This allows us to derive frequencies $f(U)$
which represent the number of times the respective set of expressions
U is instanced in a given MPC/EB/BB minute in a substantive way
that reflects their assessment of uncertainty inherent in the given economic situation. To arrive at frequency counts that can be regarded as
substantive in the sense described, raw counts of U occurrences have
to be subjected to a preliminary step of analysis that removes instances
that merely arise as part of a conditional consideration in the minutes.

In each of our three cases we have sought to use the longest available
database in which monetary policy has been subject to the same
(inflation-targeting) regime. For the Bank of England we expand the
database of Dow, Klaes, and Montagnoli (2009) from January 1999 to
December 2007, for the CNB our sample starts in January 1999, and for
the Riksbank our sample starts in February 2000. We have further
recorded the length of each minute as a word count, to be able to
control for possible change in length during particular months.[14] L_t, like
U and R frequencies, disregards the cover page and any annexes.

The derived frequency of uncertainty, $f(U)$, is then classified according to the nature of the uncertainty described. Here we consider only
two different subcategories: references to uncertainty about domestic
inflation and uncertainty on economic/output activity/growth, which
are main factors that could be considered of relevance when monetary
policy decisions are taken. Table 11.1 presents a sample of the sentences
that we consider in our indices. The data are derived from two independent passes over the minutes. The very few remaining disagreements were resolved by a third opinion.

Clearly, using such simple frequencies is only a first step; we could
go on to make a deeper analysis of the degree of the uncertainty
involved, say by taking note of the adjectives and other qualifications
used. Thus for example "particularly uncertain" should qualify as
denoting much greater uncertainty than "somewhat uncertain." We
could then have a graded scale. However, if the outlook is "particularly
uncertain," we would expect there to be far more references to uncertainty in the text than if it were only "somewhat uncertain." Hence the
extent of uncertainty would still be revealed by our frequency count.
Gradation poses its own problems. Clearly several instances of limited
uncertainty should not be equated with one instance of considerable
uncertainty. The whole range of references on each occasion would
need to be taken into account and a single graded view derived from

Table 11.1
Sample of Inflation Uncertainty and Output Uncertainty

	Inflation uncertainty	Output uncertainty
Bank of England	The overall effect of the exchange rate depreciation on inflation was highly uncertain, especially if overseas exporters' margins to the UK fell more sharply than previously expected and if retail margins were squeezed further. (June 2000)	Second, there was uncertainty about the estimate for GDP for the first quarter. (June 2002)
	The short-term outlook for CPI inflation was particularly uncertain: it was unclear how much of the recent rise in energy prices had yet to pass through the supply chain [. . .] (November 2005)	Overall, the near-term outlook for output growth had probably softened, but the extent of this was uncertain. (October 2004)
Czech National Bank	In contrast, the future development of demand inflation would be affected by strong uncertainties (downward in nature) relating especially to investment dynamics. (February 2001)	Uncertainty concerning the intensity of future economic recovery [. . .] (March 2000)
	The quantification and timing of these price effects constituted an important uncertainty surrounding the inflation forecast. (September 2002)	It was also said that the revision of the national accounts, which is currently under way could increase the uncertainty regarding the past and present development of GDP and the output gap. (June 2004)
Riksbank	The situation has changed a good deal since the spring, when a positive interest rate differential with the European Central Bank's rate was motivated by Sweden's more expansionary fiscal policy, a weak exchange rate and uncertainty about the path of domestic inflation. (October 2002)	The Executive Board concluded that economic developments continue to be marked by the great uncertainty regarding the Iraq crisis, the uncertainty regarding the strength of international economic activity and increased savings resulting from households' and companies' balance sheets adjustments after the fall in share prices. (February 2003)
	There was considerable uncertainty over how lasting the effects on inflation would be. (March 2005)	The information received since then had also to some extent dispersed uncertainty over economic activity in Sweden and abroad, and the assessment was that inflation would rise when capacity utilization increased. (December 2005)

Note: Date in parenthesis refers to the month the sentence appeared.

it. We therefore do not follow this up here, since our motive is to provide a first assessment of whether this sort of approach offers useful information on uncertainty.

11.4 Empirical Specification

Our empirical analysis is based on the forward-looking version of the Taylor rule as proposed by Clarida, Gali, and Gertler (1999, 2000).[15] It is widely accepted that the behavior of the interest rate can be described by the following policy rule:

$$i_t = a_0 + a_\pi [E_t \pi_{t+n} - \pi^*] + a_y y_t + \varepsilon_t, \tag{11.1}$$

where α_0 is a constant, i_t is the policy rate at time t, $E_t \pi_{t+1}$ is the expected level of inflation, π^* the targeted level of inflation, and y_t is the output gap. Allowing for interest rate smoothing, the above equation can be rewritten as:

$$i_t = (1 - \gamma_t)a_0 + \gamma_t i_{t-1} + (1 - \gamma_t)\{a_\pi [E_t \pi_{t+n} - \pi^*] + a_y y_t\} + \xi_t. \tag{11.2}$$

Following the theoretical literature and Martin and Milas (2009), we know that the parameters are functions of uncertainty underlying the model and the state of the economy, so that in presence of uncertainty the above equation can be rewritten as:

$$i_t = \chi a_0 + (\gamma_t + \gamma_t^{unc} u_t) i_{t-1}$$
$$+ \chi \{(a_\pi + a_\pi^{unc} u_t)[E_t \pi_{t+n} - \pi^*] + (a_y + a_y^{unc} u_t) y_t\} + \varsigma_t, \tag{11.3}$$

where $\chi = (1 - \gamma_t - \gamma_t^{unc} u_t)$ and u_t is the measure of uncertainty described in the previous section. This method allows us to test whether the response to uncertainty as communicated in the central bank minutes is reflected in the behavior of the policymakers, that is, whether in presence of uncertainty the interest rate setting adheres to Brainard's principle. If the predictions of the theoretical literature are correct, then we should expect a_π^{unc} and a_y^{unc} to take a value smaller than zero. On the other hand, γ_t^{unc} is expected to be positive since the central bank may respond cautiously to uncertainty surrounding the data (Orphanides, 2003).

Our second empirical specification considers the two subsets of uncertainty: inflation uncertainty and output uncertainty. Our second specification is therefore given by

$$i_t = \gamma_t i_{t-1} + (1 - \gamma_t)\{a_0 + \psi_1 [E_t \pi_{t+n} - \pi^*] + \psi_2 y_t\} + \xi_t, \tag{11.4}$$

where $\psi_1 = (a_\pi + a_\pi^{\pi,unc} u_t^\pi + a_\pi^{y,unc} u_t^y)$ and $\psi_2 = (a_y + a_y^{\pi,unc} u_t^\pi + a_y^{y,unc} u_t^y)$.

Here u_t^π and u_t^y are inflation and output uncertainty, respectively. As stated previously, the literature makes a clear prediction of how an optimal policy should be set. If increased uncertainty leads to a more passive response to a variable and strengthens the response to the other, we should expect $a_\pi^{\pi,unc} < 0$ and $a_\pi^{y,unc} > 0$ on the inflation side, while $a_y^{\pi,unc} > 0$ and $a_y^{y,unc} < 0$ on the output side.

11.5 Empirical Results

In tables 11.2 to 11.4 we report the estimates for the various Taylor rule specifications. The sample period goes from 1999q1 to 2007q1 for the UK and the Czech Republic, while the sample starts in 2000q2 for Sweden. We use this sample period since we wanted to exclude the financial crisis from our analysis, when monetary authorities were mainly focused on restoring financial stability and preventing the collapse of the financial system, rather than on the more traditional objectives of inflation and output stabilization. For the interest rate we use the end of the month official bank rate; the forecasts of inflation are from the Bank of England Inflation Attitudes Survey, from the CNB survery of inflation expectations of households, and from the Economic

Table 11.2
Taylor Rule Estimates—Sweden

| | Taylor rule | Taylor rule with uncertainty | | |
		(i)	(ii)	(iii)
a_0	3.266***	3.167***	3.660***	2.067***
γ_t	0.956***	0.965***	0.978***	0.971***
γ_t^{unc}		0.000		
a_π	2.884***	3.283***	2.540***	2.820***
a_π^{unc}		−0.000	0.003*	
$a_\pi^{\pi,unc}$				−0.141***
$a_\pi^{y,unc}$				0.001***
a_y	0.931****	0.151	−0.405	0.723***
a_y^{unc}		−0.001	−0.002	
$a_y^{y,unc}$				0.002***
$a_y^{\pi,unc}$				−0.001
J-stats	15.40 ($p = 0.65$)	5.79 ($p = 0.44$)	4.62 ($p = 0.70$)	4.41 ($p = 0.90$)

Note: The weight matrix is heteroskedasticity- and autocorrelation-consistent. Standard errors robust to autocorrelation and heteroskedasticity. *, **, *** denote significance at 10, 5, and 1% levels, respectively. J-stats refers to Hansen's J statistics.

Table 11.3
Taylor Rule Estimates—UK

| | | Taylor rule with uncertainty | | |
	Taylor rule	(i)	(ii)	(iii)
a_0	4.128***	4.229***	4.209***	4.913***
γ_t	0.964***	0.944***	0.944***	0.932***
γ_t^{unc}		−0.000		
a_π	2.955***	1.812***	1.840***	2.147***
a_π^{unc}		−0.006	0.007	
$a_\pi^{\pi,unc}$				−0.020**
$a_\pi^{y,unc}$				0.177**
a_y	1.880***	0.728**	0.729***	0.176***
a_y^{unc}		−0.013**	−0.013***	
$a_y^{y,unc}$				0.013***
$a_y^{\pi,unc}$				−0.035***
J-stats	21.44 ($p = 0.123$)	5.65 ($p = 0.91$)	5.649 ($p = 0.90$)	6.70 ($p = 0.80$)

Note: The weight matrix is heteroskedasticity- and autocorrelation-consistent. Standard errors robust to autocorrelation and heteroskedasticity. *, **, *** denote significance at 10, 5, and 1% levels, respectively. J-stats refers to Hansen's J statistics.

Table 11.4
Taylor Rule Estimates—Czech Republic

| | | Taylor rule with uncertainty | | |
	Taylor rule	(i)	(ii)	(iii)
a_0	3.382***	2.706***	2.823***	4.491***
γ_t	0.960***	0.958***	0.956***	0.961***
γ_t^{unc}		0.000		
a_π	2.851***	3.538**	3.780***	3.565*
a_π^{unc}		0.078*	0.090***	
$a_\pi^{\pi,unc}$				−0.019***
$a_\pi^{y,unc}$				0.027
a_y	−0.109	−0.450	−0.636*	−0.425
a_y^{unc}		−0.006	−0.019*	
$a_y^{y,unc}$				0.034
$a_y^{\pi,unc}$				−0.005
J-stats	1.45 ($p = 0.92$)	5.47 ($p = 0.90$)	4.78 ($p = 0.68$)	6.43 ($p = 0.59$)

Note: The weight matrix is heteroskedasticity- and autocorrelation-consistent. Standard errors robust to autocorrelation and heteroskedasticity. *, **, *** denote significance at 10, 5, and 1% levels, respectively. J-stats refers to Hansen's J statistics.

Tendency Survey compiled by the National Institute of Economic Research for Sweden.[16] The output gap is measured using the industrial production data detrended using the Hodrick-Prescott filter.

Each table first reports the estimates of traditional Taylor rules obtained from the generalized method of moments (GMM) estimation. There are several reasons why this is our preferred estimator. First, there is an endogeneity issue between the output gap and the interest rate. Second, even with the use of a direct measure of inflation, it is far from the only measure available to and used by the policymakers, and there might be substantial disagreement among various forecasts.[17] Third, the various measures of uncertainty in our model are clearly endogenous variables.

The estimates indicate that interest rates increase by more than two percentage points in response to a one-percentage-point increase of excess of inflation over the inflation target. The response to the output gap varies across our sample; we obtain a value of 0.931 as a response to a one-percentage-point excess of output over equilibrium output in Sweden against the 1.8 in the United Kingdom and a statistically insignificant response by the Czech National Bank. The intercept is statistically significant in all three cases, and it is very close to the interest rate average for the sample period. The parameter γ_t indicates that the interest rate is highly persistent. This is not surprising given the monthly interval of the series and that central banks tend to adjust interest rate during months when the inflation report is published, which is when new information is available.[18]

Column (i) shows the estimates of Taylor rules where all the parameters are allowed to be functions of our measure of uncertainty. We find that uncertainty does not affect the interest rate smoothing parameter, γ_t^{unc}. Hence we reestimate the model setting $\gamma_t^{unc} = 0$ (shown in column (ii)). The results using a single measure of uncertainty are not promising. The inclusion of measures of uncertainty does not support the prediction of Brainard's principle. The estimates of the parameters of interest (a_π^{unc}, a_y^{unc}) are of the opposite sign or not statistically different from zero. The reason for this could be twofold: either there is no valuable information about the uncertainty surrounding the policy decisions of the monetary policy committees, or this measure of uncertainty is too general and hides the uncertainties which have a direct impact on the members of the policy committee. Hence, these results do not shed any light on which "type" of uncertainty matters. The theoretical literature suggests that in the presence of uncertainty an optimal monetary policy should respond by decreasing the weight put on inflation when this indicator is uncertain, but it should increase the weight on the other variables (in our case the output gap). To test this hypothesis, we use our measure of inflation and output uncertainty. Results are presented in column (iii). The estimated coefficients of inflation and output uncertainty indicate that the response of interest rates to inflation is weaker when inflation is more uncertain and stronger when the output gap is more uncertain (although the latter effect is not statistically significant for the Riksbank and the CNB). For the Bank of England we also find that the response to changes in output gap is affected by the two types of uncertainty, while for the Riksbank only inflation uncertainty is statistically significant.

As for inflation expectations, at the time monetary policy decisions are taken there is a high degree of uncertainty surrounding the output gap. To correct for this well-known problem we use estimates of real-time data for the output gap for Sweden and the UK as provided by the OECD output gap revisions database.[19] The results presented in tables 11.5 and 11.6 seem to provide some support to the Brainard principle. The smaller response to inflation when inflation is less

Table 11.5
Taylor Rule Estimates with Real-Time Data—Sweden

	Taylor rule	Taylor rule with uncertainty		
		(i)	(ii)	(iii)
a_0	2.934***	3.018***	2.781***	1.995***
γ_t	0.901***	0.880***	0.872***	0.924***
γ_t^{unc}		−0.000		
a_π	2.025***	2.372***	2.776***	2.903***
a_π^{unc}		−0.000	0.000	
$a_\pi^{\pi,unc}$				−0.111***
$a_\pi^{y,unc}$				0.002***
a_y				
a_y^{unc}	0.795***	1.717***	1.549***	1.509***
$a_y^{y,unc}$		0.001	0.001**	−0.015***
$a_y^{\pi,unc}$				−0.001
J-stats	15.40 ($p = 0.65$)	5.79 ($p = 0.44$)	4.62 ($p = 0.70$)	4.41($p = 0.98$)

Note: The weight matrix is heteroskedasticity- and autocorrelation-consistent. Standard errors robust to autocorrelation and heteroskedasticity. *, **, *** denote significance at 10, 5, and 1% levels, respectively. J-stats refers to Hansen's J statistics.

Table 11.6
Taylor Rule Estimates with Real-Time Data—UK

	Taylor rule	Taylor rule with uncertainty		
		(i)	(ii)	(iii)
a_0	4.451***	4.124***	4.456***	4.962***
γ_t	0.923***	0.921***	0.936***	0.899***
γ_t^{unc}		0.000		
a_π	1.546***	2.064**	3.205**	1.381***
a_π^{unc}		0.018	0.014	
$a_\pi^{\pi,unc}$				−0.005
$a_\pi^{y,unc}$				0.167***
a_y	1.216***	0.126	−5.151	0.813***
a_y^{unc}		−0.024*	−0.146	
$a_y^{y,unc}$				−0.094***
$a_y^{\pi,unc}$				0.011
J-stats	15.76 ($p = 0.20$)	4.41 ($p = 0.98$)	1.94 ($p = 0.99$)	4.36 ($p = 0.82$)

Note: The weight matrix is heteroskedasticity- and autocorrelation-consistent. Standard errors robust to autocorrelation and heteroskedasticity. *, **, *** denote significance at 10, 5, and 1% levels, respectively. J-stats refers to Hansen's J statistics.

certain, and larger response to inflation when output is less certain, are consistent with the predictions of Peersman and Smets (1999) and Gürkaynak, Sack, and Swanson (2005).

11.6   Voting Dispersion as a Measure of Uncertainty

In this section we explore the link between the uncertainty as measured by the voting dispersion in the policy committees and the changes in the interest rate.

The rationality underlying a possible link between actual policy decisions and how members vote rests on the observation that policy committees are composed of members with different backgrounds. Recently a part of the literature has extensively investigated the implication of this diversity, suggesting the existence of heterogeneity across committee members with respect to information and preferences. For instance, studying the Bank of England, Gerlach-Kristen (2009) shows the existence of differences between internal and external members. Riboni and Ruge-Murcia (2008) and Besley, Meads, and Surico (2008) estimate individuals' Taylor rules; they suggest that long-run responses to the inflation gap are fairly homogenous, but individual characteristics are responsible for the heterogeneity in the MPC voting patterns.

In this context, it is reasonable to assume that "each member of the monetary policy committee holds a particular view of the behaviour of the economy represented by a macro model," and with it comes a level of confidence or uncertainty (Levin and Williams 2003, p. 946). Even if there is a single trusted model shared across the members, it is plausible that each member would attach an individual degree of uncertainty.

If this is the case, then each member's vote would adhere to Brainard's principle of conservatism, and as a whole a high level of committee uncertainty would be reflected in a high level of voting dispersion.

We measure voting dispersion as:

$$\frac{(total\ number\ of\ votes - majority\ votes)}{(number\ required\ for\ a\ majority\ -\ 1)}, \tag{11.5}$$

so that the variable runs from zero for full agreement to unity for the maximum level of disagreement possible.

In table 11.7 we reestimate the model replacing the uncertainty measure with the level of voting dispersion. For all three central banks, there is no evidence that voting dispersion has an impact on interest rate smoothing; this is in accordance with the estimates obtained from our derived measure of uncertainty.

Looking first at the results from the CNB, we notice that the estimates are very close to those of the Taylor rule with no uncertainty, but

Table 11.7
Taylor Rule Estimates with Voting Dispersion

	Riksbank	Bank of England	Czech National Bank
a_0	3.285***	5.318***	3.138***
γ_t	0.956***	0.965***	0.971***
γ_t^{unc}	−0.007	−0.0002***	0.000
a_π	2.823***	2.210***	2.474***
a_π^{unc}	−0.174***	−0.018***	−0.012
a_y	0.445***	2.878***	−0.613
a_y^{unc}	−0.034***	0.026***	−0.028
J-stats	13.13 ($p = 0.78$)	5.34 ($p = 0.92$)	5.45 ($p = 0.85$)

Note: The weight matrix is heteroskedasticity- and autocorrelation-consistent. Standard errors robust to autocorrelation and heteroskedasticity. *, **, *** denote significance at 10, 5, and 1% levels, respectively. J-stats refers to Hansen's J statistics.

there is no evidence that voting dispersion had any impact on the interest rate. For the Riksbank, the results suggest that uncertainty as measured by the voting dispersion has no impact on the response of the interest rate to inflation deviations from the target and the output gap. For the Bank of England, estimates of uncertainty are statistically significant, at the usual level of confidence, but only the uncertainty surrounding inflation has the expected sign.

11.7 Conclusions

In this paper we have derived three measures of uncertainty using the minutes of the monetary decision-making committees of the Bank of England, the Czech National Bank, and the Sveriges Riksbank.

We estimated the impact of uncertainty on monetary policy using the traditional Taylor rule framework. The foundation of this work rested on the theoretical literature, which suggests that in the presence of uncertainty central bankers should lower the weights on output gap and on inflation but that uncertainty does not have a direct effect on the interest rate.

We have found some evidence that monetary policy has been affected by uncertainty and that these effects are generally consistent with the predictions of the theoretical literature. The predictions made by the literature are verified for the Riksbank and partly satisfied in the estimations of the Bank of England interest rate. However, we find no role for uncertainty in the CNB. We find it difficult to believe that uncertainty has no place in the CNB committee; we can only conjecture that this lack of evidence reflects how the minutes are written.

Our work can be extended in a number of ways. This framework can be applied to other countries in order to test whether there is a clear pattern in the response of monetary policy to uncertainty and whether banks following an inflation-targeting strategy behave differently from those that adopt other strategies. It would also be of interest to analyze the impact of financial market uncertainty and investigate whether asset price uncertainty has had any impact on monetary policy. Finally, there are many more sophisticated forms of textual analysis that can be used.

Notes

We thank Petra Geraats, Cris Shore, and the reviewers and editors for detailed comments and Charlie Fahy for research assistance. We are also grateful to the participants at a seminar presentation at the Europe Institute, University of Auckland, and at the CESifo workshop "Central Bank Communication, Decision-Making and Governance" for comments and discussions. Montagnoli gratefully acknowledges financial support from the Europe Institute, University of Auckland.

1. Uncertainty as to the preferred model on which policy is to be based.

2. These results relate to what is known as additive uncertainty, i.e., uncertainty in addition to what is known. Where there is uncertainty about parameters in a model, the uncertainty is "multiplicative" and the conclusion may not be so straightforward.

3. See, e.g., Peersman and Smets (1999); Walsh (2003); Gürkaynak, Sack, and Swanson (2005).

4. There are two exceptions to this rule. The first applies in the case of imperfect or low credibility, the second when the there is uncertainty surrounding the degree of inflation persistence. In both cases policymakers may find it optimal to act more vigorously than would have been optimal in a no-uncertainty scenario.

5. See Blinder et al. (2008) for a survey of the literature.

6. These three banks are chosen simply because they offer the longest consistent sets of minutes on the inflation targeting of central banks, where the votes of the members are also published.

7. For the preliminary theoretical foundation see Dow, Klaes, and Montagnoli (2007).

8. Even in cases, such as New Zealand, where a single individual, the governor, decides on the policy setting, the degree of "soft" information employed in decision making would make it unrealistic to use a single model to represent even the most systematic individual precisely.

9. Geraats (2002) makes it clear that there is a range of aspects over which central banks try to be transparent.

10. It should be possible to extend the analysis in a different form to include some other central banks, Norges Bank for example, and we could perhaps use a more limited analysis for central banks such as the Reserve Bank of New Zealand, where extensive analyses are published, even though the minutes and voting are not. We do not consider the US Federal Reserve, as they have multiple targets and so the sources of uncertainty are rather greater.

11. Some central banks have described this more in terms of the distribution of errors that they typically make in forecasting, and this is of course correct, as the processes they use to decide how known and unknown events will affect future outcomes are themselves inevitably flawed; even after the event it is not possible to observe a pure shock and its outcome.

12. Blix and Sellin (1999) discuss the case where both upside and downside risks may be normally distributed but with different variances. Adding such distributions will generate the skew.

13. Other studies have used discursive analysis of the communication of the central bank. For instance, Bligh and Hess (this volume) build indexes of "pessimism," "certainty," and "macro" from statements and speeches of the chairman of the Federal Open Market Committee. Blix Grimaldi (this volume) uses a similar methodology to build a financial stress index of the ECB.

14. For more details on the Bank of England, see Dow, Klaes, and Montagnoli (2009). Clearly the longer a document is, the more references there can be to any word within it.

15. Clarida, Gali, and Gertler (2000) show that this interest rate rule can be obtained when a central bank maximizes a loss function over current and future output gap and inflation, subject to the linear constraint specified by the equilibrium in the goods market and the price adjustment equation. Clarida et al. also consider more flexible versions of the Taylor rule admitting expected values of the output gap a number of periods ahead. Their robustness results suggest this is an unnecessary complication. The asymmetry this specification implies seems appropriate for inflation targeting in any case.

16. With the exception of Sweden where the forecast is available monthly, the quarterly observations are interpolated to obtain monthly series, as in Besley, Meads, and Surico (2008).

17. We have of course reviewed the results from other estimators, including OLS, which would be appropriate if our more direct measures of output and inflation uncertainty accounted for all types of uncertainty and other sources of endogeneity or measurement error (Orphanides 2003).

18. On this point see Cobham (2003).

19. Data for the CNB are not available. The data are available at a quarterly frequency; hence the observations are interpolated to obtain monthly series.

References

Besley, T., N. Meads, and P. Surico. 2008. Insiders versus Outsiders in Monetary Policy-making. *American Economic Review* 98:218–223.

Blinder, A. S., M. Ehrmann, M. Fratzscher, J. De Haan, and D. Jansen. 2008. Central Bank Communication and Monetary Policy: A Survey of Theory and Evidence. *Journal of Economic Literature* 46 (December):910–945.

Blix, M., and P. Sellin. 1999. Inflation Forecast with Uncertainty Bands. [Sveriges Riksbank.] *Quarterly Review* 2:12–28.

Brainard, W. 1967. Uncertainty and the Effectiveness of Policy. *American Economic Review* 57:411–425.

Britton, E., P. Fisher, and J. Whitley. 1998. The Inflation Report Projections: Understanding the Fan Chart. *Bank of England Quarterly Bulletin* (February):30–37.

Clarida, R., J. Gali, and M. Gertler. 1999. The Science of Monetary Policy: A New Keynesian Perspective. *Journal of Economic Literature* 37 (4):1661–1707.

Clarida, R., J. Gali, and M. Gertler. 2000. Monetary Policy Rules and Macroeconomic Stability: Evidence and Some Theory. *Quarterly Journal of Economics* 115 (1):147–180.

Cobham, D. 2003. Why Does the Monetary Policy Committee Smooth Interest Rates? *Oxford Economic Papers* 55 (3):467–493.

Dow, S. C. 2004. Uncertainty and Monetary Policy. *Oxford Economic Papers* 56:539–561.

Dow, S. C., M. Klaes, and A. Montagnoli. 2007. Monetary Policy by Information. In *Open Market Operations and the Financial Markets*, ed. D. G. Mayes and J. Toporowski. London: Routledge.

Dow, S. C., M. Klaes, and A. Montagnoli. 2009. Risk and Uncertainty in Central Bank Signals: An Analysis of the MPC Minutes. *Metroeconomica* 60 (2):585–618.

Eusepi, S. 2005. Central Bank Transparency under Model Uncertainty. Staff Reports, 199. Federal Reserve Bank of New York.

Geraats, P. M. 2002. Central Bank Transparency. *Economic Journal* 112 (483):532–565.

Gerlach-Kristen, P. 2009. Outsiders at the Bank of England's MPC. *Journal of Money, Credit and Banking* 41:1099–1115.

Gürkaynak, R. S., B. Sack, and E. Swanson. 2005. Do Actions Speak Louder Than Words? The Response of Asset Prices to Monetary Policy Actions and Statements. *International Journal of Central Banking* 1 (1):55–93.

Issing, O. 2005. Communication, Transparency, Accountability: Monetary Policy in the Twenty-First Century. *Federal Reserve Bank of St. Louis Review* 87 (2):65–83.

Keynes, J. M. 1921/1973. *A Treatise on Probability*. Reprinted in *Collected Writings of John Maynard Keynes*, 8. London: Macmillan, for the Royal Economic Society.

Knight, F. H. 1921. *Risk, Uncertainty and Profit*. Boston: Houghton Mifflin.

Levin, A. T., and J. C. Williams. 2003. Robust Monetary Policy with Competing Reference Models. *Journal of Monetary Economics* 50 (5): 945–975.

Martin, C., and C. Milas. 2009. Uncertainty and Monetary Policy Rules in the United States. *Economic Inquiry* 47 (2):206–215.

Mishkin, F. H. 2004: Can Central Bank Transparency Go Too Far? Reserve Bank of Australia, NBER Working Paper, No. 10829.

Orphanides, A. 2003. Monetary Policy Evaluation with Noisy Information. *Journal of Monetary Economics* 50 (3):605–631.

Peersman, G., and F. Smets. 1999. Uncertainty and the Taylor Rule in a Simple Model of the Euro-Area Economy. Proceedings, Federal Reserve Bank of San Francisco.

Riboni, A., and F. J. Ruge-Murcia. 2008. Preference Heterogeneity in Monetary Policy Committees. *International Journal of Central Banking* 4:213–233.

Rosa, C., and G. Verga. 2005a. Is ECB Communication Effective? CEP Discussion Paper No. 682.

Rosa, C., and G. Verga. 2005b. The Importance of the Wording of the ECB. CEP Discussion Paper No. 694.

Svensson, L. E. O. 2007. Optimal Inflation Targeting: Further Developments of Inflation Targeting. In *Monetary Policy under Inflation Targeting*, ed. F. Mishkin and K. Schmidt-Hebbel. Santiago: Banco Central de Chile.

Walsh, C. E. 2003. Implications of a Changing Economic Structure for the Strategy of Monetary Policy. Proceedings, Federal Reserve Bank of Kansas City, 297–348.

12 Voting Record and Monetary Policy Predictability: Evidence on Six Central Banks

Roman Horváth, Kateřina Šmídková, and Jan Zápal

12.1 Related Literature

On the most general level the question of whether voting records of central bank boards and monetary policy committees (MPCs) reveal information about future changes in monetary policy is related to the literature on central bank communication and central bank transparency surveyed by Blinder et al. (2008) and Geraats (2002, and in this volume) respectively. The general conclusion of both strands of the literature is that the way central banks communicate to the public and the degree of their transparency matter for monetary policy. Most of the theoretical and empirical studies also indicate the benefits of more open and transparent central bank behavior. However, not all the studies reach unequivocal conclusions. For example, the model in Morris and Shin (2002) leaves open the possibility that more information provided by a central bank is welfare-reducing, while Meade and Stasavage (2008) show that the Federal Reserve's decision to release full transcripts of Federal Open Market Committee (FOMC) meetings decreased the incentives of its participants to voice dissenting opinions. Winkler (2000) draws similar conclusions and puts forward a conceptual framework to distinguish different aspects of transparency.

From the theoretical side, the question of whether the voting records of bank board members are informative about future monetary policy is virtually untouched. One of the reasons is the difficulty of modeling committee decision making with members who hold possibly different beliefs and objectives in the uncertain monetary environment. A further difficulty is presented by the dynamic nature of central bank decision making, as a policy rate adopted today becomes the status-quo policy for the next meeting.

Furthermore, it is not entirely clear what we should assume about the way bank boards reach decisions. While in reality the chairman usually holds most of the proposal power, empirical evidence in Riboni and Ruge-Murcia (2010) suggests that what they call a consensus model better captures the real-world features.

Riboni and Ruge-Murcia (2008a) try to model central bank decision making taking into account its dynamic nature. They show that even in periods in which policymakers' preferences do not differ, they may fail to reach a consensus and change the policy from the status quo, due to the possibility of future disagreement. However, it is not clear whether Riboni and Ruge-Murcia's model can support the information content of voting behavior, despite the fact that it produces persistence and strong autocorrelation of policy rates.

Disregarding the dynamic nature of central bank policymaking, Gerlach-Kristen (2008) investigates a role of the MPC chairman in committee decision making in a model that generates real-world-like dissenting frequencies. The possibility of dissent arising is due to the fact that individual policymakers receive private information about the unobserved optimal interest rate. Differences in private information sets among the MPC members then give rise to different votes by the time the policy decision is made.

The model in Weber (2010) then supports the basic intuition that the publication of voting records reveals heterogeneity in the bank board's opinion and thus provides more information to the financial markets than the publication of the final decision only. Better-informed financial markets are then able to better predict the central bank's future behavior, providing a rationale for the publication of voting records.

Similarly, the empirical literature investigating the informative power of voting records is rather scant. This is mainly due to the fact that the practice of publishing the voting records of board members has been adopted relatively recently, and several central banks make the voting records public only in transcripts of their monetary policy meetings, published with a several-year lag.

For the MPC of the Bank of England, Gerlach-Kristen (2004) shows that for the period 1997–2002 the difference between the average voted-for and actually implemented policy rate is informative about changes in the policy rate in the future, a conclusion robust to the inclusion of different measures of market expectations. In a similar spirit and using the same measure of dissent in the MPC, Fujiki (2005) reaches a similar conclusion for the Bank of Japan. For the Riksbank, Andersson, Dillen, and Sellin (2006) reach a similar conclusion.

The empirical literature trying to estimate the reaction functions of individual bank board members using information about their voting behavior is closely related. In this case information about the votes of individual members is used to predict their preferred policy rate given the state of the economy, and hence to better forecast future monetary policy decisions. For the Federal Reserve, Chappell, McGregor, and Vermilyea (2005) estimate the individual reaction functions of FOMC members. For the Bank of England MPC, Bhattacharjee and Holly (2006, 2010), Brooks, Harris, and Spencer (2008), Besley, Meads, and Surico (2008), and Riboni and Ruge-Murcia (2008b) conduct a similar exercise.

The general conclusion emerging from these studies is that there is often significant evidence of heterogeneity among the bank board members. In combination with the assumption that monetary policy is better conducted in an environment with no information asymmetry between the central bank and the markets, the publication of voting records revealing the heterogeneity of the bank board members is desirable.

12.2 Institutional Background

This section gives information on the background of central bank committees' decision making about monetary policy. The bank boards typically meet monthly and decide on the level of the repo rate. The frequency of monetary policy meetings vary, however. For example, the Bank of England and the Hungarian and Polish central banks meet monthly, the Czech National Bank used to meet monthly up to 2007 and has met eight times a year since 2008, as have the US Fed and Riksbank for the greater part of our sample period. Occasionally, the central banks hold extraordinary policy meetings.

The boards take decisions based on majority vote. In the event of a tie, the chairperson (governor, if present at the meeting) has the deciding vote. The policy decision is announced on the same day. Minutes explaining their monetary policy decision, i.e., the voting of central bankers, are published with a one- or two-week lag. Except in Poland, the voting record is an integral part of the minutes and summarizes the qualitative information contained in the minutes. In the case of Poland, the voting record appears no sooner than 6 weeks (and no later than 12 weeks) after the policy meeting.[1] In the US case, we use the data for 1970–1996 (Burns and Greenspan chairmanships) collected and coded by Chappell et al. (2005). The voting records for the US are primarily based on transcripts that are published with a several-year lag (appendix 12.1 contains further details on US data). Both US and Polish case studies document that the informative power of voting records does not depend on the ex-ante known publishing time lag. An in-depth study on voting records in Poland is provided by Sirchenko (2010).

Voting results are typically attributed, but not always. For example, the voting ratio was released for monetary policy decisions without an explicit statement on how individual board members voted in 2000–2007 in the Czech Republic. From mid-2000 to January 2006 the (unattributed) voting record was published in the minutes only, while since February 2006 the voting record has been released at the press conference that is held about three hours after the announcement of the interest rate decision. In addition, the Czech National Bank has recently published the transcripts of its monetary policy meetings from 1998 to 2001, which include the voting record as well. Hence, the Czech case offers us the second natural experiment in which we can test whether the voting ratio has informative power similar to that of the full voting record. (The results will show that it does.) The lesson learned from the Czech case is therefore to publish at least the voting ratio if considerations regarding the names are serious.

Disagreement among central bankers is common. The voting was not unanimous in 46% of the monetary policy decisions of the Czech central bank, in 70% of those of the Hungarian central bank, in 46% of those of the Polish central bank, in 19% of those of the Swedish central bank, and in 59% of those of the Bank of England during our sample period. The frequency of unanimous voting depends on the size of the bank board to a certain extent, with Hungary having more than 10 members on the board during our sample period. The typical magnitude of a monetary policy rate change is 25 basis points. Other magnitudes are less common even though central banks decreased the policy rates quite aggressively during the recent financial crisis, often by 50 or even 100 basis points at a meeting. Substantive changes of policy rate of a similar magnitude were also observed in the Czech Republic, Hungary, and Poland during the transition period to a market economy characterized by more volatile macroeconomic development. Data are further described in the appendix.

Figure 12.1 presents the link between actual voting record skew and future policy rate change. In all countries, the link seems to be positive, although there are cases when the skew can give a noisy signal about future policy, for example when the rates are not changed and one

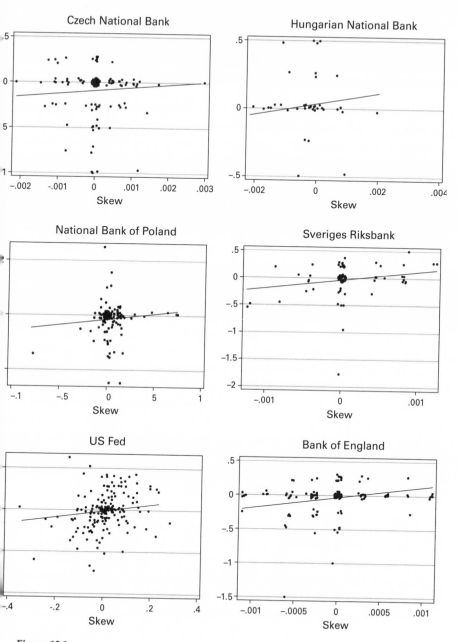

Figure 12.1
Actual voting record skew and future policy rate change. Skew, calculated as the difference between the average repo rate voted by individual members of board and actual repo rate at the next meeting, is plotted on the *x* axis. Future monetary policy rate change is plotted on the *y* axis. The jitter is used for the overlapping observations for expositional purposes.

board member dissents. When we look at various signal-to-noise ratios, we can see that there is a certain level of noise in individual members' voting records, but when more members dissent at the same policy meeting the level of noise declines, with the signal-to-noise ratio typically well above 50%.[2] We perform a regression analysis in the following section to shed light on the extent to which the voting record gives systematic information about future policy. For the regression analysis, the future policy rate change is stacked in fewer categories, as some large magnitudes of policy changes happen rarely (more on this below). As a consequence, this coding of the dependent variable substantially lowers the potential impact of vertical outliers. For the potential impact of horizontal outliers, we estimate the regressions based on various subsamples, with the results being affected minimally.

12.3 Empirical Methodology

In our empirical methodology we follow the approach developed by Gerlach-Kristen (2004) to assess the predictions of our model. Gerlach-Kristen analyzes the voting record of the MPC of the Bank of England over the period 1997–2002, while we aim to include relevant data from additional central banks to provide a more comprehensive international comparison. More specifically, we focus on the following five countries that conduct their policies within an inflation-targeting regime: the Czech Republic, the United Kingdom, Hungary, Poland, and Sweden. For comparison, we estimate similar models for the United States.

Following Gerlach-Kristen (2004), we define a measure of disagreement in the bank board, the variable *skew*, as

$$skew_t = average(i_{j,t}) - i_t, \qquad (12.1)$$

where $i_{j,t}$ is the interest rate voted for by bank board member j at a monetary policy meeting at time t and i_t denotes the monetary policy rate. We follow Gerlach-Kristen and assess whether the voting record reveals information on future monetary policy by estimating the following baseline regression model for each individual country:

$$\Delta i_{t+1} = a_0 + a_1 skew_{\tau(t)} + a_2 \Delta i_t + u_{t+1}. \qquad (12.2)$$

It is assumed in equation (12.2) that the interest rate decision is taken at time t and the votes are released at time $\tau(t)$, i.e., in the period between the interest rate decisions at t and $t+1$ (often together with the minutes, typically about two weeks after the interest rate decision at t; it is worth emphasizing that we focus on the voting record, as this is the only quantitative information in the minutes; alternatively one would have to classify the qualitative information contained in them). We estimate equation (12.2) by an ordered probit technique to reflect the discrete nature of monetary policy rate changes. It is important to emphasize that the discrete dependent variable has been stacked in fewer categories, as some magnitudes of policy changes such as 75 basis points happened rarely. Therefore, the dependent variable was coded in four to five categories depending on the country and defined as follows: large decrease, decrease, no change, hike, and large hike (changes of −50, −25, 0, +25, and +50 basis points, respectively).[3]

The coefficients a_1 and a_2 are expected to take positive values. As regards the sign of a_1, if some bank board members favor higher rates, *skew* is positive and a future interest rate hike is more likely, conditional upon the voting record being informative for future policy. As regards the coefficient a_2, it reflects interest rate smoothing and the attempt of central bankers to avoid sudden policy reversals. If a_1 is significant, we can imply that releasing voting records improves the explanatory power of a "naive" model which assumes only smoothing and reactions to shocks.

Our second baseline model extends this naive model by considering the information set available to financial markets, which we approximate from a yield curve. We can test whether the information set available to financial markets contains all information sets available to individual board members. If the financial markets have identical information sets and evaluate the information at least as effectively as the central bank, the information content of the skew indicator should be built into the slope of the term structure of interest rates. In that case, parameter b_1 would be insignificant in our second baseline model (and b_2 as well in case the interest rate smoothing is fully priced into the term structure). In the opposite case, the voting record reveals additional information to financial markets. In periods of large volatility or under some voting mechanisms, the skew may be insignificant despite the fact that individual board members have valuable information sets. To assess these considerations formally, we estimate a regression of the following form:

$$\Delta i_{t+1} = b_0 + b_1 skew_{\tau(t)} + b_2 \Delta i_t + b_3 \left(i_{x(t),L} - i_{x(t),S} \right) + u_{t+1}. \qquad (12.3)$$

As compared to (12.2), equation (12.3) now includes an additional term to control for the financial market expectations. $i_{x(t),L} - i_{x(t),S}$ represents the slope of the term structure, where L and S denote the respective money market maturities[4] and it is assumed that $L > S$ (following Gerlach-Kristen 2004, we will consider various maturities). $x(t)$ denotes the time period between the interest rate decisions, and the data on $i_{x(t),L}$ and $i_{x(t),S}$ will be from the day before the release of the voting record (thus, $x(t) < \tau(t)$).

Regarding our two natural experiment setups, we may test whether *skew* is informative in the period when the voting records are disclosed with a considerable time lag, as in the cases of Poland and the US. We may also test whether the voting ratio is informative when only unattributed voting records were available, as in the case of the Czech Republic.

We add two robustness checks to our baseline models. First, we extend the empirical specification of Gerlach-Kristen (2004) by including the measure of dispersion in voting records, which may serve as an indicator of the degree of uncertainty the board members face. We measure the dispersion of voting results by the standard deviation of individual votes:[5]

$$\Delta i_{t+1} = b_0 + b_1 skew_{\tau(t)} + b_2 \Delta i_t + b_3 (i_{x(t),L} - i_{x(t),S}) + b_4 dispersion_t + u_{t+1}. \quad (12.4)$$

The sign of b_4 is not clear-cut, although more uncertainty may trigger looser monetary policy (Soderstrom 2002; Bekaert et al. 2010; Mayes and Montagnoli, this volume). Second, we also estimate equation (12.4) based on the data before the 2008–2009 financial crisis in order to test the sensitivity of the results. Next, we also estimate equation (12.5), where we additionally control for the change in future inflation (*i* stands for 12-months-ahead inflation to reflect the forward-looking nature of monetary policy conduct in inflation-targeting central banks):

$$\Delta i_{t+1} = b_0 + b_1 skew_{\tau(t)} + b_2 \Delta i_t + b_3 (i_{x(t),L} - i_{x(t),S}) + b_4 \Delta inflation_{t+1+i} + u_{t+1}. \quad (12.5)$$

Finally, we estimate the empirical model for the US Fed, where we additionally include the committee bias. The "committee bias" is an official statement of the Fed on how the Fed is leaning in terms of its next interest rate move, and the variable is coded such that a higher value of the variable indicates an upward move of interest rates. The financial market expectations data are not included in the empirical model for the US due to significant lags in publishing the minutes, which were available only after the subsequent meeting in our 1970–1996 sample. More on the US data is available in appendix 12.1.

12.4 Empirical Results

This section gives the empirical results on whether the voting record is informative about future monetary policy. We first present our baseline estimates (equations (12.2) and (12.3)) for all countries. Alternative specifications follow.

The results reported in table 12.1 suggest that the voting record is indeed informative about future policy rate changes. Lagged repo rate change is typically significant, suggesting that the central bank smoothes interest rates, to a certain extent, and tries to avoid sudden reversals in its policies. The variable *skew* is statistically significant at conventional levels in all countries in the first baseline "naive" model as well as in the second baseline model with financial market expectations. The pseudo R-squared, the measure of regression fit, varies from 0.13 to 0.49. Our results for the UK confirm the previous empirical findings by Gerlach-Kristen (2004).

In the case of Poland, where the voting record is published with a significant lag separately from the minutes and is not available before the next policy meeting, the skew carries additional information available only to board members, not to the financial markets. The adjusted pseudo R-squared increases from 0.23 in the specification with lagged policy rate changes and term structure to 0.33 in the case of specification with lagged policy rate changes, term structure, and skew. We therefore conclude that despite the time lag the skew indicator contains additional information that can be used by board members. Releasing voting records faster would be beneficial for the transparency of monetary policy.

The results for the Czech Republic use the data only until 2006:7 in the specification with financial market expectations (column 2 in table 12.1). The reason is that, after this, the voting record was released only about three hours after the monetary policy decision was announced (as detailed in appendix 12.1). The results for the Czech Republic also point to the fact that publishing the voting ratio (without attributed voting record) may be sufficient for a better understanding of the future course of monetary policy.

Table 12.1
Does the Voting Record Predict Repo Rate Changes? Alternative Specifications—Different Maturities in Term Structure and Uncertainty

$$\Delta i_{t+1} = b_0 + b_1 skew_{\tau(t)} + b_2 \Delta i_t + b_3 (i_{x(t),L} - i_{x(t),S}) + b_4 dispersion_t + u_{t+1}$$

Country sample	Czech Republic 2000:7–2006:7		Hungary 2005:10–2009:2		Poland 1998:2–2009:12		Sweden 1999:1–2009:2		UK 1997:6–2009:2	
	(1)	(2)	(3)	(4)	(5)	(6)	(7)	(8)	(9)	(10)
Lagged repo changes (b_2)	0.08	0.45	1.22***	0.88**	0.63***	0.69***	0.92***	0.87***	1.15***	0.99***
	(0.43)	(0.42)	(0.37)	(0.40)	(0.13)	(0.18)	(0.19)	(0.21)	(0.18)	(0.19)
Skew (b_1)	0.89**	1.14***	0.50*	0.48	0.35***	0.60***	1.48***	1.29***	1.70***	1.54***
	(0.41)	(0.40)	(0.28)	(0.36)	(0.09)	(0.14)	(0.37)	(0.41)	(0.29)	(0.31)
Term structure (b_3)	10.24***	2.48**	2.10	4.67***	1.61***	1.75***	3.23**	1.24*	0.41***	1.58***
	(2.87)	(1.15)	(1.96)	(1.73)	(0.30)	(0.41)	(1.45)	(0.74)	(0.67)	(0.50)
Dispersion (b_4)		-0.93		-7.88*		-1.03		0.93		-3.99*
		(2.54)		(4.51)		(0.88)		(2.85)		(2.28)
Adjusted pseudo R-squared	0.27	0.20	0.35	0.54	0.24	0.41	0.27	0.25	0.29	0.33
Observations	75	75	40	40	142	60	90	90	142	142

Note: *, **, *** denote significance at 10, 5, and 1% levels, respectively. Standard errors in parentheses. Ordered probit estimation. "Term structure" denotes the difference between the three-month and one-month interbank rates in the odd columns and one-year and three-month interbank rates in the even columns in the given country. The data for the Czech Republic in columns 1 and 2 only until 2006:7. "Dispersion" denotes the standard deviation of individual votes on the bank board. The data on the 12-month interbank rate in Poland are available only from 2001 onward; therefore the number of observations in column (6) is smaller than in (5).

We have also carried out a number of robustness checks. In the baseline specifications, the term structure was defined as the difference between 12-month and 3-month interbank rates. Alternatively, the term structure can be based on different maturities, in the regressions presented in table 12.2 defined as the difference between 3-month and 1-month interbank rates. The results remain largely unchanged. The *skew* remains statistically significant, and the estimated size of its parameter is largely similar. Similarly, introducing the dispersion, a measure of disagreement in the board, as an additional explanatory variable does not change the interpretation of the baseline estimates. The dispersion is statistically significant at the 10% level in Hungary and the UK. This suggests that more dispersed opinion about the policy rates is associated with loosening of the policy in these two countries. The dispersion is insignificant in other countries. Table 12.2 reports the results based on a sample without the financial crisis period (up to 2007:7). Again, the results remain largely stable. Next, we also include the change in future inflation, but fail to find it significant in most countries (see table 12.3), while the results for other regressors remain largely unchanged.

The results for the US Fed, presented in table 12.4, support our findings for the inflation-targeting countries. Here *skew* is statistically significant in all cases at the 1% level even with the measure of committee bias, which in principle carries the same piece of information. The results suggest that the FOMC still has informationally independent members, despite a common perception of chairman dominance (see Chappell et al. 2005). The findings are robust to the inclusion of the future change in inflation.

All in all, the results suggest that the voting record carries relevant information about future monetary policy for all countries in our sample, and in consequence serves as a useful tool for improving transparency of monetary policy.

12.5 Median Voter Model Simulations

Lastly, we investigate whether the standard median voter model commonly used in the theoretical literature on central bank committee decision making (see for example Riboni and Ruge-Murcia 2010; Gerlach-Kristen 2008; Weber 2010) is capable of generating predictive power of the voting record for future policy rate changes. In order to address this question we need to add two components to the usual median voter setting.

Table 12.2
Does the Voting Record Predict Repo Rate Changes? Alternative Specifications—Data until Financial Crisis Only

$$\Delta i_{t+1} = b_0 + b_1 skew_{\tau(t)} + b_2 \Delta i_t + b_3 (i_{x(t),L} - i_{x(t),S}) + u_{t+1}$$

Country sample	Czech Republic 2000:7–2006:7		Hungary 2005:10–2007:7		Poland 1998:2–2007:7		Sweden 1999:1–2007:7		UK 1997:6–2007:7	
	(1)	(2)	(3)	(4)	(5)	(6)	(7)	(8)	(9)	(10)
Lagged repo changes (b_2)	1.24***	0.46	1.50***	1.22	0.64***	0.49**	1.01***	0.67***	0.99***	0.46*
	(0.31)	(0.42)	(0.47)	(0.80)	(0.13)	(0.20)	(0.23)	(0.27)	(0.21)	(0.25)
Skew (b_1)	1.66***	1.14***	0.47	1.94**	0.28***	0.62***	1.39***	0.84*	1.57***	1.28***
	(0.35)	(0.40)	(0.47)	(0.92)	(0.08)	(0.15)	(0.28)	(0.44)	(0.29)	(0.32)
Term structure (b_3)		2.53**		8.08**		2.44***		2.24**		2.99***
		(1.15)		(3.19)		(0.47)		(0.88)		(0.68)
Adjusted pseudo R-squared	0.19	0.20	0.35	0.71	0.11	0.37	0.24	0.25	0.23	0.33
Observations	87	75	22	22	114	80	79	79	123	123

Note: *, **, *** denote significance at 10, 5, and 1% levels, respectively. Standard errors in parentheses. Ordered probit estimation. "Term structure" denotes the difference between the one-year and three-month interbank rates in the given country. Data until 2007:7 to exclude the period of the global financial crisis; data for the Czech Republic in column 2 only until 2006:7. The data on the 12-month interbank rate in Poland are available only from 2001 onward; therefore the number of observations in column (6) is smaller than in (5).

Table 12.3

Does the Voting Record Predict Repo Rate Changes? Alternative Specifications—Controlling for the Change in Future Inflation

$$\Delta i_{t+1} = b_0 + b_1 skew_{\tau(t)} + b_2\Delta i_t + b_3(i_{\tau(t),L} - i_{\tau(t),S}) + b_4\Delta inflation_{t+1+i} + u_{t+1}$$

Country sample	Czech Republic 2000:7–2006:7 (1)	Hungary 2005:10–2009:2 (2)	Poland 1998:2–2009:12 (3)	Sweden 1999:1–2009:2 (4)	UK 1997:6–2009:2 (5)
Lagged repo changes (b_2)	0.02	1.42***	0.68***	0.92***	1.15***
	(0.45)	(0.41)	(0.19)	(0.19)	(0.18)
Skew (b_1)	0.78**	0.65**	0.31***	1.48***	1.72***
	(0.47)	(0.32)	(0.11)	(0.37)	(0.29)
Term structure (b_3)	10.91***	3.04	1.49***	3.24**	0.42
	(2.59)	(2.05)	(0.45)	(1.46)	(0.67)
Inflation change (b_4)	-0.34	-0.90**	-0.45	-0.02	-0.40
	(0.32)	(0.44)	(0.54)	(0.35)	(0.37)
Adjusted pseudo R-squared	0.28	0.41	0.25	0.27	0.29
Observations	75	40	142	90	142

Note: *, **, *** denote significance at 10, 5, and 1% levels, respectively. Standard errors in parentheses. Ordered probit estimation. "Term structure" denotes the difference between three-month and one-month interbank rates in the given country. The data for the Czech Republic in columns 1 and 2 only until 2006:7.

Table 12.4
Does the Voting Record Predict Repo Rate Changes? Alternative Specifications—
Controlling for the Change in Future Inflation
$\Delta i_{t+1} = b_0 + b_1 skew_{\tau(t)} + b_2 \Delta i_t + b_3 dispersion + b_4 \Delta committeebias_t + u_{t+1}$

Country sample	Burns era 1970:2–1978:2		Greenspan era 1987:8–1996:12		Greenspan era 1987:8–1996:12	
	(3)	(4)	(5)	(6)	(7)	(8)
Lagged repo changes (b_2)	0.45*** (0.08)	0.45*** (0.09)	0.41*** (0.13)	0.38*** (0.12)	0.11 (0.15)	0.06 (0.15)
Skew (b_1)	2.85** (1.12)	2.87*** (1.12)	12.25*** (2.64)	12.54*** (2.65)	9.19*** (2.83)	8.79*** (2.90)
Dispersion (b_3)		0.20 (1.08)		1.14 (2.01)		2.70 (2.14)
Committee bias (b_4)					1.08*** (0.28)	1.19*** (0.28)
Adjusted pseudo R-squared	0.13	0.13	0.18	0.18	0.27	0.28
Observations	98	98	74	74	74	74

Note: *, **, *** denote significance at 10, 5, and 1% levels, respectively. Standard errors in parentheses. Ordered probit estimation. "Committee bias" indicates how the Fed is leaning in terms of its next interest rate move, and the variable is coded such that a higher value of the variable indicates an upward move of interest rates.

Table 12.5
Does the Voting Record Predict Repo Rate Changes? Alternative Specifications—
Controlling for the Change in Future Inflation
$\Delta i_{t+1} = b_0 + b_1 skew_{\tau(t)} + b_2 \Delta i_t + b_3 \Delta inflation_{t+1+i} + b_4 committeebias_t + u_{t+1}$

Country sample	Burns era 1970:2–1978:2	Greenspan era 1987:8–1996:12
	(1)	(2)
Lagged repo changes (b_2)	0.45*** (0.09)	0.11 (0.15)
Skew (b_1)	2.84** (1.12)	9.54*** (2.84)
Inflation change (b_3)	0.13 (1.56)	−0.50 (0.40)
Committee bias (b_4)		1.09*** (0.28)
Adjusted pseudo R-squared	0.13	0.28
Observations	98	74

Note: *, **, *** denote significance at 10, 5, and 1% levels, respectively. Standard errors in parentheses. Ordered probit estimation. "Committee bias" indicates how the Fed is leaning in terms of its next interest rate move, and the variable is coded such that a higher value of the variable indicates an upward move of interest rates.

First, we need to generate an intertemporal link in the economic environment. We do this by assuming that a central bank committee composed of six members is trying to set a monetary policy rate i_t equal to the unobserved optimal monetary policy rate i_t^* which follows the $AR(2)$ process and hence is given as $i_t^* = \rho_1 i_{t-1}^* + \rho_2 i_{t-2}^* + u_t$ with the random shock u_t being i.i.d. with $N(0, \sigma_u^2)$. In the simulations we follow Gerlach-Kristen (2008) and set $\rho_1 = 1.95$ and $\rho_2 = -0.98$.

Second, we need to generate a nonuniform voting pattern among the committee members. We assume that the voting takes place between the status quo alternative x, equal to the previous policy rate, and proposed policy rate y, given as the most preferred policy rate of the median voter in the committee. Different preferences are then generated by assuming that each member in the committee receives private and noisy signals about the optimal policy rate. Hence each member j receives $i_t^j = i_t^* + v_t^j$, where the information noise is i.i.d. distributed according to $N(0, \sigma_I^2)$. We assume that the committee members learn the optimal policy rate from previous periods and form an expectation of the current optimal policy rate according to a standard signal extraction formula. With the policy rate set in integer multiples of 25 basis points, each member will then vote for an alternative x or y that is closer to his or her expected optimal policy rate.

Given the decision-making model, our simulations proceed by drawing random values for the stochastic variables, calculating an optimal policy rate and committee members' signals and ultimately their voting behavior and policy rate decisions. In an attempt to approximate standard deviation of policy rate changes, from the empirical data we set $\sigma_u = 0.05$, $\sigma_I = 0.05$ in our baseline scenario, $\sigma_u = 0.10$, $\sigma_I = 0.05$ in a high-volatility scenario, and $\sigma_u = 0.05$, $\sigma_I = 0.10$ in a bad-information scenario. For each scenario we generate 101 random 100-long paths, for each path estimating ordered probit equation (12.2) and average estimated parameters over the 101 paths while keeping values of the random variables the same for a given path across different scenarios. Table 12.6 presents results of the exercise.

What the simulation results show is that the voting pattern, in a median-voter framework combined with the $AR(2)$ process for the optimal policy rate, has predictive power for future policy rate decisions. The basic intuition behind the result is that for an optimal policy rate on, say, an increasing path, some committee members will receive signals higher than the signal of the median voter and hence will vote for the higher of the two alternatives x and y under consideration. If the

Table 12.6
Does the Voting Record Predict Repo Rate Changes? Median Voter Model Simulations
$\Delta i_{t+1} = b_0 + b_1 skew_{\tau(t)} + b_2 \Delta i_t + u_{t+1}$

	Baseline	High volatility	Bad information
Model	$\sigma_u = 0.05$, $\sigma_l = 0.05$	$\sigma_u = 0.10$, $\sigma_l = 0.05$	$\sigma_u = 0.05$, $\sigma_l = 0.10$
Lagged repo	4.24**	4.39***	3.76**
changes (b_2)	[0.73] (0.014)	[0.46] (0.000)	[0.68] (0.015)
Skew (b_1)	13.51*	12.43*	13.23
	[5.90] (0.065)	[5.21] (0.060)	[6.27] (0.104)
Observations	99	99	99

Note: Average ordered probit estimates over 101 random 100-period-long paths. [Average standard errors] and (average p-value). *, **, *** denote significance at 10, 5, and 1% levels, respectively, based on average p-value.

higher of the two alternatives is not implemented, then the skew variable in equation (12.2) will be positive and will predict a future policy rate increase, as the optimal policy rate is on an increasing path. Without going into full details, the last part of the previous sentence also suggests that the assumption of the $AR(2)$ process lies at least partially behind the predictive power of the voting pattern, as it generates much more persistent time series compared to, say, the $AR(1)$ process. Finally, what table 12.6 also shows is that the predictive power of the voting pattern is robust to increasing volatility of the economic environment in the high-volatility scenario, but not robust to increasing noise in the committee members' information in the bad-information scenario.

12.6 Conclusions

In this chapter we examine whether the voting records of central bank boards are informative about future monetary policy. For this reason, data from six countries (the Czech Republic, Hungary, Poland, Sweden, the United Kingdom, and the United States) that release their voting records are collected, and it is found that in all countries the voting records indeed are informative about future monetary policy and thus in principle improve monetary policy transparency. More specifically, it is found that if a minority votes for higher rates than the majority, it is more likely that there will be a rate hike in the following meeting. This result is robust to controlling for financial market expectations as well as different sample periods. The results for Poland as well as for the US under Burns's and Greenspan's chairmanships suggest that committee members tend to put the same effort into forming their views no matter whether their votes are published soon after the meeting or after a longer period of time. Hence, releasing voting records faster would be beneficial for both public as well as the central bank, which could gain credibility.

Like those of Gerlach-Kristen (2004), the results in this chapter hold regardless of whether the voting record is attributed or not. In consequence, in case of concern that attributed voting records may expose individual board members to some external pressure (as in the case of monetary union with board members not voting for national interests), the voting results can be published unattributed and still contribute to better understanding of monetary policy. All in all, monetary policy transparency can be improved by releasing the voting record in a timely fashion.

Appendix 12.1 Voting Records

Voting records from the following central banks have been collected (the start and end dates of the sample in parentheses): the Czech Republic (1998:1–2008:12), the UK (1997:6–2009:2), Hungary (2005:10–2009:2), Poland (2000:2–2008:12), Sweden (1999:1–2009:2), and the US (1970:2–1996:12). Typically, voting data are available at a monthly frequency. Except for those of the US, the data are publicly available at the websites of the central banks. The US data come from Chappell et al. (2005) and are only partially available at the Fed's website.

As regards the Czech Republic, the 1998:1–2000:4 voting results were available only in the transcripts that are published with a six-year delay. Therefore, the baseline estimates for this country are based on the data from 2000:7 onward. In addition, the baseline estimates for the Czech Republic are restricted to the period up to 2006:7 in the specification with financial market expectations. The reason is that from this period the voting record was released only about three hours after the monetary policy decision was announced. The monetary policy decision was typically announced around 1 p.m. and the voting ratio around 3:30 p.m. at the press conference. In principle the interbank rates could be collected at, say, 2 p.m. and therefore more recent data could have been used as well, but it has to be emphasized that the interbank market was not very liquid during the financial crisis. In light of this fact, we restrict the data for the Czech Republic to the period until 2006:7.

All US data are from Chappell et al. (2005), who code the policy preferences of individual FOMC members based on the transcripts from the FOMC monetary policy meetings. The desired federal funds rate is available directly from the records in 80.1% of cases under Burns's chairmanship and in 92.4% under Greenspan's chairmanship. By "available directly," Chappell et al. (2005) mean that the individual member explicitly stated the desired range for the policy rate or explicitly expressed a preference for a staff policy scenario or agreed with another committee member's explicit target range for the federal funds rate. Each individual's desired funds rate is calculated as the midpoint of the reported range. In the remaining 19.9% and 7.6% of cases, respectively, when the members' preferred policy rates are not directly observed, the textual record of committee deliberations (lean toward easing, lean toward tightening, or assent with staff proposal) is used to code the members' policy positions. The coding is complemented with an estimation of individual reaction functions in order to calculate expected values for desired funds rates, conditional on the information provided by leaning positions. For the US, we are able to calculate the skew both for voting members and for alternate members who are present at the policy meeting but do not have voting power. Neither of these two skew measures are available to the public in a timely fashion. Nevertheless the "committee bias" was announced from 1983 to 1999, in an official statement by the Fed of how the Fed was leaning in terms of its next interest rate move; we code this variable such that a higher value indicates an upward move of interest rates.

Interbank Rates

The interbank rates are collected in order to grasp the financial market's expectations. The source of these data is Datastream. Specifically, we collect PRIBOR rates for the Czech Republic, BUBOR rates for Hungary, WIBOR rates for Poland, STIBOR rates for Sweden, and LIBOR rates for the UK for the following maturities: 1 month, 3 months, and 12 months. The US interbank rates are not used due to significant lags in publishing the minutes as well as transcripts (both after the subsequent meeting in our sample).

Central Banks' Voting Record Release Schedules

Czech National Bank   The bank board meets on Thursdays.[6] A press conference with a presentation containing the voting ratio (without the names of the voters) takes place the same day in the early afternoon. (Until August 2006, the voting ratio was not announced at the press conference.)

The minutes are released on Friday of the following week (+8 days), containing the voting ratio, since January 2008 with the names explicitly.

Until April 2005, minutes were released on Tuesdays two weeks after the meetings (+12 days).

Bank of England   The Monetary Policy Committee decides on rates during a two-day meeting, taking place on Wednesdays and Thursdays. A press release on the committee's decision follows on Thursday noon.

The minutes are released on Wednesdays two weeks later (+13 days), containing a voting record with names.

Magyar Nemzeti Bank   The Monetary Council meets on Mondays. A press release of its decision follows on Monday at 3:00 p.m.

The minutes are released 2–4 weeks after the decision, but usually on Wednesdays. These contain a detailed voting record with names.

National Bank of Poland   The Monetary Policy Council decides on rates during a two-day meeting taking place on Tuesdays and Wednesdays. A press release of the decision follows on Wednesday.

The minutes are released on Thursdays in the week before the next meeting of the MPC, which means 3–4 weeks after the respective decision.

The MPC meeting minutes do not contain voting records. The voting records are published with a lag only in the quarterly inflation reports. If the repo rate was changed, the voting record is first published in the *Court and Economic Gazette* of the Ministry of Justice and only after that in the inflation report. Voting records in the *Court and Economic Gazette* have to be published no sooner than 6 weeks and no later than 12 weeks after voting took place.

Sveriges Riksbank   The Executive Board meets on Mondays or Wednesdays. A press release of its decision follows the same day.

The minutes are released after approximately two weeks (+14, occasionally +15 days), containing a detailed voting record with names.

US Fed   All US data are from Chappell et al. (2005).

Notes

Horváth appreciates support from the Grant Agency of the Czech Republic P402/12/G097.

1. More specifically, if the repo rate was changed, the voting record is first published in the *Court and Economic Gazette* of the Ministry of Justice, and only after that in the inflation report. Voting records in the *Court and Economic Gazette* have to be published not sooner than 6 weeks and no later than 12 weeks after voting took place.

2. More specifically, we calculate the signal-to-noise ratio as follows: When at least 25% of board members dissent—for example at least two members out of seven vote for higher rates—at a particular meeting and the rates are not changed, we classify the skew variable as giving the correct signal if the rates are increased at the next policy meeting. Calculating the signal-to-noise ratio this way, the ratio is 71% in the case of Czech Republic, 67% for Hungary, 64% for Poland, 80% for Sweden, and 54% for both the UK and US. In all cases the ratio is above 50%, indicating that the voting record gives a correct more often than a noisy signal.

3. The number of categories is set according to the log-likelihood of competing models. An alternative way would be to test whether the thresholds estimated within the ordered probit model differ significantly from each other. Note that the coding of the dependent variable substantially lowers the potential impact of vertical outliers. As concerns the potential impact of horizontal outliers, we estimate the regressions based on various subsamples, with the results being affected minimally.

4. An alternative would be to include interest rate futures or forward interest rate, but these were not available for all sample countries.

5. The share of the largest minority could serve as an alternative measure.

6. There are some exceptions to the usual organization of the monetary policy decision-making process for all central banks, typically because of national holidays. For example the board of the Czech National Bank meets on Thursday; in exceptional cases, it may meet on Wednesday instead of Thursday because of holidays. Starting in April 2005, minutes have been published 8 days after the meeting; if holidays intervene, minutes can be published more than 8 days after.

References

Andersson, M., H. Dillen, and P. Sellin. 2006. Monetary Policy Signaling and Movements in the Swedish Term Structure of Interest Rates. *Journal of Monetary Economics* 53 (8):1815–1855.

Bekaert, G., M. Hoerova, and M. Lo Duca. 2010. Risk, Uncertainty and Monetary Policy. NBER WP, No. 16397.

Besley, T., N. Meads, and P. Surico. 2008. Insiders versus Outsiders in Monetary Policy-Making. *American Economic Review* 98 (2):218–223.

Bhattacharjee, A. and S. Holly. 2006. Taking Personalities out of Monetary Policy Making. Mimeo.

Bhattacharjee, A., and S. Holly. 2010. Rational Partisan Theory, Uncertainty and Spatial Voting: Evidence from the Bank of England's MPC. *Economics and Politics* 22 (2): 151–179.

Blinder, A. S., M. Ehrmann, M. Fratzscher, J. De Haan, and D.-J. Jansen. 2008. Central Bank Communication and Monetary Policy: A Survey of Theory and Evidence. *Journal of Economic Literature* 46 (4):910–945.

Brooks, R., M. Harris, and C. Spencer. 2008. An Inflated Ordered Probit Model of Monetary Policy: Evidence from MPC Voting Data. MPRA Paper 8509. University Library of Munich.

Chappell, H. W., R. R. McGregor, and T. Vermilyea. 2005. *Committee Decisions on Monetary Policy: Evidence from Historical Records of the Federal Open Market Committee.* Cambridge, MA: MIT Press.

Fujiki, H. 2005. The Monetary Policy Committee and the Incentive Problem: A Selective Survey. *Monetary and Economic Studies* 31 (S1):37–82.

Geraats, P. M. 2002. Central Bank Transparency. *Economic Journal* 112 (483):F532–F565.

Gerlach-Kristen, P. 2004. Is the MPC's Voting Record Informative about Future UK Monetary Policy? *Scandinavian Journal of Economics* 106 (2):299–313.

Gerlach-Kristen, P. 2008. The Role of the Chairman in Setting Monetary Policy: Individualistic vs Autocratically Collegial MPCs. *International Journal of Central Banking* 4 (3):119–143.

Meade, E. E., and D. Stasavage. 2008. Publicity of Debate and the Incentive to Dissent: Evidence from the US Federal Reserve. *Economic Journal* 118 (528):695–717.

Miranda, M. J., and P. L. Fackler. 2002. *Applied Computational Economics and Finance.* Cambridge, MA: MIT Press.

Morris, S., and H. S. Shin. 2002. Social Value of Public Information. *American Economic Review* 92 (5):1521–1534.

Riboni, A., and F. J. Ruge-Murcia. 2008a. The Dynamic (In)efficiency of Monetary Policy by Committee. *Journal of Money, Credit and Banking* 40 (5):1001–1032.

Riboni, A., and F. J. Ruge-Murcia. 2008b. Preference Heterogeneity in Monetary Policy Committees. *International Journal of Central Banking* 4 (1):213–233.

Riboni, A., and F. J. Ruge-Murcia. 2010. Monetary Policy by Committee: Consensus, Chairman Dominance or Simple Majority? *Quarterly Journal of Economics* 125 (1):363–416.

Sirchenko, A. 2010. Policymakers' Votes and Predictability of Monetary Policy. Mimeo, European University Institute.

Soderstrom, U. 2002. Monetary Policy with Uncertain Parameters. *Scandinavian Journal of Economics* 104 (1):125–145.

Weber, A. 2010. Communication, Decision Making and the Optimal Degree of Transparency of Monetary Policy Committees. *International Journal of Central Banking* 6 (3):1–49.

Winkler, B. 2000. Which Kind of Transparency? On the Need for Clarity in Monetary Policy-making. European Central Bank Working Paper, No. 26.

13 A Bridge Too Far? RBNZ Communication, the Forward Interest Rate Track, and the Exchange Rate

Özer Karagedikli and Pierre L. Siklos

13.1 Introduction

The Reserve Bank of New Zealand (RBNZ) began relying on an overnight lending rate as the instrument of monetary policy in March 1999. Moreover, until 2007, the RBNZ had not intervened in foreign exchange markets since 1985. Since 1999, as shown in figure 13.1, there have been large movements in foreign exchange rate levels of the New Zealand dollar (NZD), measured either in Australian (AUD) or US dollar (USD) terms. Changes in the official cash rate (OCR), the formal name given to the RBNZ's instrument of monetary policy,[1] represent one of several means the central bank has at its disposal to inform markets about the current and possible future stance of monetary policy. Indeed, the RBNZ, arguably the most transparent central bank in the world, has become even more so in recent years (e.g., see Dincer and Eichengreen 2007, 2009; Siklos 2011).

Presumably, these developments serve to reduce, but not necessarily eliminate, the surprise element of monetary policy. This chapter has two objectives: to evaluate the role of central bank communication in mitigating monetary policy surprises, and to estimate the size of the exchange rate response to the surprise component of New Zealand monetary policy. The connection between communication and monetary policy effectiveness is of particular interest in the New Zealand case. The RBNZ is one of few central banks, though the number is growing, to publish a forward interest rate track.[2]

One way to determine whether markets may overreact to the release of an interest rate track is to examine the exchange rate response. After all, in a small, open economy such as New Zealand's, the central bank's views about the outlook for inflation and output and, by implication,

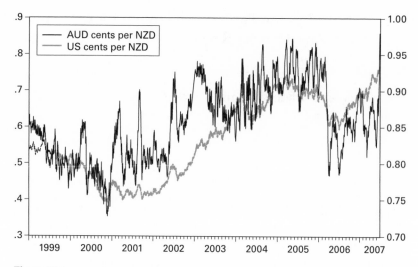

Figure 13.1
USD-NZD and AUD-NZD nominal exchange rates. Source: Reserve Bank of New Zealand. Data are at the daily frequency (7 days a week). The exchange rate is defined in terms of the foreign currency (USD or AUD).

interest rates will be partly conditioned by its views about exchange rate developments.

Why might different forms of central bank communication influence exchange rate movements beyond a surprise element, if any, in the change in the instrument of monetary policy? Consider the following illustration. On July 26, 2007, the RBNZ increased the OCR by 25 basis points, a move that was believed to have been broadly anticipated by financial markets.[3] Nevertheless, by the end of the day the NZD depreciated by just under half a percent against the Australian and US dollars. Was there anything possibly newsworthy in the RBNZ's announcement? The RBNZ explained its decision by stating that "we think the four successive OCR increases we have delivered will be sufficient to contain inflation." Even if the OCR move was widely expected, the forward-looking sentiment in the wording of the RBNZ's statement may have independently influenced market expectations of the direction of change in the exchange rate.

Ours is not, of course, the first study to quantify how the surprise component of monetary policy affects the exchange rate or the role played when a central bank becomes more transparent and communicates more often over time. However, a great deal of the literature has focused on the US experience. Moreover, as explained below, we have constructed a dataset with unique characteristics.

The publication of a forward interest rate track is not the only form of communication the RBNZ relies on. The RBNZ's Monetary Policy Statement (MPS) represents the focal point of the central bank's communication strategy, because the publication aims to inform the public about its views concerning the current and anticipated future state of the economy and the external factors that might influence it. In the present study, we also attempt to quantify the impact of any surprises this publication might contain, especially as successive MPSs reflect revisions in the RBNZ's stance about the appropriate direction of future monetary policy. There are potentially other sources of surprises that may influence exchange rate movements. Some have a direct connection to monetary policy, but others stem from announcements related to domestic economic activity as well as announcements from abroad with a potential impact on exchange rate movements around the time monetary policy decisions are made. All of these types of surprises are also taken into account.

Kearns and Manners (2006), who estimate the surprise element of monetary policy on exchange rates in four countries, including New Zealand, come closest to our study.[4] There are, however, several differences between their study and ours. Their data are coarser, and they do not estimate the separate impact on exchange rates from all sources of news; most notably, they do not allow for any role for the release of a forward interest rate track. Our study, therefore, is the first to econometrically investigate the impact of the release of a forward interest rate track for New Zealand and its impact on the exchange rate.[5] Finally, we also consider the question of whether "bad news" for inflation is "good news" for the exchange rate, or vice versa.[6] Clarida and Waldman (2008), for example, report that a 1% inflation surprise in New Zealand results in a 0.7% appreciation of the USD-NZD exchange rate in a 10-minute window around data announcements (i.e., five minutes before or after the announcement). Our estimates are not only considerably larger, albeit for a slightly longer window, but we also find that certain elements of the RBNZ communication strategy move the NZD while others do not (e.g., MPSs versus speeches by the governor). Equally important is our finding that the release of a forward interest rate track, an element of RBNZ transparency not explicitly considered by Kearns and Manners, adds only a modest amount to the surprise component of monetary policy. We believe that fears expressed by some (e.g., see Blinder et al. 2008 for a discussion of the issues), namely that releasing this type of information is tantamount to transparency gone too far, are overblown. Nevertheless, whether the release of expected future interest rates enhances the credibility of monetary policy remains in question, for reasons explained below.

The rest of the chapter is organized as follows. The next section briefly reviews the relevant literature on the connection between surprises and exchange rate movements. Section 13.3 describes the various channels used by the RBNZ to communicate monetary policy, with special emphasis on the role of the forward interest rate track and the MPS. Section 13.4 introduces the data, and the main results of the chapter are then discussed in sections 13.5 through 13.7. A concluding section (13.8) summarizes the results.

13.2   Central Bank Communication, News, and Asset Prices

There is an extensive literature dealing with the impact of surprises on asset prices. What follows then is a selective survey.[7] The early literature in this field focused primarily on the effects of news releases, typically originating from financial markets, on stock returns. More recently, attention has turned to estimating the effects from these sources on other asset prices, such as exchange rates and interest rates.

Lately, interest has also been shown in exploring how asset prices react to announcements and other forms of communication emanating from the monetary authorities. For example, Lamla and Sturm (this volume) point out that central banks can influence expectations via the media. Their application focuses on the experience in the euro zone. Similarly, Chirinko and Curran (this volume) evaluate the impact of central bank pronouncements on forward-looking interest rate data for the US. The authors conclude that their influence is subtle but, at times, can be counterproductive.

What explains these developments? First, many central banks continue to rely on an overnight interest rate, or a similar instrument, to guide the general level of interest rates. Furthermore, interest rate announcement dates are scheduled well in advance and, unless there is an emergency or crisis of some kind (as in the case of the terrorist attacks on 9/11), central banks do not deviate from the preannounced schedule.[8] Naturally, this prompts financial market participants to form expectations at predetermined intervals of time. Second, central banks in several countries are now more formally independent, transparent, and accountable to their governments.[9] Third, there is a possibility that, at times, the words of central banks can substitute for direct action (Gürkaynak, Sack, and Swanson 2005a, 2005b). Bernanke (2004) argues that the central bank can use this device to influence the likely future path of short rates as well as long rates. Indeed, central banks have generally become more talkative. As a result, there is a recognition that the monetary authority can influence markets on a daily basis.

Since financial market participants are also forward-looking, any monetary policy surprise can potentially have a deleterious impact on asset price movements. Yet monetary policy transparency is precisely intended to minimize such occurrences, unless the objectives of monetary policy are jeopardized as a result.[10] Indeed, in an attempt to provide even more guidance about the current and future stance of monetary policy, some central banks, notably the RBNZ, began to publish a forward track for short-term interest rates. In addition, the RBNZ publishes interest rate projections based on different scenarios about inflation pressure, and it is the first central bank that did so.[11] In the case of the US and the euro area, where there is arguably less central bank transparency according to some metrics (e.g., Siklos 2011; Dincer and Eichengreen 2007; Eijffinger and Geraats 2006), recent studies use interest rate futures, or forward exchange rates, to proxy future sentiment in financial markets (e.g., Connolly and Kohler 2004; Rigobon and Sack 2004; Kearns and Manners 2006; Brand, Buncic, and Turunen 2006). Whether it is possible to be too transparent is open for debate but is not the focus of this chapter (see, however, Mishkin 2004; Cukierman 2009).

A frequently used measure of "news," or surprise, is given by the following expression:

$$s_{i,t} = \frac{A_{i,t} - E[A_{i,t}]}{\sigma_{i,t}}, \tag{13.1}$$

where $s_{i,t}$ is the surprise component of announcement i at time t, and is defined as the difference between the announced value of some economic indicator, A, and its median expected value based on a forecast or a survey, given by $E[A_{i,t}]$. Equation (13.1) is divided by the sample standard error, $\sigma_{i,t}$, to standardize the measure of surprise, rendering it comparable across different types of announcements.[12] Once the surprise indicator is evaluated, it enters a regression as a determinant of some return. Denoting q as the (log) level value for a particular financial asset (in the present study, an exchange rate), a simple test of the impact of surprises consists in estimating the following regression:

$$\Delta q_t = \alpha + \beta \Delta MP_t^i + \varepsilon_t, \tag{13.2}$$

where Δq_t is the return on the asset in question, here the rate of appreciation or depreciation in the nominal exchange rate, ΔMP_t^i is a proxy for unexpected monetary policy, with the superscript highlighting the fact that such surprises may originate from several sources (as will be detailed below), while ε_t is the error term. Since the relationship between news and the exchange rate is a function of how shocks to the economy influence expectations, with good news for inflation representing bad news for the exchange rate and vice versa (Clarida and Waldman 2008) whereas standard economic theory (e.g., a relative PPP view) would suggest otherwise, namely that lower domestic inflation should, ceteris paribus, lead to a currency appreciation, the resulting asymmetry can also be examined by replacing ΔMP_t^i with $\Delta MP_t^+, \Delta MP_t^-$, which represent positive and negative surprises, respectively.

In any given week, various private- and public-sector institutions release announcements that compare actual and projected values for a large number of economic variables. In the US alone, the number of such announcements is large, with perhaps as many as 83 data-related announcements (e.g., see Siklos and Bohl 2008). With so many announcements, researchers typically have either arbitrarily chosen a subset of them, because the extant empirical literature suggests them to be statistically important, or have relied on a systematic technique such as principal components analysis to reduce the number of statistically meaningful announcements. In the case of New Zealand, there are fewer data releases. However, an important consideration for a small, open economy, generally underappreciated in the literature, is that both domestic and foreign surprises (viz., from the US and Australia) are also likely to be potentially relevant sources of shocks that can impact domestic asset price movements.

Consistent with the increased emphasis on estimating the impact of central bank policies on asset prices, researchers have also quantified statements, press releases, speeches, and other announcements emanating from the monetary authorities. Whether it is possible to objectively quantify the words of central bankers remains in question (Sebestyén 2005; Andersson 2010). Nevertheless, there have been promising efforts so far, with many studies suggesting that "verbal interventions" do move markets (e.g., Ehrmann and Fratzscher 2003). A difficulty with the interpretation of verbal announcements is that statements by central bankers may obscure the monetary authority's likely course of action, or mask the inherent uncertainty about the future course of monetary policy.[13] Yet there is also widespread acceptance of the notion that what the central bank communicates, and how, influences financial markets. This is especially true of inflation-targeting central banks whose credibility depends on meeting statutory inflation objectives.

One of the biggest challenges is identifying asset price reactions to market news from central bank announcements. For example, Gürkaynak, Sack, and Swanson (2005a) investigate whether the impact of monetary policy announcements on asset prices is adequately characterized by a single factor, the surprise component of the change in the current policy rate setting, a hypothesis that is rejected by the data. As a result, their study calls into question many single-factor studies such as Cook and Hahn (1989), Kuttner (2001), Cochrane and Piazzesi (2002), Rigobon and Sack (2003), Ellingsen and Söderstrom (2003), and Bernanke and Kuttner (2005). Gürkaynak, Sack, and Swanson (2005a, 2005b, 2007) argue that central bank communication can account for more than three-fourths of the variation in movements of 5- and 10-year Treasury yields around FOMC meeting days. Indeed, there is arguably an even more important factor to consider when investigating asset price movements, namely what the Fed might do in future. In the case of the ECB's monetary policy, yet another factor is also present due to the short time delay between the ECB's interest rate announcement and the ECB president's news conference (see Brand, Buncic, and Turunen 2006).

Given the multiplicity of factors stemming from monetary policy announcements, it is not surprising that a crucial issue is the sampling frequency. Some researchers have reported that news events can dissipate within a matter of minutes (Goodhart et al. 1993; Andersen et al. 2007). Therefore, using daily data may underestimate the short-run effects of unexpected events on asset prices, whose impact may peak within minutes of the arrival of new information, only to be reversed later the same day. Ehrmann and Fratzscher (2004, 2007) counter that intradaily data capture market overreactions, and they defend the use of daily data. Not all market participants necessarily react within a few hours. Moreover, with intradaily data, the results may be sensitive to the chosen window.

Because there may be both transitory and permanent effects as a result of central bank interest rate announcements, advocates of intra-daily data have devised new strategies to overcome some of the criticisms leveled at their estimation strategy. On balance, however, it would seem that adequately estimating the impact of the release of information by a central bank around the time of a monetary policy announcement favors an event study approach.[14] This is perhaps the most fruitful way to proceed under the circumstances. Indeed, as we shall see, the available data permits us to isolate the effects we are seeking to identify with a fair amount of precision.

13.3 Proxying Monetary Policy Surprises in New Zealand

The RBNZ communicates with the public through a variety of announcements and publications. These include: Monetary Policy Statements (MPSs), Interim OCR Reviews, speeches by the governor and the senior management, Finance and Expenditure Select Committee testimonies, and press releases.

By far the most important form of communication about monetary policy decisions in New Zealand is the MPS. The other forms of communication listed above are likely to have played a lesser role simply because of the precision and quantity of information provided by the MPS, as well as the market's advance knowledge of the timing of the release of the MPS. There are eight official cash rate (OCR) reviews a year; four are accompanied by an MPS, which represents a detailed discussion and assessment of the state of the New Zealand economy accompanied by a short overview, ordinarily one page in length. The MPS is publicly available on the RBNZ website at 9:00 a.m. New Zealand time (e.g., http://www.rbnz.govt.nz/news/2009/3724989 .html; equivalent to 3:00 p.m. of the previous day in the Eastern US time zone). The dates when these statements are released can be found at http://www.rbnz.govt.nz/news/. Each MPS also contains forecasts for a wide variety of economic time series.

While the market devotes considerable attention to what the MPS says about inflation, exchange rate, and economic growth forecasts, considerable publicity has been given to the RBNZ's publication of alternative scenarios for 90-day bank bills, conditional on different hypothesized future paths for inflation. The result is published as the forward track for short-term interest rates. The publication of the MPS is also accompanied by the data set used in its preparation. All of these documents can be readily downloaded from the RBNZ's website. Since there is considerable discussion about the advisability of releasing a forward interest rate track (e.g., see Woodford 2005), separately estimating the potential effect of this kind of information has direct policy implications. On the one hand, the release of a forward track should enhance the predictability of monetary policy and, unlike the US practice at the time of writing, the model used to obtain these forecasts is publicly available. Nevertheless, worries have also been raised over the market's ability to understand the conditionality of these forecasts. If the public takes the path as a commitment, and if the actual interest rates turn out to be different, the credibility of the bank might be impaired.

However, increased predictability is not the main reason for central bank transparency of this type. Central bankers are unelected officials and are given their mandate by legislators. There is also the matter of accountability that impels the central bank to tell the public how it is going to achieve its inflation objective, or maintain inflation around the target in the medium term. Publication of an interest rate path is one way of demonstrating the seriousness with which accountability is taken. Another purpose in publishing the endogenous interest rate path is that it helps the policymaker evaluate the implications of alternative policy paths (Archer 2005). Dale, Orphanides, and Österholm (2011) argue that central banks should communicate what they know best. Given that an interest rate is the primary tool of monetary policy, one can argue that the central bank should talk more about the interest rate path.[15] Finally, the number of central banks that have followed the RBNZ by publishing their interest rate forecasts is also an indication that central banks also find value in this approach.

The surprise element of monetary policy in New Zealand can be estimated from a few sources. One can look at the change in 90-day interest rates around policy announcements, as did Gürkaynak, Sack, and Swanson (2005a, 2005b). A surprise can also be derived from the change in futures contracts prices relative to the day prior to the policy action. Kuttner (2001) proposes the use of the futures market data to gauge the unanticipated component of monetary policy, and this approach has been typically followed in the subsequent literature. For US data, federal funds futures have been found to have good predictive content for the realized federal funds rate (Krueger and Kuttner 1996; Gürkaynak 2005; Hamilton 2009). In the case of New Zealand, a good proxy is futures on 90-day bank bills (also see Kearns and Manners

Table 13.1
Policy Events and Measures of Monetary Policy Surprises

Basis of surprise measure	First available observation	Number of observations*	Monetary policy surprise label
Change in the first contract on 90-day bank bills futures (MP_t^1)	August 16, 2000	55	MP_t^1
Weighted market expectations from Reuters (MP_t^2)	November 14, 2001	48	MP_t^2
Change in overnight index swaps (OISs) (MP_t^3)	March 20, 2002	43	MP_t^3

Note: In all cases, the last observation is the MPS release of January 27, 2007

2006), or overnight index swaps (OISs; see Choy 2003; Gordon and Krippner 2001).[16]

Bank bills futures are not directly comparable to federal funds, since the 90-day bank bills rate is not the actual policy rate. However, it is generally agreed that bank bills represent the instrument which the OCR aims to influence. First, second, third, and fourth contracts for the 90-day bank bills futures can be used to calculate different components of a monetary policy surprise in a manner described in Gürkaynak (2005; also see below). Finally, Reuters surveys market participants about the probability they attach to likely policy outcomes. A week or so before the Monetary Policy Committee of the RBNZ meets, the weighted median market expectation of the OCR is provided to the committee. This survey may or may not influence the governor's OCR decision.[17] In any event, the survey provides yet another potential source of monetary policy surprises.

Table 13.1 summarizes the surprise measures employed in this study,[18] while table 13.2 provides descriptive statistics for the three different monetary policy surprise measures defined above. Note that a positive surprise implies a higher-than-expected interest rate, hence "bad" new for inflation, while a negative surprise is the reverse and is interpreted as "good" news for inflation. Depending on the definition of the monetary policy surprise proxy, our sample begins in 2000, 2001, or 2002 and always ends in 2007.[19] The summary statistics reveal that the three surprise series are broadly comparable (we also carried out a plot of the actual surprises, not shown here). Nevertheless, the correlation coefficients between types of monetary policy surprises, while high, vary from a low of 0.72 to a high of 0.87.

Table 13.2
Summary Statistics for Monetary Policy Surprise Proxies

	Proxy		
Summary statistics	MP_t^1	MP_t^2	MP_t^3
Mean	−0.005	0.003	−0.001
Maximum	0.23	0.20	0.19
Minimum	−0.21	−0.17	−0.19
Standard deviation	0.073	0.08	0.072
Correlation matrix	MP_t^1	MP_t^2	MP_t^3
MP_t^1	1		
MP_t^2	0.72	1	
MP_t^3	0.87	0.78	1
Observations	55	45	43

An additional feature of the data is also worthy of comment. There is the possibility of a term premium. As suggested in the extant literature (Kuttner 2001; Bernanke and Kuttner 2005; Gürkaynak, Sack, and Swanson 2005a, 2005b; Gürkaynak 2005), while the term premium exists and could be time-varying, the resort to high-frequency data, namely a window of 30 minutes around policy announcements, should result in very small variations in the term premium. Piazzesi and Swanson (2008), for example, show that one-day changes in the federal funds rate futures around FOMC announcements are very small. As a result, defining a relatively narrow window around such announcements likely represents the "cleanest" way to measure surprises, as term premia that are primarily influenced by lower business-cycle-frequency movements are effectively removed (also see Gürkaynak 2005). Note also that during the first two-thirds of the period covered in this study, there was a worldwide decline in long rates. This too can be problematic, since it is unclear whether differencing of interest rates would be sensible under the circumstances. However, in an event study, this stylized feature of the data is less likely to pose a problem. We believe it is fairly safe to assume that, at the intradaily frequency, the impact of these kinds of trends would be negligible.

Figure 13.2 plots the three proxies for monetary policy surprises in a 30-minute window. As expected, surprises are positively related to interest rate movements. A positive surprise implies an expectation

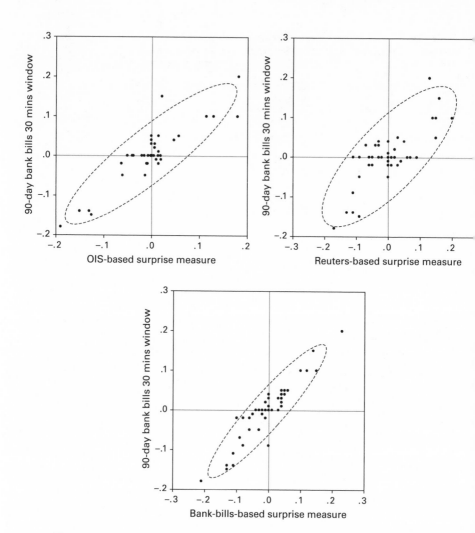

Figure 13.2
Monetary policy surprises and interest rate changes. The surprises correspond, in order, to MP_t^1, MP_t^2, and MP_t^3 in the tables and text.

that future interest rates will also rise, and by an almost equivalent amount.[20]

The literature has adopted several approaches to extracting information contained in monetary policy announcements. Gürkaynak, Sack, and Swanson (2005a, 2005b), and Brand, Buncic, and Turunen (2006) employ a recursive approach to estimating the size of the reaction to news announcements. Assume that the relevant time window is 10 minutes (denoted Δf_t^{10}). This refers to the length of time over which the implied forward rate is evaluated, and this expression defines the reaction of the market to a central bank interest-rate-setting decision as taking place over a 30-minute period (denoted Δf_t^{30}). We can write the relationship between these two measures as follows:

$$\Delta f_t^{10} = \lambda_0 + \lambda_1 \Delta f_t^{30} + resid_t. \tag{13.3}$$

Equation (13.3) hypothesizes that the size of the reaction to the setting of the interest rate is given by λ_1, which is referred to as the "jump" factor by Brand, Buncic, and Turunen (2006).[21] The residuals in the regression (*resid*) represent changes in the market's expectations about the future path of interest rates, referred to as the "path" factor.[22] In a second stage, equation (13.3) is reestimated by adding a second factor derived from the first-stage regression. Setting aside the generated regressor problem, restrictions need to be imposed to identify the sources of the shocks to interest rates not only to facilitate comparisons with the existing literature but, as pointed out in Gürkaynak (2005), because this approach also permits us to use a unique dataset from New Zealand, permitting the decomposition of the sources of surprises to the NZ dollar exchange rate.

13.4 The Impact of Monetary Policy Surprises on the New Zealand Dollar

We begin with the following regression, reminiscent of the one used in Kuttner (2001), Bernanke and Kuttner (2005), and Gürkaynak, Sack, and Swanson (2005a, 2005b):

$$\Delta q_t = \alpha + \beta MP_t^u + \varepsilon_t, \tag{13.4}$$

where Δq_t is the rate of change in the nominal exchange rate of the NZD, expressed in foreign currency units (i.e., either in USD or AUD terms), collected at various intervals. Consequently, a negative value represents a depreciation of the NZD currency. The variable MP_t^u represents monetary policy surprises as previously defined. The proxy can either be a single variable or a vector of proxies for the unexpected component of monetary policy decisions. It is important to recognize the possibility that the NZD currency will also be influenced by announcements abroad, especially from the US and Australia.

Most of the major US macroeconomic data announcements are released at 8:30 a.m. Eastern time in the US (the Consumer Price Index, gross domestic product, housing starts, jobless claims, nonfarm payrolls, etc.). Other announcements (e.g., industrial production) are released at 9:15 a.m. Eastern time. All US data announcements correspond to early morning of the following day in New Zealand. Hence, by the time an OCR announcement is made, it is unlikely that this type of news would further impact the NZD exchange rate. The FOMC releases its announcements at 2:15 p.m. Eastern time and, depending on the time of year, this corresponds either to 6:15 a.m., 7:15 a.m., or 8:15 a.m. of the next day local New Zealand time. New Zealand markets open at 8:00 a.m. local time,[23] and RBNZ announcements are made at 9:00 a.m. local time. Since our window calculations begin at 8:50 a.m. New Zealand time, we can safely assume that markets react to US news within 35 to 50 minutes of the releases, and between 35 to 50 minutes for FOMC announcements, depending on the time of year. As a result, we must also control for certain US monetary policy surprises that would overlap the 30-minute window (and, therefore, the 60-minute and one-day windows as well), our preferred choice, on the following days: October 24–25, 2006, January 27–28, 2004, August 13, 2002, March 19, 2002, October 2, 2001, May 15, 2001, April 18, 2001, October 3, 2000, May 16, 2000, November 16, 1999, and May 18, 1999. FOMC announcements on these days are temporally close to RBNZ OCR announcements. We use the Bernanke and Kuttner (2005) measure of the FOMC surprises to control for the unexpected portion of FOMC decisions.[24]

New Zealand data also pose problems on five other occasions because monthly releases of trade balance figures were announced on the same day as an OCR decision, namely April 27, 2006, April 28, 2005, October 28, 2004, April 29, 2004, and January 29, 2004. Trade balance data are announced at 10:45 a.m. local time in New Zealand. Hence, they do not coincide with the 30- and 60-minute windows employed in our regressions. Nevertheless, the mere anticipation of the release of an important piece of New Zealand economic news may well have a separate influence on exchange rate movements.

In order to ascertain the sensitivity of our results to the choice of window size, we also present results for a 60-minute window. The results for the 30-minute window are based on an interval timed to begin at 8:10 a.m. (instead of 8:50 a.m.) and 9:10 a.m. (instead of 9:20 a.m.). All times are local. For the 60-minute window, we define the window to begin at 8:10 a.m. (instead of 8:50 a.m.) to 10:10 a.m. (instead of 9:50 a.m.), again New Zealand time. In the results reported below, the impact of adding these results is negligible, in part because the net effect is to add only five additional observations. Finally, on one occasion (March 2002), Statistics New Zealand published the GDP release on its website well before the normal announcement time of 10:45 a.m. local time.[25] We also exclude from our data the OCR announcement following the September 11, 2001, terrorist attacks on the US, as this was obviously not a scheduled announcement by the RBNZ.

Table 13.3 shows the results from estimating equation (13.4), relying on the three different proxies for MP_t^u, for both the NZD-USD and

Table 13.3
Exchange Rate Responses to Monetary Policy surprises: Benchmark Specification

Coefficient	AUD-NZD			USD-NZD		
	MP_t^1	MP_t^2	MP_t^3	MP_t^1	MP_t^2	MP_t^3
Window	30 minutes			30 minutes		
β	0.033***	0.013	0.032***	0.041***	0.021**	0.039***
	(0.006)	(0.008)	(0.009)	(0.008)	(0.010)	(0.010)
Observations	55	45	43	55	45	43
R^2	0.37	0.06	0.25	0.42	0.13	0.30
	60 minutes			60 minutes		
β	0.036***	0.012	0.032***	0.044***	0.020*	0.041***
	(0.008)	(0.009)	(0.010)	(0.010)	(0.011)	(0.013)
Observations	55	45	43	55	45	43
R^2	0.35	0.04	0.20	0.36	0.08	0.24
	1 day			1 day		
β	0.035***	0.013	0.035***	0.044***	0.021*	0.043***
	(0.010)	(0.010)	(0.013)	(0.012)	(0.012)	(0.015)
Observations	55	45	43	55	45	43
R^2	0.23	0.04	0.17	0.19	0.07	0.19

Note: Estimates of β based on equation (13.4), using least squares with White-corrected standard errors. *, **, *** denote significance at 10, 5, and 1% levels, respectively. See table 13.1 for the definition of monetary policy surprises.

NZD-AUD exchange rates, while table 13.4 permits an asymmetric response of exchange rates to positive or negative surprises in monetary policy. The former represents an unexpected interest rate increase while the latter measures an unexpected decrease in the policy rate. Hence, while all coefficients are shown to be positive, the implication is that an unexpected tightening of monetary policy (i.e., bad inflation news) leads to a currency appreciation (i.e., good exchange rate news), while the opposite is true in the event that monetary policy is unexpectedly loosened. To conserve space, estimates of the constant term are omitted, but they are all statistically insignificant and economically uninteresting. Slope coefficients are highly significant and positive for bank bills futures (MP_t^1) and the OIS-based surprise (MP_t^3) measures. Therefore, the NZD appreciates in the face of a positive monetary policy surprise. If the latter is interpreted as "bad news" about inflation, this translates into "good news" for nominal exchange rate movements. For example, a 100-basis-point unanticipated monetary policy results in a 3.3% appreciation of the NZD-AUD exchange rate for the 30-minute window. A similar-sized surprise produces an even larger effect on the US dollar, at 4.1%. Differences in the USD and AUD reactions are not, however, statistically significant. It is notable that the Reuters-based surprise measure (MP_t^2) is not statistically significant in any of the NZD-AUD regressions and is significant at either the 5% or 10% levels in only a few of the NZD-USD regressions at the 60-minute and one-day windows. Since Reuters in New Zealand does not survey market participants on a regular basis, the lag between a particular survey and the actual RBNZ decision can, at times, stretch up to two weeks. Alternatively, it may be that the resort to a weighted estimate of the expectation of future OCR changes may be misleading if the weights do not properly reflect the relative accuracy or knowledge of the survey participants. Finally, also note that monetary policy surprises remain largely unchanged as the window is widened from 30 minutes to a full day. When positive and negative surprises are separately considered, as shown in table 13.4, the impact of good news on the inflation front on the exchange rate is seen to be even larger than shown in table 13.3, at least for the 30-minute window, while effects are roughly comparable for the 60-minute and one-day windows.[26] In a few cases there is some evidence of bad news for inflation leading to a currency appreciation at the 30-minute window, but the coefficients are significantly offset by the impact of good inflation news (test results not shown).

Table 13.4
Exchange Rate Responses to Monetary Policy Surprises: Asymmetric Specification

Coefficient	AUD-NZD			USD-NZD		
	MP_t^1	MP_t^2	MP_t^3	MP_t^1	MP_t^2	MP_t^3
Window	30 minutes			30 minutes		
$\beta+$	0.018**	0.002	0.00	0.024**	0.002	0.003
	(0.01)	(0.012)	(0.014)	(0.012)	(0.015)	(0.018)
$\beta-$	0.047***	0.027**	0.063***	0.056***	0.041	0.076***
	(0.047)	(0.014)	(0.013)	(0.010)	(0.019)**	(0.012)
Obs.	55	45	43	55	45	43
$\bar{R}^2$	0.41	0.08	0.47	0.43	0.14	0.49
	60 minutes			60 minutes		
$\beta+$	0.015***	0.003	−0.001	0.021*	−0.003	−0.004
	(0.011)	(0.011)	(0.012)	(0.001)	(0.014)	(0.015)
$\beta-$	0.058***	0.027	0.073***	0.066	0.046	0.089
	(0.011)	(0.017)	(0.015)	(0.013)***	(0.023)**	(0.016)*
Obs.	55	45	43	55	45	43
$\bar{R}^2$	0.40	0.06	0.47	0.39	0.12	0.48
	1 day			1 day		
$\beta+$	0.008	−0.002	−0.003	0.017	0.009	−0.001
	(0.013)	(0.015)	(0.017)	(0.017)	(0.017)	(0.015)
$\beta-$	0.060***	0.029	0.077***	0.056***	0.036	0.081***
	(0.015)	(0.021)	(0.115)	(0.019)	(0.027)	(0.022)
Obs.	55	45	43	55	45	43
$\bar{R}^2$	0.20	0.05	0.38	0.21	0.08	0.32

Note: See notes to table 13.3. $\beta+$ is the coefficient for the response of a positive MP surprise (i.e., an unexpected interest rate increase); $\beta-$ is the coefficient for the response of a negative MP surprise (i.e., an unexpected interest rate decrease). Hence, the positive coefficients indicate that bad inflation news is "good" for the exchange rate (leads to an appreciation), while the opposite holds for the case of a negative MP surprise.

To summarize, the results in tables 13.3 and 13.4 highlight two other important implications. First, monetary policy surprises have large effects on the exchange rate. Second, more precise estimates of the impact of these surprises are indeed obtained from reliance on intraday data. Notice that the standard errors are roughly 40% larger when equation (13.4) is estimated using daily data, and this, of course, is also reflected in the R^2 estimates shown in tables 13.3 and 13.4, which tend to fall as the window becomes wider. Third, the fact that monetary policy surprises are able to explain almost half of the variation in the exchange rate at the 30- and even 60-minute windows in several instances in quite impressive.[27]

13.5   Decomposition of Surprises into Level and Timing Effects

The foregoing results assume that monetary policy surprises have a single dimension, following the traditional approach used in the extant literature. However, since central banks are believed to act gradually, there is some uncertainty about whether the necessary easing or tightening will be carried out at once or over time. This implies that a surprise can carry over to more than one monetary policy decision date. In principle, then, there are potentially both a transitory and a permanent component to any monetary policy surprise. These effects are referred to as path and timing effects, respectively. For example, a surprise in the timing of a policy decision is one that leaves the expected OCR unchanged following a monetary policy announcement. In what follows, and for reasons previously discussed, we consider only surprises generated from bank bills and OIS data.[28]

To clarify our terms, suppose that a futures contract expires around the time of the next monetary policy announcement date and that this yields a surprise denoted by MP_t^i. Assuming there are no further expectations of an OCR change, the impact of the surprise is a permanent one. Therefore, we can write:

$$MP_t^i = level_t. \tag{13.5}$$

Next, suppose that that current OCR announcement contains both a transitory and a permanent component. Assuming they are additive, we can treat the transitory portion as akin to an error term in a regression of the form:

$$MP_t^u = \theta\, level_t + timing_t, \tag{13.6}$$

Table 13.5
Level or Permanent Effect of Monetary Policy Surprises on USD-NZD Exchange Rates

Monetary policy surprise	Constant	Level	$\bar{R}^2$	Observations	Wald
MP_t^1	−0.002	0.828***	0.68	55	−0.17
	(0.006)	(0.085)			(.08)
MP_t^3	−0.006	0.755***	0.80	43	−0.25
	(0.004)	(0.063)			(.06)

Note: *** denotes statistical significance at the 1% level. Newey-West standard errors in parenthesis. Equation (13.6) estimated via least squares. Results are for the USD-NZD exchange rate. See table 13.1 for the definition of monetary policy surprises. 30-minute window used.

where MP_t^u was previously defined. Substituting the right-hand side of equation (13.6) into equation (13.4), we estimate the impact of a monetary policy surprise on the exchange rate as follows:[29]

$$\Delta q_t = \beta_0 + \beta_1 \, level_t + \beta_2 \, timing_t + \varepsilon_t. \tag{13.7}$$

In equation (13.7), the regressors are estimated separately, leading to a generated regressor problem to which we return below when we discuss the possibility of bias in the coefficients. Results from the estimation of equation (13.6) are given in table 13.5.

The coefficient on the levels variable is not far from unity, implying a parallel shift in short-term interest rates.[30] Moreover, the level effect explains between 69% and 80% of the variation in surprises. Therefore, the level effect represents a much smaller fraction of New Zealand surprises than for the US (see Gürkaynak 2005). This finding is noteworthy, as the RBNZ has routinely tried to deemphasize the importance of the surprise element of monetary policy announcements. It would seem that this effort has been successful. Presumably, the release of a forward interest rate track shares in the credit for such an outcome.

Table 13.6 presents the response of exchange rate changes to both the level and timing of surprises (equation (13.7)). The results clearly show that level effects dominate. Since timing effects appear inconsequential, this suggests that the RBNZ has successfully mitigated the transitory effects of monetary policy surprises. This result contrasts with the US evidence, where timing effects are found to be significant for both interest rate and stock returns (e.g., see Gürkaynak 2005). An obvious problem with the foregoing estimation approach is that market prices may incorporate some idiosyncratic noise. In essence this is akin to an "errors in variables" problem. If the errors are of the classical

Table 13.6
Permanent and Transitory Effects of Monetary Policy Surprises on Exchange Rates

Variable	AUD-NZD		USD-NZD	
	MP_t^1	MP_t^3	MP_t^1	MP_t^3
Window	30 minutes			
Level	0.036***	0.035***	0.044***	0.043***
	(0.016)	(0.029)	(0.009)	(0.011)
Timing	0.009	−0.029	0.014	−0.037
	(0.007)	(0.009)	(0.019)	(0.031)
Observations	55	55	43	43
$\bar{R}^2$	0.44	0.45	0.47	0.52
F-Stat	21.81	22.67	17.21	18.22
Window	60 minutes			
Level	0.040***	0.038***	0.049***	0.047***
	(0.016)	(0.008)	(0.010)	(0.013)
Timing	0.008	−0.041	0.009	−0.048
	(0.008)	(0.010)	(0.019)	(0.030)
Observations	55	55	43	43
$\bar{R}^2$	0.42	0.43	0.42	0.46
F-Stat	20.92	21.11	14.18	14.93
Window	1 day			
Level	0.045***	0.043***	0.047***	0.049***
	(0.011)	(0.012)	(0.012)	(0.014)
Timing	−0.007	−0.056	0.009	−0.048
	(0.011)	(0.012)	(0.023)	(0.041)
Observations	55	55	43	43
$\bar{R}^2$	0.33	0.43	0.27	0.37
F-Stat	9.99	12.58	7.54	9.74

Note: *** denotes statistical significance at the 1% level. Equation (13.7) estimated via least squares. Standard errors in parenthesis. Controls for FOMC announcements included but coefficient estimates not shown. Standard errors are bootstrapped as described in Gürkaynak (2005), based on 1,000 replications. Results are for the USD-NZD exchange rate. See table 13.1 for the definition of monetary policy surprises. White standard errors used (conclusions are unaffected when Newey-West standard errors are used).

variety, they can bias coefficient estimates toward zero. This is known as the attenuation bias problem.[31] An appendix (not shown) demonstrates that this type of bias is a problem for survey-based measures rather than for the other proxies considered in the results just presented.

13.6 The Impact of the Forward Interest Rate Track

Since 1994, the RBNZ has published interest rate projections. The forecasting process has since gone through various changes (e.g., see McCaw and Ranchhod 2002; Ranchhod 2003). For example, until 1997, interest rate forecasts were presented without taking into account the effects of changing future interest rates on key macroeconomic aggregates. Between 1997 and 1999, when the monetary conditions index (MCI) became an instrument of policy, the RBNZ began to forecast future interest rates conditional on the impact of these rates on key variables such as inflation. The resulting interest rate forecasts came to be called endogenous policy forecast interest rate tracks.[32] The practice has continued since the OCR became the instrument of monetary policy beginning in June 1999. Interest rates are forecasted following several iterations or calibrations of the RBNZ's formal economic model, called the FPS (Forecasting and Policy System, since replaced by the KITT model; see http://www.rbnz.govt.nz/research/kitt/). Perhaps most germane to this study, assumptions about the exchange rate, as well as external forecasts of the foreign economic environment, represent significant inputs into the process (see McCaw and Ranchhod 2002, figure 2). The RBNZ publishes an endogenous interest rate track four times a year. Therefore, since our earlier proxies for MP_t^u assume eight events per year, consistent with the total number of monetary policy announcements in a year, the series of interest rate track surprises contains missing values for every second observation. As a result, the sample employed here consists only of data published in successive MPSs since August 2000.[33] We calculate the implied 90-day interest rates at 9- and 12-month horizons before the release of an MPS and take the difference between them and the RBNZ's published 90-day interest rates at the same horizons. We call the relevant series FF9M and FF12M, respectively.

The left side of figure 13.3 plots the size of monetary policy surprises estimated from the forward interest rate track. The surprises, measured in basis points, can be quite large. What is especially noteworthy is that,

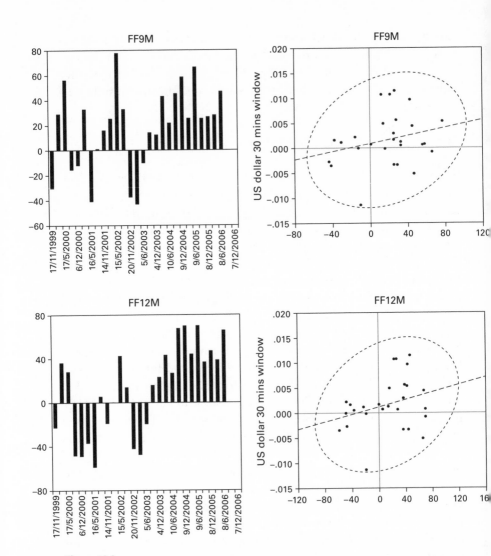

Figure 13.3
Left: Market versus RBNZ forward interest rate track differential. Right: Market versus RBNZ forward interest rate track and the NZD-USD exchange rate. FF9M and FF12M are defined in the text. Release dates (day/month/year) of MPS statements and interest rate forward tracks are shown on the bottom axes. Sources: RBNZ and authors' calculations.

during the second half of the sample, markets consistently overestimated the direction of future interest rates. Another implication of these results is that markets presumably had little difficulty in treating the projections as conditional on the RBNZ's interpretation of the existing macroeconomic environment. Of course, to the extent that there are persistent differences between the market's views of the future and the RBNZ's view, the results may also reflect a lack of credibility in the projections contained in the forward track. The right side of the figure highlights the fact that positive monetary policy surprises, namely interest rates that exceed even the RBNZ's forward interest rate track, result in a small appreciation of the NZD vis-à-vis the USD.[34] Nevertheless, the figures suggest a small likelihood that the relationship will be statistically significant. We now turn to a more formal examination of the role of these surprises.

Tables 13.7 and 13.8 report the regression results.[35] The surprise variable, MP_t^1, is statistically significant in every regression. However, FF9M and FF12M are statistically significant at least at the 5% levels for the 30-minute window and only for the Reuters-based surprise measure (MP_t^2) earlier deemed problematic. The variable FF12M is statistically significant, again for the 30-minute window, but only for the OIS-based monetary surprise proxy (MP_t^3). This means that the additional information content in the forward track dissipates fairly quickly. Nevertheless, during that interval of time, there is a further appreciation in the nominal exchange rate over and above the one due to the surprise element in monetary policy. Notice that for the 60-minute window the results differ as between the USD-NZD and AUD-NZD reactions to the interest rate track announcement. Hence, distinguishing between the two currencies can impact the interpretation of results.

In general, the size of the effect stemming from the forward track suggests that its impact is modest to insignificant. It should be emphasized, however, that the significance of the forward track is a function of how the monetary surprise variable is proxied. Indeed, interest rate forecasts affect the exchange rate only when the survey-based measure is used. Since it was suggested earlier that this measure was problematic for a variety of reasons, this suggests that a forward interest rate track does no independent harm to the exchange rate. Of course, it is not at all straightforward to separately identify the contribution of the forward track from other information contained in the monetary policy surprise variable, due to the fact that the forecasts are contained in the

Table 13.7
The Impact of the Forward Interest Rate Track on the AUD-NZD Exchange Rate

Variables	MP_t^1			MP_t^2			MP_t^3		
Window 30 minutes									
MP_t^u	0.034*** (0.010)	0.033*** (0.010)	0.032*** (0.010)	0.014 (0.013)	0.012 (0.012)	0.011 (0.012)	0.028* (0.018)	0.026* (0.015)	0.027** (0.013)
FF9M		0.003 (0.002)			0.004** (0.002)			0.003 (0.002)	
FF12M			0.003 (0.002)			0.004** (0.002)			0.004** (0.002)
R^2 / Observations+	0.31/28	0.34/27	0.35/27	0.06/28	0.13/27	0.15/27	0.14/28	0.21/27	0.26/27
Window 60 minutes									
MP_t^u	0.040*** (0.009)	0.040*** (0.010)	0.039*** (0.013)	0.013 (0.013)	0.013 (0.012)	0.012 (0.012)	0.030* (0.017)	0.027** (0.013)	0.029*** (0.012)
FF9M		0.003 (0.002)			0.005 (0.002)			0.004 (0.002)	
FF12M			0.003 (0.002)			0.004 (0.002)			0.004 (0.002)
R^2	0.34	0.38	0.40	0.04	0.12	0.15	0.13	0.20	0.25
Window 1 day									
MP_t^u	0.025* (0.015)	0.031** (0.015)	0.029* (0.015)	0.009 (0.015)	0.014 (0.013)	0.014 (0.013)	0.023 (0.020)	0.021 (0.017)	0.022 (0.015)
FF9M		0.003 (0.003)			0.004 (0.003)			0.003 (0.003)	
FF12M			0.003 (0.003)			0.004 (0.003)			0.004 (0.003)
R^2	0.11	0.17	0.20	0.02	0.08	0.11	0.06	0.10	0.14

Note: *MP* is defined in table 13.1. The estimates of the constant term are not shown to conserve space. The dependent variable is the rate of change in

Table 13.8
The Impact of the Forward Interest Rate Track on the USD-NZD Exchange Rate

Variables	MP_t^1			MP_t^2			MP_t^3		
Window	30 minutes								
MP_t^u	0.037*** (0.013)	0.036*** (0.015)	0.035*** (0.015)	0.014 (0.017)	0.012 (0.017)	0.011 (0.016)	0.028 (0.024)	0.026 (0.022)	0.027* (0.020)
FF9M		0.003 (0.003)			0.004** (0.002)			0.003 (0.003)	
FF12M			0.003* (0.002)			0.004** (0.002)			0.004** (0.002)
R^2	0.28	0.28	0.29	0.05	0.09	0.11	0.10	0.15	0.19
Window	60 minutes								
MP_t^u	0.045*** (0.014)	0.045*** (0.014)	0.044*** (0.015)	0.016 (0.018)	0.016 (0.017)	0.014 (0.016)	0.035* (0.025)	0.032* (0.020)	0.034** (0.019)
FF9M		0.005* (0.003)			0.006* (0.003)			0.005 (0.003)	
FF12M			0.004** (0.002)			0.005* (0.003)			0.005* (0.003)
R^2	0.27	0.33	0.33	0.04	0.13	0.14	0.12	0.19	0.22
Window	1 day								
MP_t^u	0.048*** (0.018)	0.051*** (0.020)	0.050** (0.020)	0.032** (0.019)	0.035* (0.021)	0.034* (0.020)	0.058** (0.026)	0.057** (0.026)	0.057*** (0.023)
FF9M		0.001 (0.004)			0.003 (0.004)			0.001 (0.004)	
FF12M			0.001 (0.003)			0.003 (0.003)			0.003 (0.003)
R^2	0.23	0.23	0.23	0.12	0.12	0.14	0.23	0.24	0.26

See note to table 13.7.

MPS which itself contains potentially many sources of surprise. In any event, the notion that releasing such information represents too much transparency—a bridge too far, so to speak—is not borne out in the data.

13.7   Other Surprises, Monetary or Otherwise

Finally, we wish to determine whether the existing specifications may have omitted other types of surprises. Here we consider an additional source, namely a quantification of the *language* used by the RBNZ to communicate its views through the MPS. To do so we interpret the commentary in the MPS according to whether the discussion focuses on output, interest rates, inflation, or exchange rate developments, as well as developments from abroad which may be seen as having a potential impact on domestic monetary policy. For example, when the outlook for each of these variables is favorable (e.g., lower inflation) according to the RBNZ, we assign a +1, while a −1 is assigned if the sentiment for any of these variables is interpreted as being negative.[36] We also attempt to assign a value according to whether there is a *bias* of some kind in the statement. That is, we separately identify commentary that explicitly indicates, following a discussion of the outlook for a particular series, whether monetary policy is likely to tighten or loosen, in which case we assign a +1 or −1 to the resulting dummy variable, respectively. Once again we are careful not to try and read too much into the MPS. Hence, the report must explicitly state whether there is a tendency or likelihood that monetary policy will change course if certain aspects of the outlook come true. This is viewed as being a statement of a change in the stance of monetary policy conditional on what is known or projected at the time the MPS is published. Otherwise, that is, when the statement is deemed neutral, the dummy is assigned a zero. *Reversal* is a 0–1 dummy that captures whether there is a change in the bias over time, as in whether a change in the RBNZ's sentiment about the appropriate stance of monetary policy shifts from one release of the MPS to the next. For example, a shift in emphasis from tightening in the previous MPS to loosening in the most recent MPS, or vice versa, would be assigned a +1. When there is no reversal in the discussion about the appropriate stance of monetary policy, a zero is assigned. Hence, equation (13.4) is modified as follows:

$$\Delta q_t = \alpha + \beta MP_t^u + \gamma_i comm_t^i + \phi bias_t + \sigma reversal_t + \varepsilon_t, \qquad (13.8)$$

where all variables, except *comm*, *bias*, and *reversal*, were previously defined. *Comm* and *bias* are dummy variables taking on the values described above, while *i* refers to whether the commentary specifically deals with output (y), interest rates (rs), inflation (p), exchange rate (q), or international developments (int). The results previously discussed are unchanged. Hence, to conserve space they are not discussed here.[37] However, it is worth noting that the *reversal* variable is statistically significant when either the Reuters survey or OISs are used to construct the proxy for MP_t^u. Therefore, there is a little bit of evidence that the foreign exchange market pays attention to the changing views of the RBNZ.

Exchange rates can, of course, also be influenced by surprises contained in regular macroeconomic announcements that are released during any of the windows defined above. To illustrate, figure 13.4 plots surprises defined as in equation (13.1) for four of the six available surprise measures, constructed from New Zealand macroeconomic data releases against interest rate changes across different windows. In general, positive surprises in inflation, GDP growth, and the trade balance lead, as expected, to positive interest rate changes. The opposite, again as one would expect, holds for a surprise unemployment rate release. Comparing actual data on these announcements against surveys from Reuters and Bloomberg, we obtain an estimate of the surprise based on the median expectation. It should be noted that expectations are based on a sample of anywhere from 9 to 15 individuals surveyed, with a mean of around 13 people surveyed. We are able to construct the resulting surprise variable for the full sample of OCR announcements. Finally, table 13.9 presents the results of equation (13.4) augmented with the additional macroeconomic announcement surprises, omitting the coefficient estimates for the constant and MP_t^u terms to conserve space. As shown, the estimates of β are unchanged relative to the earlier evidence discussed. Notice, however, that the explanatory power of the regressions is improved considerably, suggesting that such announcements have a sizeable impact on exchange rate movements. In particular, as in Clarida and Waldman (2008), bad news stemming from CPI announcements, that is, a negative surprise, represents good news for the exchange rate, a reflection of the credibility of the central bank.

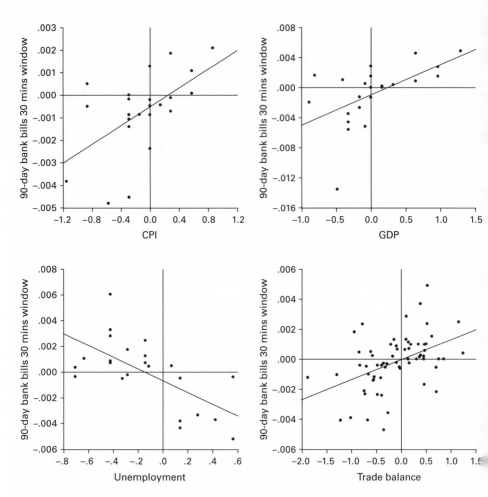

Figure 13.4
Macroeconomic announcement surprises and interest rate changes. Surprises are defined in the text. Sources: RBNZ and authors' calculations.

Table 13.9
Macroeconomic Announcement Surprises and the Exchange Rate

	30 minutes	R^2	60 minutes	R^2	1 day	R^2
Announcement	AUD-NZD					
CPI	0.0024***	0.34	0.0029***	0.42	0.0025***	0.18
	(0.0007)		(0.0008)		(0.0011)	
GDP	0.0027**	0.27	0.0036***	0.34	0.0039***	0.26
	(0.0010)		(0.0012)		(0.0016)	
CA	0.0071***	0.53	0.0074***	0.54	0.0083***	0.37
	(0.0015)		(0.0018)		(0.0028)	
RS	0.0014***	0.31	0.0016***	0.31	0.0011**	0.09
	(0.0003)		(0.0003)		(0.0006)	
TB	0.0012***	0.20	0.0015***	0.22	0.0014**	0.10
	(0.0003)		(0.0004)		(0.0006)	
U	−0.0048***	0.57	−0.0054***	0.52	−0.0054	0.30
	(0.0010)		(0.0011)		(0.0019)	
	USD-NZD					
CPI	0.0021***	0.32	0.0032***	0.40	0.0039***	0.27
	(0.0007)		(0.0009)		(0.0011)	
GDP	0.0040***	0.31	0.0052***	0.35	0.0047	0.17
	(0.0013)		(0.0016)		(0.0030)	
CA	0.0080***	0.58	0.0090***	0.61	0.0078***	0.22
	(0.0013)		(0.0015)		(0.0024)	
RS	0.0015***	0.27	0.0017***	0.29	0.0014*	0.07
	(0.0004)		(0.0004)		(0.0007)	
TB	0.0013***	0.21	0.0016***	0.18	0.0011	0.04
	(0.0003)		(0.0004)		(0.0007)	
U	−0.0046***	.42	−0.0044**	0.29	−0.0055**	0.21
	(0.0013)		(0.0016)		(0.0025)	

Notes: Equation (13.8) estimated via least squares. To conserve space, coefficient estimates for MP_t^u not shown. The independent variables include a constant and MP_t^1 (see table 13.1 for the definition), not shown to conserve space. CPI (Consumer Price Index), GDP (gross domestic product), CA (current account), RS (retail sales), TB (trade balance), and U (unemployment rate) are surprise measures evaluated as defined in equation (13.1). All announcements are for New Zealand data. The timing of the announcements is explained in the chapter. See table 13.3 for explanation of symbols for significance level.

13.8   Conclusions

This chapter estimates the impact of monetary surprises on the behavior of the USD-NZD and AUD-NZD exchange rates since the official cash rate (OCR) became the instrument of monetary policy in New Zealand. We were especially interested in separately estimating the impact from the release of an endogenously determined forward interest rate track by the Reserve Bank of New Zealand (RBNZ). Although some view the release of this kind of information as an illustration of a central bank taking transparency too far, the results of this chapter suggest otherwise. The forward interest rate track, a device now published by growing numbers of central banks, does not represent "a bridge too far." It is likely that this information is digested simultaneously with other pieces of information emanating from the central bank. For example, both the temporary and permanent surprise components of all OCR decisions are considerably smaller for New Zealand than for comparable US estimates. Nevertheless, it is found that financial markets consistently overestimated the future direction of short-term interest rates after 2003. As a result, the release of an endogenous interest rate track does result in a modest appreciation of the New Zealand currency vis-à-vis the US dollar. Therefore, one cannot entirely rule out that the release of such information reflects some residual lack of credibility in the future interest rate path. Perhaps, as is now widely believed, markets expected a tighter monetary policy than was actually delivered from 2003 to 2007. Many observers now believe that policy was too loose in many parts of the industrial world, and New Zealand may not not have been an exception. Nevertheless, future research might consider investigating the sources of the persistence errors in forecasting the future direction of a key interest rate.

Other forms of information contained in the RBNZ's Monetary Policy Statement (MPS), as well as general macroeconomic data releases, also contain quantitatively more newsworthy information that affects the exchange rate. Our results are also consistent with Clarida and Waldman's (2008) finding that bad news for inflation is good news for the exchange rate. In spite of the fact that the RBNZ appears to have done a reasonably good job at minimizing monetary policy surprises, the results based on the Reuters survey do suggest room for improvement in how monetary policy is communicated. What the present study is unable to determine is the degree to which our estimates are influenced by the manner in which the Reuters-based monetary policy surprise variable is estimated, or by the relative value of the survey and its timing, relative to other market-derived monetary policy surprise indicators used in this study. Also, the fact that we rely on an event study raises some problems. It is conceivable that a time series approach might yield additional insights into the high-frequency determinants of the exchange rate and the newsworthiness and credibility associated with an endogenous interest rate track. We leave these extensions for future research.

Notes

Pierre L. Siklos is grateful for financial support from a CIGI-INET grant.

1. New Zealand banks can borrow from the RBNZ at the OCR rate plus 25 basis points (bp) and lend at the OCR less 25 bp.

2. The Norges Bank, the Bank of England, and the Sveriges Riksbank now also provide this kind of market guidance, but they have only done so fairly recently and it is too early to estimate the impact on asset price movements. The latest addition to central banks publishing interest rate projections is the US Federal Reserve, which published interest rate projections of the members of the FOMC for the first time in January 2012.

3. This view is supported by reports on newswire immediately before the policy rate announcement.

4. Moessner and Nelson (2008) also consider the New Zealand case, but their study relies on daily data and so is not directly comparable to our approach. Also, their study is not interested in exchange rate effects from the release of this kind of information. A related piece is that of Conrad and Lamla (2010), who investigate the reaction of the euro-dollar exchange rate to ECB communication. They reach a similar conclusion to ours about the impact of surprise tightening or loosening of monetary policy on the exchange rate.

5. The original draft of the chapter, containing more results, appeared as an RBNZ discussion paper in 2008 (Karagedikli and Siklos 2008). Since then, Goodhart and Lim (2011), Detmers and Nautz (2011), and Gürkaynak and Wright (2011) have also produced studies that partly or wholly examine the RBNZ's experience with publishing interest rate projections.

6. This effect, at least in theory, is viewed as being of short duration, since purchasing power parity (of the relative kind) would predict that higher inflation leads, in equilibrium (that is, in the long run), to a depreciating exchange rate.

7. Andersen et al. (2007) and Faust et al. (2007) also provide a comprehensive bibliography of the relevant literature.

8. Many central banks publish interest rate announcements once a month, while others, including the RBNZ, make eight such announcements per year. See http://www .rbnz.govt.nz/monpol/statements/0090630.html.

9. There is an extensive literature on the sources and state of transparency among central banks worldwide. Siklos (2002) is one survey, while more recent surveys, together with empirical evidence, can be found in Dincer and Eichengreen (2007), Van der Cruijsen and Eijffinger (2010), and Siklos (2011).

10. Blinder et al. (2001) find that the improved "quality" of inflation reports can lead to smaller reactions to monetary policy actions.

11. As previously noted, there is an ongoing debate about the benefits and risks of this kind of transparency. See, for example, Woodford (2005), Blinder et al. (2008), and Goodhart (2009).

12. Monetary policy announcements (see below for the definitions used in this study) are usually expressed in percent (or basis points) and hence need not be standardized. We follow this practice here as well.

13. This is the principle of "constructive ambiguity" associated with Alan Greenspan's strategy of communicating US monetary policy in public.

14. See, however, Lahaye, Laurent, and Neely (2011) and Conrad and Lamla (2010) for a time series approach applied to intradaily data.

15. Before the RBNZ's rate decision is published, there is a running dialog between the central bank and private-sector economists about alternative interpretations of the phrasing of an upcoming policy rate announcement. This is reflected in the drafting of the press release. The RBNZ also periodically holds sessions with financial market analysts to discuss technical aspects of the forecast. Finally, many private-sector analysts in New Zealand previously worked for the RBNZ and are, therefore, familiar with the tools employed by the RBNZ in the preparation of projections.

16. Bank bills are bills of exchange issued or accepted by banks. OISs were introduced in 2003 and represent exchanges of obligations for short periods. They have proved useful to the RBNZ as a means of deriving market expectations about the OCR. See Choy (2003).

17. The governor is the only person statutorily responsible for the OCR decision.

18. That is, the numerator in equation (13.1). Also see note 10 above.

19. The onset of the global financial crisis in late 2007 may make it more difficult to extract the news from the noise element in monetary policy. Hence that period is excluded from the empirical analysis that follows. Moreover, as the governor of the Bank of Canada pointed out (Carney 2009), communicating monetary policy in a crisis may well require a rethink of central bank communication strategy. Whether this is correct is an empirical question that awaits more ample data, although it is far from clear that the essence of central bank communication has greatly changed so far.

20. A simple regression of the change in the interest rate against the three surprises yields slope coefficients of 0.85 (MP^1), 0.92 (MP^2), and 0.89 (MP^3). These are close to one, but the null that the slope is equal to one can be rejected at the 5% level.

21. Gürkaynak (2005) refers to "jumps," which may be a somewhat misleading term. For example, see Dungey, McKenzie, and Smith (2009).

22. In the case of the ECB considered by Brand, Buncic, and Turunen (2006) there is a third factor, called the timing factor, previously described.

23. See www.nzx.com/markets/key-dates/trading-hours.

24. We are grateful to Ken Kuttner for providing us with the US federal funds surprise data. For details on the construction of the series, see Bernanke and Kuttner (2005).

25. The early release concerned the December 2001 GDP figure released in early 2002. See Statistics New Zealand, "GDP Inadvertently Released before Embargo Time," http://www.stats.govt.nz/, March 2002 Quarterly Report.

26. Recursive estimates (not shown) reveal that the "good news–bad news" link reported here is statistically significant for virtually all possible subsamples. We cannot compare our results with those of Clarida and Waldman (2008). Their study only shows the combined effect of asymmetric monetary surprises across the sample of all countries considered in their study.

27. It was suggested to us that the impact on the exchange rate might also be a function of the size of monetary policy shocks. This is quite likely, and multiplicative dummies could be added to deal with this question. There is, of course, the danger that the estimated specification would be overparameterized, and there is always some arbitrariness in deciding which shocks are large and which are not. Hence, the extension is not considered but is left for future research; it would be an interesting extension once we include data following the global financial crisis of 2007–2009.

28. We rely on the second contract for bank bills futures and the three-month OIS, as these correspond to a three-month horizon following an OCR decision. There is one decision during that period. Hence, there is the possibility that markets may expect a change in interest rates. Using the third contract for bank bills and the 90-day OIS yielded very similar results (not shown).

29. Gürkaynak (2005) also introduces the notion of a "slope" effect to account for the pace of interest rate changes. We examine below the significance of this effect in the New Zealand context when we estimate the impact of the release of the forward track for the interest rate.

30. The Wald test shown in table 13.5 rejects the null that $\theta = 1$ at only the 6% to 8% levels of significance.

31. This is a somewhat neglected issue in the literature. The errors may or may not be random, and, since we look at asset prices, these may also be correlated with the right-hand-side errors. Typically, however, the measurement error problem focuses on the independent variable(s) in a regression.

32. The RBNZ also publishes scenarios for the 90-day bank bills rate conditional on different assumptions about the future course of key macroeconomic aggregates (e.g., inflation).

33. In principle, we could go back to 1997, when interest rate forecasts first appeared in the MPS. However, we would then encounter the problem of some missing intradaily data. The RBNZ also releases from time to time an endogenous interest rate track beyond the next monetary policy announcement, but there were too few such observations. Hence, only surprises based on the next monetary policy announcement are employed in the present study.

34. The results are the same for the AUD-NZD case.

35. We also generated series for the 3- and 6-months-ahead horizons implied by 90-day interest rates. The results were statistically and economically comparable to the results previously discussed. In addition, the results are practically identical when we use instead positive and negative monetary policy surprises. Versions of tables 13.7 and 13.8 that permit an asymmetric response are relegated to an appendix (not shown).

36. We are careful not to impose our own interpretation of the direction of change in a particular indicator. Rather the MPS is usually clear about whether developments are considered to be favorable or not, in order to meet the objectives of monetary policy.

37. They are, however, available on request.

References

Andersen, T. G., T. Bollerslev, F. X. Diebold, and C. Vega. 2007. Real-Time Price Discovery in Stock, Bond and Foreign Exchange Markets. *Journal of International Economics* 73 (November):251–277.

Andersson, M. 2010. Using Intraday Data to Gauge Financial Market Responses to Fed and ECB Monetary Policy Decisions. ECB Working Paper 726. *International Journal of Central Banking* 6 (June):117–146.

Archer, D. 2005. The New Zealand Approach to Rules and Discretion in Monetary Policy. *Journal of Monetary Economics* 39 (June):3–15.

Bernanke, B. 2004. Central Bank Talk and Monetary Policy. Speech at the Japan Society Corporate, New York, October 7.

Bernanke, B., and K. Kuttner. 2005. What Explains the Stock Market's Reaction to Federal Reserve Policy? *Journal of Finance* 60 (June):1221–1257.

Blinder, A., M. Ehrmann, M. Fratzscher, J. De Haan, and D.-J. Jansen. 2008. Central Bank Communication and Monetary Policy. *Journal of Economic Literature* 46 (September):915–945.

Blinder, A., C. A. E. Goodhart, P. Hildebrand, D. Lipton, and C. Wyplosz. 2001. How Do Central Bankers Talk? Geneva Report on the World Economy, no. 3.

Brand, C., D. Buncic, and J. Turunen. 2006. The Impact of ECB Monetary Policy Decisions and Communication on the Yield Curve. ECB Working Paper 657.

Carney, M. 2009. Some Considerations on Using Monetary Policy to Stabilize Economic Activity. In *Financial Stability and Macroeconomic Policy*, 297–311. Kansas City: Kansas City Federal Reserve.

Choy, W.-K. 2003. Introducing Overnight Indexed Swaps. *Reserve Bank of New Zealand Bulletin* 66 (1):34–39.

Clarida, R., and D. Waldman. 2008. Is Bad News for Inflation Good News for Exchange Rate? And, if So, Can That Tell Us Anything about the Conduct of Monetary Policy? In *Asset Prices and Monetary Policy*, ed. J. Y. Campbell, 371–392. Chicago: University of Chicago Press.

Cochrane, J., and M. Piazzesi. 2002. The Fed and Interest Rates: A High Frequency Identification. *American Economic Review* 92:90–101.

Connolly, E., and M. Kohler. 2004. News and Interest Rate Expectations: A Study of Six Central Banks. Reserve Bank of Australia Discussion Paper, 2004-10.

Conrad, C., and M. J. Lamla. 2010. The High-Frequency Response of the EUR-USD Exchange Rate to ECB Communication. *Journal of Money, Credit and Banking* 42: 1391–1417.

Cook, T., and T. Hahn. 1989. The Effects of Changes in the Federal Funds Rate Target on Market Interest Rates in 1970s. *Journal of Monetary Economics* 24:331–351.

Cukierman, A. 2009. The Limits of Transparency. *Economic Notes* 38 (1–2):1–37.

Dale, S., P. Österholm, and A. Orphanides. 2011. Imperfect Central Bank Communication: Information versus Distraction. *International Journal of Central Banking* 7 (June):3–39.

Detmers, G. A., and D. Nautz. 2011. The Information Content of Central Bank Interest Rate Projections: Evidence from New Zealand. Working paper, Free University, Berlin.

Dincer, M., and B. Eichengreen. 2007. Central Bank Transparency: Where, Why and with What Effects? NBER Working Paper 13003, March.

Dincer, N., and B. Eichengreen. 2009. Central Bank Transparency: Causes, Consequences, and Updates. NBER Working Paper 14791, March.

Dungey, M., M. McKenzie, and V. Smith. 2009. Empirical Evidence on Jumps in the Trerm Structure of the US Treasury Bill Market. *Journal of Empirical Finance* 16 (June):430–445.

Ehrmann, M., and M. Fratzscher. 2003. Monetary Policy Announcements and Money Markets: A Transatlantic Perspective. *International Finance* 6:309–328.

Ehrmann, M., and M. Fratzscher. 2004. Taking Stock: Monetary Policy Transmission to Equity Markets. *Journal of Money, Credit and Banking* 36 (August):719–738.

Ehrmann, M., and M. Fratzscher. 2007. Communication by Central Bank Committee Members: Different Strategies, Same Effectiveness? *Journal of Money, Credit and Banking* 39 (March-April):509–541.

Eijffinger, S. C. W., and P. M. Geraats. 2006. How Transparent Are Central Banks? *European Journal of Political Economy* 22 (March):1–21.

Ellingsen, T., and U. Söderstrom. 2003. Monetary Policy and the Bond Market. Unpublished manuscript, Bocconi University.

Faust, J., J. H. Rogers, S.-Y. B. Wang, and J. H. Wright. 2007. The High-Frequency Response of Exchange Rates and Interest Rates to Macroeconomic Announcements. *Journal of Monetary Economics* 54 (4):1051–1068.

Goodhart, C. A. E. 2009. The Interest Conditioning Assumption. *International Journal of Central Banking* (June): 85–108.

Goodhart, C. A. E., S. G. Hall, S. G. Henry, and H. Pesaran. 1993. News Effects in a High-Frequency Model of the Sterling-Dollar Exchange Rate. *Journal of Applied Econometrics* 8:1–13.

Goodhart, C. A. E., and W. B. Lim. 2011. Interest Rate Forecasts: A Pathology. *International Journal of Central Banking* 7 (June):135–171.

Gordon, M., and L. Krippner. 2001. Market Expectations of the Official Cash Rate. *Reserve Bank Bulletin* 64 (June):14–24.

Gürkaynak, R. 2005. Using Federal Funds Futures Contracts for Monetary Policy Analysis. Mimeo, Board of Governors of the Federal Reserve System.

Gürkaynak, R., B. Sack, and E. Swanson. 2005a. Do Actions Speak Louder Than Words? The Response of Asset Prices to Monetary Policy Actions and Statements. *International Journal of Central Banking* 1 (June):55–93.

Gürkaynak, R., B. Sack, and E. Swanson. 2005b. The Sensitivity of Long-Term Interest Rates to Economic News: Evidence and Implications for Macroeconomic Models. *American Economic Review* 95 (March):425–436.

Gürkaynak, R., B. Sack, and E. Swanson. 2007. Market-Based Measures of Monetary Policy Expectations. *Journal of Business and Economic Statistics* 25 (April):201–212.

Gürkaynak, R., and J. Wright. 2011. Market Perceptions of International Monetary Policy Dependence. Working paper, Bilkent University.

Hamilton, J. 2009. Daily Changes in Fed Funds Futures. *Journal of Money, Credit and Banking* 41 (4):567–582.

Karagedikli, Ö., and P. L. Siklos. 2008. Explaining Movements in the NZ Dollar: Central Bank Communication and the Surprise Element in Monetary Policy. Discussion paper D2008/12, Reserve Bank of New Zealand.

Kearns, J., and P. Manners. 2006. The Impact of Monetary Policy on the Exchange Rate: A Study Using Intraday Data. *International Journal of Central Banking* 2 (December):157–183.

Krueger, J., and K. Kuttner. 1996. The Fed Funds Futures Rate as a Predictor of Federal Reserve Policy? *Journal of Futures Markets* 16:865–879.

Kuttner, K. 2001. Monetary Policy Surprises and Interest Rates: Evidence from Fed Funds Futures. *Journal of Monetary Economics* 47 (3):523–544.

Lahaye, J., Laurent, S., and C. Neely. 2011. Jumps, Cojumps, and Macro Announcements. *Journal of Applied Econometrics* 26 (September):893–921.

McCaw, S., and S. Ranchhod. 2002. The Reserve Bank's Forecasting Performance. *Reserve Bank Bulletin* 65 (4):5–23.

Mishkin, F. 2004. Can Central Bank Transparency Go Too Far? NBER Working Paper 10829.

Moessner, R., and W. R. Nelson. 2008. Central Bank Policy Rate Guidance and Financial Market Functioning. *International Journal of Central Banking* (December): 193–226.

Piazzesi, M., and E. Swanson. 2008. Futures Prices as Risk-Adjusted Forecasts of Monetary Policy. *Journal of Monetary Economics* 55 (May):677–691.

Ranchhod, S. 2003. Comparison of Interest Rate Forecast Errors: Reserve Bank, ZIER, and the National Bank of New Zealand. Mimeo, Reserve Bank of New Zealand.

Rigobon, R., and B. Sack. 2003. Measuring the Reaction of Monetary Policy to the Stock Market. *Quarterly Journal of Economics* 118 (May):639–669.

Rigobon, R., and B. Sack. 2004. The Impact of Monetary Policy on Asset Prices. *Journal of Monetary Economics* 51 (November):1553–1575.

Sebestyén, S. 2005. What Drives Money Market Rates? Working paper, University of Alicante.

Siklos, P. L. 2002. *The Changing Face of Central Banking*. Cambridge: Cambridge University Press.

Siklos, P. L. 2011. Central Bank Transparency: An Updated Look. *Applied Economics Letters* 18 (10):929–933.

Siklos, P. L., and M. Bohl. 2008. Policy Words and Policy Deeds: The ECB and the Euro. *International Journal of Economics and Finance* 13 (3):247–265.

Van der Cruijsen, C., and S. Eijffinger. 2010. The Economic Impact of Central Bank Transparency: A Survey. In *Challenges in Central Banking*, ed. P. L. Siklos, M. T. Bohl, and M. Wohar, 261–319. Cambridge: Cambridge University Press.

Woodford, M. 2005. Central Bank Communication and Policy Effectiveness. NBER Working Paper 11898, December.

Contributors

Helge Berger International Monetary Fund and CESifo

Michelle Bligh Claremont Graduate University

Marianna Blix Grimaldi Sveriges Riksbank

Aleš Bulíř International Monetary Fund

Robert S. Chirinko University of Illinois at Chicago and CESifo

Martin Čihák International Monetary Fund and World Bank

Christopher Curran Emory University

Paul De Grauwe London School of Economics and CESifo

Jakob de Haan De Nederlandsche Bank, University of Groningen, and CESifo

Michael Ehrmann European Central Bank

Marcel Fratzscher DIW Berlin and Humboldt University

Petra M. Geraats University of Cambridge and CESifo

Gregory Hess Claremont McKenna College and CESifo

Roman Horváth Charles University, Prague

David-Jan Jansen De Nederlandsche Bank

Özer Karagedikli Reserve Bank of New Zealand

Michael J. Lamla KOF, ETH Zurich

David Mayes University of Auckland and CESifo

Alberto Montagnoli University of Stirling

Pierre L. Siklos Balsilie School of International Affairs and Wilfrid Laurier University, Waterloo

Kateřina Šmídková Czech National Bank and Charles University, Prague

Jan-Egbert Sturm KOF, ETH Zurich, and CESifo

Jan Zápal CERGE-EI Prague and IAE-CSIC Barcelona

Index